Captivated by Your Teachings

To Norma

May you be captivated by
our God's light + love!

Fr. Anthony J. Salim

Captivated by Your Teachings

A Resource Book for Adult Maronite Catholics

Anthony J. Salim

E. T. Nedder Publishing
Tucson, Arizona

Scripture quotations are taken from the *New Revised Standard Version Bible: Catholic Edition,* © 1989, 1993, Division of Education of the National Council of the Churches of Christ in the United States of America. Used by permission. All rights reserved.

Illustrations on pp. 1, 109, 153 and 187 are taken from *Clip Art Year A,* © 1993, Archdiocese of Chicago, Liturgy Training Publications, 1800 N. Hermitage Avenue, Chicago, Illinois, 60622-1101. Tel: 1-800-933-1800. Used by permission. All rights reserved.

Summaries of the books of the Holy Bible (Appendix VII), ©American Bible Society. Used by permission.

Imprimatur: The Most Rev. Robert J. Shaheen,
Bishop of the Eparchy of Our Lady of Lebanon of Los Angeles

Nihil obstat: Chorbishop Seely J. Beggiani, *Censor Deputatus*

© 2002 by Anthony J. Salim

Cover design: John Coury
Cover illustration credit: Zibawe-Melhem

ISBN: 1-893757-25-0

Printed in the United States of America

TABLE OF CONTENTS

INTRODUCTION

The ways by which the Traditions and Churches of the Catholic Communion express themselves are not the same always and everywhere. From the time that Christianity moved out of Jerusalem and around the Mediterranean in its great missionary effort, it encountered nations and cultures that were different from each other. As it did, the Church adapted to and was enriched by these cultures. The result has been a variety of approaches to the Faith that still marks the Church in our own times, ***while agreeing about what constitutes Catholic doctrinal teaching.***

The major differences are between East and West; within the East itself there are several liturgical traditions. The Syriac-Maronite Church of Antioch is one of these Eastern Catholic Traditions.

Maronite Tradition has deep roots in the past—which is why there is among Maronite Catholics such a strong sense of "family identity." Some of the wellsprings of this Tradition are:

1) The West Syriac expression of the great Church of Antioch, with its characteristic emphasis on the humanity of Christ, and the historical approach to Scripture interpretation.

2) The acceptance of the wisdom of the Edessan and Nisibene Church of the East, in its use of the liturgical poetic style of the **Syriac Teachers,** like St. Ephrem and others.

3) The deep and abiding influence of monasticism, which began in the East, developing in Egypt and Syria.

The presentation of the teachings of the Catholic Church, through the eyes, heart and soul of the Maronite Tradition, is what this text is all about.

Catholic Faith, Eastern-style

Our Catholic Faith is a sure expression of what God has revealed in the message and life of Jesus. It is not a blind faith. We really do grow in our knowledge of revealed truths—personally, and as a Community of Believers.

Western Catholicism has had a long-standing emphasis on the rational and systematic ordering of Church beliefs. Since the Middle Ages the approach to theology has been described as "faith seeking understanding" (*fides quaerens intellectum*). Using certain categories such as "The Trinity," "Grace," "The Sacraments*,*" *et al.*, has helped define these areas of belief rather strictly.

The Eastern Churches, however, have not usually been so similarly systematic. For us, all the truths of our Catholic heritage have been embodied and celebrated in a liturgical setting—icons, chant and more—and a rich prayer life. We have tended to sing our faith more than categorize it.

This Eastern view may be summed up in a descriptive phrase offered by Robert Murray in his book, *Symbols of Church and Kingdom*. In it he speaks of *fides adorans Mysterium*, or "faith adoring the Mystery," by which he means the Mystery of God and divine revelation. While it is true that our minds seek answers, and while it is also true that doctrinal questions have been clarified more and more through theological reflection (especially in the West—the *Catechism of the Catholic Church* is a good example), nevertheless, the East witnesses that too much systematizing produces the illusion that the Mystery of God can be exhausted through such a process. In more than one place, even the *Catechism* reminds us that the Mystery of God is inexhaustible.

Murray quotes theologian Hugo Rahner as challenging the Western notion of analytical theological reflection in this intriguing quote that makes the case. He speaks particularly of the Eastern Fathers of the Church:

> Wherever the Fathers unfold their theology with its veils of imagery, we discover a wealth of symbols and of truths clothed in symbols, **which could give new life to our modern dogmatic expressions, perhaps still all too much dominated as they are by apologetics and canon law** (*emphasis mine*). The world of imagery found in the symbols of the Church which the theology of the first ten centuries has preserved for us could bring about a renovation of our thinking about the Church, large areas of which have, from a dogmatic point of view, become sterile (*Symbols of Church and Kingdom*, p. 37).

In his apostolic letter *Orientale Lumen*, Pope John Paul II acknowledges that the East and West have used different methods and approaches in the study of revealed truth. He also expresses no surprise that one tradition may come

> ... nearer to a full appreciation of some aspects of a mystery of revelation than the other, or has expressed them better. In such cases, these various theological formulations are often to be considered complementary rather than conflicting... Indeed, in comparison to any other culture, the Christian East has a unique and privileged role as the original setting where the Church was born (¶5).

On the other hand, in these days, we see increasingly that a more systematic approach is needed for the East. Indeed, this is possible, just as the opposite is true: the West has increasingly begun to see how beneficial it is to concentrate more on the liturgical aspect of presenting the Faith. (Note the revival in the West of the Rite of Christian Initiation of Adults [RCIA], which at least is Lectionary-based.) For the *whole Church* it is very true that how we pray displays our belief system.

Catholic Faith, Syriac-Maronite-style

Maronite Liturgy teaches. In the *Qoorbono* ("Service of the Holy Mysteries," or "Divine Liturgy") as well as in the Divine Office (*Ramsho* [Evening Prayer], *Safro* [Morning Prayer] and the other Hours) and the sacramental Mysteries, all we need to know about being a faithful Catholic—Maronite-style—is clearly expressed, if only we know how to look for it. All through the Liturgical Year, as we follow the life of Christ and of his Saints, we are reminded of all that God wants us to know for our salvation.

The Church helps us to find its teachings through the Holy Scripture assigned for the days and feasts, accompanied by the prayers also assigned for the feast. These are found in the Readings from the Lectionary (see **Chapter 11, "The Lectionary"**). In these Readings God still reveals today.

In addition, the Syriac part of our Tradition gives us a clear guide to interpreting the Scriptures in a balanced and truly Catholic way by means of a special prayer of the Service of the Word called the *Hoosoyo*, or "prayer of forgiveness." This prayer, peculiar to the Syriac Tradition, expresses the theme for the day, feast or season, as it acts as a commentary on the Gospel of the day (see **Appendix IV, A Glossary of Maronite Terms**). In this way, a truly Catholic interpretation of the Word of God is possible. A very scriptural prayer, the *Hoosoyo* abounds in references to the Bible, often using the device of "typology" (see **Chapter 9, "Syro-Antiochene Tradition"**) to help us relate the celebration and teaching to the Word.

Lastly, in recognition of the fact that the Church has the gift of interpreting the Word of God through its leaders, Maronites are guided by the *Magisterium*—or Teaching Office—of the Church (see **Chapter 1, "The Teaching Office of the Church"**).

In many ways, this book attempts to break new ground in reinterpreting Maronite Catholic Tradition for our day. I hope that this work will stimulate reflection among the members of our own Maronite community. Rather than being the last word on this approach, I hope that this work will encourage other studies in Maronite catechesis, which will also define even more clearly an Antiochene and Syriac vision of the Maronite Catholic Church.

In addition, as the Syriac-speaking Churches increase their presence outside of their homelands, especially in the United States, it is my hope that this kind of work will encourage collaboration with these other Churches and leading to the possibility of a common Syriac catechism.

As we seek to understand our Faith more deeply, we pray with the Church to our God in the *Sedro* of the Finding in the Temple:

> **...Gracious Lord...[u]proot from your Church every heresy and tendency which leads to destruction, so that your Gospel may become a beacon of light and a harbor of safety....**

Rather than looking upon the doctrines of the Church as a burden, we pray, in the First Prayer of *Safro*, Thursday of the Common of the Week, Pentecost Season:

> **Draw us to yourself,**
> **enrich our voices with your praises**
> **and our tongues with inspired songs.**
> ***Captivate us by your teachings.***

The Method of This Text

It is the intention of this text to present the **basic doctrines** of the Catholic Church as understood and expressed in Maronite Tradition, particularly the liturgical tradition.

Catechetics, Eastern-style

Each of the five Traditions of Eastern Christianity has many areas that are common to all of them. At the same time there are essential differences as well. While these may be seen merely as matters of different emphases—this is often true—such differences in the last two millennia have served to distinguish one Tradition from another. In fact, this is precisely what makes the Catholic Communion of Churches so interesting and, for all the Catholic Churches, mutually enriching.

For this reason no one "universal" catechetical text can hope to serve the catechetical needs of every Tradition, or of the individual *sui iuris* Churches following a particular Tradition.

A New Direction

Sensing this truth, the Bishop of Rome, Pope John Paul II, made a welcome suggestion in an address at the Vatican in October of 1998. His concern was the proper catechetical care of Eastern Catholic Church members. Indicating a new direction for Eastern Church catechesis, he said:

> [It would likewise be helpful to prepare a Catechetical Directory that would] take into account the special character of the Eastern Churches, so that the biblical and liturgical emphasis as well as the traditions of each Church *sui iuris* in patrology, hagiography and even iconography are highlighted in conveying the catechesis (CCEO, can. 621, § 2).

Upon reflection, the implications of this deceptively simple suggestion are in fact overwhelming. Positively, the Bishop of Rome rightly recognizes that catechesis in the East is done differently than in the West, and that it is necessary to create vehicles to facilitate Eastern catechesis in an authentic manner. He explicitly suggests the creation of a *General Directory for Catechesis for the Eastern Churches*. What is necessarily implied by his words is that proper Eastern catechisms would follow.

Western Catechesis and the Eastern Churches

In recent years the publication of the *Catechism of the Catholic Church* shows quite a different situation. Despite the fact that it purports to represent Catholic teaching in a comprehensive manner, the *Catechism* pays minimal explicit attention to Eastern Tradition(s), and—as is now being recognized more—is written from a Western Church point of view. The Pope's proposal implies, of course, that the current *General Directory for Catechesis* as well as its necessary companion piece, the *Catechism*, as good as they may be for the Western Church, are not sufficient vehicles for handing on Eastern Catholic Tradition.

In this work you will find selected references taken from the *Catechism*, deliberately chosen for their relation to the Council, to Eastern Christian thought and to moral teaching. They are designated within parentheses by "*CCC*" followed by the pertinent paragraph number(s).

The Sources of This Text

The following sources guide this presentation:

1) **The Sacred Scriptures.** Central to understanding the meaning of our Catholic Faith is what God has revealed to us in the Sacred Scriptures. Our Catholic Faith is biblical faith first and foremost. Quotes from the Bible are liberally found in the text.

2) **Liturgy.** Since we are seeking to understand Catholicism through the lens of its Eastern Maronite Tradition, the attempt has been made to let **the texts of the liturgical tradition** speak for themselves, allowing them to illustrate the full range of basic Catholic teachings. In this way, Maronite Tradition may be seen more clearly as a full and authentic expression of the Catholic Faith. This method is in reality an old catechetical axiom in the Church, *lex orandi, lex credendi*—"How the Church prays reflects its belief." **Most important, however, we must recognize that liturgy is the prime way through which the Eastern Traditions "do catechesis," that is, teach the Faith.** As the "Document on the Sacred Liturgy" of Vatican II states, the liturgy is the "summit and fount" of all the Church's understanding and activity.

For this reason, the best recommendation that can be made is to **take the time to read all the liturgical quotes—always printed in bold-face type—slowly and prayerfully.** In this way, you will come to deeper appreciation for their richness, as well as appreciating the actual Divine Liturgy, Divine Office and sacramental Mysteries as you pray them.

The liturgical texts used in this book are strictly limited to the most recent edition of the *Qoorbono*, that is, the Divine Service of the Holy Mysteries (New York: St. Maron's Publications, 1993), which represents the United States' translation of the official text of the Maronite Patriarchal Liturgical Commission. Also used are the texts of the seven sacramental Mysteries. The texts of the Divine Office were not consulted because there is as yet no consensus on an official version.

3) **Maronite Tradition.** While the largest part of this work is doctrinal and catechetical, other aspects of Maronite Catholicism have been treated in some detail, such as devotional practices; liturgical customs; the moral life; saints in the liturgical calendar (hagiography); iconography. Please note that these are the very sources that John Paul suggested in his 1998 talk.

4) *Orientale Lumen.* One recent document that summarizes well the basic themes of Eastern thought is the Apostolic Letter of Pope John Paul II, *Orientale Lumen* ("Eastern Light"). In this succinct work, the reader will find a rather deep understanding of the mystical and poetic way in which the East approaches and presents the teachings of the Christian experience. The document presents them in a very understandable way and is highly recommended.

5) **The Second Vatican Council.** Pope Paul VI once called the Second Vatican Council "the great catechism of our times." The Council (from now on referred to simply as "the Council," except when referring to the Council of Chalcedon in **Chapter 4, "Jesus, Truly Human and Fully Divine"**, and Constantinople III) is abundantly represented. Such references will be indicated by their proper abbreviations and paragraph numbers in parentheses after quotes from the Council Documents. A listing of these documents—with their appropriate abbreviations, as well as a brief summary of their contents—may be found in **Appendix V.**

A Liturgical Setting

In light of the liturgical setting of this text, the four Parts of this text parallel the four basic sections of the Maronite Divine Liturgy. The internal organization of the chapters in each Part contains contents that relate to the particular section of the Divine Service. These are:

a) **Part I: Preparing for Faith/The Preparation Rites** (Lighting of the Church, Preparation of the Offerings, and the Introductory Rites, ending in the *Trisagion*)

b) **Part II: The Word of God: Foundation of Our Faith/The Service of the Word** (*Hoosoyo*, Scripture Readings, homily, Creed)

c) **Part III: God's Kingdom: the Already and the Not Yet/The Pre-*Anaphora*** (Transfer of the Offerings, Commemorations of the Living and Dead)

d) **Part IV: Our Sacramental and Moral Faith Life/The *Anaphora*** (Peace-giving, *Anaphora* proper, Communion Rite and Dismissal)

The four-fold structure outlined above relates to the catechumenate as well.

As you progress through the various Parts of the text, you may note that the four parts of the Divine Service more or less relate to stages in the journey of inquiry into the life of faith and the Church:

a) (**Part I**) One enters the church building and prepares for the hearing of the Word of the Scriptures. At this initial stage the inquirer might have questions about who God is and what the Church is.

b) (**Part II**) In the second stage the catechumen hears the Word of God proclaimed and explained. It is here that the pattern of weekly Readings presented in the Lectionary form a way to follow Jesus through the Liturgical Year. This Lectionary focus provides perhaps the greatest uniqueness to each of the many Traditions that make up the Church.

c) (**Part III**) In the third stage the catechumen explores the connections between those that make up the "saved," i.e., those already in the Kingdom (the "Righteous and the Just," or Saints), and those who on earth aspire to be in the Kingdom. It is also a time to reflect on the deeper realities of our ultimate destiny.

d) (**Part IV**) Finally, in the fourth stage the catechumen sees the demands—and the joys—of living the sacramental and moral life. With the help of the sacramental Mysteries and the teachings of the Church for life, the Christian becomes equipped to live the life of the Spirit.

You may refer to the **Bibliography** for works about Catholicism, about Eastern Tradition in general, and about Maronite Tradition in particular. This select bibliography is arranged according to the four Parts of the overall plan of this work.

Several **Appendixes** present a substantial amount of related material for understanding the main text. These should be consulted freely and are referred to frequently in the text.

- ❖ **Appendix I** presents some of the more important liturgical customs observed by Maronites, as well as laws regulating community life.
- ❖ **Appendix II** gives a good sampling of set prayer forms used in the Tradition.
- ❖ **Appendix III.** Since this is a catechetical text that is based on liturgy and the Liturgical Year, you will find in Appendix III a nine-month schedule for relating these basic doctrines to the Sunday Feasts and Commemorations of the Liturgical Year. In using this suggested plan, along with the Lectionary Readings for the Sunday, a fuller approach to celebrating the day may be made.
- ❖ **Appendix IV** contains a helpful glossary of terms from the liturgical and historical traditions.
- ❖ **Appendix V** lists the names and summaries of the 16 Documents of the Council for reference use with this text.
- ❖ **Appendix VI** lists the Eastern Catholic jurisdictions in the U.S.
- ❖ **Appendix VII** provides a summary of each of the books in the Catholic Bible.

Suggested Use of This Text

This text is helpful for someone who has no working knowledge of the Catholic Tradition, especially through the Maronite Tradition of the Catholic Communion of Churches, and who might be interested in exploring whether to enter the Catholic Church. It is also ideal as a refresher course for a Catholic who has been baptized into one of the Traditions of the Catholic Church and wishes to review the teachings of the Church.

One of the primary uses of this text will be for the baptized Maronite Catholic, who has lived the Tradition, but wishes to integrate the teachings of the Catholic Church into a deepened appreciation of the Tradition. This text may greatly help answer such questions as," What does my Maronite Catholicism mean today?" and, "How do I fit into the whole picture of the Catholic Communion of Churches?"

More specifically, this text is intended for use by directors of religious education, catechists, preachers, pastors and families:

Directors of parish school of religion programs can use this text to train new catechists in the basic teachings of the Faith, at staff meetings, workshops, days of recollection, etc. This text also works extremely well to prepare catechumens for Initiation into the Church, as well as in conjunction with the sacramental and pastoral preparation of couples in the pre-Crowning program.

Catechists need to review basic teachings in conjunction with the lessons on the elementary and high school levels.

Preachers may supplement the teaching part of their homily preparation by referring to the appropriate sections. It is also possible to present the whole range of basic teachings over a nine-month period, using the schedule in **Appendix III**.

Pastors might wish to present this text to prospective parishioners, especially if they have little or no knowledge of Maronite Catholic Tradition.

Families may find it desirable to use the text as background for their children's religious education classes or to prepare for the upcoming Sunday celebration.

Two features of this text may help facilitate these activities:

1) **Appendix III** correlates the basic teachings of the Faith to their respective seasonal Sunday celebrations and Gospels. For example, one scriptural theme of **CANA SUNDAY** (*Jn* 2:1-11) is faith in Jesus' divine power by his changing of water into wine. Maronite Tradition chooses this Gospel at the so-called "Entrance into Lent" to signify important changes: the change that will take place in Jesus in the Resurrection, (that is, *new creation*), and the process of change (*metanoia*) we must undertake during the Lenten Season. This process should lead to our own recreation by Easter, and our eventual sharing in the life of the risen Lord in the new creation. When one links this reflection to the *Hoosoyo* for Cana Sunday, one can readily see how the Tradition has interpreted *Jn* 2:1-11 in a rich way.

2) Within the text itself, the names of the pertinent Sunday celebrations are inserted, with their Gospel references. At a glance, one may find the explanation of the Teaching/Seasonal Sunday correlation.

When all members and groups of the parish community coordinate their efforts for each Sunday celebration, a most effective **Liturgy-based formation** (and not merely Lectionary-based formation) is possible. This coordination will challenge the pastoral team—pastor, other clergy, Religious Education staff and laity. In the long run, it may be the basis for true community teamwork in evangelization.

Study Questions have been added to the end of each chapter to facilitate discussion on the material.

How to Begin Reading This Text

Since this book relies upon the texts of the liturgical tradition, an understanding of the particular language and terms used in Maronite liturgy will be of great help. You can become familiar with this material by turning first to two sections:

1) **Appendix IV** contains a basic Glossary of liturgical and other terms that relate to the Syriac-Antiochene Maronite Tradition.

2) **Chapter 21** includes an outline of the Maronite Divine Service. It will be helpful to have an understanding of how the Service unfolds.

ACKNOWLEDGMENTS

A work such as this reflects the faith of a community. In a real sense, this is not just the work of one person; several individuals have contributed to the process that produced this work. They have read the manuscript with open minds and hearts (the distinction is essential) and have been voices of encouragement and skill.

I want to thank the following: Chorbishop Seely J. Beggiani, for his expertise in reviewing not only the doctrinal content but also for guiding me in the proper Eastern and Maronite expression of it. I owe a debt of thanks to him from my days at the Maronite Seminary, where it first began to dawn on me, through him, what it meant to think as an Eastern Christian and a Maronite.

To Archbishop Francis M. Zayek, retired and first eparch of the American Maronite Community, whose love for Maronite liturgical tradition caused me and others to love and respect the genius of the Liturgy in the reform of the Tradition after the Council. In many ways he was a prophet.

To Msgr. John Trad, whose pioneering translation of the Sunday Readings helped me as a young priest to realize the logic of the Maronite Liturgical Year. I consider this a watershed in my development.

To Bishop Stephen H. Doueihi, bishop of the Eparchy of St. Maron, Brooklyn, who constantly challenged me not to be satisfied with a superficial wedding of Catholic doctrine and Maronite thought, especially as it related to liturgy. He was dogged about urging me to go deeper and to "live with the text." He has always graciously made time for my questions about the Tradition.

Thanks to Fr. Francis Marini, for his help in reviewing the canonical aspects of the material, as well as for his brotherly encouragement; to Mrs. Gloria Lavender, of St. Anthony of Padua Maronite Church, Cincinnati, a supportive friend and a colleague in religious education, who brought her experience with adult catechesis to bear upon not only the content of the text but also the organization of the material; to my editor, Ms. Sandra Sabo, who put the final touches on the end of my nearly eight-year journey of faith-in-writing that is this book; and to Attorney Anthony T. Koury, of St. Maron Church, Youngstown, for his invaluable help in navigating through the complexities of computer production of the text.

To Bishop John Chedid, under whose episcopal ministry much of this book was written.

To Bishop Robert J. Shaheen, bishop of the Eparchy of Our Lady of Lebanon of Los Angeles, who gave his support to this effort as well as his approval for it to be printed.

Thanks also to Chorbishop Gregory Mansour. As friend and fellow minister Greg has always supported my fledgling religious education efforts, and now this substantial one as well.

Certain individuals helped to make the printing project a reality by their generous financial support. Thanks to Mr. John Nasseff, of the Church of the Holy Family, in St. Paul, Minnesota; to Albert and Barbara Albert, of the Church of St. George, Wilkes-Barre, Pennsylvania; and to the Board of Directors and members of the National Apostolate of Maronites.

Last, but not least, my thanks to the Holy Spirit, whose power I often felt driving me back to the work with unfailing help, insight and enlightenment. If our belief in God's Spirit means anything, it is that the Spirit aids the work of Jesus, to the glory of the Father. It is to the honor of the Trinity that this work was undertaken in the first place.

9 February 2001
Feast of St. Maron, Father of the Maronite Church

PART I: PREPARING FOR FAITH
(Divine Liturgy Focus: Introductory Rites)

Seeking Faith

On the Fourth Sunday of the pre-Christmas Cycle, as the Maronite Church is preparing to celebrate the Nativity of the Lord, the Birth of John the Baptizer is commemorated. In the *Sedro* of that feast's Word Service we hear John addressed:

> **...O Forerunner of the Word of God,**
> **hurry to us who stand like bewildered**
> **and lost children**
> **in the hope of being found....**

It is a common experience for many people to be seekers. Human beings long for something deeper in life, something that, they sense, the world cannot give, something other than the material dimension of their existence. Honest seekers throughout the ages have come to the conclusion that what they seek is beyond themselves, that their desires are fulfilled in something or Someone beyond them.

We find ourselves on a journey of faith. In this yearning, this longing, the seeds of faith are sown. There is "a hope of being found."

The Beginnings of Faith

To be sure, there are questions. We have been given the great gift of the mind with which to ask, to seek. But clearly something more than the mind is involved in our seeking.

For ages, thoughtful seekers have seen at work in the mysteries of the universe, especially in the wonders of the created world, a hand that has provided a deep reason for the fulfillment of their longing. This may not always be readily understood by the mind; but somehow the heart relates to these wonders. It is more like an appreciation of poetry in the beauty around us. This can often be true even in the face of the obvious evil around us. These glimpses into the light, into the poetry, are the beginnings of faith.

We: Adorers of the Mystery

Understanding the truths of the Faith may take different paths. In the Western Tradition of the Church, since the Middle Ages, one well-known path of doing theology has been summarized in the phrase, "faith seeking understanding." This approach has merit in that it begins with the acceptance of faith. However, its end-point, if too exaggerated, can leave one with primarily a rational point of view.

Eastern Tradition, on the other hand, recognizes that all reality is enveloped in a sense of Mystery (with a capital *M*). Some things may never be "figured out." I cannot always control my environment, my faith journey, my life; perhaps the essence of faith lies in the trusting obedience I should have when I approach the greatest Mystery of all: our loving God.

This is seen in Maronite liturgical tradition in a very interesting way in the Monday weekday text. The memorial for this day is that of the Angels. In the Opening Prayer the Celebrant prays:

> **O Eternal One,**
> *though you are concealed from the angels in heaven,*
> *you willed to assume a human body from mortal Adam.*
> **Grant that we may join in the worship**
> **of the heavenly choirs**
> **and give you thanks and praise ... .**

Strange as it may seem at first to say that God is "concealed from the angels," the Divine Liturgy is stating the essential truth about God, preserved so strongly in Eastern Tradition: God's fundamental unknowability, God's hiddenness. Even to the angels—who are, after all, creatures—God, the Infinite One, cannot ever be fully known. Yet, as the prayer recognizes, God has mysteriously shared something of the Godhead with us.

With the angels we become adorers of the Mystery.

God: The Lover of All

Throughout history, as we sought God, God found us. Our liturgical Tradition expresses this fact clearly. In the Prayer of Praise and Thanksgiving of the *Anaphora of St. James, Brother of the Lord,* the Celebrant addresses the Father in these words:

> **...You formed us from the earth**
> **and conferred on us the joy of paradise.**
> *When we transgressed your command and sinned,*
> *you neither neglected nor rejected us,*
> *but rather, like a merciful father, you sought us.*
> *By the Law you called us back;*

by the prophets you guided us;
and, at last, you sent your only Son,
our Lord and God Jesus Christ, into the world
that he might renew your image in us....

The Prayer of Praise in the *Anaphora of St. Basil* continues this theme of God finding us:

...The child you sent healed us;
he sought us out and in various ways
he called us....

In our own day, the Council, in its *Constitution on Divine Revelation* has put it this way: "By this revelation, then, the invisible God (see *Col* 1:15; *1 Tim* 1:17), from the fullness of his love, addresses men and women as his friends (see *Ex* 33:11; *Jn* 15:14-15), and lives among them (*Bar* 3:38), in order to invite and receive them into his own company" (*DV* 2).

God, in Christ, through the Holy Spirit, is still calling us today. What God asks of us is that we now seek God. In a mysterious way, our whole life with God is an ongoing quest for each other by two lovers—God and us—who already possess each other.

As the response to the post-Communion Blessing with the Mysteries states so well, using words which all Eastern Christians know:

***O Lover of all,* have mercy on us!**

Chapter 1:
Seeing the Light of Faith

Revelation and Faith

Saying that God seeks us also means that God does not want to remain far from us; God wants to be known by us in a special way. In fact, our

> **Sunday of the Birth of the Baptizer**
> **Lk 1:57-80**

faith tells us that God has always had a plan to speak with us, God's creation. This communication from God is called *revelation*, and it is a gift we should eagerly await and gratefully accept.

Our acceptance of God and the divine will, in God's revelation, is a very personal act called *faith*. "By faith one freely commits oneself entirely to God, making 'the full submission of intellect and will to God who reveals,' and willingly assenting to the revelation given by God" (*DV* 5).

The revelation of God did not happen all at once, nor did it always occur in spectacular ways. God's Self-revelation was gradual, occurring in all of creation and history, as the Syriac Teachers frequently mention. In fact, this idea of creation as an expression of the Word of God *before* the birth of Jesus is a strong theme in their teaching (compare *Heb* 1:1-2).

But God works effectively in and through human persons as well, as the Scriptures and our Liturgy testify. In fact, the Season of Glorious Birth of the Lord shows us a God who chose to be revealed through human beings, particularly the "family" of Jesus. (See the description of this Season in **Chapter 11, "The Liturgical Year."**)

One of the clearest expressions of this revelation-through-people may be seen in the Sunday of the Birth of John the Baptizer, who is called the "Forerunner" of Jesus. The texts speak with eagerness and joy of

John's birth as paving the way for the birth of the Messiah. From the
Proemion of the feast:

> **May we be worthy to praise, confess and extol**
> **the Son, the eternal Word.**
> **His Father has sent to us the messenger of his coming**
> **to prepare the way for his birth in the flesh.**
> **Let us magnify the Godhead,**
> **whose *divine and imponderable plan is announced***
> **   *this day by the birth of John the Baptizer.***
> **Glory and worship to the Good One,**
> ***for today infinity breaks the barrier of our world***
> **and fills it with the news of an astounding birth.**
> **Let us magnify him, now and for ever. Amen.**

Again, this petition is addressed to John:

> **O voice preaching in the wilderness,**
> ***fill the wilderness of our poor lives***
> ***with your happy announcement.***

Finally, in the *'Etro*, we see how the world longed for and was
ready to receive the final revelation of God's Word with a true sense of
anticipation, as today we pray to our God and anticipate the Christmas
celebration of his First Coming among us:

> **Make us worthy to approach the birth of your Son**
> ***like people waiting for a new dawn,***
> ***like a ship whose watchman has seen the land.***
> **Delight us once again with your fatherly embrace,**
> **for the announcement of the birth of the baptizer**
> **is sure hope for the salvation**
> ***you have promised from the beginning....***

Jesus is the fulfillment of God's Plan and Promise. He appeared in
God's good time, being the revelation of God to us in a very personal way.
He is still revealed to us today.

Revelation might seem to some a complex affair, a subject to be
studied in a class in theology. But as the story of John the Forerunner
shows, God has worked and works today in a way meaningful to our lives.

Faith and Doubt

A person can lack genuine faith through one's own fault; we are free—even to reject God. But when a person "doubts," we should not

> ### *Sunday of Annnouncement to Zechariah*
> ### *Lk 1:5-25*

jump to conclusions. Nor does nagging another about these doubts always help. On the contrary, it is consoling to know that God seeks us constantly until we find God.

Doubt has long played a part in the faith response to God. On the pre-Christmas Sunday of the Revelation to Zechariah—the husband of Elizabeth the kinswoman of Mary—we see Zechariah standing before the high altar of God and doubting the angel-messenger's message to him (see *Lk* 1:5-25). Zechariah's "punishment"—being mute—is only temporary, until God's message would finally be revealed through the birth of his and Elizabeth's son, John the "Forerunner."

We can be like Zechariah, as individuals and as a society. Admitting our doubt, we can still seek divine compassion. From the *Sedro*:

> **Now, on this day of the announcement of John,**
> **the Forerunner of the Lord,**
> **we approach you amid clouds of incense**
> **with the hope of gaining a kind hearing.**
> **Once again, look with kindness upon *a wayward people***
> **   *and an obstinate nation.***
> **Come once more with the announcement of the**
> **   Forerunner**
> **and send us another angel of Good News.**
> **Then, reassured of your compassion,**
> **we will praise you, now and for ever. Amen.**

A person who is seeking deeper insight into reality may sometimes have doubts, even about God. Such doubts do not necessarily indicate a lack of faith. They may be—as in the case of Zechariah—ultimately just the opposite: a sign of growing faith (see *Lk* 1:67-79).

Pope John Paul II recognized this in words from *Orientale Lumen*, section 16:

> This is what man needs today; he is often unable to be silent for fear of meeting himself, of feeling the emptiness that asks itself about meaning; man who deafens himself with noise. All, believers and non-believers alike, need to learn a silence that allows the Other to speak when and how he wishes, and allows us to understand his words.

The life of faith is very personal and delicate—and ultimately mysterious. Faith is a gift of God, and only God knows who has it. We can, however, presume that God is generous with this precious gift, and we should not presume that anyone lacks it.

Images of Light

In the midst of doubt, darkness—whether physical, or spiritual, intellectual or emotional—can be dispelled by light. Our Maronite ancestors knew this truth, and they were fond of expressing much about the spiritual life in terms of light, which pervades the whole Tradition.

As you pray the liturgical services, the image of light appears again and again. God is light; the Kingdom is one of light; faith is light in our souls. This image is prominent in the thought of the East.

Nowhere is this seen better in the Maronite Tradition than in the *Noohro*, or "Hymn of Light," in Morning Prayer of the Divine Office (*Safro*). It says, in part:

> **The light of the just and the joy of the upright is**
> **Christ Jesus our Lord.**
> **Begotten from the Father, he manifested himself to us.**
> **He came to rescue us from darkness and *to fill us with***
> ***the radiance of his light.*...**
>
> **Day is dawning upon us; the power of darkness is fading**
> **away.**
> ***From the true light there arises for us the light which***
> ***illumines our darkened eyes.*...**
> **He brings salvation and grants us life.**

He ascends to his Father on high.
He will return in glorious splendor *and shed his light*
on those gazing upon him.

This emphasis on light is not mere poetry. Light is a strong and vibrant image of the reality of God's Presence among and power in us. Most of all, its very characteristic—brightness—is cause for our hope, on many levels of our life, here and hereafter.

The Maronite Divine Service begins with the Lighting of the Church. As the lights of the church are turned on, and the candles in the sanctuary are lighted, the Congregation sings:

Alleluia!

In your light we see *light*,
Jesus, Lord of *light*.
You are true *light*
who en*light*ens all creation.
With your *light* en*light*en us,
gladden us with your bright dawn.

Pure and holy One,
you dwell in heaven's bright *light*.
Keep destructive hate and hardship
far away from us.
Help us live in righteousness;
help us purify our hearts....

The Light of Faith

Faith is a dazzling illumination within the inner self. The East cherishes this dynamic theme of illumination, for in many ways it sums up the radiant, life-giving activity of God in us.

New Sunday
Jn 20:24-31

This action of light in us, a prominent element of our Maronite Tradition, is proclaimed in numerous texts. The *Proemion* for the *Hoosoyo* for New Sunday (the Sunday after Easter), for example, beautifully illustrates the theme of illumination. While it refers specifically to the light of the Resurrection, its meaning may be extended to all godly light in us:

> **May we be worthy to praise, glorify and honor**
> **the One who renewed the world,**
> **and traced a new path of life for his creatures;**
> *Christ, the One who is light for all*
> *and who covered the universe with a new light*
> *by his glorious resurrection;*
> **the wondrous One, who performed a new wonder**
> **on this day....**

The two themes of God as the content of revelation and illumination come together in an expressive *Hoosoyo to Jesus the Light.* In it we see the redemptive power of God's light within us. From the *Sedro:*

> **O Lord,**
> *may the rays of your brightness enlighten our*
> *hearts*
> and *save us from the darkness of sin.*
> **May your rising morning be the cause**
> **of all our blessings.**
> **May our consciences be bound**
> **and our thoughts be supported**
> **by the warmth of your love....**

The fundamental reason for having God's light in us is to have wisdom for spreading of the Gospel, or *evangelization* (see **"Evangelization"** in Chapter **18**). This idea concludes this *Sedro:*

> **...By your wisdom, make us worthy**
> **to be your faithful witnesses in the world**
> **and to be renewed in our commitment**
> **to the Christian life....**

Our Christian task is to share the light of faith.

The Creed and Catholic Doctrine

Jesus taught many things in his earthly life, which were remembered and passed down to us in the Scriptures and the Tradition of the Church that he founded. From this revelation, the Church clarified the many teachings of Jesus as necessary for our salvation.

The process of understanding and clarifying Catholic teaching has been, and continues to be, a long journey of faith—of heart and mind. One result process has been a statement of Catholic belief known as a *creed*. Creeds have as their aim to summarize the beliefs of the Faith, usually to be recited in a public way, such as at the Divine Liturgy.

There have been several creeds throughout the life of the Church. Perhaps the best known, because it is recited during the Divine Service, is the Nicene Creed. Many Catholics also know the so-called Apostles' Creed.

In addition to the formulations of the creeds, there is the ongoing activity of further reflection on the truths of the faith. This is known as *theology*; its task is to continue to clarify the teachings of faith summarized in the creeds. Statements of belief are also known as *doctrine*.

Catholics believe that no new truths have been given by anyone but Jesus, the full Revealer of God's Truth; yet, the explanation of this revelation grows and develops, according to our historical time and growth in knowledge and as the Holy Spirit allows us to see these things afresh. In other words, we can come to a deeper understanding of God's revealed truth as we grow, individually and as a community in the light of faith.

In addition, theology has developed differently in various traditions of the Catholic Church. The main differing approaches have been in the Eastern Churches and the Western Church. This very text, as a presentation of the Catholic Faith through the Tradition of the Maronite Church, shows this to be true: one revelation, many approaches. Yet, despite the many different ways of expressing the same doctrines, Catholics remain united in the Faith that they cherish.

The Church's doctrinal formulas, however, are not the same as God's self-revelation; they are the *medium* through which Catholics place their faith in God. God unveils and communicates the hidden mystery of the divine life *through* Church teaching.

So, throughout the centuries, in the living Tradition of the Church, people have tried to understand God better and to express that understanding. Thus, teachings are concrete means through which we learn about God. Through the medium of doctrinal formulas we can be led to say yes to God in the personal act of faith.

The Hierarchy of Truths

Although God has revealed the fullness of the truth that God wants us to know, not all the doctrines of our Faith have equal importance. The "Decree on Ecumenism" of the Council (reaffirmed in the *Catechism*, ¶90) taught that there is a certain hierarchy, or ordering in importance, of the teachings of the Faith. In fact, it used the term, *hierarchy of truths*.

> Furthermore, in ecumenical dialog, Catholic theologians, standing fast by the teachings of the Church yet searching together with separated brothers and sisters into the divine mysteries, should do so with love for the truth, with charity, and with humility. When comparing doctrines with one another, they should remember that in Catholic doctrine there exists an order or "hierarchy" of truths, since they vary in their relationship to the foundation of Christian faith (*UR* 11).

What does this idea of "hierarchy" mean here? Simply that certain Catholic teachings are more essentially related to the core of belief than others, and which, incidentally, in light of ecumenical dialog, are the basis for a process by which all Christians can move toward unity. We are reminded that the most central teaching is the Mystery of the Most Holy Trinity:

> The Mystery of the Most Holy Trinity is the central mystery of Christian faith and life. It is the mystery of God in himself. It is therefore the source of all the other mysteries of faith, the light that enlightens them. It is the most fundamental and essential teaching in the "hierarchy of the truths of faith." The whole history of salvation is identical with the history of the way and the means by which the one true God, Father, Son, and Holy Spirit, reveals himself to men "and reconciles and unites with himself those who turn away from sin" (*CCC* 234).

Examples of how teachings relate to one another may be seen in the dogma of Mary's Assumption into heaven (her Dormition). This teaching, important to our faith life and Catholic spirituality, is to be related to more central teachings, such as the Incarnation and the dual nature in Christ. How?

For example, the teaching on Mary's Assumption is really an illustration of the central Christian belief in the Resurrection of Jesus, which is our destiny if we are faithful to Christ. Mary, precisely because of her faithful discipleship to her Divine Son, enjoyed this destiny at the very end of her life. Thus, Mary, in the Assumption, becomes a sign of hope to us of our own future with God. The central mystery is the Father's raising of Jesus in the resurrection.

The idea of the hierarchy of truths allows us to maintain a proper understanding of our Catholic teachings, for ourselves and as we dialog with other Christians.

The Teaching Office of the Church

The teaching office (that is, mandate, or ministry) of the Church is known as the *Magisterium* (from the Latin word *magister*, meaning "teacher"). It is exercised by the Bishop of Rome and the other bishops. They are the authoritative teachers in the faith and the moral life of the Church. Their teaching, guided by the Holy Spirit, is infallible, and because of this gift Catholics can be sure of the teachings of the faith, the interpretation of the Bible and the guidelines of Catholic moral living.

The *Magisterium* is exercised in two ways. In the "extraordinary" *Magisterium*, teachings are defined an ecumenical council or by the Pope personally (*ex cathedra*). By the "ordinary" *Magisterium* the Pope and the other bishops of the Church teach that which is to be held as true by all the faithful, including their day-to-day teaching mission.

Faith, Alive and Dynamic

Faith is alive and dynamic. It seeks, through grace, to penetrate the very Mystery of God. If a particular doctrine of faith no longer makes sense to a person, she or he should go on seeking. To know what a doctrine says is one thing. To gain an insight into its meaning through the gift of understanding is something else. When in doubt, "Seek and you will find" (*Mt* 7:7). The person who seeks by reading, discussing, thinking, or praying eventually sees the light. The person who talks to God even when God is "not there" is alive with faith.

STUDY QUESTIONS:

1) What is the relationship of faith to revelation? How can faith be
   compared to light?
2) In matters of faith and religion, is doubt necessarily bad?
3) Describe faith as both an act of the inner being to God and as saying yes
   to the truths taught by the Church.

Chapter 2:
The Object of Faith:
The Fathomless Mystery
of the Trinity

God-talk: Naming the Nameless One

Trying to talk about God is very difficult. The Syriac Christian world took its direction from the Israelite experience of God. The ancient Israelites refused to use the revealed Name of God, *YHWH*, using instead other terms, like *Adonai*. The Syriac Teachers, as indeed the entire East, recognized that God is essentially unknowable. No words can adequately describe the infinite majesty, mercy and love of the Divine One.

The essential unknowability of God is a favorite theme of the Eastern Church Teachers, especially the Syriac Teachers. Since God's inner life cannot be known to the human mind, questions arise: "How can we even speak of God?" "Is it possible to know anything about God?" How can we satisfy our great curiosity in exploring our relationship to the Holy One?

If they had to talk about God at all, the Eastern Teachers found it easier to describe God either in terms of what God is not, e.g., "infinite" (God is not finite), or else by poetic and analogical language. This is called *apophatic* language. They realized that all human language while sometimes eloquently, yet most often only feebly, attempts to speak about the Divine One, who nevertheless remains the essentially the Hidden One. In his *Commentary on the Diatesseron* St. Ephrem observes:

> Among the ancients, wisdom was recognized more in
> works than in words, and to the use of the tongue they
> preferred the power of the mind reflecting in silence.

From this quote we can see that it is more than the fact that words fail to describe God. For Ephrem it is better to contemplate in silence.

Pope John Paul II also acknowledged this idea in paragraph 16 of *Orientale Lumen*:

> Thus is born what is called the apophasis of the Christian East: the more man grows in the knowledge of God, the more he perceives him as inaccessible mystery, whose essence cannot be grasped. This should not be confused with an obscure mysticism in which man loses himself in enigmatic, impersonal realities. On the contrary, the Christians of the East turn to God as Father, Son and Holy Spirit, living persons tenderly present, to whom they utter a solemn and humble, majestic and simple liturgical doxology. But they perceive that one draws close to this presence above all by letting oneself be taught an adoring silence, for *at the culmination of the knowledge and experience of God is his absolute transcendence.* This is reached through the prayerful assimilation of Scripture and the liturgy more than by systematic meditation.

This is why the Syriac Tradition preferred to use poetry as the language of God-talk. First, poetry better related to the "messy and un-theological" language of the Bible than did the language of Greek philosophical thought; second, poetry uses symbolic language to express truth: metaphor, irony, symbolism, typology, paradox, and sometimes allegory.

This is also why the Tradition prefers to employ an abundance of symbolic and metaphorical titles for God. Titles such as "Holy One," "Ancient of Days," "Light (and its variants)," "King of Heaven" come directly from the Scriptures and show the strong dependence of the Tradition on the Bible. (Note in particular the titles of God in the *Trisagion*: "Holy," "Strong," "Immortal.") Other titles like "Sun of Justice," "Compassionate One," "Merciful One," "Eternal and Hidden One," "the Good One," "Exalted One," "Great Dawn," and a whole host of other creative titles reflect especially the East Syriac world view and theology of Ephrem and James of Sarug. These titles demonstrate on the one hand the reluctance of the Syriac Tradition to "explain" the nature of God by systematic (and limiting) language, and on the other hand a willingness to use creative and descriptive language to name the Nameless One.

Another important issue in God-talk today has come to the forefront with the theological thinking of women. They remind us, with justification, that all language about God is analogous—that is, it only points to the reality it is describing, in a limited way. The Old Testament—and even Jesus in his parables—did not hesitate to describe God in feminine terms on occasion (see *Lk* 15:8-10). Rightly understood, this inclusive language, while open to exaggeration, tells us of the great richness of God, who cannot be totally captured by human terms.

In the words of the *Catechism*:

> God transcends all creatures. We must therefore continually purify our language of everything in it that is limited, image-bound or imperfect, if we are not to confuse our image of God—"the inexpressible, the incomprehensible, the invisible, the ungraspable"—with our human representations. Our human words always fall short of the mystery of God (42).

The Revelation of the Trinity

God, known as the "One," is shared by the three major, monotheistic religions: Judaism, Islam and Christianity. But of the

> **TRINITY SUNDAY**
> **Mt 28:16-20**

three, only Christianity acknowledges the One God in three, divine "Persons"; we call this mystery the Blessed Trinity—from the Greek word, *tris*, meaning "three." Anyone praying the Divine Liturgy of the Maronite Church—indeed, the whole liturgical tradition—will recognize immediately that the Trinity is referred to frequently in the prayers.

For instance, every Service of the Holy Mysteries (Divine Liturgy), as well as the prayers of the Divine Office, and the sacramental Mysteries, always begins with some form of the basic Doxology:

Glory be to the Father,
and to the Son,
and to the Holy Spirit,
now and for ever. Amen.

Also, at the conclusion of the Penitential Rite in the Divine Liturgy, just before Holy Communion, the Congregation acknowledges the Body and Blood of Christ with:

> **One holy Father,**
> **one holy Son,**
> **one Holy Spirit.**
> **Blessed be the name of the Lord,**
> **for *he is one in heaven and on earth.***
> **To God be glory for ever.**

Somehow, in God's richness and bounty, the Divine One is experienced as One-in-Three. Where did we get such a notion, so difficult for our limited, human minds? How are we to understand it?

The answer is simple: **Jesus said it.**

In his prayer and teaching, Jesus revealed that he had a deep relation to the Divine One, which he expressed, in terms understood very well to his listeners, as his "Father" (see *Jn* 10:30 and *Jn* 14:10). Jesus' use of the word *Abba* is similar to our "Daddy," who bounces his children on his knee, loving them, caring for them. Jesus spoke of Two (the Father and Jesus), and he spoke of the Two as One.

Even more, when he was about to leave this earthly dimension—before his earthly passion, death, burial and resurrection—Jesus promised to send Another from the Father, to remind his followers of God's will for them, as he had taught while on earth. He called this Other the "Paraclete" (Greek for "Advocate," or also "Comforter"; see *Jn* 16:13), or "Spirit" of the Father and of Jesus, living within the Believers (*Rom* 5:5). In other words, Jesus promised that the Believers would experience the reality of this superabundant, gracious, Three-fold Divine One in their lives.

Because Jesus, God's Word, revealed this Three-ness called the Trinity, we are called to believe in him and his revelation. Yet, it has been the task of the best minds of the Church throughout the centuries to try to explain this supreme Mystery, knowing that no one explanation will ever exhaust its richness.

Two approaches have been used to try to understand the Trinity. One approach speaks of the "economic Trinity." *Economic* comes from the Greek word *oikonomia*, which means, "plan." God has always had a plan for us. The economic Trinity acts on our behalf, the Good One reaches out to us from within the Divine inner life as One who creates, redeems and sanctifies. The other approach speaks of God as the "immanent Trinity," or what the Godhead is in the threefold inner life of the relationship between Father, Son and Holy Spirit.

The Economic Trinity: God for Us

We experience the Triune God, as One who works among us for our good and our salvation, according to God's plan of salvation. This plan has been revealed to us in the Scriptures. The specific term *economic Trinity* refers to the saving plan for the created universe, over which the Lord is sovereign. We could put it another way: we know the Trinity in the divine *missions* worked among us. Even though we attribute certain missions to one of the Persons, the other Two are always fully acting as well. When the Creator created, the Word and the Spirit created. When the Word-made-flesh redeemed, the Creator and the Spirit redeemed. When the Holy Spirit sanctifies, the Creator and the Redeemer sanctify. *It is the One God who acts.*

To believe that God is Father means to believe that you are son or daughter; that God your Father accepts and loves you; that God your Father has created you as a love-worthy human being.

To believe that God is saving Word means to believe that you are a listener; that your response to God's Word is to open yourself to his liberating Gospel, which frees you to choose union with God and fellowship with your neighbor.

To believe that God is Spirit means to believe that on this earth you are meant to live a sanctifying, supernatural life that is a created sharing in God's own nature—a life that is the beginning of life eternal.

This idea of the economic Trinity is the earliest way of Christianity's knowing God, for it comes right from the New Testament's remembrance of Jesus' revelation. It is also the prime way in which the early Syriac Teachers understood the Trinity. This is still primarily how our Maronite Liturgy—indeed, the whole Eastern liturgical Tradition—prefers to understand the Trinity, that is in how the Triune God still acts for us and our salvation.

For example, the Entrance Procession Song (*Qolo*) for the Sunday after Pentecost, Trinity Sunday, speaks of this idea as the Congregation sings:

Who can comprehend the Mystery of the Trinity?
It fills heights and depths
and is beyond investigation.
The Father begot the only-begotten;
the Son, the first-born, became flesh;
the Holy Spirit, the Comforter,
        creates and perfects.
Glory to the Hidden One,
whose nature is limitless,
one Lord in three adored Persons,
who are praised by all creation.

Another example, commonly shared by all Eastern Traditions, is seen in the very form of the structure of the *Anaphora* (Eucharistic Prayer) itself. It addresses the Three Persons of the Holy Trinity in the "order of revelation": The Father (Praise and Thanksgiving Prayer, ending in the "Holy, Holy"); the Son (Narrative of the Institution of the Last Supper) and the Holy Spirit (*Epiclesis*, or "invocation"). (The Latin Tradition reverses the last two, ending with the Institution Narrative, to preserve its characteristic emphasis on Christ.)

The Immanent Trinity: God's Inner Life

As the early Church reflected more and more on the Trinity—especially in the West—it was natural that the question would arise: "What is the nature of God's inner life?" Even though the Church steadfastly maintained that God's inner life is essentially unknowable, still the realization occurred that if God could be known from the divine missions, God must have an inner life as well. In other words, if God is One, yet Three, *how are these Three related?*

In asking this important question, the best thinkers in the Church realized that the language of the Bible was not adequate to provide a response. Thus, it was to the language of Greek and Latin philosophy that the Church in her theology turned for help.

This process of reflection was not an easy one for the Church. Some great conflicts arose, dividing the Church into conflicting groups. Yet, through Church gatherings called *councils* the questions were gradually resolved. Thus, we have inherited the formulation which stands even today as the correct understanding of the *relationships* of the Divine Three to each other, while each having the totality of Divine Being: *"one 'nature' (God) in three 'persons' (Father, Son, Holy Spirit)."*

Put in these new terms, theologians expressed the inner life of the Trinity in this way: God the Father, Who has no origin, is the source of all life and being, and knows the Godhead perfectly. The Father is the Light. The *Logos* (Greek for "Word," or—to use the word of Jesus—"Son") is the One Who knows the Father, and is the "exact representation of the Father's being" (see *Heb* 1:3). The Nicene Creed calls him "Light from Light." The Holy Spirit is the perfect love that the Father and the Son have for each other. Yet, *EACH "PERSON" IS EQUAL IN ESSENCE TO EACH OTHER.* It is in the context of these relationships within the Trinity that the term "person" must be understood.

This can be difficult to understand, because in the contemporary world "person" means a self-initiating and conscious being. However, this is **NOT** the original meaning of "person" in the early centuries of the Church's history. Yet, the faith of the Church still challenges us to make our own the revelation of Jesus that somehow God is Three-in-One. In the words of the Creed of St. Athanasius: "The Father is God, the Son is God, and the Holy Spirit is God, and yet there are not three gods but one God."

This Athanasian affirmation is expressed in every Maronite Divine Liturgy at the Invitation to Communion:

>*One holy Father,*
>*one holy Son,*
>*one holy Spirit.*
>**Blessed be the Name of the Lord**
>*for he is one in heaven and one earth.*
>**To God be glory for ever.**

Although Maronite Tradition affirms that the immeasurable depths of the inner life of the Holy Trinity cannot be plumbed by mortals, yet—following the lead of St. Paul—it is the Holy Spirit who does so. At the beginning of the *Anaphora of St. James, Brother of the Lord* we read:

>**You are truly holy, O King of all time**
>**and source of holiness.**
>**Holy is your only Son, our Lord and God, Jesus Christ.**
>**Holy is your Spirit,**
>**who reaches the depths of all things,**
>*even the depth of your own Being....*

Again, this is clearly stated in the *Epiclesis* prayer of the *Anaphora of St. Sixtus:*

> **Have mercy on us, O Lord,**
> **and on your inheritance.**
> **Be pleased with this offering,**
> **by the coming of your *Holy Spirit,***
> ***who proceeds eternally from you,***
> > ***O God the Father,***
> **and who, by essence, is equal to your Son.**

St. Ephrem, Deacon and Doctor of the Church, "Harp of the Holy Spirit," uses the image of the sun to help us understand the Trinity as Three-in-One: the bright sphere we see in the sky is the origin of what we know as the sun; it is like the Father, origin of all there is. The light of the sun, coming from the origin, is what we actually see; this is like the Son, Ray and "Light of the World." We feel the warmth of the sun, also coming from the origin; this is like the Holy Spirit, the warmth of the God's Love poured out graciously upon us. Source, Light and Warm Love seem separate to us, but they are all one. One advantage of this analogy is its similarity to the references to light in the Creed.

The Economic Trinity is the Immanent Trinity
In general, the East has tended to favor the economic Trinity approach to the Blessed Trinity. In particular, the Syriac Church (including the Maronite Church) favored the economic Trinity approach, as its tradition was adamantly scriptural and initially resisted the terms used in Greek philosophy to talk about theology. The West tended to favor the immanent approach (*CCC* 236).

Today, all Traditions have elements of both approaches to help understand something that will *only be fully understood in God's Presence in the Kingdom.* For example, at every Maronite Divine Liturgy, at the conclusion of the Penitential Rite, this strong affirmation of the inner life of the Trinity is made, as the Celebrant blesses the Congregation:

> **May the grace of the most Holy *Trinity* +,**
> **eternal and *co-equal in essence,***
> **be with you, my brothers and sisters,**
> > **for ever.**

We thus realize: *The economic Trinity is the immanent Trinity*. The ancient Church expressed the truth by the Greek word, *perichoresis*, which can be understood as a *"dancing together,"* within the Godhead and as reaching out to us. What Jesus revealed to us in the words of the New Testament is nothing less than the inner life of the Divine One.

The Trinity: Center of Our Life

As baptized Christians our objective relationship to God is never vague. It is not enough to say, as many baptized Christians do today, "I believe in God—that's enough." We can remind them that Jews and Muslims believe in God as well. What is distinctive about Christianity is our belief in God *as Holy Trinity*, as revealed by Jesus the Christ. As Maronite Eastern Christians the Holy Trinity is in fact the center of our life.

The Trinity in Our Prayer Life

This devotion to the Trinity is one of the hallmarks of all the Christian East. To underestimate its importance is to misunderstand the deep trinitarian foundation of Eastern Christianity; to recognize and appreciate it is to be thoroughly enriched by the spirit of the Eastern Way.

Concretely, prayer in the East typically ends by naming all the Persons of the Trinity, while Western Christian prayer (including Protestant prayer) usually ends "in the Name of Jesus." Obviously, Eastern prayer ends with the Name of Jesus, but almost never without acknowledging the Father and Holy Spirit as well. In fact, how a prayer ends identifies it as a prayer of the East or the West. In Maronite liturgical Tradition you can always tell to whom the prayer is addressed by paying attention to the conclusion of the prayer. The Addressee (Father or Son or Spirit) is named first; the Names of the other Two then follow. Regardless of to whom the prayer has been addressed, the whole Trinity is consistently mentioned. Try to recognize this sometime!

STUDY QUESTIONS:

1) How does understanding God as a Trinity distinguish Christianity from other religions?
2) Describe the distinction between the idea of the "Economic" Trinity and the "Immanent" Trinity.
3) Reflect on how the Trinity is emphasized in Eastern Tradition.

Chapter 3:
God, the Father of Jesus

God the Father, Source of All That Is
The Teachers of the Eastern Churches consistently emphasized that God is One and the source of all that is. Of course, they believed Jesus when he spoke of the Divine Three—"Father," "Son" and "Holy Spirit." Yet they saw that Jesus proceeds from the Father, and that the Holy Spirit proceeds from the Father through the Son, a very Eastern approach to the Trinity. At all costs they wished to preserve the view that the Origin of all was to be recognized in the Father.

God, the "I AM," is bound to nothing, but binds all things to the divine life. In God's own words, "I am the first and I am the last; there is no God but me" (*Is* 44:6). We are, and will always remain God's creatures, even in the Kingdom.

God's ineffable character has always been appreciated in the East in its typical liturgical prayer, the *Trisagion* (Greek: *tris*, "three"; *[h]agios*, "holy"):

Holy are you, O God
Holy are you, O Strong One,
Holy are you, O Immortal One.
Have mercy on us!

Centuries after the revelation described in *Exodus* and *Isaiah*, the mysterious God of the burning bush did reveal his name—in Person. Shattering all human assumptions and expectations, God's Word "became flesh and made his dwelling among us" (*Jn* 1:14). In revelation that blinds the mind with its light, Jesus spoke to I AM and said: "Father, You are in me and I in you … I made known to them your name and I will make it known, that the love with which you loved may be in them and I in them" (*Jn* 17:21, 26).

I AM reveals his name in the Son. The burning bush draws you into its light.

God Chooses to Reveal

> ### Sunday of the Finding
> ### In the Temple
> ### Lk 2:41-52

When someone in an Eastern Church speaks of revelation, another familiar word comes immediately to mind: *theophany*. This word comes from a Greek word meaning "manifestation," or "revelation," of a god (or, in Judeo-Christian terms, the true God). Often, Sacred Literature tells a story in which the revelation is given in a spectacular way. Sometimes, the circumstances might even seem strange to us as well. You might be familiar with such New Testament stories as the Baptism of Jesus, for example, or the Transfiguration of Jesus on the mountain. In each, Divinity reveals something important to humanity, usually for the purpose of leading people to salvation.

The *Book of Exodus* records one of the most profound revelations in human history. Speaking from a burning bush, which "though on fire, was not consumed," God called out: "Moses, Moses!" God then told Moses to organize the Israelites and persuade Pharaoh to let him lead that enslaved people out of Egypt. Hearing the plan, Moses was apprehensive. Yet God reassures Moses by revealing that the identification of the Holy One is "I AM Who AM."

> God spoke further to Moses, "Thus shall you say to the Israelites: The LORD, the God of your fathers, the God of Abraham, the God of Isaac, the God of Jacob, has sent me to you" (*Ex* 3:13-15).

In this dialog (and in others like it—read *Judges* 13:18 and *Genesis* 32:30) God does not really reveal a "name." God refuses a label that could leave people with the impression they "have a handle" on God. God says, in effect, that the Divine One is not like any of the many gods people worship. God conceals this divinity—thereby revealing the infinite distance between all that is divine and all that we human beings try to know and control.

But by telling Moses to say, "I AM sent me to you," God also reveals something very personal. This God who "is," beyond all realities that come and go, is not unconnected with our world and us. On the contrary, this God who "is" reveals that he is *with you*. God does not tell what the divine inner life is. But the Divine One reveals *who* God is to you.

God as "Father"

The term "Father" for the First Person of the Blessed Trinity is often misunderstood. There are those who try to apply this term literally, as if the First Person produces the Second Person (the "Word," the "Son") in the same way as human fathers beget human sons. Nothing could be further from the divine reality.

On the other hand, there are many today who roundly repudiate "Father" as a "sexist" term, as if God the Father actually had a gender. They would wish to substitute other terms.

The fact is that the Gospels record that Jesus used this term, "Father," to describe this intimate relationship. He used language understandable to the hearers of his day. There is even language in the Old Testament referring to God as the "Father" of Israel.

Jesus certainly did not understand God to be his human father. But he did understand the need to express our intimate relationship with God, especially those who have been brought into a deeper relationship as daughters and sons with the Divine One through baptism in the Name of the Trinity.

The Created Universe Reveals God

We attribute the whole process of creation to God the Holy Trinity. Through the agency of the Word and in the power of the Spirit (see *Jn* 1:1-3; *Gn* 1:1-2), the Father created all that is. We are also taught that God freely and directly made all there is from nothing. Thus, many religions recognize that God is known as the *Creator*.

Further, Maronite Tradition, following the teaching of the Bible, claims that God created all from nothing. From the *Qolo* of the *Hoosoyo* for Mondays (the Angels):

> **... O Creator of all,**
> ***you established the universe from nothing,***
> **and set into it both spiritual and visible beings.**

The Syriac Teachers remind us that the revelation to Moses on Mt. Sinai is not the first revelation of God to humanity. Creation itself is an expression of the goodness of God, and in a real way reveals God to us. The Syriac Teachers suggest that from the moment of creation God was revealing, in an ever-unfolding manner, to those that could read the signs of creation. This, of course, would come to fulfillment in the Incarnation of the Word as the fullest revelation of God. But we are not to miss the gracious outpouring of the Godhead in the beauty of creation. As a stanza from the *Noohro* (Morning Prayer) reminds us:

> **Let us glorify the majesty of the Son and give thanks to**
> **the almighty Father, who,**
> ***in an outpouring of love, sent him to us*, to fill us**
> **with hope and salvation.**

The Divine Service of Pentecost manifests this theme in the special kneeling ceremony before the Communion Rite on that day. Celebrant and Congregation are asked to kneel alternately on the left knee (in honor of the Father), on the right (in honor of the Son) and on both (in honor of the Holy Spirit). A prayer for each Person of the Trinity is said each time.

Here is the first prayer, in adoration of the Father:

> **O Lord, our God, Father of mercy,**
> **we give you thanks.**
> **On Pentecost, *you completed the blessed day***
> ***of the saving resurrection of your Son.***

The italicized words speak about "complet[ing]" the blessed day of the saving resurrection of [the] Son." What is completed, in fact, is the process of the new creation, which has been seen so clearly in the existence of the risen Jesus. He (as well as his Blessed Mother, in her privileged Assumption) is now experiencing the life of the new creation, which is also our destiny, if we too are faithful.

We Are God's Creation

The Author of Life is God, who made us and to whom we belong. For those humble enough to admit it, it may be said without blush that God possesses us. Even when we come to see the blessed vision of the Trinity in the Kingdom, we shall remain God's creatures. Our task here on earth and in the Kingdom is and will ever be to acknowledge the creative sovereignty of God, and creation's glory is sharing in God's beauty and goodness. From the First Thanksgiving Prayer after Holy Communion, *Anaphora of St. John*:

> **O Gracious Lord,**
> **what return shall we make to your goodness**
> **for the salvation you have just given us?**
> *Who is able to offer the proper glory due to you?*
> *Although of little worth and according to our measure,*
> *we glorify, praise and thank you,*
> *your only Son, and your Holy Spirit,*
> **now and for ever. Amen.**

Image and Likeness

Although "of little worth," in the face of the Infinite One, and on our own, without the grace of God, human beings were nevertheless created by our loving God with dignity. In the book of *Genesis* we read:

> Then God said, "Let us make humankind in our image, according to our likeness; and let them have dominion over the fish of the sea, and over the birds of the air, and over the cattle, and over all the wild animals of the earth, and over every creeping thing that creeps upon the earth." So God created humankind in his image, in the image of God he created them; male and female he created them (*Gn* 1:26-27).

Thus, from the beginning, God wanted human creatures to be like the very Divine One. What is that "image and likeness" of God? It is certainly not any physical traits. The *Catechism* (357) states that being in the image of God means that the human individual possesses the dignity of a person, capable of self-knowledge, of self-possession and of freely giving oneself and entering into communion with other persons, a very noble condition for creatures of dignity.

Further, being created in the image and likeness of God means having *freedom* and *free will*. This is not a cheaply viewed freedom, which so easily degenerates into license. The true freedom of the children of God is to be fully human; to know the self and the Creator; and to love others wisely and fully, including the God in whose image we are made. St. John says, "God is love, and those who abide in love abide in God and God in them" (*1 Jn* 5:16b).

God has created us in such a way that we will not be forced to act in any way other than we choose. We can choose freely to accept God's way or to reject it. Of course, when we reject God and the good, we risk bringing dire consequences upon our lives and the lives of others. Choosing unwisely—selfishly—was the basis of Adam and Eve's sin. But God did not prevent their free will.

It seems as if it would be so much better if God controlled all that we do; but God does not. In acting freely (although in our case limitedly), we reflect God's utter freedom—an astonishing gift!

In God's Image Means Communion with Each Other

There is yet another way in which we are created in the Image of the Divine One. We have seen that the Trinity is a Community of divine Persons—Three in One—and live in eternal interrelation. As such, the Trinity is the model for us to live, not in solitude, but in communion with one another.

We have all heard that "human beings are social animals." Someone who chooses to live apart from one's fellow human beings except for a noble or spiritual purpose—for example, a hermit—is generally thought of as psychologically and emotionally unhealthy. On the other hand, history is full of examples of people who have been heroes in serving the needs of others in need. This heroism is not merely a human quality; rather, it is the best of humanity in the image of the God who calls us to communion as God exists in communion.

This call to communion in God's image is also the foundation of the human reality known as community. For the Christian, the highest earthly form of community is the Assembly of Believers known as the Church (see **Chapter 15, "Community as the Sacramental Context"**). This communion also finds expressions in many other ways in the lives of believers, for example, Christian marriage.

Divine Providence

> **Sunday of the Revelation**
> **To Joseph**
> **Mt 1:18-25**

In the key moment recorded in *Exodus* (and developed further in the *Book of Isaiah*, chapters 40-45), God revealed that he is *our* God, the "God of your ancestors"—the fathomless mystery who is with you through all time, with you beyond all powers of death and evil.

The God who is revealed in the Old Testament has two main characteristics. First, and most important, is the revelation that, despite the fact that God is totally the Other, totally beyond all time and space, yet the Divine One freely chooses to be personally close to us and is *our* God.

This personal characteristic of creating, sustaining and nurturing is often called *Divine Providence*. God does not just create, then leave us all on our own. No, the Loving One is always there: to light, to guard, to rule, to guide. Many people prefer superstitiously to think of the good things that happen in their lives as "good luck." To those who have faith, these good happenings are sure signs of a loving Presence who only wishes good for us, who wills life and happiness for us.

Maronites recognize the loving hand of God in the care that Joseph gave to Jesus and Mary. In the *Sedro* for the pre-Christmas Sunday of the Revelation to Joseph this providential reflection of God's care may be readily seen:

> **Is there any lofty place like yours,**
> **O honorable and righteous Joseph?**
> *You served the Lord and his mother,*
> *and were their constant companion*
> *both day and night.*
> *You carried on your arm the One who carries*
> *the whole world,*
> *and you supported the One who supports*
> *all people....*
>
> **... O innocent and righteous Joseph,**
> **we now petition you with the clouds of incense**
> **that we raise:**
> *intercede for us with the Lord,*
> *whom you served throughout your life.*
> *Implore him to watch over us in this world*
> *and to keep us from the misfortunes*
> *of soul and body....*

The story of the angel's visit to Joseph reflects this theme of God's providential care for us in another way. The angel in this Gospel, as in other places in the Bible, symbolizes the way God communicates with human beings for their good. Syriac Tradition—as other traditions—sees angels as messengers who do God's bidding. In praying for the civil leaders whose task it is to look out for us, the third intercession in the *Anaphora of the Twelve Apostles* states:

> **Remember, O Lord, our civil leaders,**
> **who watch over your people, the flock**
> **saved by your name.**
> *In your mercy forgive them, assist them,*
> *and send your angels to protect them....*

God sends us guardian angels to help and protect those for whom he cares. God's Providence takes many forms.

STUDY QUESTIONS:
1) Why was it important for Jesus to call God "Father"?
2) In what way(s) has God been revealed to us?
3) What does it mean to be created in the Image and Likeness of God?

Chapter 4:
Jesus the Christ, Divinity Joined to Humanity

Jesus, Truly Divine and Fully Human

Jesus the Christ (this second name means "Messiah," or "Anointed One") is the Second Person of the Blessed Trinity and God's "Word" (*Logos* in Greek). He is at the same time truly God and truly human. As God he has all the qualities and attributes of God. As human, he has a human body, a human soul, human mind and will, a human imagination and human feelings. While on earth, the Son of God lived a real life like our own. Even though Jesus is now glorified in heaven, his divinity does not overwhelm or interfere with his humanity—and vice versa.

The Antiochenes tried in their own way to explain how the Logos—who assumed a real human nature; and human nature—which was truly assumed by the Logos—could exist together. These Christians of Antioch tended to emphasize the *distinction* between the divine and the human united in Christ. Jealously they guarded the idea of the humanity of Christ, for they wanted to show how deeply God entered into our own existence, and how he showed us the way to fulfill our own existence in God in the Kingdom.

Although the consequences of the unity in Christ remain a mystery to our minds, the Church proclaims this unity real in Jesus, two natures in one Person (see **"The Incarnation,"** below).

The Maronite Church expresses its Antiochene roots in many places in the liturgical and spiritual traditions. Whether it is in the prayers of the Divine Eucharist—in the Service of the Word (particularly the *Hoosoyo*) or in the *Anaphora*s; in the celebration of the sacramental Mysteries; or in the prayers of the Divine Office, the Mystery of the Incarnation shines through. Maronites proclaim this belief at every Divine Liturgy just before Communion, in a prayer that all Maronites know:

> *You have united, O Lord,*
> *your divinity with our humanity,*
> *and our humanity with your divinity;*
> *your life with our mortality*
> *and our mortality with your life.*
> *You have assumed what is ours*
> *and you have given us what is yours*
> *for the life salvation of our souls.*
> **To you be glory for ever!**

This spiritual reality of the joining of the divine and human as the purpose of Christ's earthly mission is often called *divinization* by the Eastern Churches (especially the Byzantines), and is one of our strongest theological emphases. To be joined to the Trinity as fully redeemed creatures is the goal of every Christian. (More on divinization may be found in Chapter **17, "Initiation: Baptism II**.)

The statement of the Council of Chalcedon (451 A.D.) that proclaimed the true humanity and divinity of Jesus Christ became official Church teaching. The Church became divided into those who followed the teachings of the Council—known as *Chalcedonians*—and those who resisted—*non-Chalcedonians*. Bitter persecutions arose between rival groups (see **Chapter 7, "The Chaldean Catholic Church" and "The Syriac Catholic Church"**)

In time, opponents of the Council called followers of its teaching *Melkites* (from the Syriac word for "king," or "emperor") because the emperor-king in Constantinople supported the teachings of the Council. This use of the term *Melkite* was one of scorn, or at best a nickname. Pierre Dib (*History of the Maronites,* p. 47) points out that the name *Melkite* was in use in Alexandria in the 5th century and does not seem to have entered Syria until the 7th. Thus, by the 7th century even the followers of St. Maron, who were certainly Chalcedonian, were accused by resisters of teachings of Chalcedon as being Melkite.

Christ, the Revelation and Icon of God

> Long ago God spoke to our ancestors in many and various ways by the prophets, but in these last days he has spoken to us by a Son, whom he appointed heir of all things, through whom he also created the worlds. He is the reflection of God's glory and the exact imprint of God's

very being, and he sustains all things by his powerful word. When he had made purification for sins, he sat down at the right hand of the Majesty on high, having become as much superior to angels as the name he has inherited is more excellent than theirs (*Heb* 1:1-4).

The refrain of the *Qolo* for the pre-Christmas commemoration of Genealogy Sunday expresses a favorite teaching of the Syriac Church: God was revealing the Divine Presence since the beginning of time through the mystery of creation, and its culmination is the very Person of Jesus. Here again we see a theophany of the Second Person. However, unlike the spectacular details of other theophanies, this one is described so simply, so gently:

O Promise of God from age to age, O Flower of the Gospel!

In using the subtle image of a flower, the Liturgy suggests creation. As the flower unfolds, so does God's revelation. The full bloom is a thing of beauty and joy, as is Jesus for us. And as a flower cannot grow of itself, but needs to be sustained and nourished, so God sustains creation—loving, guiding and directing it, a sure sign of divine, providential care (see **"Divine Providence,"** above, **Chapter 3**).

As Image (Icon) and Light of the Father (see *Heb* 1:3), Jesus can rightly be called the Sacrament of God: "Whoever has seen me has seen the Father" (*Jn* 14:9). This incarnational view helps us to realize how good creation is (*Jn* 3:15) and highlights the Catholic emphasis on the sacramentality of the world (see the section on **"The Sacramental Life,"** in **PART IV**).

Liturgical Year: The Season of the Glorious Birth of the Lord

This lovely liturgical season helps us to reflect on the Incarnation in general and specifically to prepare for and celebrate the Birth of the Messiah. Announcing the first coming of Jesus is done in a way that highlights the ancestors and family of Jesus of Nazareth; this helps us relate this mystery to our families and ourselves. The theological mystery is that God has visited God's people in a very personal and human way, the way dear to the Antiochene part of Maronite Tradition. (See **The Lectionary** in **Chapter 11**; also **Appendix I**.)

Question: What does the preparation for and celebration of the Nativity of Jesus tell us about the Risen Christ?

Answer: It is that the One we worship in the manger is the Messiah who has already appeared to us, was born to die for our sins (this is the symbolic meaning of the gift of myrrh of the third Magi), and who was vindicated by the power of the Father in the Resurrection.

The Incarnation

> ### *Sunday of the Announcement to Mary*
> *Lk 1:26-38*

We are told in the New Testament that the Word of God became human in Bethlehem of Judea, in the body of Mary of Nazareth, who is his human mother. Historical studies tell us that the birth of Jesus probably occurred between the years 6 to 4 B.C. (This seemingly strange fact is explained by the revision of the yearly calendar in the West in the Middle Ages.) Since the Father of Jesus is God, Jesus had no human father—a miracle accomplished by the power of the Holy Spirit. We find these truths expressed for us in the first and second chapters of Matthew's and Luke's Gospels, in what are known as the "Infancy Narratives" (*Mt* 1,2; *Lk* 1,2).

God's being clothed in our humanity is called the *Incarnation*, which means, literally, "enfleshment." The Second Person of the Holy Trinity, the Word of God—and only the Word—became a human being like us in all things but sin (*2 Cor* 5:21).

Further, this event was accomplished at God's right time. These ideas are seen in the *Proemion* of the day:

> **May we be worthy to praise, glorify and honor**
> **the Ancient of Days, who is eternally begotten**
> **of the Father**

and was in due time born of a virgin;
the light and image of the Father,
who is One Being with his Father.
By his birth the sayings of the Prophets
       have been fulfilled.
To the Good One are due glory and honor
on this feast and all the days of our lives
and for ever. Amen.

In the Infancy Narratives we hear that God sent the angel Gabriel to announce this news to Mary of Nazareth and to Joseph the Carpenter. The *Hoosoyo* for the Sunday of the Announcement to Mary records her utter amazement and faith and elaborates on the angel-messenger's words:

The angel said,
"Mary, the power of God's Spirit
is now upon you.
Your son is the long-awaited hope of the Prophets.
He dwells in eternal realms,
and fiery ranks of angels accompany him,
for he is the flaming Word of God, a searing fire,
a white, hot coal."

With Mary, we also ponder the mystery (*Lk* 2:19):

Now, O Lord,
we are seized with amazement,
and like Mary, we do not understand.
With her we draw back, blinded by your eternal flame,
scorched by its touch and overcome by its power.
We know only to offer incense (He *is* God, after all!)
as a fitting response to so great a Word
who this day makes his presence among us.
We hide behind clouds of perfumed smoke,
and dare not glimpse the power
that now descends over our altar. ...

Although relatively more was written in ancient times about Jesus as an individual figure than most other ancient figures, still, very little is known about his historical life. (See **"The Quests of the Historical**

Jesus" in **Chapter 9, "The New Testament."**) The Gospels tell something about the birth and very early years of Jesus; yet, these may be more theological statements than scientific history (see Brown, *Responses*, qn. 44).

Early reflections on Jesus' life (*Phil* 2:6-11) express the conviction that he voluntarily lived a simple, even abased and misunderstood, life—leading to his shameful death. Yet God's raising up of Jesus from the grave on Easter, followed by his appearances to some of them, was undoubtedly the reason for the faith of the Apostles and Disciples. That conviction led to the establishment of the Church and served as the basis for the New Testament. The historical details, while important, are clearly secondary to the Easter faith that Christians profess.

The main focus of the Gospels hinges on the teachings and miracles of Jesus, and his Passion, Death and Resurrection from the dead. Even the Infancy Narratives express this. For example, consider these lyrics from a well-known English Christmas carol:

> I wonder as I wander, out under the sky,
> How Jesus the Savior did come for to die
> For poor orn'ry people like you and like I—
> I wonder as I wander, out under the sky.

Or again, from the modern carol, "We Three Kings of Orient Are": of the gifts the three Magi bear, one is myrrh, a burial spice. The fact of bitterness, rejection, and ultimately death, are a part of what this King (gold) and God (frankincense) must undergo.

Our Christmas *Hoosoyo* hints at this reality of salvation. In the middle of the *Sedro* we read:

> **Holy Lord, Hidden Being,**
> **you became visible at Bethlehem.**
> **Holy Lord, Fair Dawn,**
> **you enlightened the whole world.**
> *Holy Lord, Wisdom of the Father,*
> *you became a child to free the children of Adam.*

Of course, this freeing of the children of Adam—us—did not happen simply because of the *fact* of Christ's Birth; it happened through his life of sacrifice, epitomized on the Cross, and vindicated in the Resurrection.

A Will Conformed to the Divine Will in Everything

Jesus of Nazareth was a perfect human being, sinless (*2 Cor* 5:21), though tempted (*Mk* 1:12-13). It is extremely for us difficult to imagine such a person, because our inner vision is so clouded by the reality of sin in our own lives. But *the will of Jesus was fully directed toward the will of God, in perfect harmony with it*, "obediently accepting death, even death on a cross" (*Phil* 2:8b).

This was affirmed at the Third Council of Constantinople in 681. This Council taught that Christ possessed two natures and two wills, divine and human. These were not opposed to each other but cooperated in such a way that Christ willed humanly to obey the will of the Godhead perfectly in all he had decided with the Father and Holy Spirit for our salvation.

In history, some people have claimed, based on some liturgical texts they'd seen and misinterpreted, that Maronites at one time believed that there was only one will in Jesus—the divine. (This heresy is called *monothelitism*, from the Greek meaning "one will." This heresy became widespread throughout the Christian East, and there were many efforts, to reconcile opposing parties.) However, these Maronite texts only emphasize this truth: that Jesus was wholly conformed to the Divine Will, which directed and guided perfectly his human will, while leaving it free. Pierre Dib (see Bibliography) shows this accusation to be groundless.

Jesus' life was lived according to the saving will of God for all human beings. The divine "economy," or plan, of salvation, made the human Jesus what he was. Jesus accepted this will and plan and lived it out with faith and obedience to the Father. Although found in many prayers of the Tradition, the *Anamnesis* prayer of the *Anaphora of St. Mark* speaks of this plan very eloquently:

> **Lord Jesus Christ,**
> **we recall your plan of salvation for us:**
> *from your conception, birth, and holy baptism*
> *to your saving passion, live-giving death,*
> *your burial for three days,*
> *your glorious resurrection, ascension to heaven,*
> *your sitting at the right hand of the Father,*
> *and your wondrous, awesome and royal return,*
> **when you shall judge all people**
> **and separate them according to their deeds....**

Jesus, Our Redeemer

> **2ⁿᵈ *Sunday of Resurrection***
> ***Jn 3:1-6***

God's Word joined humanity and dwelt among us for our redemption, or to use another important word, our salvation.

This teaching may be seen in many texts of the Tradition. A good example is the Prayer of the Veil in the *Anaphora of St. James, Brother of the Lord*:

> **O God,**
> **in your unspeakable love for all people,**
> ***you sent your son into the world***
> ***to bring back the lost lamb to you.***
> ***Do not turn your face away from us …***

Again, we may see this idea in the admonition of the Deacon before kneeling in honor of the Son in the Kneeling Rite (after the priest's Communion) on Pentecost:

> **… Come, let us worship the true Son,**
> **sent by the Father of Light.**
> ***He knelt on our behalf,***
> ***offered prayer for our sake***
> ***and raised us up from our fall from grace.***
> ***He showed his mercy to us and forgave us.…***

Salvation from What?

Because sin was rampant in the world, and just when we needed it most (*Rom* 5:8), Christ came to save us from the slavery of sin (*Jn* 3:17). Through the efficacious action of Christ—in suffering, dying and rising—we are saved from sin and the effects of sin so rampant in the world: violence, greed, selfishness, lust and corruption. No one who reads the newspaper or watches television can be ignorant of this harsh reality.

Salvation for What?

Most often, the question of salvation is discussed only in terms of the evil from which we are saved. But there is an equally important consideration: Jesus—this Name means, "God saves"—has redeemed us *for* a purpose, too. We are chrismated people, anointed to do the divine will for God in this world. We are to be eyes, hands, feet, heart, soul and compassion of God to those who need it most here and now. This positive aspect of salvation must never be neglected (see **Chapter 18, "Our Chrismational Mission to the World"**).

The Paschal Mystery: Days of Our Redemption

The Death and Resurrection of Jesus Christ form the nucleus of the New Testament story about him. Some scholars posit that this historical kernel, the basis of the earliest *kerygma*, might be called the Cross Gospel. Upon this—coupled with the belief that Christ is risen—the Evangelists built up their narration.

Apart from the Gospels, one reason we can put our trust in the tradition about the Death and Resurrection of Jesus is from the places where these events happened: Calvary and the Tomb. Both of these sites today are within the *Anastasis*, or Church of the Resurrection, in Jerusalem. This monumental Crusader church shows the foundations of the original 4th-century edifice built by the Emperor Constantine in the Holy Land to commemorate these two sites. This evidence, confirming the witness of the New Testament itself, allows us to stand on a good historical basis for believing the Paschal Mystery. In other words tradition (in this case the places of veneration) confirms the Bible.

We call the memorial of our salvation through Jesus our Redeemer the "Paschal Mystery." It is memorialized in special ways. The Syriac Church was fond of depicting the Paschal Mystery by the icon of Jonah and the Big Fish, taken from our Lord's cue:

> When the crowds were increasing, he began to say, "This generation is an evil generation; it asks for a sign, but no sign will be given to it except the sign of Jonah. For just as Jonah became a sign to the people of Nineveh, so the Son of Man will be to this generation" (*Lk* 11:29-30).

> Jesus answered them, "Destroy this temple, and in three days I will raise it up." The Jews then said, "This temple has been under construction for forty-six years, and will you raise it up in three days?" But he was speaking of the temple of his body. After he was raised from the dead, his disciples remembered that he had said this; and they

believed the scripture and the word that Jesus had spoken
(*Jn* 2:19-22).

In this Old Testament image, Jonah is cast off into the sea,
presumably to be drowned (a seeming death); swallowed up by the big
fish for three days (a three-day "burial"), and is spewed forth from the
belly of the fish to resume the prophetic life (a kind of rebirth). Jesus
applies this myth to his life: real death, burial, resurrection.

The Paschal Mystery is commemorated ritually and dramatically
each year in Passion Week. The whole week is special, juxtaposing, as it
were, themes of sadness and joy. Even here the eyes of faith see a serene
joy in commemorating the painful sadness of Jesus'—and our—death unto
life.

Hosanna! Christ, Our King and Savior

> **Hosanna Sunday**
> **Jn 12:12-22**
> **Or**
> **Lk 19:28-40**

Setting the stage
for Passion Week is the
previous week, the last
Weekday Cycle of Great
Lent, called "Hosanna
Week." During this week
the daily Service is that of Hosanna Sunday, except, of course, that the
procession for Sunday does not take place. The Cycle ends with Hosanna
Sunday itself, a very festive day, particularly for children, and traditionally
celebrated by Maronites as a day almost equal to Easter and Christmas
(see **"Great Lent,"** in **"Customs of the Liturgical Year," Appendix I**).

Jesus said, "I am the way, and the Truth, and the life; no one
comes to the Father, but by me" (*Jn* 14:6). Christians believe that in no
other name is a person saved. For us, Jesus is indeed our King and Savior.
Our baptism is a participation in Christ's redemption.

Our joy and recognition of Christ as our King and Savior may be
seen in the texts for Hosanna Sunday. As the Opening Prayer expresses:

> **O God,**
> *make us worthy to go forth and meet you*
> *at your second coming,*
> *as the people of Jerusalem went forth*
> *to meet you.*

May we carry the banners of triumph
and the crowns of glory,
as branches of olives and palms
were once carried.
Let us join our voices and say:
"Hosanna! Blessed is the King of Israel!"
May we then enter the heavenly Jerusalem
with you and proclaim:
"Blessings and glory, wisdom and mercy,
strength and power to our God,
for ever!" Amen.

As believers in the divinity of the Son of God and hearers of his Gospel Word, Christians naturally put their King and Savior Jesus Christ above all else in their lives.

Although non-Christians, who do not serve Christ as King, may attain salvation by living their lives to the best of their understanding and ability, this is—mysteriously, the Church believes—a sharing also in the universal will of God for all to be saved, and somehow also a participation in the work of Christ (see the section on **Interfaith Dialog** in **Chapter 6**).

Nevertheless, the Catholic Church teaches that the Word of Christ be brought to all persons in such a way that anyone who hears will want to come to Christ and be baptized (see *Rom* 10:10-17), that this will and work be known and believed. This is the mission of the Church known as evangelization and it should be the desire of all committed Christians to want to tell of their Savior (see **"Evangelization"** in **Chapter 18**).

Christ Serves

As joyful as Hosanna Sunday is, the days of Passion Week are more important. The three principal days are: Thursday of Mysteries, Great Friday of the Crucifixion, and Great Saturday of the Light.

On Thursday of Mysteries the whole Church commemorates the Institution of the Holy Eucharist at the Lord's Last Supper with the Apostles. In focusing on the ritual of the Washing of the Feet, the Maronite Church emphasizes clearly the legacy of love and service that is at the heart of the meaning of the Eucharist, as well as the sacrifice of love on Calvary—with its forgiveness of sins—sacramentally re-enacted in each celebration of the Divine Service.

The blessing of water for the Foot-washing says, in part:

> **O Christ our God,**
> **you are exalted by heavenly hosts,**
> **glorified by spiritual ranks,**
> **and extolled by thousands of holy beings.**
> **You fill the highest heavens,**
> **and thousands upon thousands hasten to serve you.**
> **From the heights of heaven,**
> ***you willed to bow down and become a man.***
> **You were like us in all things but sin.**
> **Through your plan of salvation,**
> **you saved us from the captivity of the Adversary.**
> ***You have left us this example of humility***
> ***through your holy Apostles***
> ***when you washed their feet at the***
> ***Supper of Mysteries....***

Christ Dies

The first of the two main Services on Great Friday is the *Anaphora of the Signing of the Chalice.* This is one of the most ancient liturgies of the entire Church, and some form of it is prayed by all of the Churches, East and West. The focus is on the redeeming Blood of Christ, and his Body broken for us. From the *Sedro*:

> **... O merciful Lord,**
> **we now petition you and appeal to your kindness.**
> **Consecrate this chalice mixed with wine and water**
> **by the sanctifying union of your Holy Body.**
> **May it become a chalice of thanksgiving**
> **for those who drink of it.**
> ***May it become a chalice, which purifies and cleanses us***
> ***of every trace of sin....***

Typical of the prayers and tone of Passion Week—indeed, of all of Great Lent—the liturgical tradition never allows us to stop with the suffering aspect of the Cross, *but always offers the hope of redemption and resurrection.* Although many Lenten texts reflect this idea, the *Sedro* from the Service of Monday, Tuesday and Wednesday of Passion Week expresses well the contrast and the link between suffering and resurrection:

> **... We implore you, O Christ,**
> **who suffered because of your love for us:**
> *Clothe us with your passion as with a royal robe,*
> *with your humiliation as with a crown,*
> *and with your cross as a scepter,*
> *that we may become innocent, whiter than snow,*
> *and wear wedding garments at your heavenly banquet.*
> **Then we offer glory worthy of your majesty,**
> **and, in the measure of your protection for us,**
> **give thanks to you, O Christ,**
> **your Father, and your Holy Spirit,**
> **now and for ever. Amen.**

The second Service of the day is a Service of the Word: the ritual Burial of the Lord. Literal to the Gospel story of the Passion and dramatic, it invites us to be buried with the Lord, to be forgiven and rise with him (*Rom* 6:8). The first stanza of a central hymn of this Service expresses the theology of the Passion well:

> *On the Cross the Son of God gave up his life.*
> *He submitted it to God, the Lord Almighty.*
> *Tombs burst open; great rocks shook and swayed.*
> *What a wonder for all creation!*
> *Then a lance opened the side of the Lord Jesus.*
> *Blood and water flowed from him,*
> *forgiving the world!*

The response to the *Trisagion* of the day, which has been that of all of Great Lent, clearly shows its Antiochene roots, with its emphasis on the historical:

> **Holy are you, O God,**
> **Holy are you, O Strong One,**
> **Holy are you, O Immortal One,**
>
> *O Christ, crucified for us, have mercy on us!*

Christ Our Light is Awaited

On Great Saturday of the Light the Divine Liturgy is not permitted during the day. It is a quiet day that invites us to end our Lenten Fast in a spirit of anticipation for the Grandest Feast, the Resurrection. The "Service of Forgiveness" is prayed near noontime. In this communal Penance Service, we are reminded that we are to be buried with Christ if we are to rise with him, as Scripture teaches:

> Do you not know that all of us who have been baptized into Christ Jesus were baptized into his death? Therefore we have been buried with him by baptism into death, so that, just as Christ was raised from the dead by the glory of the Father, so we too might walk in newness of life. For if we have been united with him in a death like his, we will certainly be united with him in a resurrection like his (*Rom* 6:3-5).

Christ Is Risen!

> ### Sunday of the Resurrection (Feast of Feasts)
> #### Mk 16:1-8 or Jn 20:1-18

The drama of Passion Week leads, of course, to the Feast of the Glorious Resurrection, Easter Sunday. Not only in the Eastern Churches, but also indeed in all of Christianity, the Resurrection is celebrated as the "Greatest Feast."

We must remember that it is only the empty tomb that the disciples find on that Easter morning—no one actually witnessed the Resurrection event. The body of Jesus was radically changed from the battered and beaten man of sorrows to the Glorious Heavenly Being.

The response of "Believing Thomas" on New Sunday is the clearest assertion in all of the Gospels to the divinity of Jesus: "My Lord and my God!" (*Jn* 20:28). It bears repeating: liturgically, no matter what other feast or commemoration is being observed during the Liturgical Year, it is the risen Christ who is always worshiped.

The clearest example of our Church expressing its belief in the fact and mystery of the Resurrection, as well as its far-reaching effects into our own day and lives, is found in the *Hoosoyo* for the Sunday of the Glorious

Resurrection. This text reminds us of the ancient belief that Easter is at the very heart of the Christian experience. The first part:

> *Proemion*
>
> **... You, O Christ, are the light that never ceases.**
> *You were entombed like all mortals*
> *and, with your living voice,*
> *you woke all the just who were deep in sleep.*
> *You removed from creation the ancient sadness,*
> *and gathered the nations to worship you*
> *and to announce your salvation in every place.*
>
> *... as you saved us by your passion*
> *and granted us life by your resurrection,*
> *so now clothe our bodies with the power*
> *of your Spirit....*

Be His Witnesses

Christ's appearances to his friends as risen and alive form the Easter faith the Church once proclaimed and still proclaims. Since no one actually saw Jesus rise, it was the challenging task of proclaiming the risen Lord, which fell to the first witnesses of Jesus Christ alive. Our faith rests on this belief, centered on those earliest witnesses, the Twelve Apostles and Paul, and the Disciples such as Mary, Mother of Jesus; Mary Magdalene; Peter; the Beloved Disciple; James, brother of the Lord.

We then are certainly called by God to stand with those earliest witnesses to the Rising of Christ. As the *'Etro* for the Liturgy of the Sundays during the Season of Pentecost (weekly memorial of the Resurrection) states:

> *... Make us worthy to proclaim your rising*
> *from the dead with your holy angels;*
> *to announce your resurrection*
> *with your women disciples;*
> *and to rejoice in your triumph*
> *with your blessed apostles....*

Martyrs

Christian martyrdom, or giving up one's life voluntarily for the sake of Christ, is one of the earliest forms of witness to the Faith. Stories of Christians being thrown to the wild beasts (such as Bishop Ignatius of Antioch) or burned to death in spectacles of the Roman Empire abound. These brave persons were only following the lead of the Master in dying for God's cause:

> But Jesus said to them, "You do not know what you are asking. Are you able to drink the cup that I drink, or be baptized with the baptism that I am baptized with? (*Mk* 10:38)

That Jesus died for a good cause—our redemption—is expressed poignantly in the *Hoosoyo* for Fridays. Here, Jesus is described in a favorite theme of the early Church and one dear still to the Syriac Maronite Tradition: martyrdom. From the *Proemion*:

> **May we offer glory, praise and honor to Christ,**
> *the martyr,*
> *who shed his blood to give life to the blessed martyrs.*
> *He provides strength to those who fight the good fight,*
> *crowns the heroes of faith,*
> *and rejoices in their memory.*
> **To Christ, the Good One, are due glory ...**

Like other courageous Christian Traditions, the Maronite Church has had its share of martyrs for the Faith. The feast of the 350 Maronite Monks who gave their lives for the orthodox teaching of the Council of Chalcedon is observed each year on 31 July. Of note among Maronite martyrs in modern times are the three Blessed Massabki Brothers, who, among so many others, gave up their lives for the Faith in the face of Muslim persecution, in the massacres of the 1860s in Damascus. Their feast is celebrated on 10 July.

In addition to individual references to the martyrs in the liturgical calendar, the Maronite Church weekly commemorates the Martyrs on Fridays (see **"Commemorations of the *Qoorbono*"** in **Appendix I**).

Another word for someone who openly witnesses to the Faith but who does not necessarily give up one's life is a *confessor*. Although by this word one perhaps first thinks of the priest who hears confession, the idea of witnessing openly has a more fundamental meaning. Confessors to the Faith are commemorated weekly in one of two alternate texts for Tuesdays.

Liturgical Year: The Season of the Glorious Resurrection

> **Question:** What does the season of the Glorious Resurrection tell us about the Risen Christ?
>
> **Answer:** Christ is risen!

In the Maronite Tradition, the great Feast of Easter is called simply, "The Greatest Feast" (Arabic: *'Eed l'Kabeer*). In a sense, this simple title sums up perhaps the most ancient teaching of the Church: the importance of the Resurrection as the foundation of our faith. As St. Paul teaches:

> Now if Christ is proclaimed as raised from the dead, how can some of you say there is no resurrection of the dead? If there is no resurrection of the dead, then Christ has not been raised; and if Christ has not been raised, then our proclamation has been in vain and your faith has been in vain. We are even found to be misrepresenting God, because we testified of God that he raised Christ—whom he did not raise if it is true that the dead are not raised. Or if the dead are not raised, then Christ has not been raised. If Christ has not been raised, your faith is futile and you are still in your sins (*1 Cor* 15:12-17).

What Paul is trying to say in a seemingly negative way is: Christ *IS* risen; no doubt about it! Therefore, the Feast that commemorates this fact is THE biggest day of the year.

Further, it is always the risen Christ we acknowledge and worship every single moment of our lives. Even though the Lectionary sets forth a pattern of Readings that allows us to follow the chronological events in the life of Jesus, it is always the risen Lord of whom they speak. The question we always ask at the beginning and throughout each liturgical season is: What does this season of the Liturgical Year reveal to me about the risen Lord of glory? It is this focus that forms the basis of Raymond Brown's texts on the pre-Christmas Cycle (*A Coming Christ in Advent*); Christmas (*An Adult Christ at Christmas*); Passion Week (*A Crucified Christ in Holy Week*), and Eastertime (*A Risen Christ at Eastertime*) (see Bibliography for all). This question is repeated in each section on the Liturgical Year.

The hymn sung during the Communion of the Celebrant sums up the spiritual meaning of Easter and our redemption:

> **Through the resurrection of Christ the King,**
> **with true faith,**
> **let us beg for forgiveness for our souls.**
>
> **Let us all together proclaim to the Son,**
> **who redeemed us by his cross:**
> **"Blessed is our Savior:**
> **Holy are you, holy are you, holy are you."**
>
> **May the memory of Christ's mother,**
> **the saints, and all the faithful departed**
> **be honored throughout the whole world.**
>
> **Alleluia!**

During the Season of the Glorious Resurrection, Eastern Christians never tire of greeting one another with the traditional words that summarize their faith:

> **Christ is risen!**
> *He is truly risen!*

STUDY QUESTIONS:

1) Why is it appropriate that the Word *(Logos)* became human? Put in Eastern terms: How is Jesus the Icon of God?
2) In what way can Jesus be called our "Redeemer," or "Savior"? What is salvation?
3) Describe the Paschal Mystery, in Jesus' time and in ours.

Chapter 5:
The Holy Spirit:
Indwelling Love

Indwelling

There is an entirely personal presence of God within and among those who love him. Jesus himself speaks of it in the Gospel of John, where he

> **Pentecost Sunday**
> *Jn 12:31-36, or*
> *Jn 14: 23-31, or*
> *Jn 16: 1-15*

says: "Whoever loves me will keep my word, and my Father will love him, *and we will come to him and make our dwelling with him*" (*Jn* 14:23).

This special presence of the Trinity is properly ascribed to the Holy Spirit, for as Saint Paul proclaims, "The love of God has been poured out into our hearts through the Holy Spirit that has been given to us" (*Rom* 5:5). This presence of the Spirit, God's gift of love within us, is called the Divine Indwelling (*CCC* 733), a favorite descriptive term in the Eastern Churches.

The Mission of the Holy Spirit

We need to remember the way in which God has revealed the Divine Presence in salvation history to us: gradually, unfolding more and more, culminating in the Father's sending of the Spirit, who still lives with us today. St. Gregory of Nazianzus, an Eastern theologian who helped to articulate the truth of the Trinity, especially the Holy Spirit, put it this way:

> The Old Testament proclaimed the Father clearly, but the
> Son more obscurely. The New Testament revealed the Son

and gave us a glimpse of the divinity of the Spirit. Now the Spirit dwells among us and grants us a clearer vision of himself. It was not prudent, when the divinity of the Father had not yet been confessed, to proclaim the Son openly and, when the divinity of the Son was not yet admitted, to add the Holy Spirit as an extra burden, to speak somewhat daringly ... By advancing and progressing "from glory to glory," the light of the Trinity will shine in ever more brilliant rays (quoted in *CCC* 684).

The Divine Service often refers to the Holy Spirit as the "Voice." Not only does the Spirit speak for Jesus as our "Advocate" (see *Jn* 16:7), but it has been the Spirit all along, speaking through the voice of the Prophets. From the Kneeling Rite for the Holy Spirit on Pentecost:

> *Bow your heads, O Mortals,*
> *and worship God, the Holy Spirit.*
> *He speaks through the prophets;*
> *to visionaries he whispers the secrets*
> *of hidden things;*
> *and to seers he reveals the future ...*

Eastern Liturgy in general is full of references and prayers to the Spirit. Thus, at least in the public prayer of the East, the Holy Spirit is the Object of prayer and devotion.

Epiclesis and Overshadowing

One element of the Divine Service that obviously refers to the Holy Spirit is known as the *epiclesis,* a Greek word meaning "invocation." It is used of the Spirit, as the Spirit is invoked to accomplish, here and now, what the Spirit accomplished from the beginning of creation by creative overshadowing (see *Gn* 1:1, 8). Invoked in the Liturgy, the Spirit "overshadows" such elements as the eucharistic Offerings, elements used in the sacramental Mysteries, or the Congregation at prayer, and transforms them into "Holy Things." This is consistent with the scriptural approach of the East, which recognizes the Holy Spirit as having overshadowed people such as Mary at the Announcement of the Incarnation, Jesus at his Baptism, the Apostles and Mary on Pentecost.

This overshadowing as a sanctification of ordinary things is consistent with the Antiochene School, which the Syriac Teacher St.

Ephrem reflects in his poetic observation on the action of the Holy Spirit. From his *Hymns on the Faith*, 10:17:

> See, Fire and Spirit are in the womb of her who bore
>   You;
> see, Fire and Spirit are in the river in which you were
>   baptized.
> Fire and Spirit are in our baptismal font,
> in the Bread and the Cup are fire and the Holy Spirit.

Each Maronite *Anaphora* concludes the Trinitarian Prayer with an *epiclesis*. So strong is this power of the Spirit in the Eucharistic Prayer that the words signify a consecration of the Bread and Wine into the Body and Blood of Jesus. Theodore of Mopsuestia recognizes this when he tells us:

> If, therefore, the nature of the vivifying Spirit made the body of our Lord into what its nature did not possess before, we ought, we also, who have received the grace of the Holy Spirit through the symbols of the sacrament, not to regard the elements merely as bread and cup, but as the body and blood of Christ, into which they were so transformed by the descent of the Holy Spirit, by whom they become to the partakers of them that which we believe to happen to the faithful through the body and blood of the Lord (quoted in Greer 83).

This consecratory power is especially seen in Maronite Tradition in the *Anaphora of the Signing of the Chalice*.

Holy Spiritual Transformation

In Eastern liturgical tradition, two purposes of the *epiclesis* are seen: consecrating the Elements and *enlightening us* to see this power at work transforming the Gifts and ourselves. At this special moment, the Celebrant at the Maronite Divine Service kneels on both knees to invoke the Spirit, a sign of recognition of and submission to this power and Presence. Maronites are reminded of the Kneeling Rite on the Feast of Pentecost, wherein the Assembly is called upon to kneel on both knees for the Prayer to the Holy Spirit. Here is the *epiclesis* in the classic Maronite *Anaphora*, the *Anaphora of the Twelve Apostles*, emphasizing the Gifts of the Spirit:

Have mercy on us, O Lord,
have mercy on us.
Send us your life-giving Spirit from heaven
to overshadow this offering
and make it the life-giving Body and Blood
to purify and sanctify us.

And from the *Anaphora of St. Mark,* emphasizing our
transformation:

Indeed, O Lord, have mercy on us and
          hear us now.
From the heights of heaven
send forth your Holy Spirit,
who is equal to you in being and honor,
that Spirit who was seen in the likeness of a dove
descending upon your Son in the River Jordan,
and in the likeness of tongues of fire
descending upon your blessed Apostles
          in the Upper Room.
May the Spirit fill us with your abundant grace
and make us chosen vessels
for the service of your honor.

The Perfection of Creation

One of the missions of the Holy Spirit is to bring to completion the
work of the Father and of Jesus. This idea is expressed in every Divine
Service at the time before Holy Communion when the Body of Christ is
broken, a small portion of it is dipped into the Precious Blood, and three
crosses are traced in the cup:

We sign the cup of salvation and thanksgiving
with the purifying ember
which glows with heavenly mysteries
in the name of the + Father,
life for all the living;
in the name of the only-begotten + Son,
who proceeds from him,
and, like him, is life for all the living;

in the name of the + Holy Spirit,
the beginning, the end, and the perfection
of all that was and will be in heaven
and on earth,
the one, true, blessed, and exalted God,
without division,
from whom comes life for ever. Amen.

Note: the italicized words in the prayer above are exactly the same formula used to conclude the trinitarian consecration of the water used in the baptismal service, showing once again the fullness of blessing in the water, which symbolizes salvation.

Gifts and Fruit of the Spirit

Our transformation is not merely momentary, however, as if just in the Divine Service. The power of the Holy Spirit works constantly in our lives and is available to us at every moment. In Chrismation we believe that we received an even greater share of the Holy Spirit by receiving what are known as the "Gifts" and "Fruit" of the Spirit. By these, we are able to live the divine life more effectively, as they become experienced realities within our lives. (For a fuller explanation of these, see **Chapter 18, "Initiation: Chrismation."**)

Liturgical Year: The Season of Glorious Pentecost

Question: What does the Season of the Glorious Pentecost tell us about the risen Christ?

Answer: That it is through the Spirit, sent on Pentecost, that the risen Christ is made present in the ages after the event, including our own day. The overshadowing power is the same power that animates the sacramental Mysteries and the hearts of believers.

The Maronite Church celebrates the liturgical season of Glorious Pentecost until 14 September, the Feast of the Exaltation of the Holy Cross. This is a time in which to reflect upon our life in the Spirit. We also celebrate the memories of those who lived worthily the life of the Spirit on earth: the "Righteous and Just," that is, those saints who loved the Lord. These include the Mother of God, Peter and Paul, Sharbel, and others. (See **The Lectionary** in **PART II, Chapter 11**, and **Appendix I**.)

Charismatic Christianity

In recent years the Church has experienced in a remarkable way an outpouring of the presence of the Holy Spirit in what has come to be known as the "Charismatic Movement," or "Renewal." People meeting in both small group prayer meetings as well as large conferences have seen a manifestation of the Gifts of the Holy Spirit.

Non-Catholic manifestations of Charismatic Christianity have occurred in what has been known especially in the United States—but not confined there—as the "Pentecostal" Movement and Churches. However, there are clear differences between the Catholic and Pentecostal expressions.

The most significant difference is the way in which the Sacred Scriptures are read, or interpreted. In general, the Pentecostal Churches read the Bible in a literalistic, or fundamentalistic, way; whereas the Catholic Church reads the Bible in a fuller, more open way (see **Part II**). Pentecostal church organization ("ecclesiology") is more loosely characterized; whereas Catholic ecclesiology is hierarchical, that is, respecting an authority structure comprised of bishops and other clergy. Finally, Pentecostals tend to group into their own, very small, churches; whereas members of Catholic Charismatic prayer groups are always encouraged to remain in their own parishes as active members making the Holy Spirit a greater part of their Catholic life.

The Eastern Churches have an organic emphasis on the Holy Spirit in their liturgical life. The Charismatic Renewal can help Eastern Christians better appreciate their innate approach to the Holy Spirit, the "Lord and Giver of Life," as the Creed so aptly puts it.

STUDY QUESTIONS:

1) How is God present to us in the following ways: as indwelling; in *epiclesis* and overshadowing; through the Gifts and Fruit of the Holy Spirit?
2) What is (are) the "mission(s)" of the Holy Spirit?
3) How can we relate the first Pentecost to a similar experience in us today?

Chapter 6:
The Church:
Koinonia/Community of Faith

Liturgical Year: Sundays of the Church

> **Question:** What do the Sundays of the Church tell us about the risen Christ?
>
> **Answer:** First of all, the Church is the Body of Christ. Since the Body of Christ is quite literally transformed in glory with the Father and the Holy Spirit, the Church somehow participates in that glorious state, even on earth. This is a great mystery. Further, the themes of Renewal of the Church and Consecration of the Church remind us that we are in constant need of renewal of life and commitment (*ecclesia semper reformanda*), and of reconsecration to the Lord and his cause.

The Maronite Church opens its Liturgical Year at the beginning of November with the Sunday of the Renewal of the Church. In the cycle of the Lectionary

Sunday of the Renewal of the Church
Jn 10: 22-42, or
Mt 23:13-22

this annual commemoration focuses on the Assembly of Believers, in which faith is found and the Catholic Faith is practiced. The following is the first formal, liturgical prayer (after the Doxology) that the priest says to open the Year:

O Lord Jesus Christ,
by your incarnation you perfected the Old Testament,
and by your manifestation you brought forth the New
     Testament.
In your love for all people
you betrothed the Church of all nations,
and in your grace *you established its foundation*
     on Peter and the Twelve Apostles.
Now make us worthy to thank you
and exult with Simon Peter
at your heavenly banquet,
to rejoice with Paul in your paradise,
and to find happiness with John in your Kingdom.
Then, *with all who have accomplished your will,*
we will glorify you, O Christ, your Father,
     and your Holy Spirit,
now and for ever. Amen.

This beginning makes several points:

1) The *relationship of Christ to the Church is an intimate, nuptial one,* following St. Paul's imagery in *Eph* 5:25-26, 32. The Church, the Bride of Christ, dressed this day in white and green, is ready for the heavenly wedding feast.

2) Christ *established the Church on the faith of Peter, the Rock, and the Apostles.* Apostolic and guided by Spirit, the Church is infallible and indestructible. The phrase "the nations," is a favorite description of the Church's mission in the Syriac Teachers (Please consult the Bibliography for the comprehensive study by Robert Murray, *Symbols of Church and Kingdom: a Study in Early Syriac Tradition*, for an analysis of the various images used to describe the Church by the Syriac Teachers.)

3) The Church is further grounded in *the duty to evangelize,* as Paul did, in his universal mission to the Gentiles ("the nations"), and Paul's words in his *New Testament* Letters.

4) The Church is the *"foundation" of the Kingdom* of love and grace.

5) Those who have accomplished the will of Christ—therefore the will of the Father—are exulting in the Kingdom and waiting for us to join with them in happiness, a statement of the doctrine of the "Communion of Saints" (see **PART III, "Human Destiny"**).

What is the Church?

When God desired to work among us in the Incarnation, the Word took to Himself a human body like ours. With and through that body God acted in Christ during the thirty or so years that he lived in this world. He taught; he healed; he forgave; he offered Himself on the Cross for our salvation and was resurrected. Then, in the Ascension, his glorified body left this earthly dimension and was no longer active among us in a human manner.

However, after the Ascension God intended to continue Christ's work among us. To accomplish this work, God chose to use a new Body of Christ. This time it is not a physical body like the one born of the Virgin Mary. It is instead a mystical reality that St. Paul likens to a body—whose soul is the Holy Spirit—when he says, "You are Christ's body" (*1 Cor* 10:17). This is the same Body that is made present each time the Community of Believers receives Holy Eucharist. Through the Divine Eucharist Christ lives on earth again, and we are his instruments.

On Pentecost, the infant Church, born from the side of Christ on the Cross (see *Jn* 19:34), took its first pre-ordained step outward in mission. Indeed, this story (*Acts* 2:1-13) shows that the Church was, and remains, a "Church of the Nations." Not without reason is the "Constitution on the Church" of the Council aptly named *Lumen Gentium,* "Light of the Nations" (*CCC* 831). As Jesus urged us, the Church, we are to be light to unbelievers (*Mt* 5:14); or in the poetry of the Divine Liturgy (*Sedro* of the Sunday of the Consecration of the Church):

> *Arise and shine forth, O Holy Church,*
> **for the wise Architect who laid your foundations**
> **has also constructed the bars of your gates.**

> *Arise and shine forth,*
> **because God who is mighty for evermore**
> **chose you as a dwelling place for himself.**

> *Arise and shine forth,*
> **because he who chooses the living**
> **chose life for you until the end of time.**

> *Arise and shine forth,*
> **because he established your borders in peace,**
> **O Hope of the ends of the earth.**

Archbishop Angelo Roncalli—the future Pope, now Venerable, John XXIII—expresses this theme of the Church as the hope of the world in a retreat he made in 1940, during World War II:

> The Church is in the world as the community of hope. It is a sign of hope in that it proclaims to the world that in God's design nations should live in harmony (*Journal of a Soul*, p. 257).

All those Christians who have been baptized, who have received the Holy Spirit in Chrismation, who share in the life of Christ through Holy Communion, make up the Body that is to be the instrument of Christ's work on earth. The early Church used the Greek word *koinonia* ("fellowship") to describe this reality.

Insofar as God calls believers together, we recognize the Greek origin of the word for *Church—ekklesia*, or "convocation."

Another important image used to describe the Church comes from the Council: (new) "People of God" (*LG* 13). Although a limited term the Council uses this term, "People of God," very specifically of the Christian reality known as the Church. The Church is truly a People of God *in Christ*.

The Catholic Church

So far, we have seen a description of the Church of Jesus Christ as the Community of Believers in Christ. This term is at the same time specific and general: specific, in that it describes human beings who from the totality of humanity have made a choice to believe and belong to Christ and his Church; general, because among Christians there exist many different expressions of that belonging. Of all Christians, what does it mean to be a member of the "Catholic" Church?

It was the 2nd-century Syrian Christian bishop, Ignatius, from the great city of Antioch, who first referred the Church as *Catholic*:

> Where there is Christ Jesus, there is the Catholic Church.

In Ignatius' time all who professed membership in the Christian Church were members in a community that was known by the proper form of the Greek word *katholikos*, translated in English as, "catholic," or "universal." In fact, one of the great struggles of the 2nd century (and beyond) was the question of who and what idea deviates (the root of the word "heresy") from the commonly accepted set of teachings of the Faith that bind the Church together in universal understanding and charity.

It has come to be understood that *all who are united in the acceptance of Catholic teachings, including the seven sacramental Mysteries, under the presiding over the Church in charity of the Bishop of Rome, is a "Catholic,"* without prejudice to any particular Tradition.

Sad divisions within the universal Body of Christ over the centuries have resulted in the many denominations that today all call themselves Christian. Even the Catholic Church came to be more and more narrowly defined than in Ignatius' day.

The Catholic Communion of Churches

The Second Vatican Council (*UR* 3) reaffirmed that fullness of the means of salvation is to be found in the Catholic Church, in whom the one true Church of Christ "subsists" (*LG* 8).

While holding to these truths, the Council revived a view of the Church more prominent in the first Millennium, before the great Schism between West and East. Today the Catholic Church again sees herself as a "Communion of Churches," in what is known as an "ecclesiology of communion." In this view, individual Churches, from different Traditions, who have their own hierarchy to govern them, do so in communion, harmony and cooperation with the See of Rome.

This is particularly important for the Catholic Churches of the Eastern Traditions, who are not of the Latin Tradition, and who live their Catholic lives in light of their own particular heritage(s) of spirituality, liturgy, theology and Church discipline.

This concept is important ecumenically as other Churches and ecclesial communities in dialog seek to revive communion with the Catholic Church. They must and will do so in terms of their own Traditions, Traditions that, in so many cases, are identical with those found already in the Churches of the Catholic Communion. Thus, today all Christians are reaching out in dialog to each other in the sincere hope that Christian unity—a unity that has its foundation in the Trinity—may again become a reality.

Related to this idea is the now obsolete term, "under the Pope," when referring to the relation of the Eastern Catholic Churches to the Church of Rome. People used to ask members of the Eastern Catholic Churches: "Are you under the Pope?" However, in view of the richer approach of the ecclesiology of communion, we now answer that we are "in communion" with the Church of Rome, and she with us.

The Catholic Church Is a Sacramental Church and Icon of Christ

An essential teaching of the Council is that the Church is the "Sacrament" of God's revelation, that is, she is a powerful sign of Christ to the world, bringing about what Christ promised in and through her.

> The Greek word *mysterion* was translated into Latin by two terms: *mysterium* and *sacramentum*. In later usage the term *sacramentum* emphasizes the visible sign of the hidden reality of salvation, which was indicated by the term *mysterium*. In this sense, Christ himself is the mystery of salvation: "For there is no other mystery of God, except Christ." The saving work of his holy and sanctifying humanity is the sacrament of salvation, which is revealed and active in the Church's sacraments (which the Eastern Churches also call "the holy mysteries"). The seven sacraments are signs and instruments by which the Holy Spirit spreads the grace of Christ the head throughout the Church, which is his Body. The Church, then, both contains and communicates the invisible grace she signifies. It is in this analogical sense that the Church is called a "sacrament" (*CCC* 774).

Thus, if we were to describe how the Church reveals Christ to us and to the world in more properly Eastern terms, we might say that the Church is the Icon of Christ, making him present in mystery.

The Catholic Church Has a Divine Origin

While on earth, Jesus gathered around him not only his twelve closest Disciples (The "Twelve Apostles"). He also gathered other Disciples who heard his message and who, with the Apostles, came to realize on Pentecost that the Community of Faith Jesus loved—the Church—was to become his Body on earth. Through the Apostles they and we see that this Church has from before time began been established by God and is more than the sum of its members.

This divinely instituted reality of the Church seems to be indicated in each liturgical service in the greeting of the Celebrant to the Congregation before the "Praise of the Angels":

Peace be with the Church and her children!

The Catholic Church Is Organized

Upon reflection, this formula, "Peace be with the Church and her children," may, in another sense, seem somewhat redundant: Don't we, the "Children of the Church" make up the Church. Of course! Nor, however, is this an expression of a false distinction distinction between clergy and laity in the sense of only the laity being the children of the Church. This idea is false precisely because ALL the baptized who share in the Mystery of Christ are the Church. In this Mystery all—clergy and lay—have important roles to play (see **Chapter 25, "The Priesthood of the Faithful in Baptism"**).

Such metaphorical and symbolic terms as "Body of Christ," "Bride of Christ," "Church of the Nations," and "Mystery of Christ" describe a profoundly spiritual reality. However, the Church is also a very human reality with all the needs, weaknesses, and accomplishments of human organizations and societies in general.

In this rich greeting what may be at work is the realization of both the sacred and the human elements that together make up the Mystery of the Church. "Church" here also means the external, hierarchical and necessary organization of the Mystery in the human dimension where this Mystery is ordinarily experienced—most locally, the parish community; more remotely, the eparchial (diocesan) level; and furthest of all, the patriarchal level.

One of the traits of a human society is its need for organization and leadership, its need to be structured and managed. The Church is no exception. The Catholic Church is a "hierarchical" reality, a structured organization.

The Clergy

In every Maronite *Anaphora* we find General Intercessions for the needs of the faithful. The first Intercession always mentions in particular the three leaders, among others, who shepherd the Catholic Church. This example, from the *Anaphora of St. John*, is typical:

> **O Lord God,**
> **at this moment in our sacrifice**
> **we remember all your holy churches**
> **and the shepherds who dwell in them in true faith,**
> *especially, N., Pope of Rome,*

N. Peter, our Patriarch of Antioch,
N., our Bishop,
and all the bishops of the true Faith.
Along with them, we also remember
the priests, the deacons, and all in your household
who observe your commandments.
We pray to you, O Lord.

The Bishop of Rome

The Bishop of Rome—residing in Vatican City, Italy—holds a special place in the Church from ancient times, recognized even outside the Catholic Church. This is called the "primacy." It means that the ministry of the Bishop of Rome is to be concerned for the unity of the whole Church. He "presides in charity." He also acts, in John Paul's own words in *Ut Unum Sint* (¶95 §2), as "moderator" of disputed doctrinal questions for the common good of all. Although in *Ut Unum Sint* John Paul II prefers the title, "Bishop of Rome," he has many titles, including "Pope" (like the Coptic Orthodox Patriarch in Egypt, also called "Pope") and "Patriarch of the West," signifying his leadership of the Western Church. As Bishop of Rome he pastors his Diocese with local priests. The Church's central administration is called the *Apostolic See.*

As supreme Lawmaker, the Pope is responsible for approving the law codes—there are two, one for the Eastern Catholic Churches and one for the Latin Church. The official name of the law code for the East is *Code of Canons of the Eastern Churches.*

As spiritual head of the Catholic Church, the Bishop of Rome has long been recognized as someone who speaks for the truth of Christianity in a special way. For Catholics, the Pope has the important mission of being guarantor of the truth and teachings of the Faith. The "Holy Father," as he is often called, has the mandate to express the truth in a clear and final way. Catholics know this by the general term *infallibility*: of the Church in general, as the keeper of Christ's revelation in its fullness; and of the Pope in particular, such as when he makes a solemn statement of faith and morals. This he would exercise in extraordinary circumstances, and usually after consulting with his brother bishops, who help him discern the belief of the faithful. Such solemn pronouncements are rare.

In the first millennium, the governance of the whole Church, East and West, was shared more widely between the five Patriarchs of the Church. Many authors speak of this as the "Pentarchy," or, "rule of the five (Patriarchs)." Within this more varied administration of the Church, a certain, real preeminence was accorded to the See of Rome, whose most important task was seen to be as arbiter in instances of dispute over doctrinal matters. We only have to look to the great Councils of the early Church (especially Chalcedon) to see this in practice.

In the secular sphere, the Bishop of Rome is head of Vatican City State, which is in fact one of the smallest countries in the world. As such, he is sometimes called upon to negotiate in secular matters, either in person or through his diplomatic channels accredited to the Apostolic See.

Eastern Patriarchs

Other bishops in the Church serve as chief leaders of their own people within their particular Traditions. These are known as Patriarchs of the Eastern Catholic Churches (*CCC* 887). While maintaining a legal, spiritual and fraternal allegiance to and communion with the Bishop of Rome, these Patriarchs govern their faithful in Church matters according to the *Code of Canons of the Eastern Churches*.

General Eastern Law and Particular Law

In addition to this general legal code for the East, each Oriental Church *sui iuris* has its own customs and discipline, too numerous to be covered in the *Code of Canons*. These laws and customs are known as the *particular law* for that Church.

The Eastern Catholic Churches *outside their original boundaries* do not enjoy direct governance by their patriarchs or synods universally except for liturgical matters. Rather, they are under the direction of the Roman Congregation for the Eastern Churches (or, the "Oriental Congregation"), which is a department of the Roman *Curia* (a word signifying a Vatican administrative office.)

In former times people used to speak incorrectly of the Eastern Catholic Churches as being "Roman Catholic." However, in light of the newer precisions found in the "Decree on the Eastern Catholic Churches" of the Council and later documents, *it is now recognized that it is more proper to refer to the "Eastern Catholic Churches" and the "Roman Catholic Church." What pertains to all Catholics is termed "Catholic."*

Eparchs (bishops) govern their local jurisdictions, which include the clergy and other faithful of certain, clearly defined areas. An archeparch (archbishop) governs an archeparchy (archdiocese), which is larger than an eparchy, or has by virtue of preeminence in being established early. In the Eastern Churches an eparch's jurisdiction is called an "eparchy," while in the Western Church it is known as a "diocese." The chief eparch in an eparchy has ordinary jurisdiction; hence, he is referred to as the *Ordinary*. An Ordinary may have one or more auxiliary bishops, who may also serve as eparchial vicars.

The Council revived the idea of *collegiality*. By this is meant that the bishops of the world work together with the Bishop of Rome, to care for the Church's faithful, in what is called the "College (Assembly) of Bishops."

> Just as, in accordance with the Lord's decree, St. Peter and the rest of the Apostles constitute a unique apostolic college, so in like fashion the Roman Pontiff, Peter's successor, and the bishops, the successors of the Apostles, are related with and united to one another (*LG* 22).

There are other administrative titles given to bishops—such as *patriarch, major archbishop, metropolitan, apostolic administrator, exarch*—depending upon the circumstances of the jurisdiction he governs.

Bishops group together in different bodies. One body of bishops is called a *synod*, whose task it is to deliberate about matters in the worldwide particular Church. Those Eastern Churches that are patriarchal have synods over which the patriarch presides. Countries can also have a national conference. In the US, within the United States Conference of Catholic Bishops (USCCB, formerly the NCCB [National Conference of Catholic Bishops]), the Eastern Church bishops belong to the Conference called the Eastern Catholic Association (ECA). All Catholic bishops are responsible to the Pope, and report to him on the condition of their eparchies/dioceses. Eastern bishops also report to the heads of their particular Churches. Maronite bishops report to the Patriarch in Lebanon.

While other titles exist in the Church (such as *cardinal, archbishop, monsignor, chorbishop, archmandrite*), please note here that these relate to positions of administration or honor. Some of them are more ancient than others, while some were created as late as the Late Middle Ages. No matter what titles are given to ordained ministers, the fact still remains that the highest *sacramentally ordained* office in the Church is that of bishop. (See **PART IV, "Mysteries of Vocation"** for an explanation of the three Orders of the Mystery of Holy Order: bishop, presbyter [priest] and deacon.)

Most ordained presbyters are in fact *pastors*. They minister to the spiritual and material needs of God's People in Christ with the help of deacons, whose function is primarily one of service, especially to the poor. The Eastern Churches ordain *subdeacons*, who with the deacons assist the pastor in keeping the church building and people's needs in good order. Deacons and subdeacons may be ordained for their ministry permanently or in transition (in seminary) to the next level of Holy Order. In the Eastern Catholic Churches, priests, deacons and subdeacons may be married or celibate.

Pastors exercise their ministry in the structure known as a *parish*. This is a community of the faithful organized in a certain locale, whose purpose is to express the bonds of charity and fellowship among themselves and to witness in the secular community beyond the parish to the Presence of Christ in the world. Parishioners may or may not meet in a church building, but they are nevertheless a communal expression of the Body of Christ.

Members of a parish are called to be active participants on the mission of the Church (see **"The Apostolate"** below, and see also the section on **"Eastern Christian Duties"**). One is considered an active parishioner if he or she fulfills two basic requirements. The first is to worship as prescribed with enthusiasm and devotion. Ideally this is to be done weekly. People may use today's circumstances as an excuse not to attend church weekly. However, one must also be very certain that work or laziness is not simply an excuse for non-attendance.

In the cities of some countries parishes have territorial boundaries. In such a case it is presupposed that a Catholic within these parish boundaries belongs to that parish community. In the case of the Maronite Church—as with other Eastern Catholic Churches—boundaries are not so clear. (In fact, in Lebanon, one often speaks of the "village church" or even a "family church.") If a Maronite lives in a location that has a Latin or Byzantine majority, but there is a Maronite parish, he or she is still bound to attend the Maronite parish.

Second, an active parishioner contributes to the support of the parish. This is often done in a true spirit of stewardship and love, and sacrificing luxuries that take away from a spirit of detachment.

Stewardship

In fulfilling Catholic duties, the faithful Maronite Catholic willingly supports the work of the local parish, the Eparchy, the charitable works of the whole Church and the charitable works of the Holy Father.

Highlighting this important Christian obligation, the Church has recently developed an approach it calls "stewardship" (*CCC* 1351).

Various parables of Jesus speak about using our material goods for the good of others. Often these stories involve a steward—someone in charge of managing responsibly those things with which we are blessed by God. The reward for managing well is praise and promotion; the punishment for mismanagement is judgment and rejection (see *Mt* 25:14-30, for a good example).

Thus, we are called to be responsible stewards of our own goods, willingly putting an adequate portion of them at the disposal of the Church's maintenance and for works of charity on behalf of the truly disadvantaged and marginalized.

While there is no set way to do this, some well-known methods of support include: parish contribution envelopes; special collections; direct contributions; fund-raisers; tithing: giving 10 per cent of one's total income, 5 per cent directly to the Church and 5 per cent to one's favorite charities. Other, creative methods are also used, such as giving one hour's wage per week. This financial aid is an offering from one's "treasure."

In addition, affirming the need for the responsible use of finances, both on the eparchial and the parish level, the Law of the Church mandates that stewardship councils be established on both levels. By doing this, members of the Church may be assured that their voluntary financial contributions will be accounted for accurately and spent wisely.

Since the Church is largely an organization of volunteers, giving of one's time or skills is also vitally important. Helping out in this way shows a willingness to be connected in a living way to Christ and the Church:

> I am the vine, you are the branches. Those who abide in me
> and I in them bear much fruit, because apart from me you
> can do nothing (*Jn* 15:6).

Lay People

The majority of members in the Church are lay people. Since the Council, a situation that has always had some expression, but with the Council gained prominence, is the involvement of the *laity* (*LG* 33). The greater involvement of lay persons in many aspects of the Church has brought blessings. Laity are encouraged *first* to bring the message of the Gospel to the workaday world beyond the parish, and *second*, to help the pastors manage the temporal affairs and further the mission of the Church.

The term laity is here understood to mean all the faithful except those in Holy Orders and those who belong to a religious state approved by the Church: all the faithful, that is, who by Baptism are incorporated into Christ, are constituted the People of God, who have been made sharers in their own way in the priestly, prophetic and kingly office of Christ and play their part in carrying out the mission of the whole Christian people in the Church and in the world … To be secular is the special characteristic of the laity (*LG,* 31).

On a more personal level, and relating importantly to this discussion of the Church, is the role of the family. The Council documents clearly support the family as central and fundamental in society, Church and world. Indeed, one of the traditional hallmarks of Mediterranean culture in general and Maronite culture in particular has been a healthy respect for the family (see **PART IV, "Maronite Virtues: Family Life and Hospitality"**).

The Council spoke of the family as the place where the Faith and values are passed on. This is a sacred activity, and families actually carry out a ministry of the Church as they witness to the Trinity in their daily lives. In fact, the "Decree on the Apostolate of the Laity" expresses this idea positively when it calls the family a *"domestic sanctuary of the Church"* (italics mine):

The mission of being the primary vital cell of society has been given to the family by God. This mission will be accomplished if the family, by the mutual affection of its members and by family prayer, presents itself as a domestic sanctuary of the Church; if the whole family takes its part in the Church's liturgical worship; if, finally, it offers active hospitality, and practices justice and other good works for the benefit of all its sisters and brothers suffering from want (*AA* 11).

The Maronite Crowning Ritual—marriage is the basis of family life—speaks of this mission of benefiting the unfortunate in the blessing for the removal of the crown of the groom:

… May you find happiness all the days of your life.

> **May God multiply your riches**
> *and may you give aid and comfort to those who*
> *call upon you....*

The Role of Women

Among the laity, women have always had a distinctive role in the Church. The role of women continues to be evaluated, in daily life and in the highest levels of Church administration. For example, Pope John Paul II has written and spoken on this issue. The essential equality of women and men is not at all questioned (*CCC* 369).

The recent (1995) Vatican Synod of Bishops for Lebanon had this to say about the role of women:

> One of the best criteria of authenticity and family relations is respect for the dignity of the woman's role. This dignity was stated since the beginning of the *Book of Genesis*: man and woman are created as complementary to each other, and to both are entrusted not only the future of creation and family life but also the construction of the world: "Fill the earth and subdue it (*Gn* 1:28)." Christ, going beyond the norms enforced in the culture of his time, had toward women an open attitude of respect, of welcoming, of tenderness, giving them the priority on the morning of Easter, and entrusting them with the mission to bring the news of his Resurrection to the apostles. We have especially at heart in Lebanon in our own environment to promote the role of woman in the family and in society. In many areas her presence will open to debate our criteria of material rentability to the benefit of a humanization process (¶28).

The Lay Apostolate

The apostolate of the members of the Church has in its very name the reason for service: to be an apostle. As the Apostles were intimate partners of the Savior (see *Mk* 4:11), so the apostolate is meant to be a joyful sharing of what has been bestowed upon us in Initiation. Although the apostolate belongs to all, laity, clergy and religious alike, the apostolate of the laity is unique to them: by virtue of their collectively diverse circumstances, they have more possibilities for evangelization.

For Maronites in the United States, part of the work of the lay apostolate has been organized by the National Apostolate of Maronites (NAM). Serving both Eparchies, NAM seeks to encourage its lay members to foster an eparchial sense of community gathered around its two Ordinaries, encourage participation in the life of the parishes, and help to preserve the rich Middle-eastern heritage and Syro-Antiochene Tradition of the Maronite Church, adapting these to the experience of the United States. It seems likely that members of other Maronite eparchies all over the world will want to consider following suit in forming such organizations for good reasons, not the least of which is that this healthy trend of the Council has opened up a desire for Catholic laity to be a more integral part of their Church.

Men and Women Religious

Finally, congregations of women and men religious—sisters, monks and brothers—are involved in lives of Christian prayer (contemplatives) or of Christian action (teaching, hospital work, work among the poor).

The presence of religious in the Church is especially important for the Eastern Churches. All of the Eastern Churches value the monastic influence in their Traditions.

This is true for the Syriac-speaking Churches in general, from whose immediate experience monasticism arose. For example, in 3rd- and 4th-century Syria arose particular groups of ascetics known as *Bnay wBnat Qyama* ("Sons and Daughters of the Covenant").

While not organized as monks and nuns such as we know today, these people observed a strict adherence to the Gospels, based on such teachings as *Mt* 19:21: "Jesus said to him, 'If you wish to be perfect, go, sell your possessions, and give the money to the poor, and you will have treasure in heaven; then come, follow me.'" All religious observe at least the three Evangelical Counsels of poverty, chastity and obedience.

This influence filtered down into the Maronite Church, whose founding is traced to the hermit and monk, St. Maron (see **PART III, "Mary and Her Companion Righteous Ones"**).

The principal congregations of Maronite men religious in Lebanon are: the Lebanese Maronite Order (OLM); the Congregation of St. Anthony the Great (Antonines); the Mariamists, and the Lebanese Missionaries of Kraim (Kraimists). Those for women are: Sisters of St. Anthony of the Desert (Antonines); Holy Family Sisters; Sisters of St.

Theresa; Lebanese Maronite Order (OLM)—Women's Division; Sisters of Our Lady of the Meadow; the Sisters of St. John the Baptist of Hrash, and the Sisters of the Blessed Sacrament. There are also smaller groups of hermits in some countries of the worldwide Maronite Church.

The forms of liturgy and life of the Eastern Churches have been deeply influenced by monasticism. The challenge to the East, practically speaking, has been the adaptation, in modern times, to a less monastic, more parish-centered way of life in the Church, particularly the Eastern Churches in the West.

All these persons and groups together make up the Body of Christ, the Church. No one person or group is *necessarily* more important than any other. All are called to the one faith in the Lord Jesus; the Christian vocation is to follow Christ. As Catholics, we are urged to pray for vocations to the ordained ministry (priests, deacons, subdeacons) and to the religious life (sisters, brothers). But clergy and religious are constantly called to pray for the laity, in the latter's important vocation of witness to the married and single life.

Rights and Obligations in the Church

All members of the Church have rights and duties that flow from their sharing in the priesthood of Christ, by virtue of their Initiation into the Church (*LG* 33). These rights and duties are spelled out in the *Code of Canons of the Eastern Churches.*

In the ordinary living out of life in the Church, a good Maronite Catholic faithfully fulfills certain duties, some of which carry serious obligation (see **"Eastern Christian Duties,"** with their respective canons [laws], in **Appendix I**).

The Second Vatican Council (Vatican II)

> ### 3rd Sunday of Resurrection
> ### Lk 5:1-11

One of the primary ways that the Church has resolved problems and difficulties is by means of a Church council, an assembly of Christians gathered by someone in authority. Secular authority has at times convoked councils, but the main participants have always been Church leaders. When a council has had the character of being more than just a local or regional council, but rather one involving the whole, worldwide Church, it is known as "ecumenical."

From 1962-65, such a worldwide council was held at the Vatican. Called by Pope John XXIII, it drew Catholic and non-Catholic participants, as well as secular observers. 2,100 bishops attended. In fact, the scope was so broad that some consider the Council to be the first truly ecumenical council in the strict sense of being worldwide, although some Orthodox Christians dispute the ecumenical character of the Second Vatican Council.

Unlike other councils, called to answer attacks on the Church, the purpose of this Council was, in the words of Pope John, to eradicate the seeds of discord and promote the peace and unity of the entire world. Pope John wanted a reform of the Catholic Church that would update it and open it to the modern world. In other words, it was pastoral in nature. John opened the Council on 11 October 1962 with remarks that included the following:

> In the course of three years of preparatory work, a host of distinguished minds chosen from every nation and language, united in affection and determination, has brought together a superabundant wealth of doctrinal and pastoral material worthy to be offered to the Bishops of the whole world who, gathered beneath the vault of St. Peter's, will find grounds for the wisest applications of Christ's evangelical *magisterium* which for twenty centuries has enlightened the humanity redeemed by his blood.

The importance for every Christian—not only Catholics—of knowing of the Council and its work is crucial for understanding the current status of Christianity today. This was not a Council only for Catholics; its effects have positively altered the dialog that the Catholic Church has been carrying on with other Christian Churches as well as with persons of other religions.

The 16 documents of the Council reflect this effort, and it is worthwhile to spend some time in reading thoughtfully these proceedings to grasp the immense importance of the Council on our Catholic history. For your convenience **Appendix V** gives brief descriptions of the documents; however, these are not a substitute for the actual texts. As many have observed, it would not be unfair to state that there is still a long way to go in fully realizing the achievements of the Council in the life of the Church.

Church Unity

Of central importance is the movement, initiated at the Council, toward unity among Christians. We recall with pain the detrimental divisions that have occurred in the Body of Christ from the earliest days of the Church. We need only to read the history of the Church to see this.

The three major divisions are: the divisions in the East due to the heresies of the 4th and 5th centuries; the mutual excommunication of East and West in 1054; and in the West the Protestant Reformation in the 16th century.

Pope John Paul II recognized this with clarity when he stated in *Orientale Lumen* (¶17, quoting the Council):

> "Among the sins which require a greater commitment to repentance and conversion should certainly be counted those which have been detrimental to the unity willed by God for his People. In the course of the thousand years now drawing to a close, even more than in the first millennium, ecclesial communion has been painfully wounded, 'a fact for which, often enough, men of both sides were to blame.' Such wounds openly contradict the will of Christ and are a cause of scandal to the world. These sins of the past unfortunately still burden us and remain ever-present temptations. It is necessary to make amends to beseech Christ's forgiveness."

> ... Although in the first centuries of the Christian era conflicts were already slowly starting to emerge within the body of the Church, we cannot forget that unity between Rome and Constantinople endured for the whole of the first millennium, despite difficulties (*Orientale Lumen* 18) ...

The unity of the Church has its foundation in the Most Holy Trinity. The Church is one: she acknowledges one Lord, confesses one faith, is born of one Baptism, forms only one Body, is given life from the one Spirit, for the sake of one hope. The divisions of the Christian Church no longer seem to make much sense in view of the fact that the world desperately needs to see a united front among Christians, to show the world the whole, unscarred and beautiful face of Christ, who lives in the glory of the Holy Trinity.

Ecumenism

5ᵗʰ Sunday after Holy Cross
Jn 17:11-19
Or
Lk 6:43-49

Since the Council, and especially in light of the historic Document on Ecumenism, the Catholic Church seeks to enter into dialog with other Christian Churches for the sake of reuniting all Christian Believers into one Communion in Christ. This is done, knowing that there is truly a desire for it, recognizing that Christians of all denominations have much in common—most notably the Word of God in the Scriptures; and confessing to the fact that Christian unity is the will of God, as Jesus prayed in the Gospel (*Jn* 17:22-23).

This sharing has been taking place between Christians of good will. Some of the ways by which this sharing has occurred include common prayer; study—of the Sacred Scriptures and of the issues that have divided Christians—and dialog. *Ecumenical dialog* is the term used for these official common encounters.

As a result, common statements of belief have appeared. In addition to statements, ecumenical editions of and commentaries on the Holy Scriptures have appeared. Apart from the most avid fundamentalist groups (both Protestant and Catholic), Christians of many ecclesial Traditions are finding common ground in their understanding of God's Word.

Another positive area is that of official discussions, known as "dialogs," which have increased our understanding of each other and have moved us closer to the day when we shall one day again be one Church.

> "The Church has many reasons for knowing that it is joined to the baptized who are honored by the name of Christian, but do not profess the faith in its entirety or have not preserved unity of communion under the successor of Peter" (*LG* 15). Those "who believe in Christ and have been properly baptized are put in some, though imperfect, communion with the Catholic Church" (*UR* 3). *With the Orthodox Churches,* this communion is so profound "that it lacks little to attain the fullness that would permit a common celebration of the Lord's Eucharist" (Paul VI, "Discourse," 14 December, 1975; see *UR* 13-18).

Some Church leaders have often spoken of the need for the Church to "breathe with both lungs," by which is meant that both the Eastern and Western Traditions of the Church need to be recognized and promoted. On 7 December 1965, to great joy of Christians, Pope Paul VI and Patriarch Athenagoras I lifted the mutual excommunication of 1054. Later, Pope John Paul II expressed with some urgency the need to mend the breach between the two Traditions and met with the Ecumenical Patriarch Bartholomew, as well as other Orthodox representatives, on several occasions to discuss reunion. One of the most promising developments, which is more than merely symbolic, is the ongoing effort between Catholics and Orthodox to agree on a common date for the celebration of Easter. In 1995 John Paul also co-signed several "Declarations" of common belief with non-Byzantine Oriental Churches, such as the (East Syriac) "Church of the East." Of particular note here is the common declaration of understanding about the two natures of Christ united in one Person.

The Eastern Catholic Churches have been directly affected by papal ecumenical efforts, too. John Paul has issued several important documents that have as their main aim to strengthen ties to the Orthodox Churches by preparing for reunion. *Orientale Lumen* ("Eastern Light") attempts to explain for the whole Catholic Church the value of the Eastern Traditions. *Ut Unum Sint* ("That All May Be One") speaks directly to the ecumenical situation between the Catholic Communion and the Eastern Orthodox. Finally, so that the Eastern Catholic Churches may more reflect the appropriate liturgical ties to respective Eastern Catholic and Orthodox Churches (for example, Ukrainian Byzantine Catholic and Ukrainian Byzantine Orthodox Churches, Melkite Greek-Catholic and Antiochene Byzantine Orthodox Churches), the Vatican Congregation for the Oriental Churches has issued the "Instruction for Applying the Liturgical Prescriptions of the *Code of Canons of the Eastern Churches*." Clearly, Rome is working hard to invite the Orthodox to communion.

Dialogs with Rome and other Western Traditions, such as the Anglicans and the Protestants, have progressed to a surprising degree. An important declaration of agreement took place in October, 1999, between Catholics and Lutherans over the question of justification by faith (see pp. 260-61), an issue which was a central dividing point between the two denominations at the Reformation.

As Catholics we have a duty to pray for the continued success of these dialogs. (See **"The Six Rules for Ecumenism,"** p. 79.)

Intercommunion

In spite of progress toward understanding each other's Traditions, and such good efforts to try to heal and resolve them, we know—painfully—that we are still separated. In the common Christian experience, especially of the United States, a great indifference to these separating elements—often under the mask of good will—has caused many to think that anyone may receive Communion in any Christian Church at any time. Not so.

"Communion" means not only my reception of Jesus (the vertical dimension); it is also an expression of commonly held beliefs (horizontal dimension). Since we are not yet fully united—and since most Protestants do not share Catholic belief in the Eucharist—we refrain from receiving Communion in non-Catholic Churches.

When, in the Ordinary's judgment, a grave necessity arises, Catholic ministers may give the sacraments (Mysteries) of Eucharist, Penance and Anointing of the Sick to other Christians not in full communion with the Catholic Church, who ask of their own will, provided they give evidence of holding the Catholic faith regarding these sacraments (Mysteries) and possess the required dispositions (*CCC* 1401). However, as a result of the ecumenical movement, two exceptions are the Orthodox and members of the Polish National Church, who may freely share Holy Communion with us, although the Orthodox do not reciprocate.

As we are indeed encouraged to share public prayer with other Christians, we are also under the duty to pray most intensely for the day when we shall stand united as one Church of Christ—in other words, that we shall truly be "Catholic" in its most fundamental sense.

> I ask not only on behalf of these, but also on behalf of those who will believe in me through their word, that they may all be one. As you, Father, are in me and I am in you, may they also be in us, so that the world may believe that you have sent me. The glory that you have given me I have given them, so that they may be one, as we are one (*Jn* 17:20-22).

Interfaith Dialog

In its documents *Nostra Aetate* ("Declaration on the Relationship of the Church to Non-Christian Religions") and *Unitatis Redintegratio* ("Decree on Ecumenism") the Council even opened its thoughts to the religious persons of the world who do not accept Christ, such as the Jews, Muslims, and Buddhists. In these religions, the Council noted, are many good and positive things, which partake somehow in the mysterious offer of God to all people of good will for salvation.

> The Church rejects nothing of what is true and holy in these religions. It has a high regard for the manner of life and conduct, the precepts and doctrines which, although differing in many ways from its own teaching, nevertheless often reflect a ray of that Truth which enlightens all men and women. Yet it proclaims and is in duty bound to proclaim without fail, Christ who is the way, the truth and the life (*Jn* 14:6). In him, in whom God reconciled all things to himself (*2 Cor* 5:18-19), men find the fullness of their religious life.

> The Church, therefore, urges its sons and daughters to enter with prudence and charity into discussion and collaboration with members of other religions. Let Christians, while witnessing to their own faith and way of life, acknowledge, preserve and encourage the spiritual and moral truths found among non-Christians, together with their social life and culture (*NA* 2).

The Catholic Church clearly recognizes the good that is in these religions, seeing in these good elements the light of Christ. While it does not diminish our duty to share with them the Good News of the Gospel, we recognize that even if for some reason they have not accepted the Christian Message but still live out their lives according to their consciences the best that they know how (see *Rom* 2:12-16), they may be saved (*CCC* 846-48).

The Enduring Value of Judaism

One important issue that has emerged from dialog with members of the Jewish religion and others is anti-semitism. Catholics are urged today to take care to resist all forms of anti-semitism, which is at base a form of violation of human rights.

A related issue is anti-Judaism, specifically that Jews today are responsible for the death of Jesus. The Catholic Church clearly teaches that Jews today cannot be held to blame. Rather, the focus must be on our common Judeo-Christian heritage, on their status as the first to whom God made a Covenant promise, and, as Paul says, God keeps promises. The Church has always held that there is continuity between the faith of the First Covenant (i.e., the faith of the Jews) and that of the Second—or New—Covenant, Christianity. In fact, the religion of Moses and the Israelites is precisely their response to the first stages of God's revelation within the context of the First Covenant. Thus, a real respect is to be accorded to the Jewish religion on this basis.

Islam

In recent years Pope John Paul has entered into and encouraged dialog with the third of the three monotheistic religions, Islam, whose adherents are called Muslims.

The name *Islam* comes from the Arabic word meaning "to submit," namely, to the will of God, *Allah*. As such Christians share much with the intent of that word, as we ourselves seek always to discover and submit our own lives to the will of God.

Islam holds many teachings in common with Judaism and Christianity, and it often surprises those who study Islam to see how much we do share. For Islam, Jesus is not the divine Son of God. However, he is the second greatest Prophet sent by God to earth (for them, Mohammed is the Greatest Prophet). In addition, Mary, the Mother of Jesus, is to be most highly revered, as she bore the great Prophet Jesus.

STUDY QUESTIONS:

1) What is the Church? How can the Church be called the "Icon of Christ"?
2) What is the relationship of the non-Catholic Christian Churches (Byzantine Orthodox, Oriental Orthodox, Anglican, Protestant, Reformed) to the Catholic Communion of Churches?
3) How can the Church be considered a "Light to the Nations"?

The Six Rules for Ecumenism

Understanding Christians of non-Catholic Traditions takes a lot of effort, if we are to be successful in the journey towards unity. Here are some rules to remember when pursuing ecumenism:

❖ **Know your faith.** You cannot present Catholic teaching if you don't know it yourself. Others don't expect you to be an **expert**, but their legitimate questions deserve correct answers.

❖ **Know your audience**. Don't try to say too much or too little. Rather, try to answer on the level that will be most persuasive.

❖ **Be respectful**. Only if you approach the other as an equal will the dialog be fruitful. Confrontation hardly ever works.

❖ **Be responsible**. True ecumenism does NOT mean boiling things down to the least common denominator. There ARE differences between the Churches, and these must be acknowledged.

❖ **Know your resources.** Even if you don't know an answer, it makes sense to admit it, then go on to a good resource that will help. We might not know, but we can always learn!

❖ **Be patient with yourself and others.** There will be limitations on both sides of the ecumenical dialog. Be patient! Only through patience and persistence will advances be made. After all, Jesus commanded that we love one another.

Chapter 7:
The Eastern Catholic Churches

The Full Catholicity of the Catholic Church

Many different Churches, in several Traditions, make up the Worldwide Catholic Communion of Churches. The Catholic Church embraces these traditions,

> **Consecration of the Church**
> **Mt: 16:13-20, or**
> **Jn 2:13-22**

which go back to beginnings of the missionary effort of earliest Christianity. People accepted the Christian message in their own languages and in their own distinct customs and religious and philosophical outlooks. The Council, which spoke so clearly in its document, "Decree on the Eastern Catholic Churches," encourages believers to explore the Church's history and diversity in greater detail. Without at least a summary knowledge of this diversity, a Catholic has little idea of the broad scope of the Church. Put in another way, she or he does not understand the full catholicity of the Catholic Church.

What this means in real terms for the majority of Catholics, who are Latin—and for Christians in general—is that the perception of what it means to be "Catholic" must change. The prevailing perception is that the Catholic Church is synonymous with the Latin Tradition. The fact is that the *diversity* within the Church, which existed from the beginning, is the reality of the Church today. This is seen in the many Eastern Catholic Churches of the Catholic Communion of Churches. To be Catholic is to be Eastern or Latin, and all Traditions are to be equally recognized and celebrated. The Catholic Church is truly a communion of Churches. The full recognition of this basic reality about the Church will help *all* Christians in their increasing quest for unity as the worldwide Christian Church, East and West.

The Expansion of Early Christianity

The early preachers of the Gospel traveled outside of Jerusalem into the great cities and areas of the Roman Empire, such as Antioch in Syria; Alexandria in Egypt; Rome, the capital of the Empire; Armenia (in Cappadocia); from Antioch to Edessa and Nisibis, in Persia, and even into India and China. Although Christianity had been established in Byzantium (the original name for Constantinople) since the 2nd century, its expansion in Constantinople as the new, Eastern capital of the Roman—and shortly thereafter the Byzantine—Empire was a great leap forward in Christianity's history. (Bishop John Chrysostom's move from the See of Antioch to that of Constantinople in 398 A.D.—giving historical prominence to that Patriarchate—is a fine example.) In all these places the unchanging truth of the Gospel took on the cultural aspects of the peoples who received it.

Unity of Beliefs; Diversity of Worship

One important development of the expansion was worship. Taking the original, simpler celebration of the Word and Eucharist from the tradition in Jerusalem (see *Acts* 2:42), Christians developed, expanded and organized the Divine Service along the lines of their local cultures, very early in Antioch. All Christians remained for a while united in the one Faith. Even the structure of Church organization and government throughout the Empire remained faithful to Bishop Ignatius of Antioch's vision: local Communities of Faith, united under their bishops, helped by the deacons and presbyters (priests).

Soon (as early as the 2nd and 3rd centuries), however, many disagreements arose over various questions about Church belief and life. Sad divisions arose, and groups broke off from the mainstream. Naturally, these smaller breakaways troubled early Church unity, but they were not enough to cause the major rift that was to come.

The Byzantine World

In the early 4th century, while Rome remained the capital of the Roman Empire in the West, the Emperor Constantine needed a second Roman capital strategically located for governing the Eastern parts of the Empire. He chose Byzantion. Byzantion (Latin: Byzantium), a former Greek colony, was a relatively unimportant town in itself, but its location (Istanbul in modern-day Turkey) was well suited for Constantine's purposes. He completely renovated the city, calling it *Roma Nova*, "New

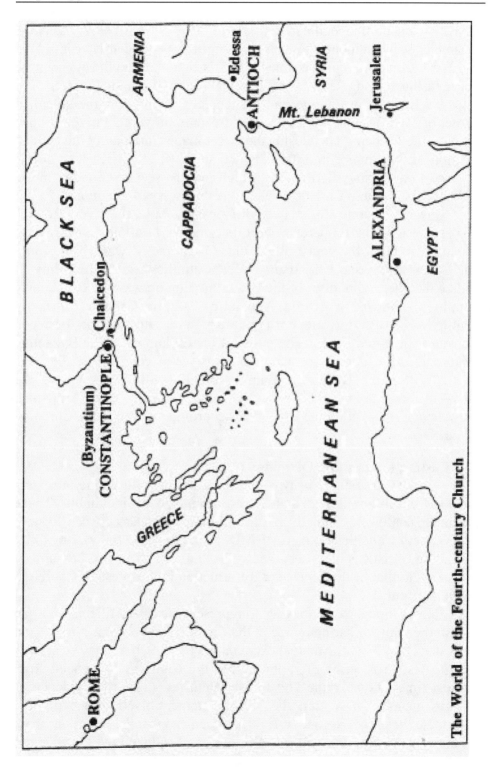

The World of the Fourth-century Church

Rome." Constantine dedicated it on 11 May 330 A.D. It was soon renamed "Constantinople." When the Empire was divided later into East and West, Constantinople became the East's capital. From the 6th century, under Justinian, and after, it was the capital of the Byzantine Empire.

Whereas Constantine had earlier decreed in 313—the so-called "Edict of Milan"—that there was to be freedom of worship in the Roman Empire, the Emperor Theodosius the Great made Christianity the official religion of the Empire in 380 A.D. The approval of Christianity in this way led to a glorious flourishing, which may be seen even today in the style of those Eastern Christians who style themselves "Byzantine."

The Byzantine Christianity of Constantinople, the "New Rome," tied as it was to the Emperor's court, became the best-known expression of Christianity in the first millennium. Of course, it was not the only one—think of Syriac Christianity. Yet, Catholics have a real duty to realize that the Catholicism of the Byzantine Empire was indeed the most populous inheritance of the Apostolic Catholic Church for many centuries—until the eleventh century and the break between Constantinople and Rome. The political reality known as the Byzantine Empire itself lasted until Constantinople was destroyed in 1453 A.D.

Within the Byzantine Empire, other Traditions—such as the Syriac-Antiochene, the East Syriac (Church of the East), the Armenian, the Alexandrine—continued to exist according to their own Christian cultures.

The Eastern (Byzantine) Orthodox Church

With Christianity in two rivaling capitals, Old Rome and New Rome (Constantinople), disputes were bound to be inevitable. These misunderstandings eventually led to a definitive break between Eastern and Western Catholicism, in 1054 A.D. From this time the vast majority Byzantine Christians have been known as "Eastern Orthodox." (Compare this break to that of the Protestant Reformation in the Western Church in the 16th century).

Even though some may try to represent the First Millennium as an undisturbed time of harmony within the Church, it simply was not so. Two facts stand out. First, the mutual excommunication of 1054 may be seen as the greatest in a series of ruptures that the Church experienced from earliest times, notably the 2nd to 5th centuries. (There is evidence of disagreements even within the New Testament itself, especially the Johannine Writings.) Second, it is now recognized that these tensions were probably as much political as religious, and who knows what could possibly have been averted through a dialog of charity? Still, from this date on, the majority of the Eastern Orthodox Churches and Latin Catholicism would continue in a tension between misunderstanding and attempts to reconcile. Despite all this, it still remains desirable, as the Churches rightly seek to restore Christian unity, to look to the first 1000 years as an example of a period when the Church seemed to enjoy greater unity than today.

Reunion and the Formation of the Eastern Catholic Churches
There were conciliar attempts to achieve reunion between East and West before the 16th century, but these were largely unsuccessful. The most notable and controversial was the Council of Florence (Italy) in 1438 A.D., with its discussions on "purgatory" and the *filioque* question.

In the 16th century, several Eastern Churches began a process of restoring communion with the Vatican in Rome, which by now had clearly become the center of the Catholic Church in the West. To some degree these newly reunited Churches retained their Eastern traditions and became known as the "Eastern Catholic Churches," as distinct from their Orthodox counterparts (see diagram, p. 98).

The only exceptions to this process are the Maronite Catholic Church and the Italo-Albanian Catholic, which claim that they have never broken communion with Rome, and which today have no Orthodox or schismatic counterparts.

"Uniatism" Unacceptable Today
The process of reunion adopted then was known as "Uniatism"; those who were reunited to the Vatican were until the Second Vatican Council known as "Uniates."

The term *Uniate* implies union, that is, with Rome. Such union was one-sided in that it meant a union on Western—Latin Church—terms. Practically speaking, this meant the loss of some authentically Eastern liturgical customs and disciplines. Examples of the first are the loss of the icon screen (iconostasis) of the Byzantine Tradition and the use of unleavened bread in any Eastern Traditions. An example of discipline —although later in history—is mandatory celibacy. Ultimately, uniatism came to be perceived as a pejorative term in both Eastern Catholic Churches as well as Orthodox Churches.

Even for the Maronite Church, not considered Uniate because of the tradition that it never broke communion with Rome, the pressure to conform to a Latin norm caused deep scars (see **"Latinization"** in **Chapter 8**).

The Council recognized that a high price was paid by the Eastern Catholic Churches in terms of latinization. Thus, the Council directed that the process of coming into communion of the Churches needs to be done differently in these days of ecumenism than had previously been done and that the terms "uniatism" and "Uniate" must never again be used—we now speak of "reestablishing communion." This attitude has strongly been endorsed by Pope John Paul II in messages to Catholics as well as in dialog with the Orthodox, particularly in Freising, Germany (1990), Arricia, Italy (1991) and the most recent (1993) meeting for this purpose at Balamand, Lebanon—documented in the "Balamand Statement."

The Council and the Eastern Catholic Churches

It is well known that Pope John XXIII had a great regard for the Eastern Churches. (This stemmed in great part from his assignment in Constantinople for many years.) Because of this regard, John wished to see the completion of a law code for the East, and he encouraged the preparation that ultimately led to the promulgation of the "Decree on the Eastern Catholic Churches" (*Orientalium Ecclesiarum*).

In this Decree the Council clearly stated the equality of all the ancient Traditions of the Church, East and West. Also, it acknowledged the need for these Eastern Churches *to reform what was needed*, so that these living Churches could be a more authentic witness to their ancient Eastern heritages. Here is a sampling of what the Decree said:

> History, tradition and abundant ecclesiastical institutions bear outstanding witness to the great merit owing to the Eastern Churches by the universal Church. The Sacred Council, therefore, not only accords to this ecclesiastical and spiritual heritage the high regard which is its due and rightful praise, but also unhesitatingly looks on it as the heritage of the universal Church. For this reason it solemnly declares that the Churches of the East, as much as those of the West, have a full right and are in duty bound to rule themselves, each in accordance with its own established disciplines, since all these are praiseworthy by reason of their venerable antiquity, more harmonious with the character of their faithful and more suited to the promotion of the good of souls (*OE* 5).

All members of the Eastern Rites should know and be convinced that they can and should always preserve their legitimate liturgical rites and their established way of life, and that these may not be altered except to obtain for themselves an organic improvement. The members of the Eastern Rites themselves, then, must observe all these. Besides, they should attain to an ever-greater knowledge and a more exact use of them, and, if in their regard they have fallen short owing to contingencies of times and persons, they should take steps to return to their ancestral traditions (*OE* 6a).

It is not merely for themselves that the Council urged the Eastern Catholic Churches to return to their roots. Especially for those that have non-Catholic counterparts—such as the Orthodox Churches—returning to authentic practices will help to foster unity.

From the earliest times the Churches of the East followed their own disciplines, sanctioned by the holy Fathers, by synods, and even by ecumenical councils. Far from being an obstacle to the Church's unity, such diversity of customs and observances only adds to the beauty of the Church, and contributes greatly to carrying out her mission ... To remove all shadow of doubt, then, this holy Synod solemnly declares that the Churches of the East, while keeping in mind the necessary unity of the whole Church, have the power to govern themselves according to their own disciplines, since these are better suited to the character of their faithful and better adapted to foster the good of souls. The perfect observance of this traditional principle—which however has not always been observed—is a prerequisite for any restoration of union (*UR* 16).

The Catholic Church Is a Communion of Churches

The "Decree on the Eastern Catholic Churches" invited the entire Church, East and West, to take a fresh look at what it means to be Church. In this regard the Council emphasized an ancient ecclesiology—this word means "study of the Church." In the early Church local Churches more readily governed themselves while acknowledging their common faith, celebrating that faith in their own unique ways. This was truly a Communion of Churches.

Taking seriously the need to heal the negative differences between the Churches while allowing an authentically more diverse system, the Council called again for what looked like a new ecclesiology but was in reality very ancient. This ecclesiology was reflected in the *lineamenta* for the Synod of Bishops/Special Assembly for Lebanon:

> ...[E]very time a Particular Church is constituted in a locality... it is the mystery of the Universal Church that becomes present in that locality... with all its essential elements present... [These Churches] are the "image of the Universal Church" and are defined as follows: "The Community of faithful Christians in communion through faith and the sacraments with their bishop ordained in apostolic succession"... [T]he Church of Christ is truly present and operative, and "in and from such individual Churches there comes into being the one and only Catholic Church."

"Rite," "Tradition," "Church"

Prior to the Second Vatican Council's "Decree on the Eastern Catholic Churches" a common incorrect way of referring to Eastern Catholics was that they belonged to a "Rite," with no appreciation of them as self-governing (*sui iuris*) Churches. In the years after the Council a better understanding—because more ancient and authentic—of Eastern ecclesiology was revived. This seemingly newer understanding appreciates more the proper distinctions that need to be observed when we talk about Eastern Catholics. The Council, then, caused us to become more precise about our individual designations by making the proper distinction between a "Rite," a "Tradition" and a *sui iuris* "Particular Church."

While it is preferable to say that an Eastern Catholic individual *is* a member of a particular Eastern Catholic Church, it is also correct to say she or he *follows a liturgical Rite* (or *Tradition)*.

Unfortunately, the *Catechism of the Catholic Church* did not employ these proper distinctions in the only paragraph in which it spoke of the Eastern Catholic Churches, i.e., ¶1203. Here, the *Catechism* inaccurately refers to the Maronite Catholic Church as the "Maronite Rite." Properly speaking, we ought to say that the Maronite Catholic Church is derived from and follows the Antiochene Rite (or Tradition).

A **rite** is a prayer ritual, or, by extension, a liturgical Tradition.

A **Tradition** has its own natural ways of expressing Catholicism according to proper language, native customs, discipline, theology, spirituality and liturgy. Tradition is broader than and includes rites, hence **it is preferable** to use the term *Tradition*, as in Byzantine Tradition.

A ***sui iuris* Church** (*sui iuris* is Latin for "in" or "according to" "its own right") is a hierarchically-organized, self-governing Church within the Catholic Communion of Churches, *derived from a particular Tradition*. By "hierarchically-organized" is meant that the individual Church has some kind of governing leader (patriarch, metropolitan, major archbishop) and makes its own decisions for governing the ordinary life of the Church.

Of the one billion Catholics in the world, almost 20 million (or 2%) follow Eastern Traditions. They are grouped into Particular Churches deriving from 5 major Traditions: 1) Byzantine (Constantinopolitan)—the largest, with 13 Particular Churches; 2) West Syriac-Antiochene, with 3 Churches; 3) the East Syriac/Assyrian "Church of the East," with 2 Churches; 4) the Alexandrine, with 2 Churches; and 5) the Armenian Church. (See also Roberson in the Bibliography.)

In the United States there are 16 Eastern Catholic jurisdictions representing 4 Traditions: 10 Byzantine jurisdictions; one Syrian (or, Syriac) Catholic jurisdiction and 2 Maronite jurisdictions (both Syro-Antiochene); and one each from the Armenian Catholic, the Chaldean Catholic and Syro-Malabar Catholic. The total Eastern Catholic population in the United States is nearly half a million. **Appendix VI** shows this population by eparchy. (See National Conference of Catholic Bishops, *Eastern Catholics in the United States* in the Bibliography.)

The following diagram of the Eastern Catholic Churches shows the current makeup of the Eastern Tradition of the Catholic Communion of Churches.

THE EASTERN CATHOLIC CHURCHES

Tradition/Rite	Sui Iuris Churches from These Traditions ✝ Denotes Patriarch as Head	Approx. Membership (See Roberson, 6th edition, 1999)
I. ALEXANDRIAN (Egypt)	1. Coptic Catholic ✝	197,000
"	2. Ethiopian Catholic	203,000
II. SYRO-ANTIOCHENE (West Syriac)	3. Syriac Catholic ✝	129,000
"	4. Maronite Catholic ✝	3,222,000
"	5. Syro-Malankara (India)	327,000
III. ARMENIAN	6. Armenian Catholic ✝	344,000
IV. CHALDEAN (East Syriac "Church of the East")	7. Chaldean Catholic ✝	304,000
"	8. Syro-Malabar Catholic (India) ✝	3,886,000
V. BYZANTINE (Constantinopolitan)	9. Belarusian Catholic	100,000
"	10. Bulgarian Catholic	15,000
"	11. Greek Catholic	2,345
"	12. Hungarian Catholic	282,000
"	13. Italo-Albanian Catholic	64,000
"	14. Melkite Catholic ✝	1,190,000
"	15. Romanian Catholic	1,119,000
"	16. Ruthenian Catholic	533,000
"	17. Slovak Catholic	222,000
"	18. Ukrainian Catholic	5,182,000
"	19. Krizevci Catholic	49,000
"	20. Albanian Catholic	?
"	21. Russian Catholic	?

Syriac-speaking Christianity

Until recent times within the Church little was known generally about the Syriac Churches, a minority among the Eastern Churches. More has been known about the larger, better-represented Byzantine Communities. In academic circles knowledge of the East was greatly helped by the pioneering work of Bishop Joseph Simon Assemani (1687-1768). Assemani was a Lebanese Maronite who lived in Rome and assembled a vast collection of Eastern works known as the Vatican Clementine Oriental Library.

The study of Syriac language, culture and Christianity gained ground in the 20th century. A revealing example is that when studying the early Fathers of the Church, theology students were most often exposed to the writings of only the Latin and Greek Fathers, but not (or, at any rate, rarely) the Syriac Fathers.

All of that changed with the historical, patristic and linguistic revival of the late 19th and early 20th centuries. Syriac versions of the Bible as well as newly discovered manuscripts of the Syriac Fathers sparked a keen interest in the ancient Syriac world. What scholars found was an expression of Christianity more closely tied to the Palestinian roots of the Church as well as its early missionary expansion into lands north and west of Jerusalem (Antioch) and further East (Persia-Mesopotamia).

In the Church, with the mandate of the Council for the Churches to return to authentic roots, the Syriac-speaking Churches began a revival in learning about the origins of their Traditions, East and West. The Maronite Church was no exception.

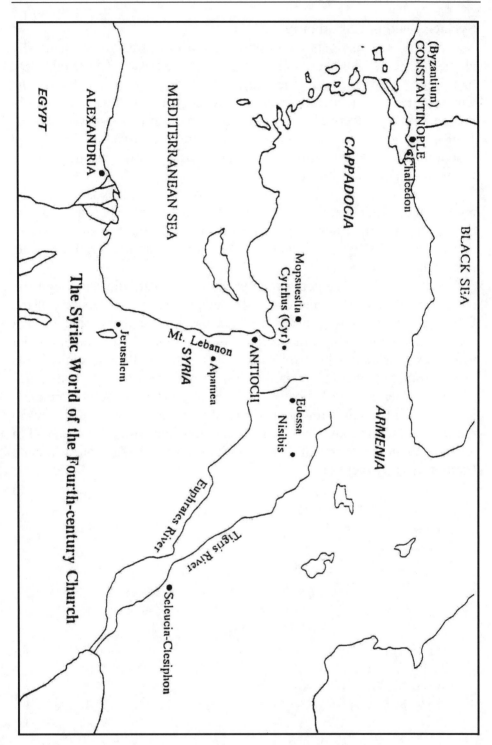

The Syriac World of the Fourth-century Church

East Syriac Christianity

The origins of Christianity in the land between the Tigris and Euphrates are also closely tied to the lands of the Bible, especially Palestine. A second-century legend holds that Abgar, ailing king of Edessa, sent a letter to Jesus himself, asking that the Savior come to Edessa to heal him. This legendary Edessan document, Jesus' reply to Abgar, represents an early text written in Jesus' name, and this legend is reported in Eusebius' *History of the Church*. Jesus writes:

> You are blessed; you believe in me, and you have not seen me. It is written concerning me, "Those who have seen me will not believe in me," and "Those who have not seen me will believe and will be saved." Regarding what you wrote to me that I should come to you, I have to complete here everything I was sent to do and, after I have accomplished it, to be taken up to him who sent me. After I have been taken up, I will send to you one of my disciples to heal your suffering and to provide life for you and those with you.

The East Syriac Church gave us the Poet Ephrem; Aphrahat "the Persian Sage" (Greek: Aphraates); James of Nisibis; James of Sarug; Isaac of Nineveh, and others. (For more information on the Syriac Teachers please consult the Bibliography, especially Beggiani, *Introduction to Eastern Christian Spirituality: the Syriac Tradition,* and Brock, *The Syriac Fathers on Prayer and the Spiritual Life*; also individual entries on St. Ephrem.)

West Syriac-Antiochene Christianity

The early Christianity of the Middle East—especially Christian Mesopotamia—thought of Antioch as the capital of "the West." Tied as it was to the central administration of the Roman Empire, by the 4th century A.D. Antioch was as cosmopolitan as Rome and Alexandria. Judging by the religious syncretism in vogue in the Empire of the time, it paralleled the other cities of the Empire in its eclectic character.

No doubt Antioch was a vibrant center of Hellenistic culture. It is no surprise that the great writers of the Antiochene Church—people like the great bishops, Theodore of Mopsuestia, Theodoret of Cyrrhus (also spelled Cyrus or Cyr), John Chrysostom—wrote in Greek. In addition, the Western form of Syriac was used extensively in this great center of learning, culture and Christianity.

The Syriac-speaking Catholic Churches

There are five *sui iuris* Churches which had the city of Antioch and Syriac language and culture as their origin. From the West Syriac Tradition come the Maronite Catholic Church; the Syriac Catholic Church, and the Syro-Malankara Catholic Church of India. Of these three, the two latter were formed from non-Catholic counterparts; Maronites hold to the tradition that they have never broken communion with Rome.

From the East Syriac Tradition come the Chaldean Catholic Church and the Syro-Malabar Catholic Church of India, both of which have been formed from non-Catholic counterparts. In all the twenty-one Eastern Catholic *sui iuris* Churches, of the three largest (in order of size)—the Ukrainian Byzantine Catholic Church; the Syro-Malabar Catholic Church (an extremely fast-growing Church) and the Maronite Catholic Church—two are of Syriac origin.

The Chaldean Catholic Church

This Catholic Church derives from the so-called Assyrian Orthodox "Church of the East." The Assyrian Church was the Church of ancient Persia (Mesopotamia), formed very early by missionaries from Antioch. Its theological centers were Nisibis and Edessa, and its later ecclesiastical headquarters was at Seleucia-Ctesiphon, on the lower Tigris River. It was characterized by the semitic theology and biblical interpretation of the Syriac Teachers, especially St. Ephrem and Aphrahat, and later James of Sarug.

Various events caused the Assyrian Church to separate early from Catholicism (431 A.D.), particularly over the issue of what language was best used to describe the double Mystery of Christ, God and Human. Some Christian thinkers wanted to understand too strict a separation between humanity and divinity in Christ. Nestorius was accused of this. Roberson (see Bibliography) mentions that this "Church of the East" gravitated to the teachings of Nestorius. The 1854 discovery of a translation of one of Nestorius' surviving works has caused serious debate today about whether he or his followers held to this strict position. The Assyrian Church today tends to downplay Nestorius' influence.

In the 17th century a part of the Assyrian Church returned to communion with Rome, and this newly formed Catholic Church became known as the Chaldean Catholic Church. Its headquarters is in Iraq.

The Syriac-Maronite Church of Antioch (See Chapter 8.)

The Syriac Catholic Church (also called Syrian Catholic Church)

The early West Antiochene Syrian Church likewise had its difficulties in maintaining understanding and agreement with the rest of the Catholic Church over the right language to use in describing the Mystery of Christ, Human and Divine. Some theologians in this Tradition tended to teach that there was a single nature in Christ, that the human part of Jesus was, as it were, swallowed up by the divine nature. This heretical teaching was known as *monophysitism* (Greek "one nature"). In the 6th century the Edessan Monophysite bishop, James "Jacob" Baradaeus, in effect took a large part of the West Antiochene Church out of communion with Catholic orthodoxy by ordaining numerous priests and bishops to serve the Monophysite Church. These Christians were subsequently called *Jacobites* after James (Jacob). The Monophysite Church was not confined to Syria, either; it was found in Egypt as well, particularly the Coptic Church.

Through missionary efforts in the 16th/17th centuries, a part of this Church returned to communion with Rome and is today called the Syriac Catholic Church.

Recent ecumenical dialogues with both the (West Syriac) Jacobite Syrian Orthodox Church and especially the (East Syriac) Assyrian Church of the East have enabled leaders of the Catholic Church and of these other Churches to find ways to come to agreement on the proper language to describe the Mystery of Christ. Also, formal, public declarations of agreement have been signed between the heads of the Churches in dialog.

The Syro-Malabar and the Syro-Malankara Catholic Churches

(Please note: because both these Churches have roots in both the Eastern and Western Syriac Traditions, they are considered together here.)

The (East Syriac-speaking) Syro-Malabar Catholic Church of India is a direct descendent of the Christian community founded by the apostle Thomas. 16th-century Portuguese Latin missionaries to India found Christians in communion with the Assyrian Church of the East but sympathetic to Rome. Unable and unwilling to accept local Malabar customs, the missionaries enforced latinizing activities that divided the Syro-Malabar Church; and in 1653 a group of these so-called *Thomas Christians* severed ties with Rome, accepting the customs, laws and traditions of the Syrian (West Syriac-speaking, Malankara) Orthodox Church. In 1930 two bishops from this Malankara Orthodox Syrian

Church reestablished full communion with Rome, thus establishing the Syro-Malankara Catholic Church, which numbers about 300,000 members, or about 10 per cent of the Syro-Malabar Catholic Church. Although the study of the Eastern Churches in India is a complex one, there is one thing for sure: the growth in Indian Syriac Christianity is considerable, especially in the Syro-Malabar Catholic Church.

The Value of the Syriac Tradition for the Catholic Communion
        The public and prominent era of the Syriac Churches as national and ecclesiastical presences had begun a decline in the tenth century; they all but ceased with the coming of the Ottomans into Syria in the fifteenth century. This does not mean, however, that the Syriac Churches disappeared. They have endured into our day.
        The value that the Syriac Churches bring to the Catholic Communion is that they offer to the wider Church religious expressions more closely related to the Palestinian beginnings of Christianity. Also, their more scriptural (and less philosophical) approach to liturgy and spiritual life witness to a desirable simplicity of Christian lifestyle—due in large part to a considerable monastic influence. In addition, the witness of writers like St. Ephrem and the other Syriac Teachers brings to the fore a poetic and mystical dimension to liturgical life often lost or at least ignored in the West in recent centuries. Finally, the historical approach to Bible interpretation—buttressed by the literal sense of Scripture—has been vindicated in our own days by the recent revival of this method of interpretation.

The Oriental Orthodox Churches
        There is a group of Eastern non-Catholic Churches called the *Oriental Orthodox Churches.* Note that although these Lesser Oriental Churches use the term *Orthodox,* these Churches are not of the Eastern (Byzantine) Orthodox Tradition. So for this reason they are also sometimes referred to as the *Lesser Oriental Churches.* Included are the Armenian Apostolic Church; the Coptic Orthodox Church; the Ethiopian Orthodox Church; the Syrian Orthodox Church; the Malankara Orthodox Syrian Church, and the Eritrean Orthodox Church.
        What sets these Churches apart is that their origins are not Chalcedonian, that is, they did not accept the *language* of the Council of Chalcedon for describing the Divine-Human Mystery of Christ. However, recent dialog between the Catholic Church and these Churches has revealed a common ecumenical ground for understanding this Mystery.

The diagram of the Eastern Christian Churches on the next page illustrates the full range of Eastern Christianity—Catholic and non-Catholic—as it exists at the present writing. For further background reading, please refer in the Bibliography to: Faris, *Eastern Catholic Churches: Constitution and Government* (chapters 1-3); Roberson, *The Eastern Christian Churches: a Brief Survey*; and the helpful video, "Eastern Churches," by Donald Sawyer. To learn about the Eastern Catholic jurisdictions in the United States, please refer to **APPENDIX VI**.

STUDY QUESTIONS:
1) In what way(s) can the Church of the first four centuries be called a pluralistic Church?
2) Describe the origins of the different Eastern Traditions.
3) How do the 21 Eastern Catholic Churches relate to their non-Catholic counterparts? Do all the Eastern Catholic Churches each have a counterpart?

The Eastern Catholic Churches: Traditions and Churches of Origin

(*) Denotes Chalcedonian Origins [451 A. D.] ("Eastern Orthodox")
(†) Denotes Pre-Chalcedonian Origins ("Oriental Orthodox")
(††) The "Assyrian Church of the East" is not designated "Orthodox"

Tradition of Origin	Church of Origin (Breakaway) (Non-Catholic Counterpart)	Eastern Catholic Church (Reunion)
Alexandrian (Egypt)	†Coptic (& Greek) Orth. Ch. (Alexandria)	Coptic Catholic Church
"	†Ethiopian Orthodox Church	Ethiopian Catholic Church
Antioch (West Syriac)	†Malankara Orthodox Syrian Church	Syro-Malankara Catholic Ch. (India)
"	†Syrian Orthodox (Jacobite) Church	Syriac (or Syrian) Catholic Church
"	No Orthodox Counterpart (no breakaway)	*Maronite Catholic Church
Chaldean (East Syriac)	††Assyrian "Church of the East" (Persia)	Chaldean Catholic Church
The Apostle Thomas	††Thomas Christians (in union w/above)	Syro-Malabar Catholic Church (India)
Byzantine (Constantinople)	*Russian Orthodox Church	Belarusan Byzantine Catholic Church
"	*Bulgarian Orthodox Church	Bulgarian Byzantine Catholic Church
"	*Patriarchate of Constantinople	Greek Catholic Byzantine Church
"	*Hungarian Orthodox Church	Hungarian Byzantine Catholic Church
"	No Orthodox Counterpart (no breakaway)	*Italo-Albanian Byz. Cath. Church
"	*Antiochene Patriarchate	Melkite Greek-Catholic Byz. Church
"	*Romanian Orthodox Church	Romanian Byzantine Catholic Church
"	*Carpatho-Russian Orthodox Church	Ruthenian Byzantine Catholic Church
"	*Orthodox Church of "Czechoslovakia"	Slovak Byzantine Catholic Church
"	*Ukrainian Orthodox Church	Ukrainian Byzantine Catholic Church
"	*Mixed Counterparts, "Croatian"	Byzantine Catholic Church
"	*Albanian Orthodox Church	Albanian Byzantine Catholic Church
"	*Patriarchate of Moscow	Russian Byzantine Catholic Church
Armenian	†Armenian Apostolic Church	Armenian Catholic Church

Chapter 8:
The Syriac-Maronite Church of Antioch

The Maronite Church has its origins in two related cultural centers. One was the Tradition that arose in the city of Antioch, with its famous "School" of biblical interpretation. This interpretation emphasized grammatical analysis of the text of the Scriptures, as well as an appreciation of the historical setting of the text. It also employed a limited use of "typology." Interpreters saw clearly how the people and events of the Old Covenant prepared the way for Christ in the New and called these events "types" (see **"Typology"** in Chapter 10). Finally, the School of Antioch fully appreciated the humanity of Christ.

The other influence was that of the Syriac world of Nisibis and Edessa, the cities of St. Ephrem the Deacon. The East Syriac world was further to the East, in Mesopotamia. In the famous ancient Christian Schools of Nisibis and Edessa, biblical interpretation made a fuller use of typology than in Antioch. In addition, in the capable hands of interpreters and commentators like St. Ephrem, biblical thought was translated into a liturgical poetry rarely equaled in the Church.

It is in this world of two cultures that St. Maron lived.

Background: Antiochene-Syriac Culture

To understand Maronite Tradition, one must go back to Antioch, an imperial city at the extreme northeastern corner of the Mediterranean Sea. Antioch's importance within the Roman Empire is well documented. In Christian terms, it was here that the followers of Jesus, the early Church, were first called "Christians" (*Acts* 11:26). Both Peter and Paul, (the "Apostles" of *Acts of the Apostles*) conducted ministries there, and here the faith of Peter took hold even before it was associated with Rome.

Antioch, one of the most important cities of the Roman Empire, was cosmopolitan, sharing the rich heritage of Greek learning with the language of Syria II, West Aramaic. This was the language of Jesus the Palestinian—even though we cannot retrieve today what that might have sounded like then. The literary form of this language, preserved by the three Catholic Churches of the West Syriac-Antiochene Rite—the Syriac Catholic Church, the Maronite Catholic Church and the Syro-Malankar Catholic Church of India—is West Syriac.

An early witness to this phenomenon of a multi-lingual Syria may be seen in the writings of a 5th-century pilgrim to Jerusalem. A Christian woman named Egeria wrote a well-preserved diary of her visit to Jerusalem, Antioch and Constantinople, and has this to report about the bishop's catechetical instruction before Easter in Antioch:

> A portion of the population in this province knows both Greek and Syriac; another segment knows only Greek; and still another, only Syriac. Even though the bishop may know Syriac, he only speaks Greek and never Syriac; and, therefore, there is always present a priest who, while the bishop speaks in Greek, translates into Syriac so that all may understand what is being explained... (*Diary of a Pilgrimage*, ch. 47).

In preserving West Syriac in the liturgy, the Maronite Church (with the other two West Syriac-speaking Churches) preserve for the entire Church the closest contact we can have to the language of Jesus.

The culture that arose due to the Syriac language was considerable, and lasted well past its 7th-century flourishing. Scripture scholars know of Syriac versions of the Bible, and a great body of non-biblical Syriac literature exists. Since the beginning of the 20th century, a considerable amount of research in English has been done on Syriac language and literature, and much more is known about Syriac culture today.

(Please refer to the Bibliography for a small listing of works about the Syriac world. Also, please refer to the map of the Syriac world at the time of the early Church [p. 92] to get an idea of the names of places important in this discussion.)

With the city of Antioch is associated the names of such great Church Fathers as John Chrysostom (before his appointment to Constantinople); Ignatius; Theodore of Mopsuestia, and Theodoret of Cyrrhus, to name just a few.

The Influence of East Syriac Christianity on Maronite Tradition

In addition to its West Syriac Antiochene origins, Maronite Tradition is influenced by elements of East Syriac Tradition. In the liturgical tradition we find the writings of poets such as Ephrem, Aphrahat, James of Sarug. They employed a distinctive liturgical verse form called *memre*. We also find the metrical forms employed by these writers used in Maronite liturgical poetry, such as found in the *hoosoyo*, innumerable *qolo*s, and other liturgical prayers.

Monasticism

Lastly, when considering the background of the Maronite Church, we cannot forget the great monastic movement, which grew up early in the 3rd century in Syria and Egypt. Associated with names such as Pachomius (Egypt), Anthony of the Desert and Simon the Stylite (Northern Syria), monasticism developed quickly and influenced greatly the mentality and spirituality of the area. It should be noted that certain groups in Syria—such as the Ebionites and the Encratites—practiced a distorted and unhealthy form of asceticism. These groups saw the body, and the material world in general, as something bad. Some of them even saw marriage as not a holy thing, and thus something to be avoided. On the other hand, others, such as the Stylites—perhaps the most famous of whom was St. Simon—inspired many pilgrims. All three important elements formed the matrix of the Maronite Community. Deeply Eastern in its roots, it shared the wisdom of West and East Syriac cultures, as well as monasticism.

St. Maron

St. Maron was born in the mid-4th century, in the northwestern part of the Roman province of Syria II. A priest and hermit, he retired to an area outside of the city of Antioch, and near the banks of the Orontes River. His life of poverty, fasting, holiness and prayer, and his ability to heal physical and spiritual illnesses, were well known.

Two sources for St. Maron exist. Bishop Theodoret of Cyrrhus (near Antioch in Northwest Syria), later wrote of Maron, in his *History of the Monks of Syria (Religious History)*, that

> ...it was he who planted for God the garden that now flourishes in the region of Cyrrhus.

R. M. Price, who has translated Theodoret's *Religious History* in to English observes:

> St. Maron emerges from the *Religious History* as the first influential hermit of the region of Cyrrhus. His pattern of life in the open air, exposed to the extremes of the climate, was imitated by many...and gave the asceticism of Cyrrhestica a distinctive character, for elsewhere hermits normally lived in cells or caves (119 n. 1).

St. John Chrysostom, exiled Bishop of Constantinople, wrote a letter—likely dated from his exile in 406 A.D.—to the hermit Maron, whom he refers to as "friend," inquiring about Maron's health and well-being and promising prayers.

The *Sedro* of the *Hoosoyo* from the Feast of St. Maron, Father of the Maronites, (9 February) eloquently speaks of St. Maron, hermit and monk:

> *Who can describe how God arrayed our Father Maron*
> *with the choicest blessings of creation*
> *and with a holy life of service?*
> *He followed the way of Christ,*
> *abandoning all else for the one pearl*
>   *of great price.*
> *His days and nights were filled*
>   *with prayer and penance.*
> *In humility he carried his cross;*
> *in dedication he became a hermit in the world,*
> *and in simplicity he praised his God*
>   *on the mountain tops...*
> *And because God graced our Father Maron*
>   *with power over body and soul,*
> *many came to follow him and to be led*
>   *by his pastor's staff.*
> *He was anointed as the Father of a great people,*
>   *a nation gathered from nations.*
> *He was his Master's plow in the garden of life,*
>   *preparing hearts for the seed of truth.*
> **Praise and thanksgiving to the One Who chose him,**
> **now and for ever. Amen.**

The Early Maronite Community: a Church Born in Orthodoxy

The Maronite Church first appeared as a distinct community within the wider Syriac-speaking Church of Antioch. Its formation was the result of a desire to defend the orthodox teachings of the 5th-century Council of Chalcedon—that Jesus Christ is fully and truly God and at the same time fully and truly human, and that Mary is properly called "Mother of God." (*Theotokos*). Thus, from the beginning the Maronite Church was thoroughly Chalcedonian.

Accordingly, Bishop Theodoret gathered the monks and hermits who followed the teachings of St. Maron into a monastery shortly after the doctrines of Chalcedon had been defined. This monastery of St. Maron prospered, and soon other monasteries were established. These evolved into centers of spiritual life, as people began to gather around them and to worship with the monks, forming the earliest Maronite Community.

The Maronite Patriarchate of Antioch

In the 7th and 8th centuries Maronites increasingly felt pressure from their neighbors: The Byzantines wanted the Maronites to follow the Greek Christianity of the Empire; and newly emerging Islam tried to force other religions to convert to it. During this time more and more Maronites moved to safety in the valleys and mountains of what was in ancient times known as "Mt. Lebanon," and what would eventually become known in modern times (1943) as the "Republic of Lebanon." They began to join fellow Maronites already there.

It was at this time, when the Patriarchal See of Antioch had no Chalcedonian Patriarch (702 A.D.), that the Maronite Patriarchate was established under Bishop John Maron. John had been bishop in the area of Kfarhai, Lebanon. Thus, while the spiritual and monastic roots of the Maronite Church go back to Maron in the 4th/5th century, the ecclesiastical organization of the Maronite Patriarchate of Antioch dates to the 8th century. In other words, from this time the Maronite Church saw itself as a self-governing (*sui iuris*) Church of the Antiochene Tradition.

Several places have served as residences for the Maronite Patriarchs over the centuries. One of the most famous is Qannoobeen, in the *Wadee Qadeesha* ("Holy Valley"). Others include Yannooh and Maifooq. Today the Patriarchal residence is at Bkirkee, Lebanon (in summer at Deemaan).

There remains to this day a Patriarch of the Maronites "and all the East," as his title expresses. Maronite Patriarchs take the name "Peter" as part of their name upon election, to show the continuous link between the Maronites and the Faith of Peter, who resided for a time in Antioch. In fact, it is the boast of the Maronite Community that it has never broken communion with the Church of Rome, while maintaining, in some measure, their proper traditions.

The Maronites in Lebanon

Maronites are survivors, despite persecutions and many changes in culture and society. In the safe, but difficult and often inhospitable valleys and caves of Lebanon, especially the Holy Valley (*Wadee Qadeesha*), Maronite faith and culture grew and flourished. As the Maronite Community developed under the leadership of the Patriarchs, the Community became known as the "Maronite Nation."

Despite pressures from outside influences, particularly Islam and the Ottomans, the Maronite Church held its own. Lebanese Maronite religious and lay leaders often served as liaisons between Church and civil society, and some even served non-Christian courts in diplomatic positions.

It is no accident that the Maronites introduced Western literacy on a large scale into the Middle East, much as their forebears the Phoenicians introduced the alphabet to the world. Due to the advanced educational background of the Lebanese (91 per cent literacy in 1997), the area became a recognized center for culture. Beirut, Lebanon's capital, was once known as the "Paris of the Middle East."

The Maronite experience in Lebanon was to a degree shaped by the wider influence of (non-Christian) Arabic culture. Yet, due to the extensive Western presence in Lebanon, Lebanese culture cannot be defined solely in terms of Arabic culture. This is largely due to the enormous influence that Maronite Catholic Christianity had in forming the Lebanese character. This in itself explains a major difference between the largely Christianized culture of Lebanon and the broader context of Islamic culture that surrounds the tiny country.

Latinization

Simply put, "latinization" means the process—imposed or voluntarily accepted—of inserting customs from the Latin Church into Eastern Church Traditions.

For Maronites, this process began far back in the Tradition. Contact with the West in the early Middle Ages (12th century), especially with the Crusaders, began the latinization process, which took its toll on

Maronite traditions. On the one hand, there was pressure from Rome for Maronite Catholics to conform to a more western model of Catholicism. On the other hand, Maronites were eager to proclaim their communion with and loyalty to Rome; thus, Maronites readily embraced Rome's latinizing.

This happened not only to the Maronites. Other Eastern Churches, for a time separated from the Catholic Communion and coming back into communion with Rome, often sacrificed some of their authentic and precious traditions, especially in the form of the Divine Liturgy and the sacramental Mysteries.

Happily, this was not to be permanent. Rome itself reversed this process (see **Chapter 7, "The Council and the Eastern Catholic Churches"**). Indeed, we have come a very long way since the Crusades, for as Pope John Paul II himself has stated, in his Encyclical Letter addressed to the whole Church about the Eastern Churches, *Orientale Lumen*:

> The Eastern Churches that entered into full communion with Rome wished to be an expression of this concern, according to the degree of maturity of the ecclesial awareness of the time. In entering into catholic communion, they did not at all intend to deny their fidelity to their own tradition, to which they have borne witness down the centuries with heroism and often by shedding their blood. And if sometimes, in their relations with the Orthodox Churches, misunderstandings and open opposition have arisen, we all know that we must *ceaselessly implore divine mercy (papal emphasis)* and a new heart capable of reconciliation over and above any wrong suffered.

> It has been stressed several times that the full union of the Eastern Catholic Churches with the Church of Rome which has already been achieved must not imply a diminished awareness of their own authenticity and originality. Wherever this occurred, the Second Vatican Council has urged them to rediscover their full identity, because they have "the right and the duty to govern themselves according to their own special disciplines. For these are guaranteed by ancient tradition, and seem to be better

suited to the customs of their faithful and to the good of their souls" ... And conversion is also required of the Latin Church, that she may respect and fully appreciate the dignity of Eastern Christians, and accept gratefully the spiritual treasures of which the Eastern Catholic Churches are the bearers, to the benefit of the entire catholic communion; that she may show concretely, far more than in the past, how much she esteems and admires the Christian East and how essential she considers its contribution to the full realization of the Church's universality (¶21).

Finally, this reversal was clearly reaffirmed by the Oriental Congregation's *Instruction* ... (see **Chapter 21**).

It still remains for the all the Eastern Churches that still cling to such latinizations to work hard to purify themselves. This is particularly necessary for any of the Eastern Catholic Churches that have a direct Orthodox counterpart, as reunion efforts between Catholic/Orthodox pairings will take latinization strongly into consideration.

Despite the 16-year war in Lebanon (1975-91), the renewal is proceeding there. It has been taking hold in other jurisdictions of the Maronite Community, notably in the United States, even longer.

The Synod of Mt. Lebanon

An important meeting of bishops (called a "synod") took place at the Monastery of Louaizee, Lebanon, in 1736. Like many such synods, there were many issues to be discussed.

The leaders of the Maronite Church were joined by representatives from Rome. Unfortunately, the agenda was skewed by the Roman legates in the direction of bringing more Latin-rite customs (beyond what was already clearly imposed) into our Eastern Church. Fortunately, the impositions were not completely successful. On the positive side, some authentic traditions were affirmed.

One of the greatest changes that this synod introduced into the Maronite Church (other Eastern Churches would follow suit) was the changeover from a largely monastic church to the diocesan model that we know today namely, the bishop residing in a fixed place within the eparchy (the episcopal "see").

To be specific, from the time of the Monastery of St. Maron and throughout the centuries, the Maronite Church was a Community formed from and characterized by the monastic tradition. People gathered in the monasteries to worship and to pray both the Service of the Holy Mysteries as well as the canonical prayer hours of the Divine Office. Bishops—including the Patriarch—were chosen from among the monks. Bishops did not always live in the center of their eparchies but often in community with the Patriarch. Often, the territories governed by various bishops overlapped. There were married priests, because the tradition had been unbroken, but monks also staffed parishes in the villages and towns.

Celibate, non-monastic clergy in the East began to be seen from this time. Though never a general Eastern Church norm, celibacy was imposed on Eastern clergy serving outside the home Patriarchate in the Roman ruling of 1929. The legislation of the Synod of Mt. Lebanon was Particular Law for the Maronite Church and guided it for more than 200 years. The promulgation of Maronite Particular Law—it is only partially approved at this writing—will replace that of the Synod of 1736, and will be in conformity with the *Code of Canons of the Eastern Churches*.

Maronites Outside of Lebanon

At the end of 19th century, the Lebanese were among the many people who emigrated from their homelands because of persecution or for economic advancement. Maronites emigrated from Lebanon and settled in all parts of the world, including Europe, Africa, North and South America, Canada, and Australia. In fact, they assimilated well, shaped by the cultures they encountered and shaping them in turn. For the Lebanese secular inculturation came easily in the first two generations in emigration. Yet, ironically this was coupled with a stubborn fondness for their Lebanese heritage. As with any immigrant population these bonds with Lebanon have weakened in succeeding generations

Like some other Eastern Catholics, Maronites were at first under the governance of local Latin bishops. Even though they would not begin to have their own eparchs and eparchies until the middle of the 20th century, the Maronites brought their own religious and cultural heritage with them and enriched the societies in which they newly resided. Clergy were sent by the Patriarchs to serve Maronite parishes. These men, frequently the most educated in the community, were suited to help these new immigrants.

After the Council several native jurisdictions were established. These were sometimes called "exarchates." As they became stable, they were elevated to the status of "eparchy."

The Maronites Today

Today, the worldwide Maronite People of God in Christ numbers well over 3 million members, and it is the third largest *sui iuris* Eastern Catholic Church. Eparchies, with their respective bishops, have been established outside of Lebanon and Syria, notably in Egypt (Cairo), Brazil (San Paulo), Canada (Montreal), Australia (Sydney), Argentina (Buenos Aires), and Mexico (Mexico City). There are Maronite Apostolic Visitators to South American countries and to Europe. Two eparchies make up the Maronite Community in the United States: the Eparchy of St. Maron, Brooklyn, New York, and the Eparchy of Our Lady of Lebanon of Los Angeles.

Inculturation and Renewal

Eastern Catholic eparchies have a real connection to the homeland of the Mother Church. In the face of renewed ecumenical dialog, the Eastern Catholic Churches will have to explore better the question of what it means to be worldwide Eastern Churches: self-governing and simultaneously in communion with the Church of Rome.

Being Maronite is not merely a matter of ethnicity, that is, being Middle Eastern. Eastern Church Tradition is a deeply spiritual reality, *adapted to the particular circumstances in which Eastern Catholics, living outside of their lands of origin, find themselves.* On this realization rests the renewal of the Maronite Church and all Eastern Churches. Maronites have begun to learn this especially since Vatican II.

STUDY QUESTIONS:
1) Identify some a) West Syriac, b) Antiochene and c) Edessan elements of Maronite Tradition.
2) Who was St. Maron? Describe separately his influence and that of St. Maron Monastery on the formation of the Maronite Community.
3) Describe the traditional link between Lebanon and the Maronite Church. Is that link exactly the same today in the Worldwide Maronite Church?

PART II: THE WORD OF GOD, FOUNDATION OF OUR FAITH
(Divine Liturgy Focus: Service of the Word)

The Bible: God's Word to Us

God's word of revelation comes to us through the words spoken and written by human beings, in response to the inspiration of the Spirit (*CCC* 105). "Sacred Scripture is the utterance of God put down as it is in writing under the inspiration of the Holy Spirit" (*DV*, 9). Sacred Tradition is the handing on of God's Word by the successors of the Apostles. "Tradition and Scripture make up a single sacred deposit of the Word of God, which is entrusted to the Church" (*DV* 10).

One of the challenges of the Council was to call the Catholic Church in general back to its rightly scriptural heritage. The reading of, love of and devotion to the Bible as a source and foundation had been in danger of being lost among Catholics since the stormy and unbalanced days after the Reformation. And although the Council's "Document on Divine Revelation" (*De Revelatione*) came as a shock to some and a breath of fresh air for others, a more solid place for the Scriptures in the lives of Catholic people has been assured.

The Maronite Church is especially devoted to the use of Scripture in its liturgy and life. The Antiochene Syriac heritage of Bible interpretation embedded within Maronite experience is strong. Especially in the earliest stages of the Tradition, our Church inherited a background that resisted Greek philosophical reflection and was focused on the Bible more directly. This approach inspired the great commentators like Theodore of Mopsuestia (considered the greatest interpreter of the Syriac Tradition) and the Deacon Ephrem, who produced liturgical language that poetically expressed the Word of the Bible.

The Service of the Word is that part of the Divine Service essentially dedicated to teaching and preaching. Whether a person is not baptized and is seeking to deepen one's knowledge of the Word of God, or already baptized and seeks to deepen her or his relationship to the Word, it happens in the Service of the Word. The Presbyter or Deacon leads the congregation more deeply into the meaning of the Bible—by means of the Lectionary—by his preaching and teaching at the pulpit.

However, it is not supposed to stop here. The Service of the Word is a limited time each week, and we are not always as receptive to hearing the Word and the preaching. As people faithful to the Word we need to amplify our study of the Bible in private reading and group study. In this way we bring so much more to the liturgical experience. Unless Christians know the Bible intimately, they cannot fully understand their liturgical life. This is particularly true of Syriac Christians because of the special liturgical prayer known as the *Hoosoyo*, which will be discussed in some detail below (**Chapter 12**).

Chapter 9:
The Sacred Scriptures

The Bible: a Sacred Library

Sacred Scriptures, the Bible, is a collection of books, a kind of library. According to the *canon* (the Catholic Church's list of books accepted as authentic), the Bible contains 73 books.

On the basis of Jewish-Hellenistic (Septuagint) tradition in Alexandria (Egypt), the Catholic Churches and some Eastern Orthodox Churches recognize 46 books in the canon of the Hebrew Scriptures. However, this listing is not shared by all the Christian Churches, especially the Protestant Churches. They follow the Hebrew Canon of the Old Testament, which contains only 39 books. The seven additional books (or sections of books) are not considered by Protestants as inspired by the Holy Spirit. This material is called by Catholics the "Deuterocanonical Books"; Protestant Christians call them the Old Testament "Apocrypha." (See the discussion below on the Septuagint.)

All of the Christian Churches recognize 27 books in the New Testament. **Appendix VII** gives a brief summary of each book of the Bible.

The Composition of the Books

The writing of the Bible occurred over a period of roughly 1,000 years, from approximately 900 B.C. to near the end of the first century A.D., with the bulk of the writing being at the time of the Septuagint (3rd century B.C.) and after.

Today, no original manuscripts of either Testament exist. The oldest ones for the Hebrew Scriptures (Old Testament) are the Isaiah texts of the Dead Sea scrolls, discovered at Qumran, Palestine, in 1947. The oldest *complete* Hebrew Bible comes from the 11th century after Christ. A fragment of John's Gospel dated to 125 A.D. appears to be the oldest New Testament text we have to date. Scholars evaluate virtually hundreds of texts and fragments of both Testaments and attempt to reconstruct the best possible sources for study and translation.

The Hebrew Scriptures (Old Testament)

The 46 books of the Hebrew Scriptures were written approximately between the years 900 B.C. and 160 B.C. The Hebrew Bible collection is made up of historical books, didactic (teaching) books, and prophetic books (containing the inspired words of prophets—people who experienced God in special ways and were his authentic speakers).

Jews today use an old, mnemonic abbreviation to remember the three, major divisions of the Hebrew Scriptures: *TaNaKh*. "T" stands for *Torah*, the first five books of the Bible (also known as the Law, or the Greek name, "Pentateuch"); "N" stands for *Nevi'im*, Hebrew for "Prophets"; and "K" for *Kethuvim*, or "Writings"—TNK. To be able to pronounce this mnemonic, they added the letter "a." It's a simple way to remember the three parts. These books, with few exceptions, were written originally in Hebrew and Aramaic.

In brief, the Hebrew Scriptures record the experience the Israelite people had of Yahweh, "the God of their ancestors" (recall *Ex* 3:13-15). As a whole, these books reveal Israel's insight into the personal reality of the one God, Yahweh, who acts in human history, guiding it with a plan and purpose. Yahweh, the God of the Old Covenant, is the same God whom Jesus, a Jew, called "Father."

The Old Testament Deuterocanonical Writings ("Apocrypha")

A word is in order about what are known as the "Deuterocanonical" Writings, or, as they have been known by Protestants, the "Apocrypha" of the Old Testament.

These are books or sections of books (listed below), which, since the controversies of the Reformation, are not accepted by Protestant Christians as the inspired Word of God. The reason for this is that they followed strictly the original Hebrew and Aramaic version of the Hebrew Scriptures. Although they do not consider the Apocrypha to be inspired by the Holy Spirit, they are of value for devotional uplift.

These two names are from the Greek. *Deutero*, meaning "second," refers to the fact that these books are considered by some Christians as being other than that which is accepted in the official canon, or listing, of books of the Old Testament. *Apocrypha* is the Greek word for "hidden," or "secret." Protestant Christians consider the Apocrypha to be, in a sense, hidden from official acceptance, although they are not forbidden to read the books of the Apocrypha.

Catholics accept the Deuterocanonical Writings as a standard part of the inspired text of the Bible. The decision for this lies with Catholic acceptance of the Septuagint listing of the Writings of the Hebrew Scriptures, which was a fuller listing.

The Deuterocanonical Writings are:

Books:
Tobit
Judith
The *Wisdom of Sirach* (*Ecclesiasticus*)
1 Maccabees
2 Maccabees
1 Esdras (*Ezra*)
2 Esdras

Sections of Books:
"Susanna"
The *Letter of Jeremiah*
The Additions to the *Book of Esther* (in the Greek version)
The "Prayer of Azariah" and the "Song of the Three Jews"
"Bel and the Dragon"
The "Prayer of Manasseh"

The New Testament

The 27 New Testament books, written originally in Greek, are made up of the Four Gospels (proclamations of the Good News), and other Writings listed below. The books of the New Testament were written approximately between the years 50 and 140 A.D.

First, in the order in which they appear in the Bible, are Gospels of Matthew, Mark, Luke and John. The first three Gospels are called *synoptic* (from the Greek, *synoptikos*, "seeing the whole together") because they tell much the same story in much the same way. The book called *Acts of the Apostles*, which follows the *Gospel of John*, is a sequel to the *Gospel of Luke*. Written by Luke, Acts continues the narrative of his Gospel. The *Gospel of John* (also called the Fourth Gospel) fills out the view of Jesus found in the three synoptic Gospels.

Each of the Evangelists wrote for a particular Christian community of faith, each with concerns common to all Christians but also with special concerns as well. These concerns are reflected in the point of view of each

Gospel writer. The *Sedro* for Thursdays, commemorating the Apostles and Evangelists, states this quite clearly:

> *...Matthew proclaimed the mystery of your*
> *mission as Messiah.*
> *Mark spoke of the mystery of your humanity.*
> *Luke announced the mystery of your plan*
> *of salvation.*
> *John reflected on the mystery of your divinity.*
> **O Christ,**
> **through the four Evangelists**
> **you gave us the Book of Life,**
> **the Gospel of your life-giving, good news,**
> **which gives life to all the faithful.**

Next in sequence come the Epistles of Saint Paul—the earliest New Testament documents—which were written in each case to meet particular situations of various local Christian communities. Most scholars today recognize that there are seven Letters authentically written by Paul; the rest are attributed to him.

The *Letter to the Hebrews* is not by Paul.

After Paul's Epistles come the Catholic Epistles. These letters are called "catholic," or "universal," because they were not written to deal with particular situations of local churches but with matters important to all Christian communities.

The final book of the New Testament is the highly symbolic *Book of Revelation*, a message of hope for persecuted Christians, promising Christ's ultimate triumph in history (see below, **"Apocalyptic Literature"**).

Old Testament and New Testament Apocryphal Writings

A number of recently discovered writings bear a strong resemblance to the writings of both parts of the Bible. Some are even quoted in the Bible—especially the New Testament—but are otherwise lost over the centuries.

These writings are called "apocryphal" writings, and are not to be confused with the seven writings of the Hebrew Scriptures (see p. 115) specifically designated by Protestants as "Apocrypha" (with a capital *A*).

These writings were never finally accepted for inclusion by any Christian group into the official texts of the Old or New Testament—a process called "canonicity." Although the reasons for exclusion are complex, the main reason is that these writings were not thought to be the revealed Word of God. In addition, when one reads the apocryphal writings in general, one sees a fanciful type of writing often hard to understand by any standards. Examples of Old Testament apocryphal writings include *Enoch*, *Jubilees* and *IV Ezra*.

The canonical—that is, accepted—writings found in the New Testament are not the only writings about the life of Jesus and the beginnings of the Church. As noted above, there are many gaps in the historical events in the life of Jesus, of the Apostles and of the earliest Church, omissions that have from the beginning of Christianity caused people to ask questions like: "Just what *did* Joseph sell in the carpenter shop?" "What Jewish lullabies did Mary sing to the infant Jesus?" "What color *were* Jesus' eyes, anyway?" "How *was* Mary's body assumed into heaven?"

It has long been known that many other so-called Christian writings sought to fill in the gaps. Such works as the *Gospel of Thomas,* the *Protoevangelium of James* (from where we get the names of Mary's parents), the *Gospel of Philip*, the *Book of Jubilees*, the *Assumption of Moses*, and the *Psalms of Solomon*, are often very fanciful, and sometimes downright unbelievable. For this reason they are called "apocryphal." Unlike the Deuterocanonical Books the apocryphal writings are still not accepted as the inspired Word of God by any Christians.

Why mention them here? First, they are imaginative attempts by Christians to tell what the Gospel didn't tell. For example, most people accept that there was an ox and a donkey in the place of the birth of Jesus; but the canonical Gospels do not mention them. (They are mentioned by the apocryphal Gospels to fulfill an Old Testament prophecy.)

Recent studies are again appreciating the role that apocryphal material has played in the popular piety of the life of the Church. Besides sporadic references within the canonical Scriptures, the writings of the era of the Fathers show some signs of quoting from non-canonical works. In the Middle Ages, in the West, we see a greater use of these non-canonical details, particularly in the medieval Christmas and Easter carols. Our era of more precision appreciates these stories less.

Second, the Church was very careful about what it finally accepted as the inspired Word of God into the New Testament.

Third, some of the apocryphal writings (such as the *Gospel of Thomas)* contain verses recorded, in many cases, *exactly* as in the accepted

Gospels. As such, they stand as a powerful testimony to the Gospels we accept and serve to confirm their authenticity. Thus, they are a help to scholars in studying the accepted—canonical—text of the Bible.

Apocalyptic Literature

There is another kind ("genre") of writing found in the Bible and that is related to the apocryphal literature. It is called "apocalyptic."

The characteristics of apocalyptic writing are that it is symbolic, often fanciful, and very dramatic. A good Old Testament example is the *Book of Daniel*. In the New Testament, the *Book of Revelation* (formerly called "The Apocalypse") stands out as the best example.

The purpose of apocalyptic writing is to be a sort of code writing for people beset by trying circumstances, often persecution for their faith. The symbols of such writing are not readily known to outsiders, particularly the oppressors. But the message of comfort and hope to the persecuted is very consoling. Thus, when one considers the overall effect of the *Book of Revelation*, the majesty and triumph of the Lamb of God, the thousands robed in white, singing God's praises, you can see how the message could, when written, and can now inspire.

Difficult symbols? Ask any Star Trek trekker, or any owner of the *Star Wars Trilogy* if he or she has difficulty getting the message in the symbols!

Versions and Translations

Because the Word of God is meant for all people, who live in the many cultures of the world, the Bible has been translated into languages other than the original Hebrew, Aramaic and Greek. These translations are called *versions*. Because the original texts of the Bible no longer exist (or have not yet been discovered), scholars rely on careful comparisons of existing versions in their attempt to reconstruct the most reliable form of the biblical text.

An important source for translating the Hebrew Scriptures are the Targums (see **Glossary**). These Aramaic translations helped Jews and Christians of Palestine read the Bible more intelligently in their native language.

A famous Greek translation of the Hebrew Scriptures was made in the 3rd century B.C. This translation, reputed to have been accomplished by 70 (or 72) scholars in Alexandria, Egypt, is called the *Septuagint*, from the Latin word meaning "seventy."

Another famous translation, dear to the Syriac Churches, is the *Peshitta* Version. This is a Syriac translation of the Bible (both Testaments) based on the original languages, dating to the 5th century. Its New Testament canon differs from that accepted by the wider Church: it lacks *2 Peter, 2 John, 3 John, Jude and Revelation.* Since the Churches of the Catholic Communion today use the Western biblical canon, the *Peshitta* is now used only by a few of the Syriac-speaking, non-Catholic Churches. It would be most interesting to consider what a Christianity would be like without, for example, the *Book of Revelation* and its confusing symbolism.

Other Syriac versions of the Bible as we know it exist. These are important because in some cases they represent some parts of the Bible that are better than an inferior Greek manuscript of the same passages. In addition, sometimes Bible quotations appear in the commentaries on the Scriptures, such as those of St. Ephrem. These often preserve for us earlier versions of the Scriptures for which the originals of the same time period of the commentaries have been lost.

For many years the Syriac Church generally used a famous version of the New Testament known as the *Diatesseron.* The word is Greek and means "the harmony of fourth," that is, of the Four Gospels. This work is a Gospel "harmony," or collation of verses into one Gospel story line. Its author was Tatian, a Syrian Scripture scholar trained in Rome.

The *Diatesseron* was not the only harmony of the Gospels, but it was certainly the most famous and most widely read in both East and West up to the 5th century. In fact, this was the Gospel of St. Ephrem, who produced a famous Commentary on it (see Bibliography).

Other Syriac versions of the Bible as accepted today (not the *Peshitta*) also exist, and they form an important part of the history of the textual criticism of the Bible.

In addition, there are versions of the Bible other than Syriac—Greek, Slavonic, Armenian, others—which scholars consult when making decisions about the text of the Bible. A famous Latin version was done by St. Jerome for the West in the 4th century. It was called the "Vulgate" Version, from the Latin phrase, *versio vulgata*, meaning "popular version." In this sense it is like the *Peshitta* for the Syriacs, since the *Peshitta* was popular version too.

The issue of reading the Bible in translation is an important one. People do not normally think of the consequences of reading the Sacred Scriptures in languages different from the original Hebrew, Aramaic and

Greek. Not many Christians are capable of reading the Bible in the originals. Reading the Bible in English, for example, is a little like the early Christians reading the Septuagint or *Peshitta* Versions: we hope that the translation we are reading comes as close to the original as possible while enjoying God's Word in our more familiar native language. We rely on the work of translators and scholars to make versions that are as accurate and readable as possible. Newly discovered information (such as the Dead Sea Scrolls, for example) enhance the possibilities for improvements in translations.

Choosing a Translation

Choosing a translation that is suitable for you demands careful consideration. People often make distinctions between texts for private, devotional reading; for Bible study—here the group must agree on the text to follow; and public reading, such as at the Divine Liturgy—usually a more formal version.

When choosing a particular translation of the Bible, you should make sure that the Apocrypha are included, so that you will be sure to have a full Catholic Bible. In a Bible from a Protestant publishing house, they are now more readily included in the listing of the Books of the Bible, and, when included, often the word *Apocrypha* is printed on the binding. The only difference is that the order will be different, since the Books of the Apocrypha will be in a separate section.

If you have chosen a Catholic translation, the Apocrypha will not be listed separately (as in Protestant translations) but printed in their Catholic Old Testament sequence.

More and more Bibles printed by Protestant publishing houses contain the Apocrypha. This is a healthy sign, in these days of reaching out to other denominations, that all Christians are reaching a better consensus of what makes up the text of the Word of God.

Two very good Catholic translations are the New American Bible (NAB) and the New Jerusalem Bible (NJB). The NAB was produced by a Committee of the National Conference of Catholic Bishops and published in 1970. The New Testament was retranslated and updated in 1986 in light of recent biblical studies and increased sensitivity to inclusive language. The Psalms were redone in 1991. The New Jerusalem Bible, first published (at the Ecole Biblique in Jerusalem) as the Jerusalem Bible (JB), was a French translation from the original Bible languages. It was soon translated into English. The NJB was retranslated directly into English from the original languages in 1985. Both the NAB and NJB are quite formal translations. The advantages of these two Catholic-sponsored versions is the addition of copious and helpful notes by Catholic scholars (notes are usually at the bottom of each column of text), as well as introductions to each major section of the Bible and to each separate Book or Letter.

A very fine (and formal) ecumenical translation—approved for use by Catholics—is the New Revised Standard Version (NRSV, 1989). Its immediate predecessor, the Revised Standard Version (RSV), had long been widely recognized as the most accurate English translation of the Bible. The NRSV still remains very faithful to the original languages; it also is conservatively sensitive to inclusive-language issues.

A widely used and very accurate Protestant-sponsored translation is the New International Version (NIV, 1978), which is rather formal. Of note is a special arrangement of the NIV that many find helpful: *The Daily Bible: in Chronological Order* (F. LaGard Smith, Editor and Narrator, Eugene, OR: Harvest House Publications, 1984). In it, Smith arranges the actual NIV text in the order in which the Bible says they occurred, and fills in the gaps with a "narration," which ties the events and periods together. This work is also divided into 365 sections, to facilitate daily reading. The value of this edition lies in offering the reader a way to read the Bible "cover to cover," in a year's time, a task that regularly discourages Bible readers when they try to read a standard edition. But caution: this edition of the NIV does not include the Deuterocanonical material (Apocrypha); and the arrangement makes no claim to present the texts *as they were probably written in history* (you need Bible study for this), rather, only as the Bible states that they unfolded. There are other similar daily Bible arrangements on the market that simply take the text as it is and divides them into 365 selections.

Two simple translations are Today's English Version (TEV, 1992) and the Contemporary English Version (CEV, 1995). All of the Protestant-sponsored and ecumenical versions named above may be purchased in editions which include the Deuterocanonical Books/Apocrypha.

The Quests of the Historical Jesus

Who was Jesus the Jew from Nazareth? How much can we know of the details of his life and ministry in what is today known as the "Holy Land"? Are the Gospels historically accurate? These are some of the questions being asked anew in our day in the so-called "Quest of the

Historical Jesus." As a topic for study, this quest has its roots in the 18th century. But as a formal study the "Quest" is a 20th-century phenomenon that has gone through three stages—"Quest"; "New Quest," and "Third Quest of the Historical Jesus."

The question is an important one, as most responsible New Testament scholars will admit. However, despite the fact that more has been written about Jesus than any other figure of the ancient world, scholars also admit that the historical data of the Gospels are limited. Discoveries such as the Dead Sea Scrolls and other writings from Palestine at the time of Jesus also help us to know more about him.

Jesus really existed. But historical details about him and his actual life situation are at best reconstructions of some Scripture scholars. The Catholic Church teaches that there is continuity between the Jesus of History and the Christ of Faith. We must never forget that the real point of the Gospels is to witness in faith to Jesus who was called "Christ" in the glory of the Resurrection.

B.C. and A.D., or B.C.E. and C.E.?
In referring to dates before and after the birth of Jesus, one often sees two systems of designations: B.C. (Before Christ) and A.D. (*Anno Domini*, "In the year of the Lord"), or B.C.E. (Before the Common Era) and C.E. (Common Era). The first set is more traditional and relates dates to the Christian idea of the centrality of Christ's birth for history. The latter—more recent—claims to be more sensitive to non-Christian religions.

Whom the New Testament Is All About
The New Testament is about Jesus Christ. Each book reveals a different side of his mystery. These sacred writings tell us not who Jesus was, but *who he is*. More than mere historical documents, these writings have the power to change your life.

STUDY QUESTIONS:
1) How is the Bible "God's Word in human words"?
2) How do Catholic and non-Catholic Christians differ in the acceptance of the canon (listing of writings) of the Bible?
3) What does the word *synoptic* mean? How do the Synoptic Gospels differ from the Gospel of John?

Chapter 10:
Holy Tradition

What is Tradition?
Tradition, in the Catholic experience, is the handing on of the Faith from Christ, through the Apostles, to all generations. The Council taught, "The Church, in her doctrine, life and worship, perpetuates and transmits to every generation all that she herself is, all that she believes (*DV, 8, #1*)."

Please note here that Tradition is being described in a very specific way. There are other uses of the word *tradition*, such as the individual Traditions in the Church that have shaped the various Catholic Communities within the Universal Catholic Church. (It is also common to speak of non-Catholic ecclesial [i.e., Church] Traditions within Christianity; but we will limit our discussion to the Catholic Communion in this text.)

Some of the ways in which the word *tradition* may be understood follow. Understanding their various meanings can help us appreciate better the richness of the Church:

❖   Tradition (with a capital *T*), the handing on of the Faith.

❖   Tradition (again capital *T*) can refer to the lived-out experience of a particular group of Christians within the larger Tradition; for example, the Byzantine Tradition; the Syriac Tradition; the Alexandrine Tradition; the Armenian Tradition; the Latin Tradition (see p. 89 and **Glossary**).

❖   Tradition (with a lowercase *t*). This refers to the many customs that enrich aspects of the various Traditions, such as sacramental, liturgical, cultural-ethnic. These often unique traditions—such as coloring Easter eggs or bringing decorated candles to the church on Hosanna Sunday (*Sha'neenee*)—differentiate the various Traditions and Churches from one another—the common ones serve to unite—and bring a great richness to the celebration of the Catholic Christian Tradition.

The importance of the Church's Tradition is not seen equally in all the Christian Churches. Its perception of importance ranges from very important (Catholics, Orthodox, some others) to hardly at all (Fundamentalists, Pentecostals, others).

Scripture and Tradition

Genealogy Sunday
Mt1:1-17

The Document on Revelation from the Council addresses the important question of the relationship of Scripture to Tradition. It affirms that both are important elements of our Christian life. Rather than being opposed to one another (as some might think), they both flow from a common source, and thus, they interact with each other to help guide us in our Christian life.

> Thus it is that the Church does not draw its certainty about all revealed truths from the Holy Scriptures alone. Hence, both Scripture and Tradition must be accepted and honored with equal devotion and reverence (*DV* 9).

We might say that Scripture lives within Tradition; throughout the centuries, our living out of the Bible, guided by the Church, has helped us to understand the Bible better. This is profoundly possible because the Holy Spirit is the inspiring force of both Scripture and Tradition.

Let's put it another way: *the Bible is the Church's Book*. It is out of the lived experience of the Covenant with God that the Israelites, God's first Chosen People, recalled, in story and worship, the Presence and Promise of God. The Second Israel, Christians, accepted this Presence and Promise as fulfilled in the mighty words and deeds of Jesus of Nazareth, whom they experienced in faith as risen and glorified after his death on the Cross. They experienced this most fully on Pentecost, when the Holy Spirit breathed into them the life of faith in Jesus the Christ. They prayed their Hebrew Scriptures, the Bible of their ancestors, as they shared the Gospel of Christ in preaching and evangelization. This "Church" then produced the New Testament. When finally added to the books of the Hebrew Scriptures, eventually this collection—called the *canon*—became accepted as the Bible we recognize today. You can always find what is the accepted canon of the Catholic Church by a simple glance at the Table of

Contents of your Catholic Bible, which is one that includes the Deuterocanonical Books (or Apocrypha).

People have reflected upon God's Words from the earliest times of the Church. Such reflection is part of Tradition. Scriptural interpretation remains one of the basic tasks of the Church.

If you are interested in delving more deeply into your understanding of the Bible and its powerful message, ask a competent Catholic pastor or religious education director for assistance. It is NOT recommended that you join just any Bible group, as you may wind up in a Fundamentalist mindset. Keep your mind and heart always open to the wider meaning of God's truth in the Bible, and do it in a Catholic way.

The Fathers/Teachers of the Church

Of special importance within Tradition is the witness of the Fathers, or Teachers (Maronite liturgy uses these terms interchangeably), in the early Church. These are believers who possessed the gift of being able to explain the Faith on which they reflected. Their writings have been of enormous importance for understanding the development of the teachings of the Catholic Faith as well as the interpretation of Scripture according to their respective Traditions within the general Tradition of the Church. Because the writings of men were considered authoritative in this area, they are often known as the "Fathers" of the Church.

Of particular importance are those Teachers who lived during the time of the Apostles and were taught by them. They are known as the "Apostolic" Fathers. Some of these include: Clement of Rome, Ignatius of Antioch, Polycarp, Papias, *et al.* The value of their writings lies in the fact that they are so close to the time of the Apostles.

In addition to these, there were other Teachers who followed the Apostolic Fathers and continued to reflect on the mysteries of the Faith and to develop its theological understandings. These so-called "Sub-apostolic" Fathers wrote in different regions of a Christianity now expanded beyond its Eastern Mediterranean origins. Included here are such people as the Syriac Teachers, which include Ephrem, Aphrahat, James of Sarug, and a host of Greek and Latin Writers.

The whole Church has always valued the writings of the Church Fathers, and they remain essential to the knowledge of the development of the Church's biblical/theological Tradition (See Oden in the Bibliography). We do well to be familiar with their writings, drinking deeply from their teachings.

Bishop Theodoret of Cyrrhus speaks poignantly of the personal difficulty in passing on the truth of the Faith in his Letter 89 to the Patrician Florens:

> We thought it useful to call your attention to the fact that those who attack our beliefs are slandering us. We ourselves, to be sure, recognize that we have made mistakes, but we have kept untainted to this day the faith taught by the Apostles ... To defend this faith, we have never stopped combating heresies of all types. It is this faith that we never cease to feed to those who have been nourished on true piety ... This teaching has been handed down to us not only by the Apostles and prophets but also by those who have interpreted their writings, Ignatius, Eustathius, Athanasius, Basil, Gregory, John and the other lights of the world and before them, by the holy Fathers gathered at Nicaea whose confession of faith we have kept intact, as the inheritance from a Father, while those who dare to violate their teachings, we call corrupt and enemies of the truth.

Theodoret understands that a bishop uses his authority as he speaks the Church's truth.

Eastern Tradition

The Catholic Tradition in general embraces—and is formed by—particular Traditions that have shaped the many Catholic Churches, East and West. Together, these make up the Universal Catholic Communion. (This is discussed in the section, **"The Eastern Catholic Churches."**)

One is often tempted to speak of Eastern Church Tradition, as if it were uniform. It is more accurate to speak of Eastern Traditions in the plural. While diverse, Eastern Catholic Traditions share much in common.

The Eastern Traditions of the Church preserve more closely the Middle Eastern origins of the Church. Included in this Eastern outlook are ancient ways (still relevant) of interpreting the Bible. The ancient centers of Christianity, such as Antioch, Alexandria, Nisibis and Edessa, were pioneers in biblical interpretation. Their lasting Traditions continue to offer a way of handing on distinct, Christian ways of understanding the Bible and living out the message of the Gospel.

Syriac-Antiochene Tradition

One important Eastern Tradition is that of Antioch, a once-proud, important political and cultural center—after Rome and Alexandria—in the Roman Empire. (See **Chapter 8**.) Its cultural and social backgrounds were the Hellenistic (Greek) heritage of Alexander the Great, and the West Syriac-speaking tradition, which embraced Greek thought patterns.

The Historico-grammatical Approach

A "School" of biblical interpretation developed at Antioch that specialized in the historical approach. This approach respected the authors of the books of the Bible (especially the Old Testament) and their meanings for the audiences of their ancient day (the *literal sense*). In addition, the Antiochene School analyzed the grammar and linguistic structures of the texts to a fine detail.

Typology

Further, the Syriac Teachers developed to an art the ability to see in the events and persons of the Old Testament a foreshadowing of events and persons that were fulfilled in the New Testament. These former events were called *types*; and their fulfillment in Christ—in light of his person and teachings—were called *antitypes*. The method is known as "typology" (see Zaharopoulos 115-16.) Typology was even extended into sacramental theology, whereby events in the life of Christ were types of the Church and the sacramental Mysteries.

The *Catechism* recognizes this biblical and Syriac method of typology thus:

> It is on this harmony of the two Testaments that the Paschal catechesis of the Lord is built, and then, that of the Apostles and the Fathers of the Church. This catechesis unveils what lay hidden under the letter of the Old Testament: the mystery of Christ. It is called "typological" because it reveals the newness of Christ on the basis of the "figures" (types) which announce him in the deeds, words, and symbols of the first covenant. By this re-reading in the Spirit of Truth, starting from Christ, the figures are unveiled. Thus the flood and Noah's ark prefigured salvation by Baptism, as did the cloud and the crossing of the Red Sea. Water from the rock was the figure of the

spiritual gifts of Christ, and manna in the desert prefigured
the Eucharist, "the true bread from heaven" (*CCC* 1094).

Underlying this valuable tool of biblical interpretation are two
related ideas. First, there is continuity between the Hebrew Scriptures and
the New Testament. In other words, God really was preparing the world
for the entrance of his Divine Son into human history. The events of the
Old prepare for the New.

Second, history is not merely human history. God, wishing to save
humanity from all that is destructive, brings about "salvation history." In
this deeply faith-filled view, history has meaning, and this meaning may
be seen in the texts sacred to the Jews and to Christians.

Paradox

Even though typology indicates continuity, religious expression
cannot always find harmony. The Syriac Teachers, with their sensitivity to
the Inexpressible Mystery, struggled to express—particularly by apophatic
language (refer to **"God-talk: Naming the Nameless One,"** in **Chapter
2**) the gaps they found between the divine world of the Logos and our
human nature which the Logos assumed.

Related to the appreciation of this distinction is the Antiochene use
of paradox. In biblical commentary and in liturgical expression, these two
(seemingly) contrasting worlds meet. Thus, Christ the majestic agent of
creation, is quietly cradled at the breast of his mother Mary. Or we see
Joseph as the guardian of the One who providentially holds the universe.
The literary device of paradox requires us to reflect upon—and struggle
with—the mystery of divinity touching humanity.

Theodore of Mopsuestia

One of the most famous exegetes, or interpreters, of the
Antiochene School was Theodore, bishop of the city of Mopsuestia (see
Appendix IV). The Antiochene-Syriac world considered him to be THE
Interpreter of the Bible. (It should be noted that in recent years there has
been a revival of interest in the person and work of Theodore. For more
information please refer to Rowan Greer, *Theodore of Mopsuestia:
Exegete and Theologian*, in the Bibliography. Many of the quotes from
Theodore cited in this text come from Greer.)

Theodore reacted to the theologians of Alexandria, Egypt, who
aggressively sought to tie their interpretation of the Scriptures to the Neo-
platonic philosophical categories of the Hellenistic spirit of the day. In so

doing, the Alexandrines overused the literary device of allegory in explaining the Word of God, and risked distorting the original semitic flavor of the Bible.

Theodore was an Antiochene through and through. He sought to preserve the Bible's semitic character by never importing Greek philosophy into his interpretation. Thus, Theodore read the Scriptures in the "literal" (not literalistic) sense (see **Chapter 12, "The Senses of Scripture"**). While this did present some limitations for the further growth of theology in general, it did rightly remain faithful to the Bible's own ways of expressing the Christian Mystery. In the words of Rowan Greer:

> ...Theodore's literal explanation of the Old Testament, preserving the relationship between Old and New Testaments, but guarding the original application of the Old to Hebrew history, represents an outstanding exegetical contribution (p. 104).

Central to Theodore's historical understanding of the Bible's message was his use of typology. Theodore himself offers a definition of what typology is (quoted in Greer, p. 109):

> One and the same is He who rules over the Old and the New Testaments, God the Master and Maker of all things; to one end of ends He distributes both in the former and the latter.

> To be sure, the Law had the shadow of all things that would happen; but the people became worthy of God's providence because of the expectation of what would appear at the coming of the Lord Christ.

It should be noted that Theodore used typology rather sparingly (see Zaharopoulos 130). For example, he only thought Pss. 2, 8, 45 and 110 referred to Christ. Yet it cannot be doubted that he preferred this literary device to the allegorizing of the Alexandrines. Theodore adamantly avoids allegory. Diodore of Tarsus, teacher of St. John Chrysostom, sums up the Antiochene interpretation method in this way:

> We do not forbid the higher interpretation and *theoria*, for the historical narrative does not exclude it, but is on the

contrary the basis and substructure of loftier insights.... We must, however, be on our guard against letting the *theoria* do away with the historical basis, for the result would then be, not *theoria*, but allegory (quoted in Greer, p. 93).

St. Ephrem, Deacon, "Harp of the Spirit"

Also famous was St. Ephrem, Deacon, "Harp of the Spirit," who bequeathed to the Church a great heritage of liturgical poetry, which also served as a commentary on the Scriptures. Ephrem's basic poetic form is the *memra* (pl.: *memre*, pronounced, "memray"); he also composed prose works. Ephrem comments on the richness of the Word of God thus:

> Who is capable of comprehending the immensity of the possibilities of one of your utterances? What we leave behind us in your utterances is far greater than what we take from it.... Many are the perspectives of his word, just as many are the perspectives of those who study it.... His utterance is a tree of life, which offers you blessed fruit from every side.... The thirsty one rejoices because he can drink, but is not upset if unable to render the source dry. The well can conquer your thirst, but your thirst cannot conquer the fountain (see McCarthy 19).

Whereas Theodore used typology sparingly, the East Syriacs—such as Ephrem, Aphrahat, and James of Sarug—used it abundantly. Nevertheless, all the Syriac Teachers saw the importance of typology as a method for interpreting the Bible.

Theologically, the School of Antioch was famous for its emphasis on the *humanity* of the Mystery of the Word-made-flesh, and of the incarnational aspect of the Church and the sacramental Mysteries (see the introduction to **Part IV, "Syro-Antiochene Incarnational Theology"**).

Maronite Tradition

Out of the Tradition of Antioch, from the region of Northwest Syria, are found the origins of the Maronite Tradition. Possibly knowing the East Syriac Schools of Edessa and Nisibis (notably St. Ephrem), the monk and hermit, Maron, known to us by the writings of Bishop Theodoret of the Eparchy of Cyrrhus, came to settle near the Orontes, away from bustling Antioch. His later followers in the Monastery of

Maron established a self-governing Tradition (8th century) within the Catholic Communion (see **"St. Maron"** in **Chapter 8**).

Chiefly from the liturgical texts they left behind, we can perceive the true Antiochene character of the Maronite Tradition. It preserves the liturgical poetry attributed to Ephrem, while making creative use of typology in its expression, which forms its way of interpreting the Bible. In addition, Maronite use of *paradox*—especially in the tension between the human and the divine—influences liturgical expression. Two stanzas from the *Qolo* of the *Qoorbono* daily text from Wednesdays illustrate this:

> **Blessed are you, Mary!**
> **From your own flesh**
> *you were able to feed the Preserver,*
> *who supports the whole creation.*
> **Blessed are you, Mary!**
> *You carried in your lap*
> *and held in your arms the Son*
> *of the Most High,*
> *who is attended by the heavenly hosts.*

STUDY QUESTIONS:

1) What is "Tradition" as applied to the Bible and the life of the Church?
2) What is the relationship of Scripture to Tradition? Why isn't it enough to say that all we need for the Christian life is the Bible alone?
3) What characteristics define: a) Eastern Tradition; b) Syriac-Antiochene Tradition, and c) Maronite Tradition?

Chapter 11:
The Maronite Liturgical Year

The Lectionary

As with all other Traditions, the Maronite Church organizes its biblical life around the pattern of Scriptures found in a Church book known as the Lectionary (a general word used in the whole Church from the Latin, *lectio*, meaning "reading," or "lesson"). With Readings for every day of the Liturgical Year, the Maronite Catholic walks with Jesus and his earthly life and Resurrection (Seasonal Cycle), and with the "Righteous and Just" (the Saints), in the Sanctoral Cycle, or *Fenqitho*, in the life of the Spirit in the Church.

This liturgical tracking of the Divine and saintly life is called the *Liturgical Year*. By becoming more conscious of Christ in this way, a Christian cultivates a different way of observing life. As Paul admonished in the *Letter to the Philippians*:

> Let each of you look not to your own interests, but to the interests of others. Let the same mind be in you that was in Christ Jesus (*Phil* 2:4-5).

As we follow the mind and life of Christ and the Saints in the Liturgical Year, our own daily life is seen through the lens of the Bible's vision and we more readily seek the heart of Christ. Specifically, we do this largely in the context of personal reading and study of the Scriptures, but also in the context of worship. We not only grow as Christian individuals but as communal members of the Syro-Antiochene, Maronite Church, hearing the Word in church with other believers.

The process of the development of the use of lectionaries may be seen in three stages:

Stage One: We know from Scripture studies that the earliest forms of the Gospel were collections of sayings of Jesus, written and preached. For example, scholars have theorized the so-called "Q" Source as such a collection. Other, non-accepted "Sayings Gospels" were developed at the time of the writing of the accepted Gospels (especially the Synoptics), such as the *Gospel of Thomas* and the *Protoevangelium of James* (see **Chapter 9**). What impresses one when reading these is that there is no basic story line to the words of Jesus, as well as many other strange features. It is quite difficult to recognize these as the same kind of Gospel as the four Gospels we know, and they aren't.

Stage Two: The Evangelist called Mark made an immense contribution to the Church when he took the ideas of the Sayings collections and fashioned them into a rather coherent story line from the Baptism of Jesus to the Passion and Resurrection. The vast majority of Bible scholars today acknowledge that from Mark, Matthew and Luke composed their Gospels along the same, basic story line and focused on their respective listening audiences. Studies have shown that it is legitimate to speak of the different "churches" that developed from not only the Synoptics but from the *Gospel of John* as well. Other church groups developed from the guidance of Paul.

The early Churches were organized along the lines of the different perspectives of the Bible. Later on, in the 2nd and succeeding centuries, rival and even heretical church groups arose (for example, the Gnostics). Yet, different orthodox (authentic) churches also developed, especially in the great centers of the Roman Empire, as the Church's mission expanded (see the description of this expansion in **Chapter 7, "The Eastern Catholic Churches"**).

Stage Three: The various lectionaries of the individual Traditions of the third/fourth-century—and in the case of the Maronites, post-5th-century—were composed. Thus, the pattern of biblical Readings used in worship developed according to the liturgical vision lived out by a particular Tradition.

In the case of the Maronites, the Lectionary drew from the richness of the West Antiochene Tradition, not ignoring elements from the East Syriac Tradition, but shaped, ultimately, according to the way Maronites came to structure the Liturgical Year as they prayed it.

In every sense, the Bible is the Church's Book, developed in Holy Tradition and experienced fruitfully in this context today.

Typical of many other places in the liturgical tradition, the first *Anamnesis* prayer of the *Anaphora of St. Mark* clearly expresses this following of Christ throughout the year, as it recounts the important events on the life of the Savior:

> **Lord Jesus Christ,**
> **we recall your plan of salvation for us:**
> *from your conception, birth, and holy baptism*
> *to your saving passion, life-giving death,*
> *your burial for three days,*
> *your glorious resurrection, ascension to heaven,*
> *your sitting at the right hand of the Father,*
> *and your wondrous, awesome and royal return,*
> **when you shall judge all people**
> **and separate them according to their deeds...**

The Lectionary attempts to integrate the writings of the Old and New Testaments into the yearly pattern of Readings. This pattern is determined by several liturgical "seasons," i.e., periods of time that together allow the worshiper all through a year's time to follow the life of Christ and the life of the Spirit and the example of the Righteous and the Just (i.e., the Saints in glory).

Since this work is fundamentally based on an understanding of Maronite Liturgy and the Liturgical Year, a synopsis of the Cycle is now given.

THE LITURGICAL YEAR: A SYNOPSIS

Sunday(s) of the Church

One or two Sundays of the Church are celebrated each year: Renewal of the Church and Consecration of the Church. If 1 November occurs on a Monday or Tuesday, only the Consecration of the Church is celebrated, with its proper ceremony.

Although not a liturgical "season" as such, this Sunday (or Sundays) begins the Liturgical Year by focusing on the Church. It is a time when, as the Gospels focus on the Jewish Temple and Jesus as the New Temple (see *Jn* 2:19), we are asked to renew our lives and reconsecrate ourselves to Christ and his life of redemption. We also remember that in the Universal Church we are members of an Eastern Tradition. It is a fitting (liturgical) New Year's beginning.

Season of the Glorious Birth of the Lord (Season of *sooborey*, or "Happy Announcements")

The pre-Christmas Cycle has six Sundays, which all focus on the unfolding revelation of the Birth of the Messiah. This is done in the context of the immediate family of Jesus, centering on Mary and Joseph (*Mt* 1, 2; *Lk* 1, 2). This is certainly in line with the Antiochene emphasis on the humanity of Jesus and its appreciation of the historical aspect of Scripture. The greatest Announcement, of course, is that of the angels on Christmas.

There are one or two Sundays after Christmas (depending upon the day of the week that Christmas occurs), one of which is always celebrated: the **Finding in the Temple.** On 1 January the liturgical commemoration is **Feast of the Circumcision (Naming) of the Child Jesus**, with a second commemoration of the common Eastern observance of St. Basil.

The Sundays of this Season are:

> *Announcement to Zechariah*
> *Announcement to the Virgin Mary*
> *Visitation to Elizabeth*
> *Birth of John the Baptizer*
> *Revelation to Joseph*
> *Genealogy Sunday*
> *The Finding in the Temple*

In celebrating the Finding in the Temple (Sunday after Christmas) the Maronite Church uses the 3rd Infancy Narrative of *Luke* (chapter 2) to parallel closely the Gospel development of Jesus' own growth. He is seen in the Temple, recognizing his true "Father" (his divine Origin) and preparing himself for his Baptism and public life. In addition, Joseph disappears from all the Gospel narratives: Joseph's earthly fathering is done, and Jesus will now proclaim the heavenly Father. The Twelve Days of Christmas take us to the Feast of the Epiphany (Theophany).

Season of Epiphany (Theophany; Syriac: *Denho*)

Taking the Baptism of Jesus (6 January) as the model, the Maronite Church celebrates our new life of Baptism and Chrismation in this Season. In Syriac it is called *denho*. For some Syriac Churches, this season is the traditional time of reception of catechumens into the Church. But for all Syriac Christians, *denho* is a time to reflect on our baptism.

During the first three days of the Sixth Week of Epiphany (Monday-Wednesday) the Maronite Church observes **"Nineveh Days."** These three days are penitential and serve to anticipate the Season of Great Lent. In one form or another, these days are observed by all the Syriac Churches, East and West.

Three special Sunday commemorations are made at the end of the Epiphany time: for **Deceased Priests,** for the **Righteous and Just** (All Saints), and for the **Faithful Departed** (All Souls) in general. These commemorations of the Departed are to be seen in the context of the Epiphany emphasis on the chrismational mission of all Christians. Those who have died to this life are on the next stage of their journey to the Kingdom. If they have died faithful to the Gospel commandment to love, they will one day be called to the Eternal Light by Christ, the "True Hope who never fails."

During the closing of this Season—or the beginning of the Lenten Season, if it begins early—the obligatory **Feast of St. Maron** (9 February), patron of the Maronites, is celebrated.

The Sundays of this Season are:

First through Sixth Sundays of Epiphany
Sunday of Deceased Priests
Sunday of the Righteous and Just (All Saints)
Sunday of the Faithful Departed

Great Lent

Lent is, throughout the Church, a special time of fasting and abstinence designed to lead us to personal and communal conversion. It has been traditionally honored as a great opportunity to do penance (see the Lenten Fasting and Abstinence Rules in **Appendix I, "Our Maronite Customs"**).

In addition, in some of the Churches Great Lent was a time of purification for catechumens receiving instructions to be baptized.

There are two basic liturgical cycles within the Lenten Season: the Sunday Cycle, focused on the Resurrection, and the weekday cycle, which is penitential. (For a fuller explanation of these cycles, please refer to **"Commemorations of the *Qoorbono*,"** in **Appendix I**).

The Sunday Cycle begins with **"Cana Sunday"** (*Jn* 2:1-11), also called "Entrance into Lent." The wedding at Cana, an epiphany of Jesus, closes the previous season and opens this next one. Its theme is transformation. On the one hand we see this pattern: in the Gospel water becomes wine; in the Liturgy bread and wine become Jesus' Body and Blood. On the other hand his physical body, changed in the Resurrection, the greatest miracle, a new creation, is symbolized by the water-made-wine. This focus on change should lead us to make the changes necessary in our own spiritual lives. All the other Lenten Sunday celebrations highlight the movement toward Resurrection. We move from an earthly wedding story to considering our life at the eternal Wedding Banquet.

The Sundays of this Season are:

> *Cana Sunday/Entrance into Great Lent*
> *Sunday of the Man with Leprosy*
> *Sunday of the Hemorrhaging Woman*
> *Sunday of the Prodigal Son*
> *Sunday of the Man Who Was Paralyzed*
> *Sunday of the Man Who Was Blind*
> *Hosanna Sunday*

Passion Week

Passion Week, characteristically Antiochene, is very literal and dramatic in following the human passion and death of Jesus. The first three days of Passion Week are marked by the celebration of the Service of "Coming to the Harbor" (Monday and Tuesday), and the "Service of the Lamp" (Wednesday). **Thursday of Mysteries** is commemorated by the Washing of the Feet. **Great Friday of the Crucifixion** sees the praying of the **Liturgy of the Pre-Sanctified Offerings** (or *"Anaphora* of the Signing of the Chalice,"** see **Chapter 21**) in the morning (or noon); and the liturgical **Service of the Burial of the Lord,** prayed properly at noon, but due to pastoral circumstances, quite commonly in the evening. On Great **Saturday of the Light,** no Eucharist is permitted during the day. Strictly speaking, there can be no Vigil Liturgy of the Resurrection; this liturgy must take place at midnight or in the early hours of Easter Sunday.

Season of the Glorious Resurrection (Pascha)

This Season extends from the celebration of the Easter Liturgy until the end of Pentecost week, which closes the Easter Season.

Easter—called *Pascha* by many Eastern Christians—celebrates the central Christian mystery: Christ is risen. Since the risen Jesus bestowed his heavenly peace on this day, Maronites celebrate the **"Ceremony of Peace"** in the Easter Service. Peace is the Maronite Church's wish for the world. At his **Ascension** (40 days after Easter) Christ's humanity entered into God's glory and we are urged to carry on Christ's mission.

Pentecost (50 days after Easter) sees the commemoration of the Holy Trinity, through the manifestation of the Holy Spirit: when the Spirit appeared, believers realized that there is a Trinity of Persons in God. Also, the **Rite of Genuflection** is done near the end of this liturgy. Water is also blessed on this feast, as on Epiphany.

The Sundays of this Season are:

> ***Sunday of the Glorious Resurrection***
> ***New Sunday***
> ***Second through Sixth Sundays of the Resurrection***
> ***Pentecost Sunday***

Season of Glorious Pentecost

This is a time when Maronites commemorate life in the Spirit, which is the life we now lead. This Season contains celebrations for the Saints, especially Peter and Paul, Sharbel, and, of course, Mary (focusing on the Feast of the Assumption, one of the oldest and dearest feasts of the Maronites), and other Saints (see **"Other Righteous and Just"** in **Chapter 13**). In fact, many of the feasts of the Saints may be transferred to the closest Sunday, and this provides a variety to the observance of this rather long Season. The Pentecost Season extends to Holy Cross.

Of special note is the observance of the Friday of the week after Pentecost, a day called **"Gold Friday,"** from the first Reading of the day (*Acts* 3:1-10). In this Reading Peter observes that he has neither silver nor gold, but rather that he gives the knowledge of the Gospel of Jesus.

The Sundays of this Season are:

> ***First Sunday after Pentecost (Trinity Sunday)***
> ***Second through Eighteenth Sunday after Pentecost***

Season of the Glorious Cross

The Feast of the Holy Cross is celebrated on 14 September. Based in the story of the return of the true Cross to Constantinople, this feast celebrates the salvation wrought through the Cross. This Season focuses on our life as we await the Second Coming of Christ to be lived in the light of the glorious Cross. Maronites end the Liturgical Year awaiting Christ's Second Coming but will soon begin the Liturgical Year (in November) anticipating the commemoration of His First Coming (in the Season of the Glorious Birth of the Lord.

The Sundays in this Season are:

> ***First to Seventh Sundays after Holy Cross***

Preaching the Word of God

To think "Lectionary" is to think preaching. The first activity of the early Church, after believing that Christ is risen, was preaching the

Good News of the Gospel. This preaching is often identified by the Greek word *kerygma*. It still remains one of the essential tasks of the Christian Community and is the prime task of the presbyter (priest)(see *Acts* 6:2).

With the Council there has been a general revival in Catholic preaching of the Scripture. Seminaries have again become better training grounds for effective *kerygma*.

In preaching, a distinction is often made between a "homily" and a "sermon." A homily is a relatively brief (7-10 minutes) explanation of the Word of God for the day, given in a conversational, easy-to-grasp style.

A sermon, on the other hand, is less closely tied to the texts and more to the special event commemorated (graduations, commencements, anniversaries, and the like).

Preaching a successful homily is not to be taken lightly. Careful preparation is needed to discover the clearest exegesis (interpretation and background) of the texts; proper illustrations—often from real life and the faith experience of the preacher and the hearers—and suitable application to the hearers' Christian life are needed as well.

In *Preaching as Art and Craft,* Walter J. Burghardt, the dean of Catholic preachers, provides an excellent summary of the present challenge facing homilists:

> The wine of the Gospel is always and everywhere new. But "new wine must be put into fresh wineskins" (*Lk* 5:38). A homilist's risk and joy is the effort to do for God's people in our time what preachers like Jeremiah and Joel, Peter and Paul, did for God's people in their time: express God's inexpressible Word in syllables that wed felicity to fidelity, that flare and flame, that captures minds and rapture hearts, syllables charged with the power of God. Such an art falls under Bonhoeffer's "costly grace." If Catholic preaching remains at low ebb, an overriding reason is that homilists either see the sermon as a product that comes cheap or, conceding its high cost, are reluctant to pay the price. Effective preaching is not an option, not primarily a privilege; it is a vocation that may not be refused.

Preachers should be aware that preaching at sacramental occasions should take the form of homilies, basing their remarks on the Readings of the sacramental celebration. It is especially important for preachers to realize that even at funeral, where there is a great temptation to give a eulogy (the Greek word means a "speaking well"), proper preaching focuses on the message of hope convincingly communicated in a homily on the Readings.

John Chrysostom describes the grace of effective preaching to his congregation in the following quote:

> Preaching improves me. When I begin to speak weariness disappears; when I begin to teach fatigue too disappears. Thus neither sickness itself nor indeed any other obstacle is able to separate me from your love ... For just as you are hungry to listen to me, so too I am hungry to preach to you. My congregation is my only glory and every one of you means much more to me than anyone of the city outside (quoted in Carroll, p. 107).

The Council clearly expressed the preference of the homily as the more common way for the Gospel to be preached (*SC* 52).

Central to the efficacious passing on of any Particular Catholic Church's Tradition is the preaching of the texts in their proper contexts in the Lectionary. That is why it is so important to understand the flow and unfolding of the Liturgical Year as found in the Lectionary. For Maronites, understanding the pattern of the Lectionary defines who one is as an Antiochene Syriac Catholic, following the Maronite Way.

STUDY QUESTIONS:
1) What is a lectionary?
2) How does a lectionary help a Catholic follow Christ and the Saints through the liturgical year?
3) Name the seasons of the Maronite Liturgical Year.

Chapter 12:
The Interpretation of Scripture

What is Bible Interpretation?
In the words of the *'Etro* for Thursday:

> **O Lord,**
> **through the prayers of your holy Apostles and**
> **four Evangelists**
> *enlighten our minds,*
> *that reading their holy writings*
> *we may realize the power enshrined in them….*

The Bible is not an easy collection to interpret. Despite a popular claim of some Fundamentalist Christians—that all you have to do is pick up the Bible at any point, and the Holy Spirit will automatically give you the exact meaning—the text of the Bible is complex. It requires much study, prayer and reflection just to begin to know its meaning. We call this looking at the many meanings of the biblical text *interpretation*.

As the prayer after the *Trisagion*, which closes the Introductory Rites in each Divine Service, implores the Lord:

> **O Holy and Immortal Lord,**
> *sanctify our minds and purify our consciences,*
> *that we may praise you with pure hearts*
> *and listen to your Holy Scriptures.*
> **To you be glory, for ever. Amen.**

Difficulties in Determining Composition
The Bible may be thought of as a vast library, spanning many times and situations, expressed in many styles and literary forms. Although God's truth of the Bible is timeless and lasting, the world of the Bible has come and gone. Imagine how much easier, for example, the task

of writing down God's inspiration would be if the Bible writers could have used a computer word processor. But the fact is that the majority of people in the Old Testament were illiterate. And we know that the bulk of the material from the Hebrew Scriptures weren't scriptures at all for centuries, but rather passed on by word of mouth, sung at worship (especially the Psalms), and thus kept alive. This is also true of the New Testament, although the New Testament was oral tradition for a shorter time than the Old Testament. Only later learning, with greater literacy, produced the first written forms of the Bible.

All of this could lead to a kind of distortion of these human expressions, as comparing various ancient manuscripts of the Bible shows. Scholars must work hard at making the right choices for an accurate text. This is why, for example, the recent study of the Dead Sea Scrolls is important.

Given these problems—and a host of others—Bible scholars do the best they can to get a reliable text even before they try to figure out its meaning, or rather, to interpret it. However, we are in a very good position today, perhaps the best in history since the texts were initially written, to get a fairly accurate biblical text, although scholars will always be quick to admit the limitations involved.

The Inspiration of the Holy Spirit

Many of these considerations have been from the human side of the Mystery of the biblical Word of God. Are these human things somehow to downgrade the legitimate role of the Spirit in scriptural interpretation? On the contrary! It is only through the illuminating power of the Holy Spirit that we can understand anything at all about the Bible (see *Jn* 16:12-15). But the Spirit doesn't excuse us from using the God-given minds with which we were born, and with the help of the Holy Spirit we can begin to explore the Word of God.

On Thursdays the authors of the Holy Bible, especially of the New Testament, are commemorated. Most especially, the inspiration for the Sacred Scriptures, namely the Holy Spirit, as well as the proclaimers of the Word of God, namely the Prophets and the Evangelists, are mentioned in the *Qolo* of the day:

> *The Holy Spirit, the Spirit of Jesus,*
> *breathed into the prophets...*
> *The Spirit revealed and perfected the chosen Apostles....*

Thus, the focus of this text is the Word of God as an activity of the Holy Spirit. It is thus fitting that we should we pray, before reading the Holy Scriptures: *"Come, Holy Spirit, fill the hearts of your faithful, and kindle in them the fire of your love."*

The *Magisterium*, a Sure Guide

The Teaching Office of the Church is called by a special name—the *Magisterium* (**see Chapter 1**). This important teaching function exists to ensure that we read the Bible (and understand our Faith) with certainty, under the guidance of the Holy Spirit. This is what is behind all the copious notes that appear on virtually every page of Catholic editions of the Bible. We can thus be sure that we are getting the best interpretation, and being guided in a correct way to understand God's Word, approved by the Church's Teaching Office.

The goal of reading the Bible for our best benefit—truth and edification—can be achieved by proper interpretation, and this takes hard work and diligent study. Two terms are used to designate Bible interpretation: *exegesis* and *hermeneutics*. A reliable dictionary of the Bible can further help you with these and other terms.

A very good, recent example of a document from the Teaching Office of the Church on biblical interpretation is entitled, "The Interpretation of the Bible in the Church" (see the Bibliography). It is the fruit of the dynamic movement of Catholic entrance into the field of recent biblical interpretation. This Vatican document is worth every bit of time you can put into reading and understanding it.

In addition, the sections on biblical interpretation in the *Catechism of the Catholic Church* are excellent (¶¶101-141). Both of these resources, as well as works mentioned in **Part II** of the Bibliography will help you in your study of as well as your spiritual reflection on God's Word.

The Teachers of the Church Help to Interpret

This attitude of working hard at interpreting correctly is a hallmark of contemporary Catholic scriptural exegesis. As Catholics, we have much help, because we can rely on the best teachers in the Church—not only those who are contemporary but also those who have gone before us.

Throughout the ages, from the time of the Fathers and Teachers of the early Church until today, thinkers in the Church's Tradition have tried to express the Mystery of God's revelation in a way that the faithful might best understand these truths. Some men and women—like St. Ephrem and

Theresa of Avila—are referred to as "Doctors" of the Church (from another Latin word *doctor,* meaning "teacher"). Such people represent the best minds in Catholic history who have struggled, like us today, to understand and live according to the revelation of God's Word to us.

Scripture Interprets Itself

Of course, one of the main interpreters of Scripture is Scripture itself. The Bible writers did not write in a vacuum. They were always aware that they wrote in a context of a rich, traditional heritage of revealed truth. Often, when writing down the patterns of revealed truth, they recalled that God had communicated similar ideas before them. We often find in the Bible verses so similar to others that they seem copied *verbatim*. Some were. This is true of both Testaments. Again, you are directed to the reference sections found at the bottom of the columns of the biblical text (or sometimes on the side margins, as, for example, in the New Jerusalem Bible Version). You should take the time to look up such parallels, for it will increase your understanding of the text by helping to see the connections the authors made between the Testaments.

In addition to individual verses shedding light on other verses, we should try always to put a verse *into its own context.* This is extremely important. If we try to isolate a verse or passage from its context, we can easily run the risk of missing its true meaning. We can immediately relate to this from our own experience: when we remark to others that our words "were taken out of context," we say we were misunderstood. This is also true of the Bible. Using a good commentary will help us see a verse or passage in its proper setting. Consequently, words that may seem obscure on first reading may become clearer in their (intended) context.

The Senses of Scripture

Another idea that is very important in interpreting a verse or passage is what Scripture scholars describe as the *senses* of Scripture. By this they mean that the Bible is so rich that indeed a passage or verse can have many meanings and interpretations, meanings which went far beyond the time in which they were originally written.

"Sense" in this sense (pardon that pun) is used to describe a particular way of understanding a biblical passage: the "spiritual" sense, the "typological" sense (especially esteemed and used in the Syriac Tradition), the "allegorical" sense, the "spiritual" sense, or the "literal" or "historical" sense (there are others). The *Catechism* recognizes this in paragraph 115 and describes the other senses of Scripture in paragraph 117.

Of particular note is the literal sense. Let us be clear about what is NOT meant by this term. The literal sense of Scripture is not the same as the literalist, or Fundamentalist, interpretation of the Bible. The fundamentalist approach says that every word of the Bible is literally true exactly as expressed, as if it had been dictated, word for word. This is a particularly late way of interpreting the Bible (19th century), and is popular with many televangelists. Fundamentalism has a host of problems associated with it, and is NOT the way the Catholic Church interprets the Scriptures.

The literal sense of the Bible explores the actual text of the Bible for grammar and syntax—a very literary approach—as well as the historical setting of the biblical text, according to sound interpretation.

This most basic and important historical approach seeks to discover just what the author of a biblical book meant at the time he wrote, how he was hearing God's true word, in the time- and culture-bound setting of his day, and how his hearers grasped the meaning of his expressing God's revelation. Of course, we know that God's Word had wider implications, for prophecies were fulfilled, and we still live our lives by the ancient Word. (This wider application is sometimes referred to as the *fuller sense* of Scripture.) However, to discern this original meaning, we need all the tools and skills described earlier.

The distinction between the literal sense and the literalist (or Fundamentalist) interpretation of Scripture is very important to bear in mind.

This appreciation for the literal sense and historical approach is important for Maronite Tradition. The historical approach was the hallmark of the Antiochene Tradition, which is an essential element in the background of the Maronite Tradition of scriptural interpretation.

Critical Methods

Catholic scholars recognize the validity of going back, as best we can, to the original, intended meaning of a biblical passage by the endorsement officially given by Pope Pius XII in 1943, in a document called in Latin, *Divino Afflante Spiritu* ("Inspired by the Holy Spirit"). In it, the Church encouraged scholars to use everything helpful at their disposal—archeology, history, philology, anthropology, and other pertinent sciences—to understand the Holy Bible. It was a big step

forward in Catholic Scripture studies and signaled the entrance of the
Catholic Church in a prominent way into contemporary biblical studies.

The Second Vatican Council affirmed this endorsement in its
document on Divine Revelation entitled *De Revelatione*. The Document
put it this way:

> In determining the intention of the sacred writers, attention
> must be paid, among other things to *literary genres* ... The
> fact is that truth is differently presented and expressed in
> the various types of historical writing, in prophetical and
> poetical texts, and in other forms of literary expression.
> Hence, the exegete must look for the meaning which the
> sacred writers, in given situations and granted the
> circumstances of their time and culture, intended to express
> and did in fact express, through the medium of a
> contemporary literary form. Rightly to understand what the
> sacred authors wanted to affirm in their work, due attention
> must be paid both to the customary and characteristic
> patterns of perception, speech and narrative which
> prevailed in their time, and to the conventions which people
> then observed in their dealings with one another (*DV*, 12).

One of things that the Document recognizes is the matter of
literary forms. While the historical sense is fairly commonly accepted
today, "literary criticism" of the biblical text has also gained ground. Since
the Document other interesting methods of criticism are also being applied
to the Bible. (See **"On the Interpretation of Scripture,"** in the
Bibliography, for a summary of the various methods being used today.)

Another positive outcome of the Council's concern for ecumenism
is dialog with other Christian Churches and Communities. Probably in no
other area than biblical criticism has there been such a great cooperation
among the scholars of the Churches. This seems to be a sure sign of the
working of the Spirit in our day.

Eastern Approaches to Biblical Interpretation

In the early centuries of the Church, Bible interpretation in the East
was lively and creative. Even though there are many points of similarity
among Eastern approaches, there are differences as well. In the 4th
century two Schools of biblical interpretation predominated: the
Alexandrine and the Antiochene. Biblical interpretation is a good place to

see some basic differences in the ways that theology developed in Antioch (and the Syriac School) and in Alexandria (which influenced Byzantine thought).

A key difference between these two approaches lies in the way(s) in which each School reacted to Greek philosophy. From the outset the Church took root in a world permeated by the rich heritage of Greek civilization, known also as *Hellenism* (the adjective is *Hellenistic*, from the Greek word for Greece). This included the large body of writings left by Greek philosophers. The Romans may have conquered the Greeks, but Hellenism inspired the best of Roman thought.

Representative of Greek philosophical thought—but by no means limited to them—were Plato and his followers, the so-called "Neo-Platonists." These thinkers envisioned a separate world of "Ideas," the "really real" that was permanently valid—above, and beyond, the world inhabited by humans and other created material realities. In other words, the starting point for all that is true is from above.

The Egyptian capital of Alexandria, with its famous Library, was a vibrant center of Neo-Platonic thought. A large community of Jews had already settled there before the time of Jesus. The Jewish community, like others in Alexandria, had adapted to Hellenistic ways in only a few generations. The Greek translation of the Old Testament—known as the *Septuagint*—was made there. The biblical interpreter and philosopher Philo (a Jew) was a leading figure in Greek thinking. His interpretation of the Old Testament influenced many of the Church Fathers, including Origen.

It was natural that Christianity at Alexandria would take on a heavily Greek flavor. The Church at Constantinople—hence, the Byzantine Tradition—would align itself with Alexandria and also adopt a Hellenistic theological system. It is not difficult to see from this how the theological emphasis of the Byzantine Tradition is on the divinity of Jesus as the starting point for theological discourse, including the allegorical interpretation of the Bible.

The approach of the Antiochenes, on the other hand, was rooted in a clear sense of history and how God works in history. To put it in today's terms, history is not merely secular; it is, rather, "salvation history." The Antiochenes insisted that God works in creation, and that creation reveals the hand of the Father. In fact, the history of creation is a history of the gradual revealing of God's Word, who is finally shown forth definitively in the Jew from Nazareth, Jesus. Divinity is joined to humanity; but humanity is the dwelling and revelation of divinity.

From the stories and Scriptures of the Israelites may be found examples of persons and events that foreshadow those of the New Testament, even Jesus himself. These examples they called types. These were fulfilled in later events known as *antitypes*. The Antiochenes in the "West"—that is, nearer to Antioch itself—made less use of typology. The East Syriacs, such as St. Ephrem and Aphrahat, made much greater use.

Rather than opposing the Platonic view of the Alexandrians with another Greek philosophical tradition, the biblical interpreters and theologians of the Antiochene School preferred the Semitic world view of the Bible, a view that was not affected—at least in the beginning—by Hellenistic thought.

These approaches can still shed light on the way we read the Bible today (see **"The Senses of Scripture,"** above).

Liturgical Interpretation of the Bible

Another very important way to read the Bible is through the guidance of the Lectionary. This patterning of the biblical texts, with the characteristic emphases of a Tradition, clearly identifies the themes of the Tradition and shows how to read God's Word in the context of that Tradition. In other words, the prayer of the Church (the Service of the Word of the Divine Liturgy) shows how the Word of God is to be understood. This is characteristic of the Eastern approach in general.

For the East this is very true: unless we know the Scriptures well, we will not fully appreciate the richness of the Divine Liturgy. Conversely, by being attentive to the rhythms of our Eastern liturgical prayer life, we can enter more deeply and more effectively into the Mystery of the Word of God.

The *Instruction* for the Eastern Catholic Churches recognizes the rich diversity of prayer forms in Eastern liturgies, seeing in them a retelling of Scripture. Even though referring specifically to the "Divine Praises" (the Divine Office), the following description (¶97) illustrates the point well:

> The celebration of prayer in time is permeated by the Holy Scripture, the Word given by God for "reproof, for correction, for instruction in righteousness" (*2 Tim* 3:16). The meal of the Word is not only consumed by means of the Lectionaries, which gather biblical texts to be

proclaimed, and present them organically throughout the liturgical year, but also by means of the very rich collection of liturgical hymns, of which all the Eastern Churches are justly proud, and which are "the continuation of the read, assimilated and, finally, sung Word... a sublime paraphrasing of the biblical text, filtered and personalized through the experience of the individual and the community.

Maronite Liturgical Interpretation of the Bible

Having seen the various elements that lie at the heart of the Maronite Experience, namely, origins and Liturgy, we can now see that it is possible to read the Bible through Maronite eyes. This reading, of course, is done in solidarity with the Church, namely, with legitimate methods that the whole Church recognizes. Nevertheless, Maronite Catholics interpret God's Word in the context of the Syro-Antiochene Tradition.

Although the following items are not meant to be an exhaustive list, nevertheless, some basic elements that will help the Syriac-Maronite reader of God's Word include:

❖ A general background in contemporary methods of Bible interpretation. There are many good texts today—both Catholic and ecumenical from which to choose. Please see the Bibliography for some suggested texts.

❖ A working knowledge of Antiochene and Syriac principles of interpretation. These will include knowledge of what is meant by the literal sense of the Scriptures; and of typology: how it was employed by the Fathers (such as Theodore of Mopsuestia and St. Ephrem), especially in their commentaries and poetry.

❖ A thorough knowledge of the Lectionary and Liturgical Year of the Maronite Church. An outline with a basic description of the Liturgical Year has been given above. However, the best way to learn the Lectionary is to experience it on a weekly (even daily) basis.

❖ A good knowledge of the structure and function of the *Hoosoyo*, especially as it is used in the Maronite liturgical tradition.

❖ Sincere prayer to the Holy Spirit for illumination.

The *Hoosoyo*

Of special note here is the typical Syriac prayer form in the Maronite Word Service known as the *Hoosoyo*, or "Prayer of Forgiveness" (see the Glossary in **Appendix IV** for a helpful description of the structure and parts of the *Hoosoyo*). This central prayer of the Introductory Rites of the Divine Service (as well as of other Syriac Churches) is key to understanding the theme of the liturgical celebration. Often composed with abundant scriptural references, it invites the worshiper to reflect deeply upon the use it makes of Scripture. In other words, while praying the *Hoosoyo*, we are, in the very act of praying, engaged in the interpretation of the Scripture it contains.

While the *Hoosoyo* functions in the Liturgy primarily as a prayer, the fact that it helps us understand the Bible better—and in a more properly Syriac-Antiochene Maronite way—justifies its being included here under the section on interpretation. Unless one knows the Scriptures intimately, much of the meaning of the *Hoosoyo*—not to mention the focus and spirit of the liturgical celebration—may be lost.

Through Maronite Tradition, which includes a highly scriptural liturgical tradition, embracing the uniquely Syriac *Hoosoyo* and the typical principles of the Antiochene School, such as typology and paradox, anyone willing to work a little with the Lectionary and the Tradition will find a satisfying way to read the Word of God as embodied in a particular Tradition of the Church.

STUDY QUESTIONS:

1) What are some of the difficulties in saying that all one need do to understand the Bible is simply to open it up at random and the meaning will automatically be clear?
2) In Catholic Tradition, who or what helps us to interpret Scripture?
3) How is the *Hoosoyo* of help in understanding the Readings of the Maronite Lectionary?

PART III: GOD'S KINGDOM: THE ALREADY AND THE NOT YET
(Divine Liturgy Focus: Transfer of the Offerings, Commemorations)

The Kingdom
Every time Christians pray the Lord's Prayer, we profess profound beliefs about the afterlife. When we express the desire, "(May) your Kingdom come," we are really saying that we believe that God's Kingdom exists in two dimensions—in the life beyond us (ahead of us in time and vision) and in our present journey on earth, here and now. It is as if we are saying, "May your Kingdom where you dwell in glory beyond our earthly existence erupt forth into our lives, so that we might experience its effects." To put it another way: The Kingdom IS ALREADY, and at the same time NOT YET FULLY, existing on earth, even though we get glimpses of it from time to time.

Theodore of Mopsuestia once put it like this:

> ...the future age, or the life which is after this, will furnish us also that which we were by no means capable of attaining by ourselves.... Therefore, because Christ came, pointing out and directing through His resurrection those things, which are future, He offers indeed to us, too, promise of these things. All of us who in this present life believe in Christ are, so to speak, in the middle of this present life and of the future one... (Quoted in Greer, p. 75).

Christians are, therefore, people with feet in both places. As such, we live our lives (the Already) in the light of the knowledge of the Trinity, union with Whom (the Not Yet) is our goal.

When we reflect upon the Kingdom, it is not only upon God that we focus our thoughts. There are also, the Church believes, those who have completed their earthly journey and are recognized in a public way by the Church to be with God. Our Maronite Tradition calls these Saints the "Righteous and the Just." They are commemorated as a community on the second Sunday before Cana Sunday (see **Chapter 11**, **"The Liturgical Year: a Synopsis."**) They not only stand as sterling examples of lives of holiness in the Spirit but also beckon us to be one day with the Lord. In Catholic Tradition in general, but in the East especially, and very much in Maronite Tradition, Mary the Mother of God stands out as the shining example of the Righteous and Just.

In addition, when we take the afterlife seriously, we readily think of what our ultimate destiny will be: eternal life with or without God.

This is radically our own free choice: God will not prevent us from rejecting him; but God will also help us turn toward heaven at any moment we want.

Liturgical Transition to the *Anaphora*

> **The Lord reigns, clothed in majesty, Alleluia!**
> **I am the Bread of Life, said our Lord.**
> **From on high I came to earth so all might live in me.**
> **Pure Word without flesh I was sent from the Father.**
> **Mary's womb received me,**
> **like good earth a grain of wheat.**
> **Behold! The priests bear me aloft to the altars.**
> **Alleluia! Accept our offerings.**

With this chant, which accompanies the Transfer of the Offerings from the Altar of Preparation to the Altar of Sacrifice (after the Service of the Word), the third part of the *Qoorbono* begins. As you chant during the Divine Service, you can easily see that the symbolism revolves around Jesus the Word of God as a "grain of wheat," which "falls" into Mary, who is described as fertile, "good earth," in which the Word/Grain takes root. It is a central chant that is very well placed in the flow of the Divine Service. When the Offerings are brought to the Altar, the Celebrant chants the Commemorations of the Faithful Living and Departed for whom the Eucharist of the day is prayed.

These commemorations take place in chiefly two sections of the Maronite Divine Service, although references to the repose of the departed occur in prayers too numerous to mention. The first important place is the Commemoration prayers mentioned above. The second major commemoration of the Living and the Dead is in the Intercessions, which close the *Anaphora* (see **"Praying for the Living and the Dead," Chapter 14**).

With regard to the first point, the Catholic teaching on the Saints is well exemplified by considering Mary, Mother of God; Saints in Maronite Tradition will be discussed as well. In connection with the second point, we also consider our own destiny after physical death. More will be said in the section on **"Human Destiny."**

The catechumen journeying toward union with the Church will seek good examples of faith, here and in the Beyond. Also, with all thoughtful persons he or she will think about the ultimate destiny of humanity faithful to God.

Chapter 13:
Mary, Mother of God, and Other Righteous and Just

Mary in Maronite Tradition

Next to the Lord Jesus, there is no one in heaven or in our spiritual lives whom devout Maronites wish to remember more than the Lady Mary, "Mother of

> **Sunday of the Righteous and Just**
> Mt 25:31-46

God," (Syriac: *Yoldat Aloho*; Greek: *Theotokos* [literally, "God-bearer"]; Arabic: *Oom Allah*). In this deep veneration, we share solidly with our Eastern sisters and brothers. Often our prayers mention this powerful Intercessor with the Lord, who is at the same time called "mother" and "sister." In this the *Qoorbono* echoes St. Ephrem in a meditation in which he addresses Christ:

> For she is Your mother—she alone—
> and Your sister with all. She was to You mother;
> she was to You sister. Moreover, she is Your betrothed
> with the chaste women. In everything,
> behold, You adorned her, Beauty of Your mother.
> (*Hymns on the Nativity*, 11.2)

Mary is first among the "Righteous and Just," (the Saints). Their lives on earth so clearly reflected the Gospel that the whole Church publicly recognizes them as eminently worthy of imitation by us on our own spiritual journey.

Titles of Mary

Our liturgical tradition has numerous texts honoring God through Our Lady. In fact, the East gave the rest of the Church the earliest devotion to Mary, especially the feasts of the Mother of God. Maronites receive this love of the Mother of God from our Syriac heritage, especially from Teachers like the Deacon Ephrem and James of Sarug. From this rich Marian tradition comes a wealth of titles for Mary, such as "Mother of (Jesus) the Light," "Cedar of Lebanon," "Cedar of our Catholic Faith." From this heritage we also see a wide range of symbols and typology so characteristic of the Syriac Tradition in general.

We should see in these titles for Mary a deeper meaning, for they express deeper theological truths about the work of salvation of her Son and her role in God's Plan. (The same holds true for the titles of Jesus in the Scriptures.) In fact, properly seen, the devotional life of prayer through Mary or any of the Saints must always be seen in the wider context of God's will to save all humanity through Jesus.

> ...She conceived, gave birth to, and nourished Christ, she presented him to the Father in the Temple, shared his sufferings as he died on the cross. Thus, in a very special way she cooperated by her obedience, faith, hope and burning charity in the work of the Savior in restoring supernatural life to souls (*LG* 61)....

There is always a deeper focus on Jesus as we think of his Mother.

Mother of God

Of all titles for Mary of Nazareth, "Mother of God" holds a special place in Catholic Tradition. We must look at this title in the broadest way, namely, for what it says theologically about Jesus Christ, the Divine Son of God.

God the Trinity has no mother. God is a spiritual Being, without beginning or end, eternal. However, when one of the Trinity—the Word—graciously assumed our humanity, he did it through the humanity of Mary. This mystery is referred to as the Incarnation.

Early theologians rightfully reflected on this mystery. They soon realized this logic: if God the Word became human, he had to have a mother. This mother was Mary of Nazareth. If Jesus the man is the divine Word, that is, God, then in a real sense Mary can be called "Mother of God," insofar as Jesus is truly God.

Some of our Antiochene predecessors, especially Patriarch Nestorius, grappled with this amazing idea. In his view the full human qualities of Jesus Christ must not be compromised by favoring considerations of Christ's divine side. But he went too far: he refused to teach that Mary is the Mother of God (*Theotokos*); rather, she is only the mother of the human Jesus.

At the Council of Ephesus in 431 A.D. the teachings of Nestorius were condemned. But the heresy that arose because of Nestorius gave the Church the opportunity to reflect more deeply than ever on the mystery of the Assuming Word and Assumed Humanity. The Council of Chalcedon, in 451 A.D., expressed clearly and solemnly for the Church that Jesus was truly God and truly human, in the one Person of Jesus, by the formula that guides authentic Catholic teaching to this day. In referring to Mary as the *Theotokos*, then, what the Church was really saying was that One of the Trinity actually took on our flesh, lived the life we all lead (except for sin) and that we are saved by One who as a human knows us as we know ourselves.

Mary, Symbol of the Incarnation

Thus, calling Mary the Mother of God tells us clearly about who Jesus is for the Believer. Mary, then, might rightly be considered a symbol of the Incarnation. The fondness that the East has for depicting the "Madonna and Child" is not mere sentimentalism. These icons tell us about the true humanity of the Word. Even the mother of Jesus worships him. For this reason, properly speaking, any depiction of Mary Mother of God should always include her Divine Son. In his *Hymns on Virginity* (25.9) St. Ephrem speaks of the awareness of the Incarnation manifested between Our Lady and the Beloved Disciple (of St. John's Gospel):

You, Lord,… they saw…
while observing one another:
Your mother saw You in Your disciple
and he saw You in Your mother.
The seers who at every moment
see You, Lord, in a mirror
manifest a type so that we, too, in one another
may see You, Our Savior.

Ever-virgin

Catholic Tradition also teaches that Mary remained physically a virgin before, during and after the birth of Jesus. This teaching is reflected clearly in Maronite Tradition. There are constant and numerous expressions of this in the prayers of our Church, as, for example, in the often-repeated title "Ever-virgin." We see this expressed in the *Sedro* of the *Hoosoyo* for Mary on Wednesdays as a typical example:

> **With spiritual hymns,**
> **may we praise and glorify the blessed,**
> ***ever-virgin Mary*, Mother of God...**

And again in the *Qolo* of this same *Hoosoyo*:

> **Hail, Mary!**
> **In your virginity**
> **you became the mother of the Mighty One:**
> **he fills heaven and earth.**
>
> **Hail, Mary!**
> **in your virginity**
> **you became the mother of the Ancient of Days:**
> **his name was before the sun.**
>
> **We now bless your virginity**
> **as we bow and beseech you**
> **to intercede for us.**

This traditional recognition of Mary's consecration to God should be seen in the context of the Antiochene/Syriac emphasis on virginity in the beginning stages of the Syriac Tradition, and from the area of Syria that, with Egypt, gave the Church the birth of the monastic tradition. (Please refer to the discussion on monasticism in **Chapter 12**).

All-holy

Jesus, God's eternal Word-made-flesh, is the Holy One prophesied in the Scriptures. However, the Scriptures, and our frequent prayers, witness that Mary too is "all-holy." In the familiar prayer "Hail, Mary" (taken from *Lk* 1:28), and from the clear witness of the Syriac

Fathers—particularly Ephrem and James of Sarug—we see that God chose Mary from time immemorial in the divine Plan to be the sinless Mother of the Redeemer.

In view of her Son's Redemption and Resurrection, Catholic Tradition believes that certain blessings were bestowed on Mary. Among them is that other than her Divine Son, Mary was the only human being preserved from the effects of Adam and Eve's Fall from grace, thus becoming a "pure vessel" for giving a perfect humanity to the Incarnate Word, Jesus of Nazareth. We might think of it this way: Because of this blessing for Mary of freedom from sin, the Word could take on a sinless humanity by *nature*. Thus, aside from our first parents (created perfect) both Mary and Jesus were the only other two perfect human beings to have lived on earth. The ramifications of this fact are enormous, and we do well to reflect upon the truth of it.

The sixth-century Syriac Writer, James of Sarug, saw it this way:

> And this is why He chose her, pure and full of beauty. He came down from his abode and dwelt in the Blessed among women, because there was no other woman who could be compared to her. She was humble, pure, beautiful and immaculate—so to be the worthy one to become His mother and no on else (quoted in Zayek, p. 36).

This teaching of Mary's sinlessness, according to the "hierarchy of truths" (see **Introduction**), is to be understood in terms of what is revealed to us about God, and specifically in this case, about Jesus. Mary's sinlessness tells us that God's universal, saving will is focused on all who come into this world; in other words, God wishes that all be saved. Of course, unlike Mary (who did respond), or as committed Christians (who should), not all choose to respond positively to God. But God's will is clear nevertheless:

> This is right and is acceptable in the sight of God our Savior, who desires everyone to be saved and to come to the knowledge of the truth (*1 Tim* 2:3-4).

Thus, in view of God's saving will and plan that Jesus be the agent of that salvation, Mary is privileged to be spared from the darkness of sin.

While we cannot know this fact about Mary directly from the Bible, the New Testament directly relates the fact of the sinlessness of Jesus:

> For we do not have a high priest who is unable to sympathize with our weaknesses, but we have one who in every respect has been tested as we are, yet without sin. Let us therefore approach the throne of grace with boldness, so that we may receive mercy and find grace to help in time of need (*Heb* 4:15-16).

This is interestingly expressed in the petition for the Faithful Departed in the *Anaphora of St. Peter, Head of Apostles*:

> **...O Lord, lover of all people,**
> **receive into the bosom of Abraham**
> **all those who lived their life in true faith.**
> **Remove and forgive all our, and their, transgressions,**
> *for no one is free of sin*
> *except our Lord God and Savior, Jesus Christ.*
> *Through Christ and because of him,*
> *we hope to find compassion*
> *and the pardon of all our faults.*
> **And we pray to you, O Lord.**

The Tradition here is clearly focusing on Jesus as The Sinless One. Taking its cue from *Heb* 4:16, the Tradition sees why Jesus can forgive: Having experienced the dark side of life as we do, but not capitulating to it, he can understand our weakness and be compassionate.

St. Ephrem recognizes the compassion of God as it is extended to Mary in a special way. He states that even she needed to be redeemed, as seen in his *Hymns on the Nativity* (16.9-10). Mary speaks:

> What can I call You, a stranger to us,
> Who was formed from us? Shall I call You Son?
> Shall I call You Brother? Shall I call You Bridegroom?
> Shall I call You, Lord, O [You] Who brought forth His mother
> [in] another birth out of the water?
> For I am [Your] sister from the House of David,
>   who is a second father. Again, I am a mother

because of Your conception, and bride am I
because of Your chastity. Handmaiden and daughter
of blood and water [am I] whom you redeemed and baptized.

If in this Eastern prayer from the *Anaphora of Peter* Mary is not mentioned explicitly as also being sinless, let us not forget that the entire Church was not asked to assent to this formally until the 19th century—late in Christian history—with the proclamation of the doctrine of the "Immaculate Conception," bearing in mind that this is a Western formulation.

Jesus' First Disciple

The Bible, particularly in the Gospel of Luke, tells us that Mary was a woman of faith and discipleship. Her "yes" at the moment of the Incarnation marked her as having taken the Eternal Word into her heart before the Word was even formed in her body. The prayer at the Transfer of the Offerings shows this relationship of Mary to the Word:

> **The Lord reigns, clothed in majesty, Alleluia!**
> **I am the Bread of Life, said our Lord.**
> **From on high I came to earth so all might live in me.**
> **Pure Word without flesh I was sent from the Father.**
> **Mary's womb received me,**
> **like good earth a grain of wheat.**
> **Behold! The priests bear me aloft to the altars.**
> **Alleluia! Accept our offerings.**

Liturgically this prayer is fittingly placed: after our hearing of the Word of Scripture—like Mary, a hearer of the Word—and before the Eucharistic Prayer and Holy Communion, whereby Christ is sacramentally and mysteriously incarnated for us today, as he once was in his Mother. The chant is thus pivotal: it looks back to the Word Service, wherein the Word is heard, and looks forward to the Word incarnated in the Eucharist, our Bread of Life and our nourishment.

First Sharer in the Resurrection

Although not explicitly stated in Scripture, the doctrine of the "Assumption" (or *Dormition*: "Falling asleep") of Mary, body and soul, into heaven at the end of her earthly life comes from Tradition. This event,

Mary's share in the Resurrection, is celebrated with much devotion among Maronites and other Eastern Christians.

Many of the prayers of the Service of the Word for this feast either imply or symbolically express the favor God bestowed upon Mary in the Assumption. The second strophe of the *Qolo* of the day is a good example:

> **Alleluia!**
> **Blessed are you, O Mary,**
> **for God, who feeds all creatures,**
> **was nourished by you**
> **and rested on your breast.**
> **O Wonder!**
> **The Son of God was nourished**
> **by a human creature!**
> *He assumed what is ours*
> *and gave us what is his.*
> **On his mother's memorial let us proclaim:**
> **Glory to you, O Lord!**

The italicized words will be recognized as part of the Incarnation prayer before Holy Communion in the *Qoorbono* ("You have united..."). What else has the Lord given in our baptism but a real share in the divine life: for us, in our baptism, and for Mary in her Assumption? In Baptism, our involvement in the effects of the First Sin was washed away. In Mary, who had been preserved from that sin, and remained an obedient listener of her Son all her life, the share in the Resurrection—that is, the assuming of Christ's risen life—was immediate at the end of her earthly life. This is the obvious intent of the Alleluia verse, a quote from *Ps* 45:9:

> **Alleluia, Alleluia!**
> The King's daughter stands in glory,
> the queen stands at your right hand.
> **Alleluia!**

Mother of the Church

As First Disciple, Mary is also appropriately called "Mother of the Church." Standing with the Beloved Disciple under the Cross (*Jn* 19:34-35), she witnessed the birth of the Church in water (Baptism) and blood (Eucharist), flowing from her dying Son's side. Again, she gathered with the Apostles and the Disciples on Pentecost to receive the Spirit (*Acts* 2:1-4). Reflecting on these things, the *Constitution on the Church* fittingly closed with its Chapter 8 on Mary, declaring her to be "preeminent and... a wholly unique member of the Church, and... outstanding model in faith and charity. The Catholic Church taught by the Holy Spirit, honors her with filial affection and devotion as a most beloved mother" (*LG* 53).

As Mother of the Church, one of Mary's everlasting tasks is to present the Savior to his people, who, as the Community of the Saved rejoice in his presence. (See the discussion on **"Evangelization"** in **Chapter 18**.) This is seen poignantly in the pre-Christmas Feast of the Visitation of Mary to Elizabeth. Our liturgy presents an icon of the whole Church gathering to experience the Lord: the elderly, the young, and the unborn. From the *Sedro*, (which addresses Christ):

> **You traveled with your mother, Mary,**
> **to visit the aged Elizabeth,**
> **and she rejoiced at your coming...**
> **Your mother went quickly to the dwelling**
> **of Elizabeth,**
> **and you accompanied her...**

Intercessor

Unless another feast is celebrated, on every Wednesday the Maronite Church honors Mary the God-bearer. In the *Proemion* of this commemoration we hear:

> *May we offer glory, praise and honor*
> *to the exalted One, who humbled himself*
> *and exalted the humble Virgin,*
> *to God, who became flesh*
> *and saved our human race;*
> *to the Most High, who lowered himself*
> *and raised up the lowly.*
> **To Christ, the good One, are due glory and honor,**
> **on this day and all the days of our lives,**
> **now and for ever. Amen.**

Of course, these words are addressed to Christ who is eternally the supreme Intercessor to God for us.

The *Hoosoyo* concludes thus:

> *'Etro*
>
> **O radiant Lily and fragrant Rose,**
> **the aroma of your holiness fills the whole universe.**
> *Pray for us,*
> *that we may be the sweet perfume of Christ,*
> *reaching throughout the whole world.*
> *May our incense be for the salvation of the departed*
> *and for the preservation of the Faith among the living,*
> **that we may inherit eternal happiness,**
> **and sing praise to the Most Holy Trinity,**
> **now and for ever. Amen.**

Clearly her role as Intercessor — standing with us in prayer to Jesus, her Divine Son is seen here. Mother, yet Ever-virgin, she reflects God's everlasting care for all creation.

Cedar of Our Faith

In Lebanon stand the famous cedars of Lebanon, ancient and massively strong. They are known from the Hebrew Scriptures, as Solomon chose them for the building of the Temple. They are symbols of everlasting strength.

Maronites have for centuries recognized the Mother of God under the title of "Cedar of Lebanon." For us, she represents a strong and enduring faith, which does not break under adversity.

> Everyone then who hears these words of mine and acts on
> them will be like wise man who built his house on a rock.
> The rains fell, the floods came, and the winds blew and
> beat on that house, but it did not fall, because it had been
> founded on rock (*Mt* 7:24-25).

Other Righteous and Just

If Mary is the first among the Righteous and the Just (the Saints), she nevertheless stands both at the head of and with others in glory who are intercessors for us and whose lives of faith and obedience are worthy of imitation. The *Sedro* of the Sunday of the Righteous and Just expresses it well:

> We worship and glorify you,
> as we joyfully celebrate the Feast of all the saints
> in your holy Church.
> We present them to you on the clouds of this incense
> *as our intercessors.*
> Establish peace and tranquility in your Church.
> Glorify it with bishops, priests, and teachers.
> *Make your Church a holy people, a saved gathering,*
> *and an apostolic branch*
> *that will grow and bear fruit by the power of your*
> *Holy Spirit.*
> *Grant us to follow your chosen saints*
> *and to live righteous and just lives.*
> *Make us worthy to enter the dwelling place of the saints*
> *in the world…*

And in each Divine Service, during the incensing at the Pre-*Anaphora*, we may sing:

> **Alleluia!**
> *We remember Mary, Mother of God,*
> *the prophets, the Apostles, the martyrs,*
> *the just, the priests, and the children of the Church,*
> from one generation to another,
> to the end of time. Amen.

Maronites have their own calendar of Saints, with proper Services (contained in a liturgical source known in Syriac as the *Fenqitho*, or "Treasury of Feasts").

Some of the more important Saints venerated in the calendar are:

❖ **St. Maron (Feast Day obligatory in Maronite Particular Law: 9 February)**(see **Chapter 8**).

❖ **St. Ephrem the Deacon, "Harp of the Holy Spirit" (28 January).** Also honored in the East Syriac "Church of the East," Ephrem is among the greatest liturgical poets of the Church. His poetry—and the hymnody based upon it—safeguarded doctrinal orthodoxy against the heretical teachings of his time and inspired the chant of other Churches.

❖ **St. John Maron (2 March).** John was a Maronite bishop living in Kfarhai, Mt. Lebanon. When the Catholic See of Antioch was left vacant (8th century), John was elected by his people to be Maronite Patriarch of Antioch. It is from this time that the Maronite Community was established as a self-governing (*sui iuris*) Church within the Catholic Communion of Churches.

❖ **St. Sharbel (23 July).** To Sharbel, hermit and monk, were attributed many miraculous cures and events, even during his lifetime. His life was one of gradual movement from conventional monasticism to the life of the hermit. From his death in 1898 to the close of the Second Vatican Council in 1965, when he was beatified, his body did not decay. He was the first saint from the East to be canonized (recognized as a saint) by the process of the Vatican.

❖ **Saint Rebecca (Rafqa) (23 March).** Rebecca was a nun and spiritual mystic. During her lifetime she went blind and also suffered ill health. Still, she lived a life of extreme asceticism characteristic of holy men and women in Maronite Tradition. As with others, miracles have been attributed to her intercession.

❖ **The Massabki Brothers (10 July).** These three Syrian Maronite lay men, two of them married and family men, were martyrs for the faith in Damascus in the fierce massacres by the Muslims in the late 1800s. They are designated for the Maronites in the United States as patrons of laity.

Some Saints are honored in common with those from other Traditions. The Transfer chant commemorating Mary characteristically expresses the rich theology of the East regarding the Saints. They are not venerated in and for themselves, as if they were divine; rather, they lead us specifically toward Jesus, whom they now worship with us, and to the Father, the goal of our longing, as we pray in the Holy Spirit.

This teaching is often quite misunderstood by fellow Christians who do not share the same outlook. One often hears from Fundamentalist Christians:

"Why do you Catholics worship the Saints?"

Our answer to this is easy:

"We don't. Like you, we worship God alone."

The other question often heard is:

"Why do you pray to the Saints; why not go directly to Jesus, the One Mediator between us and the Father?"

The answer to this is simply:

"Of course, we can. But don't you often ask your friends to pray for you? If they with their sins are worthy of your trust to pray for your needs, how about those whom (you claim) have already entered the Kingdom immediately after death, and are now enjoying the vision of the Lord? They are certainly closer to God than we or our earthly friends!"

Catholic teaching about the Saints, including the Mother of God, might be summed up in the following simple prayer: "O Mary (or "O Saint [N.]"), please pray to Jesus, and ask him to take our prayer to the Heavenly Father."

To put it another way, we depend on "friends in high places."

This last is especially true of the Mother of God. On earth she was privileged to know her Son more intimately than anyone else (except perhaps St. Joseph). Why should anyone be tempted to think that this intimate knowledge was destroyed at her death? If anything, we might speculate that it is intensified in their new, heavenly relationship.

All things have been handed over to me by my Father; and no one knows the Son except the Father and anyone to whom the Son chooses to reveal him (*Mt* 11:27).

In a special way Mary—with Joseph—reflects her Divine Son's everlasting and providential care for God's created universe. In this she is worthy of all devotion, and Catholic Tradition in general has never been afraid to celebrate this. A healthy Catholic faith recognizes that the more we think about the Mother of Christ, the more we must honor the One she bore.

Devotion to Our Lady and the Saints

In Maronite Tradition, devotion to the Mother of God and to the Saints has taken many forms. The liturgical tradition is a very important source for authentic Eastern thinking about and devotion to them. In the various forms of the Liturgy—the *Qoorbono*, Morning Prayer (*Safro*) and Vespers (*Ramsho*), the seven sacramental Mysteries—there are countless references to Mary in the prayers and hymns. (The Wednesday commemoration for the *Qoorbono* is to the Mother of God.) Here, the references rarely focus on Mary for her own sake but rather refer to her role in God's divine plan of salvation in Jesus. When praying thus, one strongly forms an image of the Mother and Child found in icons.

One type of devotion to Mary and the Saints (Righteous and Just) is the service of blessing with the icon. Another devotion traditionally dear to the hearts of Maronites, as with many other Eastern Christians, is the recitation of the Rosary.

Two testimonies to the love for Mary and the Saints may be seen within in and outside Lebanon: In addition to the major place of pilgrimage at Hareessa, in Jounieh, countless wayside shrines to Mary (and the Saints) dot roads throughout the country. Also, many churches are named after the Mother of God under various titles.

STUDY QUESTIONS:

1) How does the chant at the Transfer of the Offerings ("The Lord Reigns") relate the Service of the Word and to the *Anaphora*?
2) How do the titles of Mary show us something necessary about Christ and the Church?
3) What is the correct, Catholic understanding about Mary and the Saints?

Chapter 14:
Human Destiny

Living between the Two Appearances of Christ

It has been said that Christians are those who live between the two Appearances of Christ: between his Birth and the end of the world as we

> ### 1st Sunday after Holy Cross
> ### Lk 17:20-37

know it, when he will come again to judge us and transform the world (the Final Judgment) to bring all to the Father (*1 Cor* 15:23-28). This final Coming and judgment is often referred to as the *Parousia* (Greek: "an appearing in power"). Justin, a well-known martyr of the early Church, put it this way:

> … (T)he prophets have proclaimed two advents of His: the one, that which is already past, when He came as a dishonored and suffering Man; but the second, when according to prophecy, He shall come from heaven with glory, accompanied by His angelic host… (*1 Apol.* 52.3).

This is distinctively expressed in the Maronite form of the "Holy, holy," at the beginning of each *Anaphora*:

> **Holy, holy, holy mighty Lord, God of hosts!**
> **Heaven and earth are full of your great glory.**
> **Hosanna in the highest!**
> **Blessed is he who *has come***
> ***and will come* in the name of the Lord!**
> **Hosanna in the highest!**

Maronite Tradition strongly reflects its Syriac background in its clear emphasis on the Second Coming of Christ. In fact, one of the themes of the Season of the Exaltation of the Glorious Cross is this focus on the Second Coming. The second *Anamnesis* prayer of the *Anaphora of St. Peter*:

We remember, O Lord,
your saving second coming,
and we glorify you and your majesty.
On that fearsome and awesome day,
when you will separate the just from sinners...

Theology uses the word *eschatology* (Greek: "study of the final things") to describe talk about the events of the final time. This term helps us to recognize that our final goal, our destiny, is a very good one for all who remain faithful to the words of Christ in the in-between time.

Liturgical Year: The Season of the Glorious Cross

Question: What does the Season of the Glorious Cross tell us about the risen Christ?

Answer: The Feast—indeed the whole Season—of the Glorious Cross is a pointer to the realm beyond us in which the Lord of Glory, Jesus, dwells in the majesty of the Trinity. From here he beckons us, through our belief in the power of the Cross, through a life lived in faithful witness, and to a happiness beyond the grave. The risen Jesus calls us to be with him one day in that glory of the Resurrection.

For the Maronite Church, these considerations of the final things are focused in the last season of the Liturgical Year, the Season of the Glorious Cross. The actual feast day that begins the season is the Exaltation of the Holy Cross, celebrated on 14 September. In this season we look to the Cross not in its sorrowful aspect of Passion Week but rather to the triumph of the Cross by which Christ directs our life. This is cause for celebration, as we glory in the Cross of Christ, as St. Paul says (*Gal* 6:14). As the *Sedro* of the Feast of the Holy Cross puts it:

> *As we call to mind*
> *the sweet memory of the cross of our salvation,*
> *we celebrate with praises and hymns*
> *the day of its finding.*
> *We rejoice at its ineffable and glorious mysteries.*
> *The sign of the cross is the victory*
>   *and pride of those who worship it...*

Thus, the Season of the Glorious Cross becomes, in reality, a symbol for our entire life as we live it now in the light of the Cross.

Individual Death and Judgment

Our bodies die. Yet, because we have the promises of Christ to his faithful, we can know something of what awaits us, even if it ultimately is

> **Sunday of the**
> **Faithful Departed**
> **Lk 12:32-40, or**
> **Lk 16:19-31**

beyond our limited, human comprehension. We can think about what awaits those who are not quite prepared for the Eternal Light, who need the full forgiveness of sins and further purification. We can also know what awaits those who outright reject the overwhelming gift of God's love and mercy.

Since the choices of our lives determine our eternal futures, the Church teaches that we shall be judged according to life in this dimension. From the *Sedro* for the Sunday of the Faithful Departed:

> **O Christ our God,**
> **you will come in glory on the last day**
> **to judge the living and the dead.**
> **All people will stand before your almighty Throne**
> **to hear your judgment and to receive your reward.**
> *On that day the light of truth will shine forth*
> *revealing every inner conscience and*
> *dividing all people to the right and to the left.*

Thus, the clear light of God's knowledge will reveal the lives of all, including that final choice that was made at the moment of death—in a life lived for or against the love of God, our Just Judge.

The "Dew of Mercy"

Moreover, hope is rightly founded on the great mercy of a Loving God. This idea is traditionally expressed in the Maronite Tradition as the "dew of mercy." God's merciful loving-kindness is like refreshing dew upon the soul of the believer awaiting the dawn of eternity. The following *Qolo* is sung at the cemetery:

> **May the *dew of mercy*,**
> **showered by the Father**
> **and sprinkled over the young men**
> **in the furnace of corruption,**
> **overshadow the departed**
> **in the dark depths of the nether world....**

If we have been constant in living a life of virtue and faith, we can expect a good reward. As the Prayer for the Imposition of the Hand in the *Anaphora of St. Sixtus* expresses:

> **Send your blessing upon us, O Lord,**
> ***that we may be worthy of the happy death***
> ***reserved to men and women of peace.***
> **We will glorify you, O God,**
> **now and for ever. Amen.**

Between Death and the Kingdom: Purifying Journey

> ### Sunday of the Man
> ### With Leprosy
> #### Lk 5:12-16, or
> #### Mk 1:32-45

What happens to an individual after death has been a question in many cultures throughout history. The legends of these cultures describe this journey from physical life to the condition of afterlife in many interesting ways. Catholic Tradition has had something to say about the journey of the soul to final happiness in the Kingdom.

Although the Fathers of the early Church, including St. Ephrem, attest to the reality of the soul's need for purification after death, the widely known <u>term</u> *purgatory* is not explicitly stated in the Scriptures. The term comes from Western Tradition, and did not even appear in it until the 11th century at the earliest. The *formulation* of the teaching became a source of controversy between Greek East and Latin West; the Syriac Churches, including the Maronites, never became involved in the controversy. In any case, since the 16th century the Catholic Church officially teaches that the departed stand in need of purification from whatever keeps them from full union with the Trinity in the Kingdom and is wisely silent about further details about the nature of that purification.

We must remember that what is being described is a *state* of the soul, not a place. (Contemporary theologian Karl Rahner has offered the term "The Intermediate State.")

Maronite Tradition repeatedly expresses two ideas about the Faithful Departed. The first is that not all the dead have yet completed their journey to the happiness of the Kingdom. They are "at rest" and "awaiting" the final saving action of the Lord. Second, they need our prayers for the forgiveness of their sins and purification. The *Hoosoyo* for the Sunday of the Faithful Departed says in part:

> *...May they rest in the dwelling places*
> *prepared for them in the heavenly Jerusalem,*
> *the city of the Saints.*
> *In your mercy, accept what your Church offers to you*
> *on their behalf—alms, prayers and offerings.*
> *Through the intercession of your Mother*
> *and your Saints,*
> *deliver them from their suffering....*

The Hope of the Saved

The prayer above acknowledges that the departed are still somehow suffering by atoning in some way for their sins on earth. However, like the man in the Gospel story for the Second Sunday of Great Lent—who needed purification from his disease—that suffering is made easier to bear in view of the *hope* that the dead will be united to the Lord in the Eternal Light, which somehow they experience, for *they are saved.* This aspect of hope is central to Christian life. The Departed already experience the overwhelming love of the Trinity, but their "temporary" separation from the fullness of that love only adds to their pain. Yet they see their (our) destiny as a great Wedding Banquet to which we are all invited in our wedding garments. (The Syriac-Maronite Tradition recognizes this image of the Wedding Banquet from the Scriptures and uses it in instances too numerous to mention.)

The hope clung to by the Departed was nourished in life by the Eucharist, which was their "pledge" (Syriac: *ra'bono*) of eternal happiness, even its foretaste. Hope—and our prayers—sustains them.

For the faithful Christian believer death is not an abandonment to nothingness but rather the ultimate instance and fulfillment of hope. The human side of us experiences the utter separation from this earthly dimension, although we do not lose all connection (see **"The Communion of Saints"** below). But the faithful who are passing into the Kingdom focus more directly on the Lord. As the first stanza of the *Mazmooro* for the Sunday of the Faithful Departed expresses it:

> **From my youth until the present**
> **my eyes look to you to save.**
> *Now I sleep in hope of you,*
> *grant me rest among the saints.*

What is also clear here is the great mercy of God. We constantly ask the Lord to be merciful not only to us but to our departed.

The Need for Divine Protection

This process of purification is seen as part of the journey to the Kingdom. The prayer below implies that the journey is difficult and never free of danger until the end. (Compare the Intercessions for Evening Prayer for Wednesday of Week III in the Latin Office.) One is reminded of the troubles of the hero in the great English allegory by John Bunyan, *Pilgrim's Progress*. In Maronite Tradition, this aspect is highlighted in the *Sedro* for the Sunday of the Deceased Priests:

> **…Grant peace and serenity to the priests**
> **who have gone before us to your holy dwellings.**
> **May their works precede them as a record**
> **of their faith**
> **and a memorial of their lives.**

> *May the Evil One flee at the sight of their coming*
> *from the path that leads to you.*
> *Let none of your deceased ministers be tempted*
> *by the devil and his legions.*
> *May the marks of your holy Mysteries*
> *shelter and protect them on their journey to you....*

Strong is the power of Satan. Stronger yet is the power of the risen Savior, who seals them and all the faithful departed with the "marks of the Holy Mysteries," the Holy Eucharist, which the priests have brought to the faithful at the Divine Service. These "marks" may also be a reference to the nail marks of the crucifixion, still visible to Thomas in the risen Christ (*Jn* 20:27). The death and resurrection of the Lord is celebrated in the Divine Eucharist, which guards the faithful.

The Intercessions: Praying for the Living and the Dead
There is a value to praying for the dead. Only in a way that the Father knows best will this kind of prayer be helpful. Prayer for the Departed is an ancient practice in the Church and is based on *2 Macc* 12:46.

The Intercessions are prayers, which are offered by the Deacon on behalf of the worshiping Assembly for the needs of the Church and are a standard part of the Divine Service. In the absence of a deacon other members of the Assembly, such as a subdeacon or even the laity themselves may offer the Intercessions.

In the Maronite Divine Service these are prayed after the *Epiclesis* and close the *Anaphora*. Placed thus, our petitions are offered in the presence of the Eucharistic Christ, who will, we trust in faith, hear our prayer.

The structure of the Intercessions is very simple: an opening petition for the leaders of the Church (Pope, Patriarch, local Bishop); middle petitions for the whole Church members on earth (the Living); a petition for the intercession of the Righteous and Just, and a closing petition for the Departed, who are alive in God.

We demonstrate a desire to make offerings to the Church and to the priest for this purpose by giving "alms, prayers and offerings," as the prayer suggests. Such acts of sacrifice have traditionally been thought to benefit the Faithful Departed. The Church also teaches that such actions as giving alms, fasting, and doing acts of charity can benefit the living as well. By making atonement and reparation for our sins, we learn to distance ourselves from the earthly attachments from which we are purified. Thus freed from any obstacle to our soul's vision, we are finally ready for the full sight of God's heavenly glory.

One other traditional custom is offering "stipends" (free-will, monetary offerings, see p. 365) to the priest for the praying of the Divine Service. This custom even draws the priest into the process.

The Communion of Saints

This communion extends even beyond earthly existence. The Church teaches that there is solidarity between the living and the dead, as expressed in the Creed by the phrase, "the communion of saints." We really do have a beneficial connection to the faithful who have passed on, a communion of faith, hope and love. One day we expect to be reunited to them for ever. The Council focuses on this bond of union by saying that it "accepts with great devotion the venerable faith of our ancestors regarding this vital fellowship with our brethren who are in heavenly glory or are still being purified after death" (*LG* 51).

Hell

3rd Sunday after Holy Cross
Lk 13:1-9

Because we possess free will, we can choose not to serve God in this life and also to reject him at the time of death. This choice, being ours, separates us from the God who is light and life. The *Anamnesis* prayer of the *Anaphora of St. John the Apostle* expresses this poetically, yet firmly:

> **...When you come in glory with your holy angels,**
> **O Lord,**
> **and all look for the reward they deserve,**
> *let us not be strangers to your household.*
> *Do not turn your face away from us,*
> *nor let our sins and offenses touch*
> *your holy heart.*
> *Do not reject us from your presence,*
> **for we have known your holy name**

> and professed our faith in your divinity.
> Rather, forgive our sins, pardon us,
> and have mercy on your inheritance....

Just what the exact nature of the punishment of hell is has never been specifically defined by the Church, despite a long tradition of the image of burning flames. The *Anamnesis* prayer of the *Anaphora of St. Peter* refers to it this way:

> ...On that fearsome and awesome day,
> when you will separate the just from sinners,
> do not hand us over to the *burning flame*
> *that causes weeping and mourning, affliction*
> *and torment,*
> because of our sins and the evil we have done;
> rather, have mercy on us, O Lord, and forgive us ...

The image of flames is not to be taken literally: fire was once feared as ultimate destruction. What is clear, however, is that hell is the total absence of God and divine love and mercy, a burning pain far worse than fire. It is the result of an intentional choice to reject God. The destruction of ourselves due to rejection of God is far more intense.

The Kingdom of Heaven

> But, as it is written, "What no eye has seen, nor ear heard, nor the human heart conceived, what God has prepared for those who love him"—these things God has revealed to us through the Spirit; for the Spirit searches everything, even the depths of God (*1 Cor* 2:9-10).

St. Paul appears to be a realist in attempting to describe the indescribable: the joy and happiness of our union with the Divine One, the Holy Trinity,

> **6ᵗʰ Sunday of Resurrection**
> **Jn 14: 1-14**

cannot even be imagined. What a wonderful surprise this will be! Perhaps we should be content to accept this insightful Pauline teaching as he presented it.

For now we see in a mirror, dimly, but then we will see face to face. Now I know only in part; then I will know fully, even as I have been fully known (*1 Cor* 13:12).

However, it is human to inquire into the nature of things, especially into the Ultimate Destiny of Good, heaven. Even Jesus offered earthly comparisons:

The kingdom of heaven may be compared to a king who gave a wedding banquet for his son (*Mt* 22:2).

One needs to be prepared for the banquet, wearing one's wedding robe, another favorite metaphor from the Tradition:

… and he said to him, "Friend, how did you get in here without a wedding robe?" And he was speechless (*Mt* 22:12).

Heaven's inhabitants are intimate with Christ:

And I saw the holy city, the New Jerusalem, coming down out of heaven from God, prepared as a bride adorned for her husband (*Rev* 21:2).

Thus, following Scripture, the Tradition speaks of heaven, using terms that are both scriptural and poetic, among them joy and light (see **Chapter 1, "Images of Light"**). These descriptions of the Kingdom as a state of joy, filled with light, are not, of course, confined to Maronite Tradition. All Traditions use these terms. For example, the formula, "Eternal rest grant unto them… let perpetual light…," is familiar to Catholics of the Latin tradition.

In Maronite Tradition one of the clearest places in which the themes of light and joy are expressed can be found in one of the *Mazmooro* verses for the Sunday of the Faithful Departed:

The Cross is a lighthouse scattering the darkness death brings, for the face of the Savior *lights the way and leads us on to his place of joy.*

Finally, heaven is our home:

> In my Father's house there are many dwelling places. If it were not so, would I have told you that I go to prepare a place for you? (*Jn* 14:2)

We shall indeed be safe and happy—immeasurably happy—in the presence of the Trinity forever. As the ending of the well known and comforting *Psalm 23* puts it:

> Surely goodness and mercy shall follow me all the days of my life, and I shall dwell in the house of the LORD my whole life long (*Ps* 23:6).

The *'Etro* for the feast of the Ascension expresses the hope for a heavenly home well:

> **O Lord,**
> **accept the incense and prayers we offer you**
> **on the feast of your Ascension.**
> **Make us ready to receive the Spirit you promised,**
> *that we and to dwell in that place you set aside for us*
> *near your Father,*
> *may meet you in the heavenly dwellings*
> **and praise you, O Christ,**
> **your Father, and your living, Holy Spirit,**
> **now and for ever. Amen.**

Thus, as faithful believers, we put our trust in the Gracious One, who will favor us beyond our wildest imaginings.

A New Earth and a New Heaven

As Christians trying to live faithfully between the two appearances of Christ, we await the day when he will return in glory to bring about the transformation of the world, and us with it.

> *Cana Sunday*
> *(Entrance into Great Lent)*
> *Jn 2:1-11*

When will that day come? The Council addresses this question and expresses the Church's vision:

> We do not know the moment of the consummation of the earth and of humanity nor the way the universe will be transformed. The form of this world, distorted by sin, is passing away and we are taught that God is preparing a new dwelling and a new earth in which righteousness dwells, whose happiness will fill and surpass all the desires of peace arising in human hearts (*GS* 39).

Surely this is an extension of the miracle of Easter, in which Jesus himself was transformed into the glory he now enjoys at the right hand of his Father. The expression "at the right hand" is a biblical metaphor for being in glory. This is a doctrine of the utmost hope.

Our Maronite Church begins its Lenten journey to Easter with the feast of the Wedding at Cana in Galilee. The Evangelist John records that at this event, Jesus performs his first public "sign," or miracle by changing water into wine, thus making known the beginning of his "hour" of glorification:

> Jesus did this, the first of his signs, in Cana of Galilee, and revealed his glory; and his disciples believed in him (*Jn* 2:11).

Our Church uses this sign of transformation to begin a series of Lenten Sunday celebrations that highlight other transformations, both physical and spiritual. This series culminates in the greatest miracle story of all: the Resurrection, the sign of the new Earth and the New Heaven, the New Creation. The first of the *Mazmooro* verses states it well:

> **You gave joy to your guests, O Lord,**
> **by the water you changed into wine.**
> *Give joy to us in your paradise*
> *on the day of your manifestation.*

Pneumatization: Transformation into Spiritual Beings

This "sign" of turning water into wine is a liturgical symbol, as the feast day celebration uses it, of our own anticipated transformation. As

Jesus was once transformed by the Father into a glorious, risen humanity, so too do we hope for this for ourselves. The *Sedro* for Cana Sunday points to this:

> **O Lord,**
> **source of all generosity and goodness,**
> **we now implore you:**
> **in your grace, shine upon us.**
> **Open the treasure of your abundant compassion to us.**
> *Enrich us with your good gifts*
> *and delight us with your true promises.*
> *Seat us at the table of your kingdom*
> *and let us drink from your new wine.*
> *Give us the joy of your eternal feast*
> *and let us rejoice in the splendor of your face.*

This process of transformation from the merely bodily form to the form of the "spiritual body," as St. Paul calls it (*1 Cor* 15:44), is called *pneumatization.* The term comes from the Greek word, *pneuma*, which means, "spirit."

Becoming spirit does not apply only to individuals. It also applies to the whole created universe. Pope John Paul II comments:

> The liturgy reveals that the body, through the mystery of the Cross, is in the process of transfiguration, pneumatization: on Mount Tabor Christ showed his body radiant, as the Father wants it to be again.
>
> Cosmic reality also is summoned to give thanks because the whole universe is called to recapitulation in Christ the Lord. This concept expresses a balanced and marvelous teaching on the dignity, respect and purpose of creation and of the human body in particular... The world is destined to be assumed in the Eucharist of the Lord, in his Passover, present in the sacrifice of the altar (*Orientale Lumen* 11).

A liturgical note: Since Cana Sunday is the "Entrance into Great Lent," and its first Sunday, we might be tempted to expect a clearly penitential theme. While, in fact, the penitential is not absent from the text (note the *'Etro*), the clear thrust of the Maronite Lenten Sunday Cycle is that of the evolving sense of transformation in the Gospel stories of Christ's curing of both physical and spiritual diseases (especially sin). Also important in this Cycle is the overcoming of the alienation from community that the diseases effect: as those in the Gospels are cured, they are reconciled to the community and consolation of others. The supreme reconciliation, of course, is brought about by the Death and Resurrection of Jesus. The full reconciliation of the Paschal Mystery is seen on Easter Sunday, when Christ breathes his Resurrection Peace upon the Disciples.

Another important illustration is seen in a liturgical symbol of the new creation. On Easter Sunday morning, the flowers that were used in the Great Friday Service of the Burial of the Lord are distributed to the faithful. Just as the human body of Jesus was transformed into the "spiritual body" of heaven, so we look forward to being with him one day in Paradise. These flowers, with their natural fragrance and beauty, are symbols of the new creation. This is very much in line with St. Ephrem's sensory images, used in his poetic writings, as this selection from the *Hymns on Paradise*, stanza 7, shows:

> Do not let your intellect
> be disturbed by mere names,
> for Paradise has simply clothed itself
> in terms that are akin to you;
> it is not because it is impoverished
> that it put on your imagery;
> rather, your nature is far too weak
> to be able
> to attain to its greatness,
> and its beauties are much diminished
> by being depicted in the pale colors
> with which you are familiar.

This transformation is nothing less than the *restoration to glory* that was lost by the First Sin of our ancestors, or, as the Mystery of Baptism puts it, the putting on again of the "robe of glory" (see **Chapter 17, "Initiation: Baptism II"**).

This longing to have the goodness of creation restored at the Second Coming of Christ is what the Faithful Departed cling to in hope, just as we live out our lives in hope. We Maronites celebrate this hope in the Season of the Holy Cross, which concludes our Liturgical Year.

May we cry out each day, as does the end of the Book of Revelation, the Syriac petition,

Marana tha, "Our Lord, come."

STUDY QUESTIONS:
1) What does it mean to be "living between the two Comings of Christ"?
2) Describe what happens after we die.
3) Is pneumatization, that is, the process of spiritual transformation, limited only to the afterlife?

PART IV: OUR SACRAMENTAL AND MORAL FAITH LIFE
(Divine Liturgy Focus: *Anaphora*, Communion, Dismissal)

The Sacramental Life
The Author of the Fourth Gospel states quite clearly:

> For God so loved the world that he gave his only Son, so
> that everyone who believes in him may not perish but may
> have eternal life (*Jn* 3:16).

**1ˢᵗ Sunday of Epiphany
Jn 1:29-34**

Most readers of this verse are encouraged to focus on believing in Jesus as the One who saves us. The *response* of the believer to the sending of the Son is certainly a big part of the meaning of this verse. But there is a deeper aspect to this biblical thought that remains necessary and precious to Catholic theology. It has to do with *God's love for the world.*

Because God's creation was good in the first place, and despite humanity's corruption of it through prideful sin, God continued to love creation. As we saw in Chapter 3, God chose to reveal the divine life through creation.

> Long ago God spoke to our ancestors in many and various
> ways by the prophets, but in these last days he has spoken
> to us by a Son, whom he appointed heir of all things,
> through whom he also created the worlds (*Heb* 1:1-2).

This process of revelation came to full expression in the birth and life of Jesus, the *Icon of God.* Jesus is God's most eloquent Word spoken to us. In Jesus we see the Father and hear God speaking to us:

> Jesus said to him, "Have I been with you all this time,
> Philip, and you still do not know me? Whoever has seen me
> has seen the Father. How can you say, 'Show us the
> Father?'" (*Jn* 14:9)

Syro-Antiochene Incarnational Theology
The Incarnation, the "making flesh," of God is, so to speak, God's act of faith in his creation and us. Jesus is the connecting point between God and humanity. The Syriac Teachers call this a *rozo* (E. Syriac, *raza*),

or symbolic "mystery." Our God is so good, so loving, that we are able to glimpse heaven by seeing and listening to the One sent by the Father.

We call this way of looking at God's loving action in Jesus "incarnational" theology. It means that we humans, who live by signs and symbols, have the ability to look beyond these earthly indicators to the life beyond, to which we are destined. But it also helps us to appreciate the very signs and symbols that point to the beyond. We call this vision based on holy signs and symbols *sacramentality*. Through earthly things that have ordinary meaning for us here, we can catch a glimpse of what is behind them, namely the life of the Kingdom beyond, where God waits for us to join the Trinity and be unfathomably happy for ever.

This respect for and insistence upon the human dimension of the Mystery of Jesus, the Word-joined-to-humanity, colors many aspects of the Antiochene Tradition. It is why we find Syriac Writers of poetry and prose using the device of paradox (see discussion in **Chapter 10**).

As the Icon of Christ, the Church is the place above all in which the contrast between the divine and human is seen. Yet, it is precisely in the interplay of divine and human that the Church exists. No wonder that the Tradition of the Church never seems to exhaust the possibilities of describing this rich and deep Mystery called "Church." It is in and through this Body, the Church, that the sacramental Mysteries are found.

What Is a Sacramental Mystery?

Although Eastern Church theology does not easily provide strict definitions of spiritual things, the writers of the Eastern Church did at times help to clarify. Theodore of Mopsuestia explains to us in an Antiochene way what a sacramental Mystery is:

> Every sacrament consists in the representation of unseen and unspeakable things through signs and emblems. Such things require explanation and interpretation, for the sake of the person who draws nigh unto the sacrament, so that he might know its power. If it only consisted of the (visible) elements themselves, words would have been useless, as sight itself would have been able to show us one by one all the happenings that take place; but since a sacrament contains the signs of the things that take place or have already taken place, words are needed to explain the power of signs and mysteries (quoted in Greer, p. 78).

The Holy Spirit and the Sacramental Mysteries

These Mysteries are accomplished by the energizing power of God's Holy Spirit, whose mission it is to sanctify the Church. By our *epiclesis,* and by the Spirit's consequent overshadowing—as over Mary at the Annunciation, Jesus at his Baptism, and as at the Pentecost—the Spirit enables the Mysteries to change our lives.

This is affirmed in paragraph 1152 of the *Catechism*, which speaks clearly of the Spirit's power and role in the sacramental Mysteries.

The Passive Voice

Because God initiates these mighty works—God's grace is indeed a free gift—we must recognize this in gratitude and humility as we celebrate this in ritual. In the Eastern Churches, the liturgical prayer form of the Mysteries is expressed in the passive voice, to show that God is indeed doing the works, through the humble hands of the celebrant. For example, we hear "...The servant of God *is baptized...*," "...*is crowned...*," "...*is forgiven....*"

The *Catechism* also affirms this central Eastern sacramental principle in paragraph 1127.

The Sanctification of Life

Why do we celebrate the sacramental Mysteries at all? Why did God, through the Church, give them to us? It is because the Holy One wishes that we taste divine holiness even here and now. In doing so, we in fact live out our spiritual rebirth, begun in our Initiation and aided by the power of the Mysteries. Our lives are elevated above the merely human and joined to the divine. The second Thanksgiving Prayer (after Communion) of the *Anaphora of the Twelve Apostles* puts it this way:

> **O Lord our Savior,**
> *you became flesh*
> *and by sacrificing yourself for us you saved us.*
> *Redeem us now from eternal damnation,*
> *make us temples of your holy name...*

The graphic at the beginning of this **Part IV** illustrates this well. It is the Washing of the Feet at the Last Supper, the First Eucharist. As we will see later, Jesus shows us a powerful example of humility and service in the Eucharistic action. It is a divine oxymoron: "powerful humility." In the sacramental Mysteries, the Spirit touches us so that we might touch the lives of others. In fact, through the sanctifying power of the Holy Spirit, all earthly liturgy is Christ's own prayer, continued at the Father's right hand.

This making-holy extends over the whole span of our lifetime, "from womb to tomb." God wants nothing less than to touch our WHOLE lifetime, even into eternity. From the beginning of our lives, when we are tiny babies, and beyond the moment of our death, God's Providence is upon us.

The Sacramental Mysteries as Liturgical Actions

Recognizing the sacramental dimension of existence, the Church teaches that certain times within its life—the corporate Church life of the believer—are expressed as liturgical celebrations of the encounter with God.

The Mysteries form the heart of the life of the Church and are to be seen as an essential part of its liturgical life. Thus, some of the Mysteries are Services of the Word: Initiation (Baptism-Chrismation) and Holy Crowning. (Although not a sacramental Mystery, the *Jinnaaz* [funeral] Service may also be seen as a Service of the Word.) Others are related to the Eucharist: the *Qoorbono* itself, especially the *anaphora*; Penance (just before Holy Communion in the *Qoorbono*, where Eucharist is seen as the forgiveness of sin); Ordination to Holy Order (celebrated at Communion time during the Divine Liturgy).

The Eastern Churches call these seven celebrations the sacramental "Mysteries." They are:

Mysteries of Christian Initiation:
Baptism
Chrismation
Holy Eucharist

Mysteries of Healing:
Penance (Reconciliation)
Anointing of the Sick

Mysteries of Vocation:
Holy Order
Holy Crowning

Chapter 15:
The Mysteries of Initiation

The Baptism of the Lord as a Model for Initiation
The Gospels speak of his baptism in the Jordan River as the first event of Jesus' adult life. In fact, both Mark and John begin their historical treatment of Jesus' life with the events surrounding the Baptism. (Only Matthew and Luke tell us about the Birth and Infancy of Jesus. Luke adds the theological account of the Finding in the Temple and moves from Jesus at 12 years old to his adult baptism. There is no need to ask what happened to Jesus between twelve and thirty; Luke just says that Jesus lived obediently in Nazareth.)

The importance of the Baptism story, from a Gospel standpoint, is that Jesus is *revealed* as Messiah and divine Son of God (also a new phase in his ministry) and sent by the Spirit to the desert to ponder in depth his mission in the Plan of the Father.

For the East the Baptism of Jesus, with its voice from the Father in Heaven and the appearance of the Holy Spirit "like a dove," is a "theophany," or revelation of the divinity of Jesus. (The Western emphasis at Epiphany on the visit of the Magi to the stable to worship the same divine Child serves the same purpose—Christ is the "Light to the Nations" [*Is* 42:6b].)

As an analogy in the life of the Christian, our baptism elevates us to a new relationship with the Trinity and to the Church. Our Chrismation gives us a deeper share in the Gifts of the Holy Spirit and propels us on our missionary goal of living and sharing new life in the Spirit. This might be termed our "Chrismational" calling.

The Liturgical Year: *Denho*, the Season of Epiphany
The Eastern Churches in general begin the post-Christmas Season of Epiphany with the commemoration of the Baptism of the Lord in the Jordan River (6 January). (The West celebrates the Baptism slightly later.) At one time this feast was not separate from Christmas but became distinct

when the Church began to celebrate the Birth of the Messiah on 25 December.

The Maronite Church values the Epiphany Gospel truth so much that a whole liturgical season is built around it. It is a time when the Maronite Church takes between two to six Sundays (depending on how early or late Lent begins) to reflect upon the consequences of Initiation for the Christian.

Both feast and season are important from the point of view of the catechumenate as well. The tradition of some of the Syriac Churches sees the Feast of the Baptism of the Lord as the proper day of reception of catechumens and of candidates (note the distinction) into the Church. (Any catechumenate process yet to be developed for the Syriac East will have to take this into account.)

Question: What does the Season commemorating Christ's Baptism (*Denho*) tell us about the risen Christ?

Answer: Jesus did not need John's baptism, which was for the forgiveness of sins. He comes to John to signal the end of John's ministry and the beginning of his own. Like the Resurrection above all, Jesus' Baptism is a revelation of his divinity, of his being the Messiah and of his being One of the Trinity.

Initiation: Incorporation into the Body

The Church is the Body of Christ, made up of many members:

For as in one body we have many members, and not all the members have the same function, so we, who are many, are one body in Christ, and individually we are members one of another (*Rom* 12:4-5).

As it is, there are many members, yet one body (*1 Cor* 12:20).

St. Paul here is telling us very insistently that the image of the body and its members is appropriate to describe the reality of the way Christ lives on earth today. This is a mystery, of which we have a real share, and a great responsibility: What Christ looks like to the non-initiated is shown by us initiates by how we live Christ's words and life.

Yet, unlike initiation into other organizations or clubs, sacramental Initiation into the Body means coming into an Assembly of those who believe in the God of Jesus Christ, who is the Father; the Son of the Heavenly Father, Jesus, whom the Father sent; and the Spirit of God, who is also sent by the Father and who reminds us intimately of the words and deeds of Jesus. It is also Initiation into the new life of the Holy Trinity, and a life-giving share of grace, which is nothing less than the Divine Life itself.

To be initiated into the Community of Believers, to be incorporated—this word means to be em-*body*-ed—is one of the central aims and realities of the Mysteries of Initiation (*CCC* 798).

This Initiation has three stages and three particular rituals: Baptism with water; sealing with Myron (Chrism) in Chrismation, and the reception of the Holy Eucharist. It is a mystical, sacramental, yet nonetheless real meeting with God, who calls us to life and salvation. The *Catechism* describes Initiation in this way in paragraph 1212.

Community as the Sacramental Context

The sacramental life is liturgical life: The seven Holy Mysteries are always celebrated in and as a liturgical context. Although the effects of the life of grace—which the Mysteries build up—are expressly experienced in our daily living, the rituals are experienced among the Community of Believers at prayer.

Further, the Mystery of the Divine Eucharist is the foundation of the Church and of the whole sacramental life (see **Chapter 19, "Initiation: Eucharist"**). The Church, the Body of Christ, is nothing less than the *Community* of Believers.

As public worship undoubtedly shows, liturgy is the prayer of the Community, the praying Body of Christ. If you listen carefully to the prayers of worship, you will almost never hear references to "I" or "me." Liturgy is the prayer of "we" and "us." In public worship, it is the task of the Celebrant to lead the prayer of the whole Church gathered at that particular time. Please bear this important point in mind as you read the sections below on the seven sacramental Mysteries.

The Catechumenate

According to the earliest practice of the Church, a person interested in exploring the possibility of a life commitment in faith in the Church was called a *catechumen*. This word comes from the Greek word *katecho* meaning "to echo." In handing on the Faith believers echo in an effective way the teachings that have been passed down to other believers throughout the centuries (see **"Tradition"** in **Chapter 10**). Therefore, this word—and others in English derived from it, such as *catechesis*, *catechism*, *catechetical*, *catechumenate*—has come to mean, "to instruct."

In the early Church a catechumen underwent a period of introduction to the local faith community and instruction in the mysteries of the Faith, lasting up to two years. Then the candidate received the Mysteries of Initiation—for the greatest part, such as those Christians of Rome, Antioch and Constantinople, this was at the Easter vigil. By these three he or she became a full member of the Church. A period of follow-up (Period of *Mystagogia*) ensured that the newly Initiated received the support needed to strengthen the bonds of faith and love further.

The Western Church has revived this program of the Catechumenate in its Rite of Christian Initiation of Adults (RCIA). This is laudable, and we in the Eastern Churches ought to study how to adapt the process for use in our own Communities, perhaps in the form of a Rite of Eastern Christian Initiation of Adults (RECIA). **Can. 617** of the Eastern Code puts it in general, but clear terms:

> Each Church *sui iuris* and particularly their bishops have the serious duty of providing catechesis, by which faith matures and the Disciple of Christ is formed through a deeper and more systematic knowledge of the teaching of Christ and through an increasingly stronger commitment to the person of Christ.

STUDY QUESTIONS:
1) What is a sacramental Mystery? What elements make up a sacramental Mystery? (See Introduction to **Part IV**, p. 189).
2) Reflect on the centrality of the Baptism of Jesus as a model of our own Initiation.
3) Why is the Christian Community so important for the Mysteries of Initiation?

Chapter 16:
Initiation: Baptism I, Response to Sin

Baptism is the gateway to the other sacramental Mysteries. In other words, one must be initiated by holy baptism as a member of the Church—which

2nd Sunday of Epiphany
Jn 15:1-8

membership is begun through Baptism—before one can participate in the remaining Mysteries. Although Baptism is not the fundamental Mystery—the Eucharist is—still, one makes a beginning in the new life of the Trinity and of the Church through Baptism.

For the Eastern Churches, Baptism and reception of the Holy Spirit find their "type," or prime example, in the Baptism of the Lord Jesus in the River Jordan. The parallel between the Baptism of Jesus and our Baptism is not precise—Jesus willingly submitted to John's baptizing for another purpose: This event reveals Jesus as the Messiah and Lord. It is designated by either of two Greek words, *Epiphany*, or *Theophany*, meaning "manifestation," or "revelation." In Syriac the season is called *Denho*.

The *Hoosoyo* for the Sundays of Epiphany well expresses the main themes that are important in the Holy Mystery of Baptism. Here it is in part:

Sedro

O God,
you became man out of your love for us.
You were born of the flesh to gather all people
  into *the adoption of your Father*,

and to make them his children through water
*   and the Holy Spirit.*
O Creator of life,
you became man in order to renew the image of Adam,
which grew old and distorted because of sin.
Newness of life came through baptism,
the pure fire and spiritual light.
You had no need for baptism,
yet came to be baptized and to sanctify
*   the waters of the Jordan...*
Bless your people and guard your inheritance.
You have clothed us with your baptism:
the robe of glory and the seal of the Holy Spirit.
You have called us to be spiritual children
through the second birth of baptism,
which purifies all sinners....

The Robe of Glory

Catholic teaching affirms that human nature was privileged from the very outset to be perfect, even in the natural state. Maronite liturgical tradition describes this original goodness and happiness in a particularly vivid image from its Syriac heritage: the "robe of glory." This is expressed in many places, but the conclusion of the Anointing with Holy Chrism in the Mystery of Chrismation states it well, as the newly Initiated is addressed:

You have been clothed with the living Father,
you have received Christ, the Son,
you have put on the Holy Spirit,
and you have been given the robe of glory,
which Adam once laid aside.

Even outside of the text for Initiation the idea is found. See, for example, the *Qolo* for the Common of Prophets, the Just and Confessors (Tuesday), Strophe I:

Your Church throughout the universe
sings you praise, O Lord,
for you exalted her and clothed her

with the robe of glory.
In her midst, all nations adore you,
for you redeemed them with your blood
and saved them by your cross.

Such a beautiful image, the robe of glory, graphically captures the intimate desire of God to identify humanity with divinity. This doctrine also inspires hope, for it shows the clear intent of God not only to create from nothing, but also to create everything good:

> God saw everything that he had made, and indeed, it was very good. And there was evening and there was morning, the sixth day (*Gn* 1:31).

Our first parents, however, did not take care of this robe. Adam (meaning "earth") and Eve (meaning "mother of all the living") stained it by the worst possible form of ingratitude to the Creator, and in their pride, they brought sin into the world. This entry of sin into the world, which was personal sin for them, infected the rest of humanity so deeply that no one born into this world—except the Incarnate Son of God, Jesus, and by the grace of God, the Mother of Jesus, Mary—escapes its sad effects. As the choice of *Psalm 51* for the Word Service of Baptism appropriately demonstrates:

> Wash me thoroughly from my iniquity, and cleanse me from my
>   sin.
> For I know my transgressions, and my sin is ever before me.
> Against you, you alone, have I sinned, and done what is evil in
>   your sight,
> so that you are justified in your sentence and blameless
>   when you pass judgment.
> Indeed, I was born guilty, a sinner when my mother conceived me.
> Purge me with hyssop, and I shall be clean; wash me, and I shall be
>   whiter than snow.
> Let me hear joy and gladness; let the bones that you have crushed
>   rejoice.
> Hide your face from my sins, and blot out all my iniquities.
> Create in me a clean heart, O God, and put a new and right spirit
>   within me (*Ps* 51:2-5, 7-10).

Our Tradition says poetically (losing the "robe of glory") what the Scriptures say metaphorically about the image of God. This latter is echoed in the Divine Liturgy, in the prayer after the "Holy, holy…" of the *Anaphora of St. John:*

> **…You sent your Son for our salvation.**
> **He descended, became flesh, suffered,**
> **and was crucified for us,** *who have corrupted his image….*

Traditional Eastern theology—particularly that of the Byzantine Tradition—expresses this idea in terms of humans being created in God's image, but by sin damaging God's likeness. Though God's image is not destroyed, God's likeness in us must be restored. Both Traditions, Syriac and Byzantine, see that sin demands constant renewing in us of God's life.

More will be said below about sin in **"The Mysteries of Healing,"** **Chapters 23** and **24**). However, it is because of this introduction and compounding of sin in the world that the Mystery of Baptism was established by the will of God in Christ, through the Church.

The New Adam

It was and remains the mission of the Word-Who-Assumed, Jesus, to redeem us from this state of affairs (see **PART I, "Jesus, Our Redeemer"**, p. 40). Just as Adam and Eve brought sin into the world, so the Tradition of the Church calls Jesus the "New Adam." He cancels this debt to sin and brings the world new life and salvation. (See *CCC* 683).

This theme of the Old Adam and the New Adam comes from the writings of Paul. It is one of the earliest uses of typology in Christianity and occurs in all Traditions. *Adam* stands for all human beings. Since Jesus is the New Adam, he restores all humanity, through Baptism, to a glory that surpasses even the primordial glory of our first Parents.

Washing Away Sin

Water cleanses. In the baptismal service, water is used to signify the washing away of the effects of the First Sin (in an infant), and also any personal sins of an adult. If the candidate is immersed in the water, to the sign of washing is added the deep symbolism of our dying and rising with the Lord—our dying to a life of sin, and our rising to a life of grace and blessing:

Do you not know that all of us who have been baptized into Christ Jesus were baptized into his death? Therefore we have been buried with him by baptism into death, so that, just as Christ was raised from the dead by the glory of the Father, so we too might walk in newness of life (*Rom* 6:3-4).

The themes we have seen so far are well expressed by the Prayer of Blessing of the Water in the baptismal ritual:

> *O Lord,*
> *drive away the rebellious power*
> *of the enemy from these waters,*
> **from those who enter them to be baptized,**
> **and from this place.**
> **Bestow upon them the**
> **power of the Holy Spirit....**

A New Womb for Spiritual Children

The Syriac Tradition adds the concept that the waters of baptism are a womb, from which will be born new and spiritual children. Thus, the waters of birth are given a dramatic redefinition:

> *As the womb of our mother, Eve,*
> *gave birth to mortal and corruptible children,*
> *so may the womb of this baptismal font*
> *give birth to heavenly and incorruptible children....*
> **And as the Holy Spirit hovered**
> **over the waters at the work of creation,**
> **and gave birth to living creatures and animals**
> **of all kinds,**
> **may he hover over this baptismal font,**
> **which is a spiritual womb.**

> *Instead of an earthly Adam,*
> *may it give birth to a heavenly Adam.*
> *May those who enter it to be baptized*
> *be permanently changed and receive a spiritual nature,*
> *instead of a corporal one;*

> *a participation in the invisible reality,*
> *instead of the visible one;*
> **and instead of the weakness of their spirit,**
> **may the Holy Spirit abide in them.**

The Problem of Evil

When we realize how a great a gift God has given us in Jesus' taking away the effects of sin through our baptism, we also need to reflect that the problem of evil also remains. We rightfully ask, for example, "Why do bad things happen to good people?" Thinkers have never satisfactorily explained the existence of evil. Evil, and its other face, sin, is a mystery indeed. As the *Catechism* (¶385) urges, "We must therefore approach the question of the origin of evil by fixing the eyes of our faith on him who alone is its conqueror."

Two kinds of evil seem to exist: natural disasters or tragedies, and moral evil. The first kind—which includes disasters such as earthquakes and tornadoes—is the result of the natural processes of the earth's continuing growth and development. When these happen, we are tempted to attribute it to evil; in such cases, however, we are too often the passive recipients of what is actually part of nature.

The latter—moral evil—is easier to understand, if more harmful, for we are responsible for it. Homicides and other kinds of murderous, violent actions are the result of our own sinful actions, directly or indirectly intended. Accidents, for example, are in fact often caused by extreme carelessness, drunkenness, improper use of drugs, and so forth. When innocent people, even the environment, are harmed by such irresponsibility, we rightly express this as evil. No amount of rationalizing can excuse it.

What—or who—is the cause of this sin in us? St. Paul, in a classic passage, wonders:

> I do not understand my own actions. For I do not do what I want, but I do the very thing I hate. Now if I do what I do not want, I agree that the law is good. But in fact it is no longer I that do it, but sin that dwells within me. For I know that nothing good dwells within me, that is, in my flesh. I can will what is right, but I cannot do it. For I do not do the good I want, but the evil I do not want is what I do. Now if I do what I do not want, it is no longer I that do it, but sin

that dwells within me. So I find it to be a law that when I want to do what is good, evil lies close at hand. For I delight in the law of God in my inmost self, but I see in my members another law at war with the law of my mind, making me captive to the law of sin that dwells in my members. Wretched man that I am! Who will rescue me from this body of death? Thanks be to God through Jesus Christ our Lord! So then, with my mind I am a slave to the law of God, but with my flesh I am a slave to the law of sin (*Rom* 7:15-25).

Paul sees Sin (with a capital *S*) almost as a fierce actor on the stage of his soul, violently turning him away from the very God he wants to serve. Sin is overwhelming.

Tradition, taking its lead from the many references in Scripture to the action of a personal Evil One and its demons, has identified the personal source of evil as the "Devil," "Satan" or "The Evil One" (*CCC* 391). Although limited in influence over human beings (*CCC* 395), nevertheless, he is to be guarded against, lest we fall prey to his attraction:

And no wonder! Even Satan disguises himself as an angel of light (*2 Cor* 11:14).

Not for nothing does the Lord's Prayer end with the direct petition to God: "… but deliver us from the Evil One.…"

Even sickness, including terminal diseases, is the result of sin. When we hear others ask why someone had to die, for example, because of illness, especially sudden illness, we find ourselves so often unwilling to accept that we are not perfect—even as we may be in the process of being perfected by God—and that the effects of the First Sin are very present, very current and very strong.

For all who eat and drink without discerning the body, eat and drink judgment against themselves. For this reason many of you are weak and ill, and some have died. But if we judged ourselves, we would not be judged. But when we are judged by the Lord, we are disciplined so that we may not be condemned along with the world (*1 Cor* 11:29-32).

What, then, is the answer to the problem—the mystery—of evil? God, who looks after us in loving care, in providence, does not wish us to suffer evil and tragedies. However, he does *permit* such things to happen, and many times only God knows the reason. Also, many times the reason only surfaces much later; it may take the eyes of faith to recognize the answer. Only people of faith and humility can accept this, for the world only laughs at such acceptance:

> I have said this to you, so that in me you may have peace.
> In the world you face persecution. But take courage; I have
> conquered the world!" (*Jn* 16:33).

The other answer is that God knows how to bring good out of evil. Since evil has entered the world by a hand other than God, only the Gracious and Compassionate One can reverse it. As our Liturgy expresses it, in the embolism prayer from the *Anaphora of St. Sixtus*:

> *Hasten, O Lord,*
> *to change all that is detrimental and harmful*
> *into that which will help and benefit us,*
> **and we will glorify you,**
> **now and for ever.**

This is one result of the new life of faith through Baptism. It is one way that God clothes us again in the robe of glory; but it takes time to dress properly!

Warding Off the Power of the Evil One

As Christians who pray daily the prayer that Jesus taught us, the "Our Father," we petition our God to "...deliver us from the power of the Evil One." As people who read the Word of God, we know that a personal agent of evil seeks mightily to turn us from God's Kingdom of Light to its Kingdom of Darkness. In addition, as we have seen above, this life into which we are born is tainted by the reality of sin and evil. One of the purposes of Baptism is to liberate us from sin and bestow new life.

For once you were darkness, but now in the Lord you are light. Live as children of light (*Eph* 5:8).

Wouldn't it be grand if we could avoid all evil and simply live the new life of God! However, the experience of the Church is that, having been given the gift of free will (see **Chapter 3, "Image and Likeness"**), we participate in the evil of the world.

In this context the Maronite Baptismal Ritual speaks, in many places, of petitioning God to ward off the evil we know exists. From the *Epiclesis* over the baptismal water:

> **O Lord,**
> **may the Holy Spirit come and abide**
> **in these waters.**
> *May he drive away from them*
> *the power of the enemy.*
> **May he enkindle them**
> **with an invincible strength.**
> **May he bless + them**
> **sanctify + them**
> **and make them like the waters**
> **which flowed from the side of your only**
> **Son on the Cross...**
> *May they be clad against the attacks*
> *of the evil one with heavenly vesture*
> *and with the shield of faith.*

From the blessing before the first anointing:

> **Indeed, O Lord,**
> **bless + him/her in your name,**
> *and protect him/her with your Cross*
> *from the Evil One and his powers,*
> **now and for ever. Amen.**

Baptism includes four prayers of exorcism, and they all clearly invoke the mighty power of God over the forces of evil. These are to be heeded, not as hyperbole but as a real recognition of the evil that still exists in our world, and of the existence of its Perpetrator.

Lastly, the parents and Godparent(s)—all present may participate—are asked formally to make a renunciation of Satan on behalf of the candidate (if an infant), or the candidate is asked directly, if adult:

> **I renounce you, Satan,**
> **all your angels,**
> **all your powers,**
> **all your worldly pomp,**
> **all your corrupt teachings**
> **and all that is from you.**

Those involved in the Initiation ritual should be reminded clearly about just what they are uttering at this point: The renunciations stand at the heart of the Christian response to God in faith, through these sacramental Mysteries of Initiation. If an adult catechumen is involved, the reality of a sinful life will be enough to allow him or her to see the value of this renunciation.

STUDY QUESTIONS:
1) Reflect on the relationship of the Mystery of Baptism to sin.
2) What is the significance of the Syriac theological symbol of the "Robe of Glory"?
3) Reflect upon the role of Baptism in understanding the problem of evil.

Chapter 17:
Initiation: Baptism II, New Life in God

The Gift of Faith

Opposed to the battle with Satan is the great gift of faith and the new life that comes with it. The Bible—both the Hebrew Scriptures as well as the New Testament—is full of references to faith. (The NRSV uses the word *faith* and its derivatives 542 times.) In fact, from the human point of view, we must say that faith is the message of the Bible: God speaks to humanity and invites a response of and in faith.

Faith is one of the three "Theological Virtues" (see *CCC* 1814). Faith is celebrated in Baptism. Given as a gift through the cooperation and consent of parents and Godparent(s), the newly Initiated grows in the life of faith, nourishes the gift and makes it one's own. By faith, a person comes to respond to the Word of God, and to the life of the Trinity given at Baptism.

In handing on—this is the root meaning of "Tradition"—the Faith, parents must realize that they are the child's first religious educators. The task of the godparent(s) is to support the child's parents in this mission. Parents and godparents need to understand this before the Initiation takes place, particularly in the pre-Jordan classes.

Grace as Indwelling of the Trinity

Thomas Merton once said, "The things we really need come to us only as gifts." He was expressing a truth about a reality in which we participate by being joined to the Trinity in Baptism: We experience and live the life of grace, which is a gift of God.

What is grace?

St. Paul speaks eloquently of grace in the context of salvation:

> But the free gift is not like the trespass. For if the many died through the one man's trespass, much more surely have the grace of God and the free gift in the grace of the one man, Jesus Christ, abounded for the many. And the free

gift is not like the effect of the one man's sin. For the judgment following one trespass brought condemnation, but the free gift following many trespasses brings justification (*Rom* 5:15-16).

But God, who is rich in mercy, out of the great love with which he loved us even when we were dead through our trespasses, made us alive together with Christ—by grace you have been saved—and raised us up with him and seated us with him in the heavenly places in Christ Jesus, so that in the ages to come he might show the immeasurable riches of his grace in kindness toward us in Christ Jesus (*Eph* 2:4-7).

Grace is, above all, a gift. In fact, the Greek word for grace conveys the idea that it is something that is freely given. Eastern Tradition sees this gift as no less than God's life itself—this is grace. The idea is expressed in the Eastern Teachers as the "indwelling" of God, the Holy Trinity.

A good example from our Divine Liturgy can be seen in the closing of the Penitential Rite (just before the Invitation to Communion). The Celebrant blesses with:

> *May the grace*
> *of the Most Holy Trinity* +
> **eternal and co-equal in essence,**
> **be with you, my brothers and sisters,**
> **for ever.**

Baptism, in giving us a share in the life of the Trinity, gives us a share in the life of grace. The text of the Mystery of Holy Baptism expresses it thus in the Rite of Admission of the Candidate. The following prayer is said over the mother, but could well apply to both parents:

> **... Send the grace of your Holy Spirit upon her.**
> **Sanctify her body and soul**
> **and adorn her with holiness.**
> *Make her a pure vessel*
> *for the glory of your divinity*

and enable her to enter your holy temple....

It is clear from this prayer that it is possible for us creatures of God to have divinity reside in us. God's Presence is grace. Thus, men and women have become brothers and sisters in the Lord through the life of the Trinity given in Baptism. The *Catechism* also expresses this Eastern theme in paragraph 1997.

This is a very personal way of thinking about grace. In the Maronite Divine Liturgy grace is poignantly described in the *Qolo* for the commemoration of the martyrs on Fridays:

> **For their love of the cross**
> **the martyrs bore all hardships,**
> *and like a mother, the grace of the Lord*
> *sustained them at the hour of their death.*

In a secondary way, the life of the Trinity is expressed in the liturgical tradition by the plural: "graces." This term conveys the blessings that come to us as daily gifts and helps for Christian living. Although many examples could be given, the final blessing of the Divine Liturgy expresses this idea well:

> **Go in peace, beloved brothers and sisters,**
> *accompanied by the nourishment and graces*
> *you received from the forgiving altar of the Lord.*
> *May the blessing of the Most Holy Trinity remain*
> *with you:*
> **the + Father, and the + Son, and the + Holy Spirit,**
> **one God, to whom be glory, for ever. Amen.**

Participation in the Mystery of the Life of the Trinity

We are transformed in grace. The Syriac Antiochenes prefer to speak of our *participation* in the divine life of the Trinity. The Greek Fathers,

5ᵗʰ *Sunday of Resurrection*
Lk 5:27-39

by contrast, use the term *divinization*, (the Greek word is *theosis*).

In both Traditions (as for all), the end result of the Christian life is the same: union with God. By our participation in God's life, we become truly Godlike. This is what Adam and Eve tried so arrogantly to achieve, but they lost their glorious robes in the attempt. Now, by the grace of God in Christ, we can recover the robe of glory. We do not actually become God, for we shall always remain God's creation; but we intimately share the divine life mystically here on earth and will share it fully as creatures transformed in the Kingdom that is to come. In and through the Holy Mystery of Baptism, we are given a profound share in the life of grace; and the life of grace profoundly assists in our Christian life.

The following prayer of the Congregation before Communion in the Divine Service expresses this idea well:

> **You have united, O Lord,**
> **your divinity with our humanity**
> **and our humanity with your divinity;**
> **your life with our mortality**
> **and our mortality with your life.**
> ***You have assumed what is ours,***
> ***and you have given us what is yours,***
> **for the life and salvation of our souls.**
> **To you be glory for ever. Amen.**

The Necessity of Baptism

The Church has always taught that Baptism is necessary for salvation. The Gospels record: "Jesus answered, 'Very truly, I tell you, no one can enter the kingdom of God without being born of water and spirit'" (*Jn* 3:5; see also *Mt* 28:18-20; *Ti* 3:4-7 *Ti* 3:4-7;). As the *Catechism* affirms:

> Baptism is necessary for salvation for those to whom the Gospel has been proclaimed and who have had the possibility of asking for this sacrament (*CCC* 1257).

This puts the burden of preaching Christ to others and to preach effectively and convincingly. When this happens Baptism with water is necessary and appropriate.

Other Forms of Baptism

In addition to Baptism with water the Church has always recognized two ways other than the ritual pouring of water by means of which baptism may be received: baptism of blood (*CCC* 1258), for those who die for the faith before ritual baptism (see **"Martyrs"** in **Chapter 4**), and baptism of desire (*CCC* 1259), for catechumens who die before they are baptized ritually and who have repented of their sins.

The traditional recognition of other ways of receiving baptism has always signaled a broader vision of the Mystery than the pouring of water. In this context the former Western idea of *Limbo* has finally been put to rest in the *Catechism* (*CCC* 1261). The idea of *Limbo* was a theological thought of the Latin Church of the Middle Ages and never a formal doctrine. The *Catechism* expresses the hope for the salvation of these souls based on the great mercy of God, as it recalls the words of Jesus, "Let the little children come to me, do not hinder them…" (*Mk* 10:14).

There are proper effects in each of the Mysteries. Baptism washes away sin, thus recreating us and restoring our nature to the state for which we were destined by God at creation. This is symbolized by the image restoring the robe of glory. Baptism also puts us into a new relationship to God, the Holy Trinity, by which our lives are set in the direction of glory in the Kingdom (divinization). Too, it incorporates us into the Body of Christ, which is the Church. This is the beginning of our Initiation. As the *Sedro* from the ritual states:

> **… Lord God,**
> **now extend the right hand of your mercy**
> **upon your servant who is prepared**
> **for holy baptism.**
> *Sanctify, purify and cleanse him/her*
> *through your forgiving hyssop.*
> *Bless and protect your people and your inheritance.*
> *You have clothed us, through your baptism,*
> *with the robe of glory*
> *and with the seal of the*
> *Holy and life-giving Spirit.*
> *and called us to be spiritual children*
> *in the second birth of holy and*
> *forgiving baptism.…*

Canonical Considerations

Because Baptism imparts on the soul an indelible spiritual sign, a character that is a consecration of the person for Christian worship, Baptism and Chrismation may not be repeated. (Parents and catechists of all Eastern Catholic children must remember this, especially if children are enrolled in a Roman Catholic school or religious education program, lest the children be presented for Chrismation along with their class.)

In order for Baptism/Chrismation—indeed, all of the sacramental Mysteries—to take place, certain regulations must be observed. This has been made clear in the recent promulgation of the *Code of Canons of the Eastern Churches,* which lists such regulations and laws. A summary of these for the Initiation Mysteries appears in **Appendix I: "Our Maronite Customs."**

STUDY QUESTIONS:
1) How is faith a gift from God?
2) Reflect upon grace as indwelling of the Trinity in the life of the soul. How does a baptized and chrismated believer "participate" in the Divine Life?
3) What are the two forms of Baptism other than Baptism with water?

Chapter 18:
Initiation: Chrismation

Seal of the Spirit on Our Baptism

Immediately following the bestowal of the Mystery of Baptism, the Celebrant anoints the newly baptized with Holy Myron, also known as Chrism (hence "Chrismation"), three times while praying the following:

> **With the Myron of Christ our God,**
> **sweet fragrance of the true faith,**
> **seal and fullness of the grace**
> **of the heavenly Spirit,**
> **N., the servant of God, is sealed**
> **in the name of the + Father,**
> **and of the + Son,**
> **and of the + Holy Spirit.**

This formula of Chrismation teaches us that this sacramental Mystery is a "seal" put upon Baptism. It completes the next stage of what was started in Baptism and looks forward to the completion of the Mysteries of Initiation with the reception of Holy Communion.

In paragraphs 1293 and 1294 the *Catechism* describes the idea of anointing as "sealing," healing and consecration.

Effects of Chrismation: Fullness of the Spirit

Sometimes Chrismation is popularly associated exclusively with the Holy Spirit, as if there were no other connection to the Spirit in the other Mysteries of Initiation. We must remember, however, that during Baptism, the newly baptized is in fact initiated into the divine life of the Trinity: Father, Son *and Holy Spirit*. As the text expresses, the candidate now receives the "'fullness' of the grace of the heavenly Spirit." What does this mean?

The Liturgy for Pentecost tells us in the *Qolo* for the day:

> ... **In the likeness of tongues of fire**
> **the Spirit of consolation came down.**
> **He overshadowed the assembly of the apostles,**
> **gathered in the Upper Room.**
> *By his overshadowing,*
> *they were filled with light.*
> *They came out announcing to the world:*
> *The Son has risen from the tomb,*
> *in the glory of his divinity....*

The italicized lines of the first strophe state three important things about the work of the Holy Spirit in us:

❖ When an *Epiclesis* of the Third Divine Person is made, the Spirit overshadows us, just as at Pentecost, at Jesus' Baptism and at the Divine Liturgy.

❖ The candidate is given *light*, a foreshadowing of the Kingdom.

❖ The candidate is given power and strength to witness to Christ in the world.

Perfecting the Priesthood of Jesus Christ

Through the indwelling of the Spirit, especially as the candidate is being initiated into the Body of Christ, a share in the priesthood of Christ is given (*CCC* 1305), as the author of First Peter tells us:

Come to him, a living stone, though rejected by mortals yet chosen and precious in God's sight, and like living stones, let yourselves be built into a spiritual house, to be a holy priesthood, to offer spiritual sacrifices acceptable to God through Jesus Christ (*1 Pt* 2:4-5).

(The Priesthood of Christ will be discussed later, in **Chapter 25**.)

Gifts, Charisms, Fruit of the Spirit

The Holy Spirit bestows two kinds of gifts. The first kind is intended for the sanctification of the person who receives them. They are permanent, supernatural qualities that enable the graced person to be especially in tune with the inspirations of the Holy Spirit. The first kind of gifts are *wisdom* (which helps a person value the things of heaven—see *Sir* 1:12), *understanding* (which enables the person to grasp the truths of religion), *counsel* (which helps one see and correctly choose the best practical approach in serving God), *fortitude* (which steels a person's resolve in overcoming obstacles to living the faith), *knowledge* (which helps one see the path to follow and the dangers to one's faith), *piety* (which fills a person with confidence in God and an eagerness to serve God), and *fear of the Lord* (which makes a person keenly aware of God's sovereignty and the respect due to God and divine laws)(*CCC* 1830-31).

A second kind of gifts of the Spirit is called charisms. They are extraordinary favors granted principally for the help of others. *1 Cor* 12:6-11 mentions nine charisms. They are: speaking with wisdom, speaking with knowledge, faith, healing, miracles, prophecy, discerning of spirits, tongues, and interpreting speeches.

St. Paul tells us in the *Letter to the Galatians* (5:22-23) of the "fruit" of the Spirit that result from the Christian's response the Spirit: love, joy, peace, patience, kindness, goodness, faithfulness, gentleness and self-control. Surely these are also signs that the Holy Spirit of God dwells within us (*CCC* 736).

These Gifts, Charisms and Fruit of the Holy Spirit are not only for our upbuilding, however important and necessary this is. The power of the Holy Spirit is given to help us accomplish the chrismational mission of the Church in bringing the Gospel and the name of Jesus to the world—that is, to *evangelize*. As Jesus moved forward in his ministry from his baptism by John in the Jordan River, so in a similar way, we are called to go out to the world to do God's work.

Discipleship

Another word for following Christ in his work of sanctifying the world by spreading the message of the Gospel is *discipleship*. We are to follow the Master, listen to his word, and put it into practice. This is the message of the Gospel for the 3rd Sunday of Epiphany.

3ʳᵈ *Sunday of Epiphany*
Jn 1:35-42

Like Martha of Bethany, sister of Mary and Lazarus, we can be busy about many practical things that may or may not be related to the Gospel. But Jesus tells Martha that the real task is to listen to his words:

Now as they went on their way, he entered a certain village, where a woman named Martha welcomed him into her home. She had a sister named Mary, who sat at the Lord's feet and listened to what he was saying. But Martha was distracted by her many tasks; so she came to him and asked, "Lord, do you not care that my sister has left me to do all the work by myself? Tell her then to help me." But the Lord answered her, "Martha, Martha, you are worried and distracted by many things; there is need of only one thing. Mary has chosen the better part, which will not be taken away from her" (*Lk* 10:38-42).

It is true that we must responsibly live out our lives by performing many tasks. But Jesus tells us that these necessary tasks must not deter us from the prior task of following him first above all. This message is stated in the New Testament in many different ways; following Jesus in discipleship is the heart of the Gospel and the result of our Chrismation.

Evangelization

> **Sunday of the
> Visitation to Elizabeth
> Lk 1:39-56**

If we become disciples by the Mysteries of Initiation, and thereby hear the Word of the Lord, we may not afford ourselves the luxury of thinking that hearing the Word is enough. By our Chrismation the Holy Spirit sends us out on mission—to share the Good News of Christ with others. This is called *evangelization*, or, *Gospelling*.

Therefore, as Christian disciples we ought to have a good knowledge, a correct interpretation and a deep love of the Holy Scriptures, especially the Gospels (see **Part II**). They are, after all, God's Word of salvation to us, as well as the foundation of all that we are and do. So, they should have a very direct and important influence on our lives. We look to the Word of God not only for inspiration but for true instruction in living God's Way:

> All scripture is inspired by God and is useful for teaching, for reproof, for correction, and for training in righteousness, so that everyone who belongs to God may be proficient, equipped for every good work (*2 Tim* 3:16-17).

We are called to be like Mary, who shares the Word in her womb with her cousin Elizabeth, and like John, who, in his mother Elizabeth's womb, jumps for joy at the coming into his home of the Word. This portrait in Luke's Gospel symbolizes and involves the young and the elderly in a community presentation of and response to God's revelation in Jesus.

> For, "Everyone who calls on the name of the Lord shall be saved." But how are they to call on one in whom they have not believed? And how are they to believe in one of whom they have never heard? And how are they to hear without someone to proclaim him? And how are they to proclaim him unless they are sent? As it is written, "How beautiful are the feet of those who bring good news!" But not all have obeyed the good news; for Isaiah says, "Lord, who has believed our message?" So faith comes from what is heard, and what is heard comes through the word of Christ (*Rom* 10:10-17).

As this Bible passage shows—and with it a wealth of official teaching in Church Tradition—our Gracious God wills that all persons come to salvation through hearing and believing in the truth of God revealed in Jesus.

Especially since the Council, the Church has realized that it must use all that is available in today's world to spread the Word of God effectively. This includes all the technological means of communication at our disposal. We are encouraged in this by the Council's Document, "Decree on the Instruments of Social Communication" (*Inter Mirifica*). What is amazing is the burgeoning of technology since the publication of the Decree in December of 1963, particularly the use of cyberspace. This can only mean that there are even more ways now to spread the Word of God and the teachings of the Church in an effective manner.

Maronite Tradition is strong in expressing its gratitude to those who have labored to pass on the Faith. These are referred to as "teachers" and are most often included with our relatives in prayers of remembrance. The fifth Intercession in the *Anaphora of the Twelve* expresses this poignantly:

> **Remember, O Lord, assembly of our ancestors and *teachers of the true faith*,**

who have kept your truth safe,
and have borne sufferings on behalf of your
Church.
Grant us to preserve their truth on our lips,
to follow in their steps ...

By sharing the Word in a gentle, yet powerful and persuasive way, we follow in the steps of Mary, Elizabeth and John the Forerunner, who were, from the beginning of the Christian adventure, teachers and evangelists.

STUDY QUESTIONS:
1) What is the relationship of Chrismation to Baptism?
2) In what way(s) can Chrismation be considered a "personal Pentecost"?
3) What are the effects of Chrismation?

Chapter 19:
Initiation: Eucharist

The third Mystery of Initiation is the Holy Eucharist. Every time we receive it, we participate fully in the membership of the Church. We not only receive the Body of Christ but also mystically affirm ourselves as members of the Body of Christ. Our Initiation is complete, but our mission continues.

4ᵗʰ Sunday of Epiphany
Jn 15:1-8

Anamnesis

The words of the First Eucharist are recorded in four places in the New Testament: three times in the Synoptic Gospels and once in a letter of St. Paul:

> While they were eating, he took a loaf of bread, and after blessing it he broke it, gave it to them, and said, "Take; this is my body." Then he took a cup, and after giving thanks he gave it to them, and all of them drank from it. He said to them, "This is my blood of the covenant, which is poured out for many (*Mk* 14:22-24).

> While they were eating, Jesus took a loaf of bread, and after blessing it he broke it, gave it to the disciples, and said, "Take, eat; this is my body." Then he took a cup, and after giving thanks he gave it to them, saying, "Drink from it, all of you; for this is my blood of the covenant, which is poured out for many for the forgiveness of sins (*Mt* 26:26-28).

> Then he took a loaf of bread, and when he had given
> thanks, he broke it and gave it to them, saying, "This is my
> body, which is given for you. Do this in remembrance of
> me." And he did the same with the cup after supper, saying,
> "This cup that is poured out for you is the new covenant in
> my blood (*Lk* 22:19-20).

> For I received from the Lord what I also handed on to you,
> that the Lord Jesus on the night when he was betrayed took
> a loaf of bread, and when he had given thanks, he broke it
> and said, "This is my body that is for you. Do this in
> remembrance of me." In the same way he took the cup also,
> after supper, saying, "This cup is the new covenant in my
> blood. Do this, as often as you drink it, in remembrance of
> me" (*1 Cor* 11:23-25).

Even though they differ slightly in wording, these four recordings
show that the Last Supper was important enough for the early Church to
commit them to writing. However, this was no mere memory of an event
that they recorded, as if done once and then merely remembered. This
remembering was powerful enough to be recognized as a real recreating of
the Last Supper every time the words are spoken. Indeed, not only the
events of Thursday of these Mysteries, but also Great Friday's witnessing
of the death of the Lord. It is, in Eastern Church terminology, *anamnesis*,
a Greek word meaning "remembrance."

Anamnesis is a mysterious, sacramental, making-present of the
saving events of our redemption, and not a mere recalling. This sacrifice
was real and unrepeatable in terms of salvation. What Christ did for us on
the Cross was enough for all time to keep on saving us to the end of time:

> For Christ did not enter a sanctuary made by human hands,
> a mere copy of the true one, but he entered into heaven
> itself, now to appear in the presence of God on our behalf.
> Nor was it to offer himself again and again, as the high
> priest enters the Holy Place year after year with blood that
> is not his own; for then he would have had to suffer again
> and again since the foundation of the world. But as it is, he
> has appeared once for all at the end of the age to remove
> sin by the sacrifice of himself (*Heb* 9:24-25).

However, as Jesus is quoted at the Last Supper, we are urged again and again to repeat the sacramental ritual of the Eucharist, knowing that these events are spiritually and mystically re-enacted for our sake. Thus, when we celebrate the Eucharist at the Lord's command, we remember his Death and Resurrection until he comes again: as Paul quotes of Jesus, "...in remembrance of me." As the first *Anamnesis* prayer of the Congregation in every Divine Liturgy says:

> *O Lord, we remember your death,*
> *we witness to your resurrection,*
> **we await your second coming,**
> **we implore your compassion,**
> **and we ask for the forgiveness of our sins.**
> **May your mercy come upon us all.**

Christ Among Us

It is not only, however, that the Paschal Mystery is made present among us when we remember the death of the Lord; Christ himself dwells among us in a true and real manner. Even though we receive what appears to us as bread and wine, we believe in faith that it is the Body and Blood of Jesus, Redeemer and Bread of Life. As St. Ephrem reminds us, the Eucharist is "the same reality in a different garment." In another place Ephrem describes the Mother of Jesus speaking to him in the Divine Eucharist:

> I see you, my Son, under the species of bread,
>> as I saw you in the crib.
> Is it only to me, O Son,
>> that in two images you show your beauty?
> The bread manifests itself
>> as well as the Spirit.
> Remain in the bread
>> and in those who eat it.
> In what is seen and unseen,
>> may the Church see you as your Mother does.

The prayer that the priest proclaims before the Congregation, after the distribution of Holy Communion is completed, shows this belief in the Real Presence clearly:

> **We render always glory**
> **and thanksgiving to you, O Lord,**
> *for giving us your Body to eat*
> *and your Blood to drink.*
> **O Lover of all,**
> **have mercy on us!**

The belief in the Real Presence of Christ in the Eucharist is at the heart of Catholic teaching and faith. Curiously, those who claim to read the Bible literally do not believe the words of Jesus when it says that Jesus took bread and wine and changed them into his own Body and Blood. As Catholics we have always taken these words literally.

As we gaze into the sanctuary and see the sanctuary candle lighted before the Tabernacle (where the Eucharist is kept), we are always reminded that the Lord Jesus is present among us as our Light and Life.

The Fundamental Mystery Creates the Church

The fundamental sacramental Mystery of the Church is the Eucharist because it is truly the Body and Blood of Christ—the way Christ dwells among us today.

Look at it in this way: because Christ is present in his Church as the Eucharist, he forms his Body of Believers, called the Church. Since the Church exists as the sacramental Presence of Christ, the Church, therefore, is the context wherein the other Mysteries are celebrated. We enter through Baptism, we are strengthened for mission and service by the chrismational Gifts of the Spirit, and we are nourished by the Eucharist of God in Christ (*CCC* 1396). Only when we receive the Divine Eucharist is our membership in the Assembly of Believers complete.

This is seen ritually as well, in an expressive liturgical gesture within the regular celebration of the Holy Mysteries (just before Communion), as well as in the ordination rites. The Celebrant of the Service touches the paten and chalice holding the Body and Blood of Jesus with his left hand and extends his right hand over the congregation (or the ordination candidate) and prays over them (him). The intimate relationship between the power of the Eucharist to those whom it is directed can thus be seen. In the case of the Divine Liturgy, this action makes the congregation one in the love of the Lord; in ordination, this eucharistic power creates ministers to serve the Church as ordained, and in turn to make the Eucharist available to the rest of the Church.

"O Bread of Life"

A well-known hymn of our Church celebrates Jesus as the "Bread of Life," a theme taken from the sixth chapter of St. John's Gospel (*Jn* 6:48-51). We sing:

> **O Bread of Life, O Food of Souls,**
> **the pledge of heavenly joy:**
> **the Son of God and Son of Man,**
> **the Merciful Lord...**

The Gospel remembers and the Church witnesses to the fact that the Eucharist is real food for our souls. Just as the Israelites needed to eat the manna that God sent them to live in their desert wandering, and just as we need to be nourished by food and drink to continue to exist physically, so we need the Bread of Life for the life of our souls. As the *Catechism* expresses it:

> *Holy Communion augments our union with Christ.* The principal fruit of receiving the Eucharist in Holy Communion is an intimate union with Christ Jesus. Indeed, the Lord said: "He who eats my flesh and drinks my blood abides in me and I in him" (*Jn* 6:56). Life in Christ has its foundation in the Eucharistic banquet: "As the living Father sent me, and I live because of the Father, so he who eats me will live because of me" (*Jn* 6:57).

Then in the same paragraph the *Catechism* quotes from the Syriac Office of Antioch:

> On the feasts of the Lord, when the faithful receive the Body of the Son, they proclaim to one another the Good News that the first fruits of life have been given, as when the angel said to Mary Magdalene, "Christ is risen!" Now too are life and resurrection conferred on whoever receives Christ (*CCC* 1391).

This aspect makes the Mystery of the Eucharist the third Mystery of Initiation. The first post-Communion Thanksgiving prayer of the *Anaphora of St. Sixtus* expresses this idea well:

O Lord,
our mouths, used to earthly food,
give you thanks for your grace
which enables us to receive the divine gift
of the Body and Blood of your only Son.
With Christ and through him,
glory, honor, and power are due to you, O Father,
and to your Holy Spirit,
now and for ever. Amen.

By thus becoming full members of the Church in the reception of the Holy Eucharist, we can go on being nourished by the frequent, even daily, reception of Communion, provided we are in proper relationship to the Lord. This means that we are free from serious sin and have a sincere desire to receive the Lord Jesus into our bodies and souls.

Ra'bono: Pledge of Eternal Life

A second important theme of our Church about Eucharist contained in the hymn "O Bread of Life" is expressed in the phrase, "… the pledge of heavenly joy …" In Syriac the word "pledge" is *ra'bono*. Since we are pilgrims passing through this earthly dimension on our way to our Heavenly Home, the Kingdom (see **Chapter 14, "Human Destiny"**), we strive daily to nurture our contact with Living God. In this life we "walk by faith, not by sight (*2 Cor* 5:7)." On our walk with the Lord, we need the assurance often that the promise of the Lord will be fulfilled. We trust; still, a frequent assurance will bolster our trust and our faith.

The assurance, the pledge, of eternal life—the contact with the Lord for which we long—is found in the Eucharist. By our fruitful reception of the risen Lord in Holy Communion, we know he not only comes to us today but also waits on the Other Side, ready to meet and greet us conditioned by our earthly faithfulness to him. The *Catechism* quotes the Antiochene Bishop Ignatius as he comments precisely on this point:

> There is no surer pledge or clearer sign of this great hope in the new heavens and new earth "in which righteousness dwells (*2 Pet* 3:13)," than the Eucharist. Every time this mystery is celebrated, "the work of our redemption is

carried on" and we "break the one bread that provides the medicine of immortality, the antidote for death, and the food that makes us live for ever in Jesus Christ (*CCC* 1405).

The Divine Liturgy often expresses this idea of the Eucharist as pledge. A good example of this may be seen in the closing of the Trinitarian Prayer of the *Anaphora of St. John*:

> **May these Mysteries sanctify the bodies and souls**
> **of those who participate in them,**
> **for the purity of their hearts,**
> **the cleansing of their thoughts,**
> **the holiness of their souls,**
> ***and as a pledge of the heavenly kingdom***
> **and a new life, for ever. Amen.**

"Fire and Spirit"

Another important Syriac theme used to describe how the mystery of the Eucharist is linked to the power of the Holy Spirit comes from the writing of St. Ephrem, who loves to use this metaphor for the power of the Eucharist:

> The Prophets have called the Most High a fire
> "a devouring fire," and "who can dwell with it?"
> The people were not able to dwell in it;
> its might crushed the peoples and they were confounded.
> In it, with the anointing you have been anointed;
> you have put him on in the water;
> in the bread you have eaten him;
> in the wine you have drunk him;
> in the voice you have heard him;
> and in the eye of the mind you have seen him!
> *(Hymns for the Feast of the Epiphany, #22)*

This Syriac idea is reflected in many places in the Maronite liturgical tradition. One example appears in the *Qolo* for the *Hoosoyo* for the Sunday of the Renewal of the Church (first Sunday of the Liturgical Year):

> **Blessed are you, O holy and faithful Church:**
> **the Bridegroom who betrothed you**
> **offered you good and rich pastures;**
> **he brought a beverage to your wedding banquet**
> **which satisfies the thirst of your guests for ever.**
> **Come forth:**
> ***eat fire in the bread***
> ***and drink spirit in the wine.***
> ***It is in fire and spirit that you shall be glorified***
> **and enter the kingdom in his company.**

"Holy Things for the Holy": The Eucharist as Forgiveness of Sins

A standard Eucharistic phrase in Eastern liturgies is "Holy Things for the holy…" The first part of the phrase ("Holy Things" with a capital *H*) refers to the Eucharistic Species, and the latter ("…for the holy," small *h*) refers to those who *have been made worthy*—holy—to receive the Holy Things. The Maronite Divine Service has the Celebrant hold up the Eucharist before the Congregation just before the distribution of Communion and proclaim:

> **Holy Things for the holy,**
> **with perfection, purity and sanctity.**

Having completed the Rite of Forgiveness of the Service, those who are properly disposed to receive Jesus are invited to do so. What is important here is the double use of the word "holy" in English; these two uses of the term are not, strictly speaking, equal. "Holy Things" are nothing less than Jesus Present in Mystery—as God, the Source of all holiness. If we are holy, it is only that God has made us such, that is, by God's initiative, God's grace. Here is deep theology in a brief phrase.

Put in another way, *the Eucharist forgives sin.* This aspect of the Eucharist is central to its many meanings and should never be forgotten. This can be seen in Jesus' own words about the cup he shared at the Last Supper: "Drink from it, all of you; for this is my blood of the covenant, which is poured out for many for the forgiveness of sins" (*Mt* 26:27b-28).

Our Divine Liturgy expresses this theme of the Eucharistic forgiveness of sins well, in the various *Anaphorae*. In the prayer following the *Epiclesis* of the *Anaphora Twelve Apostles* it couldn't be more clearly stated:

> May these holy Mysteries
> *be for the pardon of our faults,*
> the cure of our souls and bodies,
> and the strengthening of our consciences,
> so that none of your faithful may perish.
> Rather, may we live by your Spirit,
> lead a pure life,
> And give you glory,
> now and for ever. Amen.

Thursday of the Mysteries: the Eucharist as Service to Others

As a Church of the Syro-Antiochene Tradition, our Maronite Church generally reflects the parent Tradition in paying attention to the human side of the mystery of the Incarnation, stated more clearly in the Synoptic tradition of the Gospels of Matthew, Mark and Luke.

Curiously, however, on Thursday in Passion Week the Service commemorating the Institution of the Eucharist reflects the Tradition of the Gospel of John. During this Service the emphasis on the Body and Blood of Christ as Bread of Life at a meal is equaled by the emphasis on *service to others in humility* as the direct consequence of the love of Christ in the Eucharist. This is seen most clearly in the texts of the Service of the Word: Christ's washing the feet of the Apostles. The *Proemion* of the day expresses this theme beautifully:

> May we be worthy to praise, glorify, and honor
> Christ, the most High and exalted One,
> *who willed to humble himself* and accept death...
> He humbly washed the feet of his disciples
> and taught them the great and hidden mystery
> of his descent to our human weakness.
> *In so doing, he imparted an authentic example*
> *to be handed down to his Church.*
> Glory and honor to Christ,
> now and for ever. Amen.

We are truly called to be other Christs today, in service and love. We accomplish this by a life that seeks not our own selfish gain, but rather the good of others. The Church teaches us how to do this in many ways. One good way is by practicing the Corporal and Spiritual Works of Mercy (see this in **Chapter 28, "Living a Moral Life II"** below).

The Eucharist: the Humility of Our Savior

In the *Proemion* for Weekday Wednesdays (Memorial for the Virgin Mary), we pray:

> **May we offer glory, praise and honor**
> *to the exalted One, who humbled himself*
> **and exalted the humble Virgin;**
> **to God, who became flesh**
> **and saved our human race;**
> *to the Most high, who lowered himself*
> *and raised up the lowly.*
> **To Christ, the Good One, are due glory and honor,**
> **now and for ever. Amen.**

Reflection upon the Mystery of the Eucharist needs to be linked to reflection upon the mystery of the Incarnation, in this fashion (see *Phil* 2:6-11): the pre-existent, eternal and glorious Word of the Father "condescended" to become human. In doing so, he willingly set himself up to be misunderstood and rejected, as the Gospels record (see especially the Gospel of Mark). Even further, he allowed himself to be abused and debased in the human shame of the crucifixion. But God the Father vindicated Jesus as the Christ (*Rom* 6:4).

Yet, even though in glory now, the Risen Christ still willingly submits to humility in every Eucharist. Think about it: When he was on earth, people could see a human Jesus and the possibility that he was sent to earth by God, for he told us that he had divinity residing in him. But this is not so easy to see in the Eucharist. In the Eucharist we need the supreme act of faith that the fullness of Christ's divinity rests in what looks like ordinary bread. Jesus is not only the Bread of Life; Jesus, the risen Lord, is very life itself.

Whenever we are tempted to receive the Eucharist without utter faith and devotion, we risk subjecting our witness to Jesus to indifference. Christ humbly submits to us. Receiving the Eucharistic Bread in all its humility is a lot like the shepherds at the birth of Jesus: they witnessed an infant who was divinity in a tiny bundle. Or can we say with the centurion under the Cross: This was truly the Son of God (see *Mk* 15:39)? Do we truly believe? The *Qolo* for Mondays (Commemoration of the Angels) reminds us:

> *Behold, Christ is distributed by human hands.*
> *He allowed himself to become a sacrifice*
> *for the sake of sinners*
> **that they may live by him.**

Approaching the Eucharist with Reverence

First-time visitors to an Eastern Rite Liturgy often remark upon the real sense of reverence with which the Divine Service is conducted. This reverence is felt in the inspiring prayers, too. Eastern Rite "natives" often remark, after a vacation, how much they missed their own Liturgy, how they sometimes felt like they "hadn't gone to church" by worshiping at another church. The Liturgy of the East has this sense of awe and reverence built right into its very character. That's why it should never be rushed, either by clergy or laity. (No Catholic Liturgy should!)

In addition, the issues of dressing properly, arriving several minutes early and staying until the very end of the Divine Service are not so much signs of show or even of discipline (though they are that, too) as much as an external acknowledgment that worship is the noblest and holiest thing that a human being can do. These simple things say that we indeed reverence the One who has created, redeemed and sanctifies us.

As we approach to receive the Eucharist, we are in holy company. As the hymn which is sung during the Celebrant's reception of Holy Communion expresses:

> *Hosts of Heaven*
> *stand with us*
> *at the altar.*
>
> **They carry in procession**
> **God's atoning lamb**
> **sacrificed before us.**
>
> **Let us all approach**
> **and receive Him**
> **for our forgiveness.**
>
> **Alleluia!**

This respect for the Body and Blood of Christ is why we are still asked by Church law to fast for one hour before receiving. Fasting enables us to be properly disposed to receive this precious Gift, the very Son of God, made present for us in the mystery of the Holy Mysteries. In addition we must be sacramentally absolved of serious sin before we may take Holy Communion.

After all, we have, as humans, been entrusted with the greatest responsibility. Again, as the *Qolo* for Weekday Mondays observes:

> **O Savior of all,**
> **you chose us to minister at your mysteries,**
> **to carry your body and blood within the church**
> ***with solemnity and dignity.***

STUDY QUESTIONS:
1) Explain how the Eucharist is the Real Presence of Christ.
2) How is the Eucharist the fundamental Mystery that creates the Church?
3) Explain the relationship of the Eucharist to the forgiveness of sins.

Chapter 20:
The Worship That Is Due to God

Why Worship?

It is not enough to say that one is a Christian. One must show forth a godly life in Christian love and concern. Repeatedly the Lord warned against mere lip service to faith and community belonging:

> None of those who cry out "Lord, Lord," will enter the kingdom of God, but only the one who does the will of my Father in heaven (*Mt* 7:21).

Another action marks someone who realizes the right relationship of himself or herself to the Creator: worship of God with all one's heart because this is due to the One who created us and dwells in majesty above all (*CCC* 2096). We should know this from the First Commandment as well. Majesty belongs to the Lamb:

> Worthy is the Lamb that was slain
>   to receive power and riches,
>   wisdom and strength,
>   honor and glory and praise!
>   (*Rev* 5:12)

Constantly, Maronite liturgical tradition calls attention to this central fact of existence: *God, the Mighty One, yet Compassionate and Merciful, is to be adored.*

We are encouraged by professing our faith openly in a welcoming and like-minded assembly of fellow believers when we are worshiping God together:

> Where two or three are gathered in my name, there I am in their midst (*Mt* 18:20).

In a world characterized by a variety of religions other than Christianity, or in the face of increasing atheism and indifference to religion, many still feel a need to share Christian faith. Christians in general need to recognize that it is in our churches that we may freely express our common beliefs to and with one another. Worship time is fundamental to the mutual support of believers in the Holy Trinity: Father, Son, and Spirit. *With our brothers and sisters in the Faith, we hear the Word of God proclaimed and explained, and we receive the Lord in a Communion with God and our fellow believers.*

When we come to worship on the weekend (recall always that the Saturday vigil is in fact a Sunday celebration), we recognize that we are celebrating Easter. This special recognition of Sunday is one of the oldest traditions of the Christian Church. Since the Lord Jesus was raised from the grave on a Sunday, each Sunday is like a little Easter. The verses chanted before the First Reading at this liturgical time reflect this belief:

He who rose on a Sunday made this day a feast so great that the Angels, rejoicing, join with us to celebrate.

The Church believes that its nature requires it to celebrate the saving work of the divine Bridegroom by calling it to mind on certain days throughout the year. Every week, on the day that it has called the Lord's Day, it commemorates the Lord's Resurrection. It also celebrates it once every year, together with his blessed Passion, at Easter, that most solemn of all feasts …In the course of the year, moreover, it unfolds the whole mystery of Christ from the Incarnation and Nativity to the Ascension, to Pentecost and the expectation of the blessed hope of the Coming of the Lord (*SC* 102).

Even though the Season of Glorious Pentecost follows The Great Feast of Easter, on each post-Pentecost Sunday the Congregation hears a *Hoosoyo* that reminds them that every Sunday commemorates the Resurrection, regardless of any other commemoration. From the *Sedro*:

…Mind and tongue fail to describe the wonders you accomplished *on that holy and wondrous day, the Sunday of your resurrection from the dead.*

With the Psalmist David we proclaim:

This is the day the Lord has made,
Let us rejoice and celebrate.
This is the day which has no equal
in the past nor in the future.
This is the great feast day,
crown and glory of all other feasts....

Celebrating the Faith: Liturgy

Many studies have shown that human beings are religious beings. This is seen not only in the expressions of hope and trust reflected in writings left behind in the record of civilization but also in the ritual actions indicated by history. The Psalms are a good example of acts of faith and worship in a liturgical setting. It seems that if we believe, we ritualize our beliefs by worshiping. Christians call this *liturgy*.

For Catholics, especially of the Eastern Traditions, liturgy is essential. The Council recognized this in its "Constitution on the Sacred Liturgy" when it stated:

> ...[T]he liturgy is the summit towards which the activity of the Church is directed; it is also the source from which all its power flows. For the goal of apostolic endeavor is that all who are made children of God by faith and Baptism should come together to praise God in the midst of the Church, to take part in the Sacrifice and to eat the Lord's Supper.

Then it continues in the same paragraph:

> The liturgy, in its turn, moves the faithful filled with "the paschal sacraments" to be "one in their commitment to you"; it prays that "they hold fast in their lives to what they have grasped by their faith." The renewal in the Eucharist of the covenant between them and the Lord draws the faithful and sets them aflame with Christ's compelling love (*SC* 10)....

Truly, these words from the Council are ones to which Eastern Christians can relate. Liturgy teaches us about our Faith, about how to draw closer to the Trinity, and how to live. In liturgy Eastern Christians see the action of the Holy Trinity in the worship of the Church. Nothing could be more important in the life of the Christian than to praise and worship that Loving Trinity.

The liturgy of the Church takes many forms. Yet everyone in any Tradition of the Catholic Communion will agree that the supreme liturgical act is the Divine Liturgy, for it is here that we meet our Lord in the Word and in the Eucharist. In fact, no matter what form the Divine Liturgy takes, what makes it Catholic is the insistence that the hearing of the Word of God and the making present of the Eucharist are *both* celebrated.

Divine Worship: Mystical Invitation

Like every other Tradition, the Service of the Word in the Maronite Divine Liturgy is structured around Scripture Readings that are organized in a pattern found in the Lectionary (see **Chapter 11** for a discussion of the Lectionary and the Liturgical Year). By means of this the Maronite Catholic discovers who she or he is by following the pattern of Scriptures that celebrate the life of Jesus and the Spirit throughout the whole Year. In addition, by means of a prayer unique to the Syriac Tradition, the *Hoosoyo*, we see how our Church interprets the Scriptures, especially the Gospel, in our Maronite Tradition.

Maronite Tradition uses many Eucharistic *Anaphorae* for the Divine Service. The *Anaphora of Peter, Apostle III* (*Sharrar*) is especially ancient. William Macomber comments on this *Anaphora* (also known as *Anaphora of the Apostles*) in *East of Byzantium*, p. 73 (see Bibliography):

> The original form of the *Anaphora of the Apostles* has been the object of great speculation, and justly so. It is clearly one of the most ancient eucharistic prayers still in use today; it was, or at least became, the principal anaphora of those Syriac-using churches that were least influenced by the Hellenistic culture of the Roman Empire; and it can be considered a representative expression of the Judeo-Christianity of the early centuries of the Christian era...and the probabilities are much greater that its composition took place during the third or early fourth century.

Like all Eastern *Anaphorae*, those of the Maronite Church express the Trinitarian Prayer portion in the traditional order of: Father (Prayer of Praise and Thanksgiving), Son (Last Supper Institution Narrative) and Holy Spirit (*Epiclesis*).

As the "Service of the Holy Mysteries," our Divine Liturgy invites us, in a mystical and effective way, to draw more closely into intimacy with the Trinity, who renew richly the Divine Life with us at worship. Immediately before the dismissal, the Celebrant gives a fitting summary of why we have been together at prayer. He prays from the *Anaphora of the Twelve*:

> **We thank you, O Lord God,**
> **and we ask that this Divine Communion**
> **be *for the forgiveness of sins,***
> ***the glory of your holy Name,***
> ***and that of your only-begotten Son,***
> ***and of your Holy Spirit,***
> **now and for ever. Amen.**

Eastern Liturgy

In *Orientale Lumen* John Paul II takes great care to show the particular character of Eastern liturgical prayer. He accurately describes it in this way:

> Within this framework, liturgical prayer in the East shows a great aptitude for involving the human person in his or her totality: the mystery is sung in the loftiness of its content, but also in the warmth of the sentiments it awakens in the heart of redeemed humanity. In the sacred act, even bodiliness is summoned to praise; and beauty, which in the East is one of the best loved names expressing the divine harmony and the model of humanity transfigured, appears everywhere: in the shape of the church, in the sounds, in the lights, in the scents. The lengthy duration of the celebrations, the repeated invocations, everything expresses the gradual identification with the mystery celebrated with one's whole person. Thus, the prayer of the Church already becomes participation in the heavenly liturgy, an anticipation of the final beatitude (11).

Faith Response: Prayer and Praise

Prayer is the raising of one's mind and heart to God or the requesting of good things from God.

Our relationship to God is expressed by a life of prayer. This prayer life may be private—such as meditation, or prayerful reading of Scripture—or it may be public at times, such as at common worship. We may use well-known, learned prayers, or the public prayer of the Church's liturgy (Eucharistic Liturgy, Divine Office, the sacramental Mysteries, devotions).

As the sixth-century Syriac Teacher Babai expressed it:

> Make it your care to pray without ceasing, for prayer is light to the soul, and it acts as a guard to the body. Pray not just when you are standing in prayer, but also when you are moving around or doing something, and even when you are asleep, and when you are eating. When your mouth is occupied with nourishment, let your heart be occupied with prayer. While your right hand is looking after your body's needs at table, let your mind be given to praise and thanksgiving to him who provides for your needs. In this way your food will be blessed and hallowed in your body, without your being concerned with this.

Types of Prayer

The basic Christian response is *adoration and praise*. This is the first task of those who recognize the grace and privilege of being called in Christ's Name and God's love, yet also realize their humble existence as creatures before the Sovereign Lord of all. The statement characteristic of one full of praise for God is "God, I praise you for who you are."

The praise and glorification of God's holy Name is fundamental to Maronite prayer tradition. Hardly a prayer goes by without some reference to giving the Trinity praise, glory or honor. Almost every *Hoosoyo* begins with these words, and to quote the number of prayers from the liturgical tradition that mention praise and glory would be impossible here. Because of the divine initiative, God's offer of salvation, we are able to find the words to glorify the One who deserves glory each and every moment of our lives. Praise characterizes the public worship of the Trinity. This only deepens our desire to praise God in everything that we do, in public or in solitude.

In *prayer of petition* we beseech the Good God for forgiveness, for our being delivered to the Kingdom, and for the various needs we have in our hearts. Even though our prayer is all too often selfish and imperfect, our God knows what we need even before we ask it (*Mt* 6:8). If we did not get what we asked for, we must realize that what we have petitioned God for might not be what we need for our best interests or our salvation. Perhaps, also, we have not prayed with the right spirit. We might also find that we need to pray for an openness to *God's will for us, not our selfish, short-sighted will*: This kind of prayer is that of the mature and trusting servant of the Lord. It is the same kind of prayer uttered by the leper who approaches Jesus in the Gospel story: "Lord, if you choose, you can make me clean" (*Mt* 8:2b).

Recognizing this fact gives God the credit for his loving-kindness toward us, and acknowledges that God has our best interests in mind. Instead of asking God to change the divine mind in our favor—though this is indeed possible—we should rather recognize that more often *prayer changes us*. If we can see this important point, then we can better accept what the Lord is teaching when he said:

> But strive first for the kingdom of God and his righteousness, and all these things will be given to you as well (*Mt* 6:33).

A *prayer of intercession* is said on behalf of another. It is the kind of prayer that Jesus prays, as he is the one Mediator between God and human beings.

> Therefore confess your sins to one another, and pray for one another, so that you may be healed. The prayer of the righteous is powerful and effective (*Jas* 5:16).

Intercessory prayer is so necessary to the praying Church that it is built into its liturgy. In the Maronite Divine Service, the Intercessions occur after the Trinitarian Prayer of the *Anaphora*—right after the *Epiclesis*, in the Eucharistic Presence of Jesus. It is here that the needs of the Community and the Church at large—even the legitimate human needs of the world—are made public. Included are prayers for the living and for the deceased (see **Chapter 14**). This kind of prayer is used when we pray through the Saints to Jesus, who in turn takes our prayer to the Father.

The First Intercession of the *Anaphora of St. Peter* is a good example. In it God is asked to strengthen bishops:

> *... so that they may stand before you in prayer*
> *and intercede for us....*

Lastly, there is *prayer of thanksgiving*. In this kind of prayer, the grateful Believer acknowledges one's debt to the God whose bounty is infinite. For every good thing, the Christian can say, "Thank you, my God." So important is it to give thanks that the name of the central prayer of the Christian's life, the Holy *Eucharist*, comes from the Greek word for "to give thanks."

Prayers in the Western Traditions (Catholic, Anglican and Protestant) typically end in a phrase similar to "We pray in Jesus' Name." This is quite consistent with Latin theology and its Christological emphasis on Jesus.

Eastern prayer, by contrast, focuses more on the Holy Trinity, and mentions the three Divine Names more regularly. Eastern prayer acknowledges Jesus' precious presence, but it also expresses the fuller belief in our triune God who is so unfathomably rich in grace and life.

In our liturgical tradition we can readily know to whom a prayer is addressed by observing how it ends. Since the Trinity is so important in our prayer life, any one of the Divine Persons may be being addressed. Noting this at prayer makes sometimes makes an astonishing difference in our perception of the prayer.

Some of the various forms of both common Catholic and specifically Maronite prayers are treated in **Appendix II: Our Prayer Tradition.**

The Psalms

Among fixed prayers, the Psalms have a special importance. This collection of 150 liturgical poems is found as its own book with the Hebrew Scriptures (Old Testament).

In the currently accepted (Western) canon of Bible books, the Book of Psalms numbers 150. It is well known, however, that this number is an approximation. Other Churches, such as some Orthodox Churches, list a different number. In the (Syriac) Peshitta version of the Bible the number of Psalms is significantly greater.

The Psalms express a wide range of human emotions and aspirations and reflect all types of prayer. The Psalms form the backbone of the Divine Office, but they also serve well as a source for personal prayer and meditation on their own.

The Psalms are very important in Maronite Liturgy. For example, there is a Psalm assigned to every Service of the Word. This is meant to be chanted or recited by the Congregation in an alternating form reminiscent of the way it is done in the monasteries.

Syriac poetry—such as *memre* and *midrashe*—used by St. Ephrem and developed by his successors, is based on the biblical metrical pattern of the Psalms. In this way the Syriac Liturgies in their own style this special prayer form of the Bible called *psalmody*.

The Lord's Prayer

Taught by Jesus, the *Lord's Prayer* is unique. In fact, it may be said that the Our Father may be called the quintessential prayer of the Church and indeed a summary of the whole Gospel (*CCC* 2774).

Another reason that the Lord's Prayer is so central is that essentially, all prayer is addressed to the Father. Even when we pray to Jesus, the one Mediator between us and the Father, he takes our prayer to the Father. Prayer to the Holy Spirit is effective, for it is the Spirit who plummets the depths of God. Even prayer directed to the Saints is offered to Jesus, who presents these needs to the Father.

From the Lord's Prayer we learn many things. Because it is addressed to the Heavenly Father, we can see in it Jesus' unique relationship of intimacy with the Source of all there is (see *Jn* 10:30). Further, because Jesus taught *us* to pray this prayer, he indicates that we too have a Heavenly Father by adoption through Baptism. Thus praying the Lord's Prayer brings us into communion with the Father and the Son and draws us into the special relationship they enjoy. Realizing that we are indeed God's children should make us want to develop in us the will to be like Jesus and to foster a humble and trusting heart. As Jesus enjoined, we ought to adopt the attitude of little children if we would enter the Kingdom of Heaven (see *Mt* 18:3).

The Lord's Prayer is structured on seven petitions. The first three are centered on the glory of the Father:

❖ The sanctification of the Name of God ([1] "… hallowed be your name")
❖ The coming of the kingdom ([2] "… Your kingdom come")
❖ The fulfillment of God's will ([3] "… will be done").

The last four present our wants to God:

❖ Spiritual and physical nourishment ([4] "…Give us this day our daily bread")

❖ The healing of our sin ([5] "…And forgive us our debts/trespasses")

❖ Victory in the struggle between good and evil ([6] "…And do not bring us to the time of trial/ [7] but rescue us from the Evil One").

The "Prayer of the Faithful" (Divine Office)

In union with the wider liturgical tradition of the Catholic Church, Maronites consecrate other times of the day with prayer. Most notable is the Divine Office, a prayer which is built around the praying of the Psalms, and prayed at certain, specified times of the day. Evening Prayer, called *Ramsho*, is prayed at sundown, which (following ancient Jewish tradition) begins the next day. (Thus, the prayer of *Ramsho* will always be for the next day of the week following the evening it is prayed: for example, Thursday *Ramsho* is prayed on Wednesday evening.) Morning Prayer is said at the beginning of the day and is called *Safro*. In the monasteries and congregations of men and women religious, other times of the day have their set prayers from the Divine Office as well. The structure of the Divine Office parallels the Word Service of the *Qoorbono*.

The Maronite Divine Office is called "Prayer of the Faithful," and we are reminded that *all* Maronites—not just clergy and religious women and men—are called to sanctify the day with prayer.

The Seven Sacramental Mysteries

The other liturgical actions that draw us into the mystical life of the Trinity are the seven Mysteries of the Church (treated separately).

Devotions and Customs

The liturgical experience also includes certain devotions and customs, seen in more detail in **Appendixes II** and **III**.

STUDY QUESTIONS:

1) Why is it necessary that human beings worship God?
2) What is liturgy? How is liturgy a "celebration of faith"?
3) Name and describe the four basic types of prayer.

Chapter 21:
The *Qoorbono*/Divine Service of the Holy Mysteries: The Prayer *Par Excellence*

Maronite Liturgy

The Syriac Liturgy finds its beginnings in the liturgy that the Apostles brought from Jerusalem to Antioch (see **Chapter 8**). With its development in the region straddling Antioch and Edessa, the Maronite Church absorbed both Traditions. As the 1993 English translation of the Introduction to the 1991 revised text of the *Qoorbono* states:

> When the Maronites emerged as a Christian Syriac Antiochene community, during the fifth century and later, the Antiochene rites were under the influence of those of Jerusalem. However, the Maronites also had a liturgical tie to another important center, that is, the Syriac center of Edessa.... They were not influenced by the Hellenistic Greek legacy as was the Antiochene rite of Jerusalem; rather, they preserved their own distinctive features and expressions, which were closer to the Holy Scriptures and to the original Christian theology (p. 12).

The *Qoorbono*: "Offering"

In the Maronite Tradition, the Divine Liturgy is most properly known as the Divine Service of the Holy Mysteries. In the ancient language of this West Syriac Tradition, it is known as the *Qoorbono*, a word that means "Offering." It is here that Christ is offered to the Father, at the same time as he does the offering; this is accomplished by the overshadowing power of the Holy Spirit.

In the prayer of elevation before the Lord's Prayer in the Communion Rite at each *Qoorbono*, the Celebrant prays silently:

> **You, O Lord, are the pleasing victim,**
> *who was offered for us;*
> **you are the forgiving sacrifice,**
> *who offered yourself to your Father.*
> **You are the Lamb of sacrifice,**
> *and yet also the priest who offered himself for us.*
> **May our prayers be like incense in your sight**
> **as we present them** *through you and with you*
> *to your Father.*

Undoubtedly, the chief characteristic of the Syriac Church is its sense of awe and wonder before the divine Mystery. The Syriac liturgical tradition is dominated by the vision of the prophet Isaiah, when he saw the Lord on a lofty throne in the Jerusalem temple, and heard the angels crying, "holy, holy, holy" before him. This scene is recalled at the beginning and the end of every office of prayer and the sense of mystery that inspires it fills the whole liturgy. Together with this sense of awe in the presence of God's holiness is a profound sense of human sin. As the prophet was led to cry out, "Woe is me, for I am of unclean lips and I dwell among a people of unclean lips," so the Tradition is filled with this sense of human sin and unworthiness and one of the principal themes of the liturgy is that of "repentance." But this sense of sin and the need for repentance is accompanied by, or rather is actually an expression of, the awareness of God's infinite love and mercy, which comes down to human need and raises us to share in his own infinite glory. Thus there is a wonderful balance of dreadful majesty and loving compassion, of abasement and exaltation.

The Structure of the Maronite *Qoorbono*

The *Qoorbono* has four basic parts. Its clear order shows two parallel sections: an introduction to the Service of the Word, followed by the Word Service itself; and the pre-*Anaphora*, followed by the *Anaphora* itself. (A fuller explanation of the Divine Service is found in Beggiani, *The Divine Liturgy... [Revised Edition]*; see Bibliography.) An outline of the *Qoorbono* may be found on pages 244-45.

The four parts of the *Qoorbono* have a simple parallelism when viewed as the two larger parts of the Divine Service—the Service of the Word and the *Anaphora*. Each part is really composed of a section that introduces the main part and the main part itself.

In the Service of the Word, we need to prepare appropriately for the hearing of God's Word. Thus, we enter the church singing, then hear the *Hoosoyo* chanted. The purpose of this prayer, as noted in **Chapter 12**, is to focus on the commemoration and to call us to ask for God's help to "make us worthy" to hear the Word. These Introductory Rites conclude with the *Trisagion*. (However, a case can be made for the *Trisagion* beginning the Word Service proper). Thus, having been properly prepared, we hear the Word of God proclaimed and preached.

The transition from the Service of the Word is made by the theologically rich Transfer Hymn ("The Lord Reigns"), which shows Mary as the Hearer of the Word (taking us back to the Word just heard by us) and as Bearer of the Assuming Word (inviting us to take the Incarnate Word in Holy Communion).

The Pre-*Anaphora* commemorates the intentions of the Divine Service by naming them. We are reminded that there is a communion, or bond, between us and those faithful who have gone to their rest. It is our hope also to be with the Lord and with them one day too.

The Offerings of the *Qoorbono* become the Supreme Offering, Jesus Himself, in the *Anaphora*. Here, the Word is once again dwelling among us under the form of Bread and Wine, in utter humility.

Having received the Eucharist, we are blessed and dismissed to love and serve the Lord and others.

The Style of the Celebration of the *Qoorbono*

Since the Eucharistic Service is the highest form of prayer that we can offer, it is always worth celebrating it in the best way possible. Eastern and Western liturgies do this in different ways, usually recognized in the style of praying the Service.

All Eastern Liturgies in general are traditionally chanted from beginning to end. Outside of the homelands of the East—particularly in Western culture—adaptations have been made, especially in that some parts of the Divine Liturgy are recited. Nevertheless, chanting as much of the Divine Service is still a goal to be striven after.

It has recently been suggested that if not all of the *Qoorbono* is chanted, at a minimum the Celebrant would chant: in the Service of the

OUTLINE OF THE MARONITE *QOORBONO*

I. Introductory Rites
    Preparation of the Offerings
    Lighting of the Church
    Chant for the Entrance to the Church
    Dialog for the Entrance to the Sanctuary
    Doxology
    Opening Prayer
    First Greeting of Peace
    Hymn of the Angels
    Prayer of Forgiveness (*Hoosoyo—4 parts:*)
        Proemion (Introductory Doxology)
        Sedro (Order of Prayer)
        Qolo (Hymn)
        'Etro (Acceptance of Incense)
    Trisagion

II. Service of the Word
    Psalm of the Readings (*Mazmooro* chant)
    First Reading(s)
    Alleluia and Chant (*Fetgomo*)(Procession with the
        Scriptures)
    Gospel
    Homily
    Creed*

---

*Please note that the placement of the Creed here in the current order of Maronite Divine Liturgy is not the oldest placement and currently parallels the Roman placement. In earlier times the catechumens in the whole Church were dismissed after the Service of the Word, for they had not yet made a public Profession of Faith at their individual Baptism nor received Holy Communion. The Creed was part of the Pre-Anaphora, which only the fully Initiated members of the Community were permitted to recite regularly at that point, rather than at the conclusion of the Service of the Word.

III. Pre-*Anaphora*
Approach to the Altar, with Dialog
Transfer Procession of the Offerings, with Hymn ("The Lord Reigns")
Commemorations
Incensing of the Offerings and Hymn

IV. *Anaphora*, Communion and Dismissal
Rite of Peace
Prayer for Peace and Exchange of Gesture of Peace
Prayers for Imposition of the Hand and for the Veil

Eucharistic (Trinitarian) Prayer
Prayer of Praise and Thanksgiving to the Father
"Holy, holy"
Narrative of the Institution of the Eucharist
Memorial of the Plan of the Son (*Anamnesis*)
Invocation of the Holy Spirit (*Epiclesis*)
Intercessions

Communion Rite
Pauline Blessing (*2 Cor* 13:13)
Breaking and Signing of the Sacred Bread
Commingling of Species and Elevation
The Lord's Prayer
Penitential Rite
Invitation to Communion ("Holy Things...")
Communion of the Celebrant and Congregation
Blessing with the Eucharist
Post-Communion Prayers

Blessing and Dismissal

Word the *Hoosoyo*; the *Trisagion* (in Syriac, according to the instructions of the Patriarch), and on special feasts the Gospel; in the *Anaphora* the Trinitarian Prayer (from the Praise and Thanksgiving [to the Father] through the end of the *Epiclesis*). This includes the Institution Narrative, which, at the word of the Patriarch, is to be in Syriac. The parts of the Deacon (and Subdeacon) to be sung are indicated in the official liturgical texts.

As for the Congregation, there are the sung responses to the parts stated above, as well as the other hymns that accompany the various liturgical actions: Opening Psalm; various *Qolo*s [especially the *Qolo* of the *Hoosoyo*]; Alleluias after the First Reading; Transfer of the Offerings; Peace-giving; Response to the Intercessions; Breaking of the Bread; Priest's Communion; Congregation's Communion; and Recessional.

In general, the *Qoorbono* of the Maronite Church has always been prayed in the vernacular, with a varying degree of use of the Syriac in every age. The first languages of the Divine Liturgy were, of course, Greek and Syriac (the two early forms of the *Anaphora of St. James* well attest to this). When it became prominent in the Middle East, the Arabic language came into use in the *Qoorbono*. Syriac was the language used longest in Maronite liturgical history. Today, in a worldwide setting, other vernacular languages are permitted and used.

Until very recently the Maronite Celebrant faced East for the Service of the Word and the *Anaphora* with the people. The idea is that all expectantly face Christ, the "Sun" of Justice, who arises in the East.

The most recent reform of the *Qoorbono* suggests that the Service of the Word ought to be chanted from the Celebrant's place on the Gospel side of the sanctuary. This is to highlight the teaching aspect of the Service of the Word. The Patriarchal Commission recognizes the traditional facing East for the *Anaphora*, but for now leaves it up to each bishop in his own eparchy to determine the orientation of the Celebrant for the *Anaphora*.

Because the *Instruction* for the Eastern Catholic Churches (see below) was issued after the most recently reformed text of the *Qoorbono*, it yet remains to be seen what the Patriarchal Liturgical Commission might decide about facing East for the *Anaphora* again universally.

The Liturgy of the Pre-Sanctified

This special Eucharistic liturgy, also known as the *Anaphora of the Signing of the Chalice*, is celebrated only on Great Friday of the Crucifixion in the Maronite Church (compared with the Byzantine Churches, who celebrate it on all the Wednesdays and Fridays of Great

Lent). The structure of this service is recognized as that of the Divine Liturgy, with the following differences: there are more litanies prayed by the deacon; and there is no *Epiclesis* for the bread, only of the wine. That is because the Body of Christ has been reserved overnight from the Service of Thursday of the Mysteries and is brought to the altar for this Service. An *epiclesis* is invoked and the chalice is "signed," that is, traced with the sign of the Cross by the Eucharistic Bread, for later distribution to the faithful.

This Pre-Sanctified Liturgy is based on the *Anaphora of Sharrar*, the oldest in the Church. Its prayers recall the memory and work of the earliest ecumenical councils as well as the early bishops, martyrs and other saints of Christianity.

Recent Reform of the Divine Liturgy

Since the "Constitution on the Liturgy" of the Council focused on the liturgical life of the whole Church, it called for the reform of the liturgies of all the Traditions of the Church, East and West.

For the Eastern Catholic Churches, the Council produced a separate document to treat these Eastern Traditions. It was called the "Decree on the Catholic Churches of the Eastern Rite" (*Orientalium Ecclesiarum*). This document particularly stated that if these Eastern liturgical traditions had been influenced by unauthentic influences, particularly by the Latin Church (the word "latinization" was coined at the time of the Council), they were to return to their venerable "ancestral traditions":

> All members of the Eastern Rite should know and be convinced that *they can and should always preserve their legitimate liturgical rite and their established way of life, and that these may not be altered except to obtain for themselves an organic improvement.* All these, then, must be observed by the members of the Eastern Rites themselves. Besides, they should attain to an ever greater knowledge and a more exact use of them, and, *if in their regard they have fallen short owing to contingencies of times and persons, they should take steps to return to their ancestral traditions (OE 6)(emphases mine).*

Thus in 1971 the Oriental Congregation produced an experimental reformed text of the Maronite *Qoorbono*. The Maronite Patriarch issued an experimental text in 1972. These reforms were not uniformly implemented in all parts of the Maronite Church.

Twenty years later, in 1991, the Patriarchal Liturgical Commission issued the current reform of the text Divine Service. It follows in essence the reformed text of 1971 and is mandated for Maronites worldwide.

Prior to the reform, some Byzantines thought that the Maronite *Qoorbono* was a deviation from their own Tradition, not always understanding that the Syriac-Antiochene Tradition—parent Tradition of the Maronite Church—is older than the Byzantine. Nor have they understood the authentic character of the Syriac-Antiochene Tradition.

By contrast, the Byzantine Tradition took on the characteristics of the royal court at Constantinople, moving from the simple rite from Jerusalem and Antioch to quite a more elaborate ritual. Since the reform, the authentic form of the Maronite *Qoorbono* should be recognized as deriving from the simpler, *common* Antiochene liturgical ancestor.

Reform of the Sacramental Mysteries and the Divine Office

Some of the texts of the seven Mysteries have been revised and others are in the process. Needed reform of the Office presents challenges.

The *Instruction* for the Eastern Catholic Churches

In order to support efforts of reform in all the Eastern Catholic Churches, the Oriental Congregation issued in 1996 an *Instruction for Applying the Liturgical Prescriptions of the* Code of Canons of the Eastern Churches. This document reaffirms the principles from the "Decree on the Catholic Churches of the Eastern Rite" of the Council, but in stronger and clearer language: If reform has not yet taken place, it now must.

STUDY QUESTIONS:
1) What does the Syriac word *Qoorbono* mean? Explain how it appropriately describes the Eucharistic worship service.
2) Name the parts of the Maronite *Qoorbono*.
3) Briefly trace the reform of the Maronite *Qoorbono* since the Second Vatican Council.

Chapter 22:
The Mysteries of Healing: Confronting Sin and Its Effects

The Reality of Sin

Sin is almost universally recognized as some type of offense. Sadly, our lives are not perfect. The woman who had the bleeding control problem in Mark's

> ### Sunday of the Hemorrhaging Woman
> ### Mk 5:21-34

Gospel knew the reality of sin on three levels: the general sin of the world; personal sin and communal sin. Her sickness—like all sickness—was due to the consequences of the First Sin brought into the world by our first ancestors. Since that great mistake, people have suffered the ravages of sin and death. Although this Gospel story says almost nothing about the woman's personal sin (Jesus focuses on her faith), nevertheless, he tells her that she is saved—and he came in the first place to save us from sin.

In addition, her illness kept her apart from the Jewish Community. Somehow, the Mosaic Law judged that she offended that which guided the rest of her faith Community (Israel). We can be almost certain that she was shunned actively by the "righteous" among them. She was judged to have committed a communal sin.

Sin is a reality in our lives. The *Sedro* of the Sunday of the Birth of John the Baptizer expresses this reality:

> **...And now, O Lord,**
> **let the right hand of your mercy and compassion rest upon us,**
> *for we are shaken like reeds in the desert of life.*

> *We are overcome with fear as the sands of sin*
> *and the winds of discontent encroach*
> *on our feeble lives ...*
> **Delight us, once again, with your fatherly embrace,**
> **for the announcement of the birth of the baptizer**
> **is sure hope *for the salvation* you have promised**
> **from the beginning....**

The "sands of sin" blow abrasively through our souls, causing discontent—a discontent not always recognized as an offense against our God or our brother and sister, but deeply hurtful nonetheless.

The First Sin in Every Sin

All sin is rooted in the selfishness of our ancestors and their turning away from God, seeking to become gods themselves:

> Sin is an offense against God: "Against you, you alone have I sinned, and done that which is evil in your sight" (*Ps* 51:4). Sin sets itself against God's love for us and turns our hearts away from it. Like the first sin, it is disobedience, a revolt against God through the will to become "like gods" (*Gn* 3:5), knowing and determining good and evil. Sin is thus "love of oneself even to the contempt of God." In this proud self-exaltation, sin is diametrically opposed to the obedience of Jesus, which achieves our salvation (see *Phil* 2:6-9)(*CCC* 1850).

The First Sin, while personal to our first ancestors, is not a personal sin that we commit. (The Western term, *Original Sin*, is foreign to the thought of the East, especially in the way the Western Father, St. Augustine formulated it.) Simply being born into human life catapults us into the battlefield of sin, in which we must struggle our whole life long. By the First Sin we are touched by that which would draw us from God, and it leaves these negative, soul-scarring effects on us and our human nature weak and vulnerable.

Yet, thanks to our loving God, we are not left completely at the mercy of these negative effects. Through Baptism we are freed from the First Sin and pointed to God, even as we struggle with its effects in our life. However, that is not the end of the story...

Personal Sin

The *Supplication of St. James*, in the ritual for the first weekday of Great Lent ("Ash Monday") shows this clearly as the Congregation sings:

> **I yearn for your pardon, O Lord! Give me tears to repent**
> **in this season of Lent. Lord, have mercy!**
> **I beg for your favors, O Lord. For your mercy I thirst,**
> **for your kindness and love. Lord have mercy!**
>
> **Against you, O Lord, I have sinned. Hear the cry of my voice,**
> **turn your ear to my prayer. Lord, forgive me!**
> **O wash me, O Lord, from my guilt. Purify me and I**
> **shall be whiter than snow. Lord, forgive me!**
>
> **O Jesus our Lord and our God, you have served all your flock**
> **in your mercy and love, O Good Shepherd!**
> **You came to return all the sheep who had wandered and**
> **strayed from the love of our God, O Good Shepherd!**

The reality of sin is personal as well. Sometimes, as Paul experienced, sin is a powerful, incomprehensible, overwhelming and frustrating thing, as he tells us in *Rom* 7:15-24.

One of the clearest themes in the Scriptures is that of personal sin. Sin has been described as "missing the mark" of our aiming toward God's law. We are called by God to strive for perfection but don't always succeed (see *Mt* 5:48).

At some early stage of our life, we normally come to a point—called the "age of reason"—when we are fully capable of choosing against God and the divine law. This is what sin is. Against whatever good our parents, our Church, our consciences tell us is right, we choose the opposite.

Syriac-Maronite Tradition uses a variety of words to name sin. A few of these words are given in English here, with their respective Syriac equivalents (in italicized phonetics): the most common word for "sin" is *hteeto* (singular); other words are: "faults," *htohay* (plural); "transgressions," *met'abronwoto* (pl.); "offenses," *sakhelwoto* (pl.); "failings," *boosoray* (pl.).

Although sin is an intimately personal act, there are sometimes circumstances that lessen the responsibility for the seriousness of the sin committed (and even times when sin may not be present in the act). These include: ignorance, duress, fear and other psychological or social factors.

Communal Sin

In the recent past, there had been an exaggerated sense of sin as a quite private affair: we often asked God to forgive "my sins," as if our sins didn't hurt anyone but God, and possibly ourselves. We cannot deny that our sins somehow wound our relationship with our loving God. Yet today we have again recovered a sense of the parallel reality: that sin is an offense against others—both as individuals *and as a community.*

Saying yes to this idea presupposes that we understand the importance of community in our relationships, our families, our school, our work, our churches, our cities and our world. Hence, we might be tempted to think that considerations such as nuclear limitation, war and peace, the environment—because they may be popular—are not the "stuff" of sin. However, when seen in the light of the communal and social responsibility demanded by the Gospel message, they are crucial. When we offend a part, we offend the whole.

Our Maronite tradition of sin has something to say about this sense of social sin. Repeatedly, it is expressed in the prayers and is rooted in the profound sense of community that is at the heart of Christian reality. Rarely do the prayers of the liturgical tradition speak in terms of the first person singular—"I." It is almost always "we" who sin. We think of our sinful actions—as well as our service—in terms of our being in a family. We love or offend each other and God as members of God's Family in Christ and the Spirit.

Sin Has Hidden Consequences

Curiously, the Tradition also acknowledges sins done in ignorance, or at least without full knowledge, yet harmful to God and others. The Prayer of the Veil, in the *Anaphora of St. Mark*, for example, illustrates this theme:

> **... We beseech you, O Lord,**
> **to accept this awesome and unbloody sacrifice**
> **from our sinful hands,**
> **and through it forgive our sins**
> **and hidden offenses....**

While it may be argued that the prayer is simply acknowledging personal and non-public sin, the implication may be more, especially when compared to other texts. For example, every *Anaphora* in the Tradition concludes the last Petition for the Departed in the Intercessions with the following. This revealing prayer is a standard response prayed by the Congregation:

> **Grant them rest, O Lord,**
> **and forgive all our sins and failings:**
> *those sins we have committed knowingly*
> *and those things we have done without knowledge.*

Even more intriguing is the petition for the Departed in the *Anaphora of St. James, Brother of the Lord*:

> **Give us rest and absolve us, O Lord.**
> **Remit the offenses we have committed** *with consent*
> *and without consent,*
> *knowingly and unknowingly,*
> *in thought and in deed,*
> *those done with foreknowledge or in error,*
> *and those known to you alone.*
> **For the forgiveness of our sins, we pray to you,**
> **O Lord....**

These prayers express the idea that in fact hurtful consequences of our sins and failings can result even without our full knowledge of the sin.

Who of us, for example, can deny that a careless and thoughtless comment more often than we would like comes back to us, whether in the form of a reported hurt or a payback? Particularly in regard to gossip, or broken confidences no matter how well intentioned, for example, the consequences are more than we thought at the outset. With regard to the environment, we are now beginning to see what we have done to this beautiful gift of creation thoughtlessly and with dire results (*CCC* 2415).

In the end, St. Paul might have agreed with the Prophet Jeremiah: The heart is devious above all else; it is perverse—who can understand it? (*Jer* 17:9)

Serious Sin and Less Serious Sin

Sin can have degrees of seriousness, or, as it also described, of "gravity." God calls us to life and relationship to the Trinity. Serious sin is deadly *because it totally breaks our covenant relationship with God and puts one in serious danger of eternal life without God ("Hell").*

> If anyone sees his brother sinning, if the sin is not deadly, he should pray to God and he will give him life. This is only for those whose sin is not deadly. There is such a thing as deadly sin, about which I do not say that you should pray. All wrongdoing is sin, but there is sin that is not deadly (*1 Jn* 5:16-17, NAB).

The English translation of the *Code of Canons of the Eastern Churches* speaks of "serious" sin. While not categorizing any other sin than serious, the law does imply the existence of less serious sin.

Less serious sin does not completely destroy our relationship to God, but harms it. Love can still exist despite less serious sin, which can be repaired by charity. If repeated, less serious sins lead to other vices.

Maronite liturgical tradition often links two traditional terms in an often-used phrase: "sins and faults." At least in the English translation of the liturgical texts a real distinction seems to occur here between serious sin ("sin") and less serious sin ("fault").

The *Catechism* has attempted to put forth a number of sins considered serious, taking into account of the circumstances of today's condition of life (some of these are listed in the section on the Ten Commandments in **Chapter 27**).

Even though the attraction of evil to itself and away from God can be either a serious matter or less serious one, we must never forget that all deliberate sin is wrong and partakes of the life of the Evil One. We must try to work our whole life at trying to conquer sin.

The only way to restore our broken relationship to God, the Church teaches, is the sincere conversion (*metanoia*) back to God. If serious sin is involved, the sacramental confession of sin is necessary.

Metanoia/Conversion

Let us return for a moment to Paul's dilemma in *Romans* 7:

> For I delight in the law of God in my inmost self, but I see in my members another law at war with the law of my mind, making me captive to the law of sin that dwells in my members. Wretched man that I am! Who will rescue me from this body of death? (*Rom* 7:22-24).

Paul sees that he cannot go on feeling wretched. He knows that a change must happen for him to be once again at peace.

When we sin and feel the weight of guilt within us, we know that we must "turn things around" in our lives. Actually, this common, English idiom is a very good description of what it means to experience a conversion from our sinfulness. The Greek word *metanoia* expresses this well: a 180-degree turnabout from our sinful walk, like the Prodigal Son. Two strophes of the *Qolo* of the Lenten Sunday of the Prodigal Son express this well:

> **The prodigal son *wanders far* from the warmth**
> **of his home.**
> **He *flees far* from home to a life**
> **of risk and hazard.**
> **But while he is away, an obliging heart**
> **is filled with perfect love for him.**
> ***He returns*, his own heart broken,**
> **to seek the source of health.**
> **And his father rejoices,**
> **for his son *has returned*.**

Conversion is at the heart of the Christian life. In conversion, much is shown about the one who seeks peace through repentance, and much is said about the One who bestows the forgiveness. This is perhaps why the Parable of the Prodigal ("extravagant") Son (or, as it is sometimes called, "the Forgiving Father") has always had such influence on its hearers—great repentance rewarded by great forgiveness is truly moving.

Conversion-in-humility is indeed necessary for forgiveness. Unfortunately, especially as preached by some televangelists, the turn to God seems so easy that we miss the deep sense required for true conversion. Above all, we must constantly evaluate our radical orientation to God and live all aspects of our life in accordance with that radical choice for God. When we inevitably fail—for it is human to fail—we can turn back to our Loving Father. Repentance was the theme of John the Baptizer, a message that Jesus took up in his early public ministry:

> From that time Jesus began to proclaim, "Repent, for the
> kingdom of heaven has come near" (*Mt* 4:17).

Conversion is perhaps second only to the theme of God's love in the teaching of the Fathers of the Church. They understood it so clearly. Ironically, a great saint such as Anthony of the Desert, who is traditionally portrayed as being beset by all manner of demons, realized that the more one tries to purify oneself, the more one is aware of the dangers of temptation. Like Paul, we can almost feel overwhelmed and helpless; but the Church and the Bible offer hope and a challenge:

> I appeal to you therefore, brothers and sisters, by the mercies of God, to present your bodies as a living sacrifice, holy and acceptable to God, which is your spiritual worship. Do not be conformed to this world, but be transformed by the renewing of your minds, so that you may discern what is the will of God—what is good and acceptable and perfect. For by the grace given to me I say to everyone among you not to think of yourself more highly than you ought to think, but to think with sober judgment, each according to the measure of faith that God has assigned (*Rom* 12:1-3).

Liturgical Year: Great Lent

Question: What does great Lent tell us about the risen Christ?

Answer: It may seem ironic, but Great Lent and even Passion Week are not exclusively about the suffering and death of Jesus. Actually, that is only part of the Paschal Story. Knowing that his Death led to his Resurrection, the Church never sees the texts of Lent and Passion Week about suffering and death without recognizing the light of the Resurrection shining out close behind. Without this Easter perspective, the story of the death of Christ would be merely the tale of the death of a well-intentioned preacher who failed.

One observance common to all the Traditions of the Catholic Communion of Churches is Great Lent. This is a time of purification and reflection before the wondrous celebration of the Glorious Resurrection.

Lent has a fascinating history. It was not always the lengthy time that it is today nor was it observed in a uniform manner (nor is it today, either).

In addition, in some parts of the Church Great Lent was the time when those desiring baptism were undergoing the period of preparation leading up to their Initiation into the Church at the Easter Vigil.

Yet, in view of our common sinfulness and need of purification, the season is as relevant now as ever.

Fasting

One remedy for sin that the ancient Christians saw as helpful was fasting. This is what Simon the Stylite was doing at the top of his pillar in the North Syrian wilderness; what Anthony was doing in the desert; what Maron did in the open air, also subject to all the changes of weather; what Sharbel did at his hermitage; and what countless others did, in order to elevate their thoughts and souls to God.

Maronite Tradition has always encouraged heroic fasting, and our ancestors excelled at it, often restricting or forsaking nourishment on Wednesdays and Saturdays as well as Fridays as a regular practice. We are obligated today to fast only minimally, especially during Lent, but we should reconsider this practice.

Although the way for serious sins to be forgiven is through the sacramental Mystery of Penance (Reconciliation), less serious offenses may be atoned for by such voluntary acts as fasting. Other traditional ways include almsgiving to the poor, prayer, and positive works of charity.

St. John Chrysostom expresses this in a homily:

> Would you like me to list also the paths of repentance? They are numerous and quite varied, and all lead to heaven.
>
> A first path of repentance is the condemnation of your own sins: *Be the first to admit your sins and you will be justified.* For this reason, too, the prophet wrote: *I said: I will accuse myself of my sins to the Lord, and you forgive the wickedness of my heart.* Therefore, you too should condemn your own sins; that will be enough reason for the Lord to forgive you, for a man who condemns his own sins

is slower to commit them again. Rouse your conscience to accuse you within your own house, lest it become your accuser before the judgment seat of the Lord.

That, then, is one very good path of repentance. Another and no less valuable one is to put out of our minds the harm done us by our enemies, in order to master our anger, and to forgive our fellow servants' sins against us. Then our own sins against the Lord will be forgiven us. Thus you have another way to atone for sin: *For if you forgive your debtors, your heavenly Father will forgive you.*

Do you want to know of a third path? It consists of prayer that is fervent, careful and comes from the heart.

If you want to hear of a fourth, I will mention almsgiving, whose power is great and far-reaching.

If, moreover, a man lives a modest, humble life, that, no less than the other things I have mentioned, takes sin away. Proof of this is the tax collector who had no good deeds to mention, but offered his humility instead and was relieved of a heavy burden of sins (*De Diabolo Tentatore 2,6*).

Jesus says:

But when you give alms, do not let your left hand know what your right hand is doing, so that your alms may be done in secret; and your Father who sees in secret will reward you (*Mt* 6:3-4).

STUDY QUESTIONS:

1) Describe the relationship of the First Sin ("Original Sin") to every personal sin committed.
2) What is the meaning of *metanoia*, and why is conversion necessary for the forgiveness of sins?
3) What is the relationship of fasting to the Season of Great Lent?

Chapter 23:
The Mysteries of Healing I:
Penance (Reconciliation)

Paul does not end his lament in *Romans* with despair:

> Wretched man that I am! Who will rescue me from this
> body of death? Thanks be to God through Jesus Christ our
> Lord! (*Rom* 7:24-25a)

The grace given by and through Jesus Christ frees Paul and us
from sin. This grace is nothing less than the indwelling of the Trinity, the
light of our souls. Paul might have enjoyed this contemporary description
of finding the good out of the evil: sin opens our eyes to the beauty of
grace.

> But God proves his love for us in that while we still were
> sinners Christ died for us. Much more surely then, now that
> we have been justified by his blood, will we be saved
> through him from the wrath of God. For if while we were
> enemies, we were reconciled to God through the death of
> his Son, much more surely, having been reconciled, will we
> be saved by his life. But more than that, we even boast in
> God through our Lord Jesus Christ, through whom we have
> now received reconciliation (*Rom* 5:8-11).

To be reconciled to God and the Church, Christ has given us the
Mystery of Penance (or as it sometimes called, "Reconciliation"). Through
the Church's bishops and priests the Holy Spirit forgives sins. Through
Penance we are reconciled to God and recover grace and gain strength in
the battle with sin. Eternal punishment for serious sin is remitted, and

temporal punishment (in part) for less serious sin. Joyfully, we gain peace of conscience and spiritual consolation.

Because serious sin offends the Church, Body of Christ, one must confess serious sin in the Mystery of Penance to be reconciled.

Currently, the ritual of private confession to a priest with absolution in the Maronite Church has yet to be reformed (see **Appendix I, "Our Maronite Customs," #10**).

Liturgy: the Penitential Rite

Very strong in the Tradition is the forgiveness of non-serious sin in the Service of the Holy Mysteries, during the Penitential Rite before Holy Communion. The structure is clear (refer to the outline of the *Qoorbono* in **Chapter 21**). This rite follows the praying of the Lord's Prayer, in which we ask to be forgiven as we forgive others. The Celebrant begins with a greeting of peace, a hope for reconciliation. The Deacon then invites the people to bow their heads "before the forgiving altar" (emphasizing the forgiving power of the Eucharist). The Celebrant then prays a prayer of forgiveness (varying with each *Anaphora*) that acts, in effect, as an absolution. A Trinitarian blessing is given, and then the Holy Things (i.e., Eucharist) are held up before the faithful as an invitation to Communion.

Our Basic Unworthiness

No one can pray the liturgical texts of the Eastern Churches in general, or the Maronite Tradition in particular, without recognizing that one of the great themes of the Liturgy is the unworthiness of humanity before God. Contrary to the great attributes of God in the *Trisagion*, we are sinful, weak and mortal. Time and time again we pray that God will "make us worthy" to come before the Divine Throne of Mercy to petition the Lord.

This is seen above all in the Syriac Tradition in the *Sedro* part of the *Hoosoyo*. Regularly, the *Sedro* begins with the words, "Make us worthy." In this case, we are praying to be worthy to hear the Word of God and be purified by it.

In petitioning God to effect our worthiness, we recognize the fundamental teaching of the Bible and the Church on grace: It is God who takes the initiative in justifying us, not any works that we can do *prior to that free gift of grace.* Our acts of goodness are important, indeed essential to our living out of the Christian life. But in no sense can we ever hope to win God's grace by these acts; they are a result of the life of grace.

This teaching may be seen in several places in the *Anaphora of St. James, Brother of the Lord*. The Prayer of the Veil is typical:

> **O God,**
> *in your unspeakable love for all people,*
> *you sent your Son into the world*
> *to bring the lost lamb back to you.*
> **Do not turn your face away from us**
> **as we offer you this reasonable and unbloody**
> **sacrifice.**
> *We rely not on our own righteousness*
> *but on your kindness.*
> *We implore your goodness, O God,*
> *so that this mystery, prepared for our salvation,*
> *may not result in the condemnation of your people,*
> *but in the pardon of our faults...*

This is not a matter of denying the benefit of good works to the exclusive consideration of grace—that, in its strictest form, was the interpretation of the classical Protestant position. But the *Letter of James* puts it pointedly:

> Do you want to be shown, you senseless person, that faith apart from works is barren? Was not our ancestor Abraham justified by works when he offered his son Isaac on the altar? You see that faith was active along with his works, and faith was brought to completion by the works. Thus the scripture was fulfilled that says, "Abraham believed God, and it was reckoned to him as righteousness," and he was called the friend of God. You see that a person is justified by works and not by faith alone. Likewise, was not Rahab the prostitute also justified by works when she welcomed the messengers and sent them out by another road? For just as the body without the spirit is dead, so faith without works is also dead (*Jas* 2:20-26).

As a result of God's justification, and in light of it, our works honor God and help the Church. Recognizing this is important, especially in light of the official 1999 Joint Declaration on the Doctrine of Justification, between the Catholic and Lutheran Churches. This consensus statement expresses the agreement between the Lutherans and us on the central question that divided the two Churches at the time of the Reformation.

This idea of the need to be justified couldn't be any more clear than in the prayer that all recite, with palms uplifted, just before the distribution of Holy Communion, now said as a petition to be made worthy to receive the Divine Eucharist:

> **Make us worthy, O Lord God,**
> **to sanctify our bodies with your holy body**
> **and to purify our souls with your forgiving blood.**
> **May our communion be for the forgiveness of our sins**
> **and for eternal life.**
> **O Lord our God, to you be glory for ever.**

God: Great Mercy; We: "Lord, Have Mercy!"

If God's grace has been bestowed upon us, then it is an act of Divine Mercy. Many times in the Gospels Jesus speaks of the mercy of the Father in sayings and especially in parables. The Eastern Churches consistently recognize the great mercy of God, and thus with confidence we can approach the Divine Mercy Seat.

What is our response? "Lord, have mercy!" Typical of the East, this is rarely said just once; usually it is triple—an intense plea for compassion. One good example of this idea is found in the *Anamnesis* prayer from the *Anaphora of St. Mark:*

> **We beseech you, O Lord,**
> **at the fearful hour and moment of trembling,**
> *to forgive our sins in your kindness*
> *and wash our faults* **into the depths of your compassion.**
> **Wipe away our transgressions with the hyssop of your**
> **mercy.**
> **For this reason, through you your Church and your**
> **flock implores your Father...**

Another prayer, the second *Anamnesis* prayer from the *Anaphora of St. John the Apostle* is almost an Act of Contrition. In the context of the Eucharistic Prayer, it certainly invites one to conversion:

> ...When you come in glory with your holy angels,
> O Lord,
> and all look for the reward they deserve,
> let us not be strangers to your household.
> *Do not turn your face away from us,*
> *nor let our sins and offenses touch your holy heart.*
> Do not reject us from your presence,
> for we have known your holy name
> and professed our faith in your divinity.
> *Rather, forgive our sins, pardon us,*
> *and have mercy on your inheritance....*

If God makes us holy, we are holy and can live a holy life.

"Holy Things for the Holy"

If we have understood the teachings involved in the liturgical Penitential Rite, it will come as no surprise that the Celebrant will lift up the Holy Communion and say,

> *Holy Things for the holy,*
> with perfection, purity and sanctity.

Please recall the discussion of this prayer above, in the context of the Eucharist forgiving sins. There, the emphasis was on the Eucharist Itself as the Holy Things (capital *H, T*) of the Body and Blood.

Here, the emphasis is on us being made holy (small *h*), made worthy, and prepared to receive the Holy Things. By the grace of God, we share in the Divine Life.

STUDY QUESTIONS:

1) Why does Maronite liturgy (*Qoorbono*, sacramental Mysteries, Divine Office) emphasize our basic unworthiness?
2) Why is it so important for us to know of God's great mercy?
3) In the phrase, "Holy Things for the holy," what is understood by the fact that we are to be holy before receiving the Holy Eucharist? In other words, how are we made holy enough to receive Jesus in Holy Communion?

ST. EPHREM'S PRAYER
FOR STRENGTH IN WEAKNESS

Lord Jesus Christ,
King of kings,
you have power over life and death.
You even know things
that are uncertain and obscure;
and our very thoughts and feelings
are not hidden from you.
Cleanse me from my secret faults,
for I have done wrong
and you saw it.
You know how weak I am,
both in soul and body.
Give me strength, O Lord, in my frailty
and sustain me in my sufferings.
Give me a prudent judgment, Dear Lord,
and let me be always mindful
of your blessings.
Until the end let me retain your grace
that has protected me until now.

AMEN!

Chapter 24:
The Mysteries of Healing II: Anointing of the Sick and Dying

The Opening Prayer for the Second Weekday Cycle of Great Lent (called the "Weeks of Miracles") illustrates well the aspect of healing intimately related

> **Sunday of the Prodigal Son**
> **Lk 15:11-32**

to the Holy Mystery of Anointing. By it we pray:

> **O Lord,**
> **you are rich and abound in good gifts,**
> **make us worthy to praise and thank you**
> **for *your wondrous and saving deeds on our behalf:***
> ***You granted speech to those unable to speak,***
> ***hearing to people unable to hear,***
> ***sight to those who were blind,***
> ***cleansing to people with leprosy,***
> ***movement to those who were paralyzed,***
> ***strength to the sick,***
> ***and resurrection to the dead...***

Christ's Mission of Healing

Even a superficial reflection on this inspirational prayer will reveal in it the Scriptural basis from both Isaiah—who uttered this prophecy about the work and the mission of the Messiah—and from Luke, who sees in Jesus the fulfillment of the prophecy:

> The spirit of the Lord GOD is upon me, because the LORD has anointed me; he has sent me to bring good news to the oppressed, to bind up the brokenhearted, to proclaim liberty

to the captives, and release to the prisoners; to proclaim the year of the Lord's favor, and the day of vengeance of our God; to comfort all who mourn; to provide for those who mourn in Zion—to give them a garland instead of ashes, the oil of gladness instead of mourning, the mantle of praise instead of a faint spirit. They will be called oaks of righteousness, the planting of the LORD, to display his glory (*Is* 61:1-3).

And he answered them, "Go and tell John what you have seen and heard: the blind receive their sight, the lame walk, the lepers are cleansed, the deaf hear, the dead are raised, the poor have good news brought to them (*Lk* 7:22).

Miracle healing was not unique to Jesus; others brought healing to the sick as well. The difference in the Gospel accounts between the miracles of Jesus and the healing of others was the important dimension of faith that Jesus demanded of those he healed.

The Miracles as Signs of the Kingdom

Jesus' healing affected not only the body but also the spirit. The story of the healing of the Paralytic, whose sins were also forgiven (*Mk* 2:1-12) is a good example. People healed only of physical ailments would get sick again, perhaps with even less trust in a gracious God. People healed in spirit knew that even when the end came, there was a "Father" waiting to receive them, much as the father in the story of the Prodigal Son (*Lk* 15:11-32). What an even greater gift than mere healing of the body! This was the real work of the Kingdom.

Through the miracles and stories of healing presented in the Maronite Lenten Gospels, we journey to the greatest miracle: the Resurrection. Called the "New Creation," the Resurrection is characterized by complete wholeness of spirit and body. The closing prayer of the *Epiclesis* in the *Anaphora of St. Peter, Head of the Apostles* reflects this:

May those who participate in these Mysteries
be healed from all wounds of body and soul
and receive life and forgiveness,
now and for ever. Amen.

Because the role of Holy Anointing has been misunderstood, its effect has not been appreciated as it ought. Although this Mystery is given to a person at the point of death (old Latin Rite name, "Extreme Unction"), Holy Anointing is appropriately given whenever a serious healing is desired. The ritual includes the confession of sins and priestly absolution, if possible, as well as the reception of the Eucharist. Thus, freedom from one's sins brings about the peace of spirit, which can open the door to healing.

Prayer and Healing

A significant number of professed Christians either do not believe in the healing power of prayer or underestimate it. Pressure from the unbelieving sector of modern science in recent decades has discouraged some believers.

However, contemporary scientific and medical studies have begun to show a fascinating and provable correlation between the phenomenon of prayer for those who are ill and the higher incidence of recovery for those being prayed for as compared to those who have no one to pray for them.

This is not news to the faithful Christian. Prayer is a result of faith. And those who have faith rely on Divine Providence and power to be able to bring about the possibility of healing. Christians should always pray with the idea that prayer may be answered in this direct way, if God, who sees the whole picture, as we cannot, wills the healing. The trusting believer also knows that real healing may take other forms and accepts that the more important healing may be that of the soul.

Faith-filled prayer is not to be seen as merely one tool among many for healing. The committed Christian always turns first to the Divine Healer and keeps prayer as the first priority. Medical means are legitimate and not to be abused, but they should never be seen as a substitute for the power of God. In addition, many Christians pray for their medical advisors and care givers, hoping that God will help them in their important task of healing.

Anointing as a Sign of Hope

It has been recognized for centuries that anointing with oil has a restorative—even curative—effect. From the beginning the Church incorporated this idea of strengthening and healing into its sacramental life.

Even more, the Mystery of Anointing always carries with it a great hope that God, who knows the depths of our need better than we do, will do what is best for us. We never forget that hope is one of the three "theological" virtues.

The liturgical Tradition reflects this hope-filled theme of healing in the Sunday Cycle of the Lenten Season, as a quick glance at the Lenten Sunday Gospels will reveal (see the summary of the Liturgical Year in **Chapter 11**.)

The *Sedro* for the Weeks of Miracles draws out the ideas of the Opening Prayer:

> *Glory to you, O heavenly Physician.*
> *With your remedy, you healed our wounds,*
> *for you are the source of healing*
> **and bestow your gifts upon all....**
>
> **...We implore you, O Lord,**
> **with the fragrance of our incense,**
> **and we ask your compassion:**
> *heal our sick and the oppressed among us.*
> *Sanctify our souls and bodies.*
> *Clothe us with the robe of glory....*

The Body-Soul Unity

Although we speak of the person as composed of both body and soul, it is important to remember that both aspects form a reality that is a unity. The contemporary recognition of this fact is undoubtedly behind today's notion of *holistic*. Yet it is worthwhile noting that Christian writers in ancient times also recognized this basic idea as well. The Antiochene writer, Nemesius, a contemporary of Theodore of Mopsuestia put it this way:

> (T)he vital power which is pre-requisite to feeling is acknowledged to be derived by the body from the soul. It is legitimate to speak of the soul's "sympathy" with its body. Thus recognizing that while soul and body are not partners on equal terms, in this respect, they are partners.... Therefore, if the soul is said to be in a body, it is not so said in the sense of being located in a body, but as being in a habitual relation of presence there, even as God is said to

be in us. For we may say that the soul is bound by habit to the body, or by an inclination or disposition towards it, just as they say that a lover is bound to his beloved, not meaning physically, or spatially, but habitually. (Quoted in McLeod, "Theodore … Revisited," p. 469.)

Wholeness of Body-Soul

Wholeness of both body and soul is the desired effect of the Mystery of Anointing. Put crassly, even in the face of death, Holy Anointing is a "win-win" situation for the one who truly sees with the eyes of faith; even if the Lord does not permit the body to respond to the anointing, with the forgiveness of sin and reception of the Eucharist, which is a *zwodo* (see **Glossary**), or *viaticum*, the soul is made ready for its last part of the journey to the Kingdom. As the Prayer of Blessing/Anointing in the ritual expresses:

> **O Holy Father,**
> **Divine Physician of souls and bodies,**
> **who sent your Son, Our Lord Jesus Christ,**
> **to heal all sickness,**
> **and to bring deliverance from death and evil,**
> **+ through the grace of Christ, your Son,**
> *may this Holy Anointing*
> *heal your servant from every sickness*
>   *of soul and body,*
> **and enable him/her, with Christ,**
> **to give honor to you and the Holy Spirit,**
> **now and for ever. Amen.**

In this world and the next, our destiny is to glorify God.

The Mystery of Holy Anointing and Its Effects

The actual anointing is done by tracing the Oil of the Sick in the form of a cross, starting with the forehead, down over the nose, lips and chin; then from the right ear, across the eyes, and ending at the left ear. Thus, the senses, by which sin enters our lives, are anointed, as the priest asks God to heal the recipient. The prayers of the current ritual highlight several of the miracle healings of Jesus, some of which are also read during the Sundays of Great Lent, to which this Mystery is to be linked.

The effects of Holy Anointing include: the uniting of the person with the passion of Christ, for the recipient's sake and that of the Church; the strengthening, peace and courage to endure, in a Christian manner, the sufferings of illness and old age; the forgiveness of sins, if confession wasn't previously available—for this reason the proper minister of Holy Anointing is the priest, for he has the duty to administer Penance; the restoration to good health, if it is conducive to the salvation of the recipient's soul, and, if not, the preparation for the ultimate passing over into the glory of the Kingdom.

Holy Oils

Oil was used in ancient times as a natural element that gave strength and healing. We also use oil—and forms of medicine derived from it—today to aid us in health and healing.

While blessed oil is an essential sign in the Mystery of Holy Anointing, this sacramental Mystery is not the only one that uses blessed oil—it is also used in Baptism, Chrismation and Holy Order.

During Passion Week the bishop blesses three kinds of oils to be used in the bestowing of the sacramental Mysteries. They are: Holy Chrism, Oil of Catechumens and Oil of the Sick.

The word *chrism* comes from the Greek for "anointed." In the Old Testament, for example, religious leaders—such as the high priest—and civil leaders—such as the king—had oil poured over the head to signify that they were chosen to lead (see *Psalms* 23:5 and 133:2). In the New Testament Jesus is referred to as the Messiah. *Messiah* is derived from the Hebrew word for "anointed"; the Greek for this word is *Christos*. Thus from this Greek word we get many others in English: Christ, Christian, Christianity, Chrism, Chrismation, Christmas; even names derived from it, such as Christine, Christopher. The Arabic word for chrism is *Myroon*, hence the English alternative for chrism, Myron.

The Oil of Catechumens reminds us of those adults who prepared for Initiation into the Church. Today it is also used as the first anointing of Baptism. In the case of infant baptism the use of this holy oil reminds parents and godparents of the obligation to rear children in the Faith.

STUDY QUESTIONS:
1) How are the miracles of Jesus signs of the Kingdom of God?
2) Discuss the relationship between spiritual health and bodily health.
3) What are the effects of the Anointing of the Sick and Dying?

Chapter 25:
The Mysteries of Vocation I: Ordained Ministry

The Priesthood of the Faithful in Baptism

No discussion of vocation in the Church in general, or of vocation as illustrated by the two Mysteries of Vocation specifically, can take place without first considering the common

> *3ʳᵈ Sunday of Resurrection*
> *Lk 5:1-11*

priesthood of the Initiated Faithful. This reality was made clear again for the Church in the "Dogmatic Constitution on the Church," *Lumen Gentium*. In this important document the Church once again teaches the truth that *all baptized believers* share in the priesthood of Jesus in the spirit of the New Testament:

> Come to him, a living stone, though rejected by mortals yet chosen and precious in God's sight, and like living stones, let yourselves be built into a spiritual house, to be a holy priesthood, to offer spiritual sacrifices acceptable to God through Jesus Christ (*1 Pet* 2:4-5).

The Council teaches that all who share in the life of Christ through Initiation carry on the mission of his Church in a three-fold manner: the prophetic ministry, whereby the Word and will of God are made manifest to the world (*LG* 34); the priestly ministry, whereby the worship of God is carried out (*LG* 35); and the kingly ministry, in which the baptized work toward making the Kingdom of Heaven more and more a reality in the world (*LG* 36). In this context every Initiated believer bears the right and duty to be Christ and Church in an effective way, especially with the help of one's Chrismation.

Appropriately, the Concluding Prayer of the Rites of the Mysteries of Initiation says:

> **O Lord,**
> **enlighten the heart of your servant, N.,**
> **who has just received baptism.**
> **As you enabled him/her to become**
> **a son/daughter of your grace,**
> **in your merciful kindness keep him/her firmly**
> **in the ranks of your children.**
> **Grant, O Lord, that after being purified**
> **with the waters of your covenant,**
> **he/she may be a member of**
> ***a royal priesthood,***
> ***a holy nation,***
> ***a blessed community.***

Within this priestly community, special roles are reserved for certain members. Put another way, there are specific ways in which members of Christ's priesthood carry out his prophetic, priestly and kingly mission. Two of these special paths have been established in the Church's tradition as sacramental Mysteries: Holy Order (the ordained ministry) and Holy Crowning. They are neither incompatible nor mutually exclusive.

Why Holy *Order*?

Ordained ministry in the Church is known as *Holy Order*. From the beginning of the Church's Tradition, found even in the New Testament, is a certain ordering of the ministry for service to the People of God in Christ. Among his followers Jesus chose twelve special men, from various walks of life, to be his intimate friends, and with whom he shared his revelation in a deeper way. These are known as the Twelve Apostles, sometimes just "The Twelve." Maronite Tradition respected this important group of Jesus' followers by naming its oldest authentic Eucharistic *anaphora*, the *Anaphora of the Twelve Apostles*, after them.

Even among the Twelve certain ones were singled out by Christ. At times Peter himself is addressed by Jesus for certain things (see *Mt* 16:13-20). At other times he takes three of them—Peter, James and

John—with him (see *Mt* 17:1-8; *Mk* 14:32-42). There is a certain ordering taking place here.

One of the words to describe process of ordering persons or things in priority, for a special purpose, is *ordination.*

By means of the Mystery of Holy Order the service and administration of the persons and works of the Church is ordered. There are three levels of Holy Order: bishop, priest, and deacon.

The Order of Bishop

The Greek word for bishop is *episkopos*, meaning "overseer." It is the task of a bishop to see that the "local Church," that is, the eparchy, is administrated according to the mind of Christ (in Christian love), in harmony with the wider Church and according to its law.

In the New Testament bishops were the ones who directed the life of the early communities of the Church, aided by the deacons. Today, bishops oversee eparchies, and they may also serve on various Church committees outside of the eparchy for the work of the wider Church.

There is no higher sacramental Order in the Catholic Church than bishop. The bishop receives the fullness of the Mystery of Holy Order, which integrates him into the episcopal "college" (i.e., worldwide assembly of bishops) and makes him the visible head of the Church entrusted to him, i.e., the eparchy. As successors of the Apostles and members of the college, bishops share in the apostolic responsibility and mission of the whole Church under the authority of the Bishop of Rome, the Pope, the successor of St. Peter.

The Order of Presbyter (Ordained Priest)

A priest is known in the New Testament by the Greek word *presbyter*, meaning "elder." Presbyters make up the second of the three Holy Orders. Presbyters are the bishop's prudent co-workers, and they extend the authority of the bishop as well as the concern for those in the bishop's care within the eparchy. Around their bishop ordained priests form a "presbyterate," or assembly of fellowship

Presbyters receive from their bishops a call to serve the People of God in many capacities. While most serve in parishes as pastors, presbyters may be in such special ministries as teaching, administration, chaplaincy programs, prison ministry, counseling. Candidates train for the priesthood in a seminary, according to standards set in Church Law, by episcopal conferences and eparchies.

The Order of Deacon

    A deacon was known in the early Church by the Greek word *diakonos*, meaning "servant," or "helper." According to *Acts* (see *Acts* 6:1-6) the ministry of the growing Church was getting to be more than the elders could manage. To help, seven upstanding men were chosen to assist with the poor, with the needs of widows, and with the other needs of the Community of Believers. Thus, the office of deacon, or the *diaconate*, was established.

    In the earliest layers of the organization of the Church, deacons served in a more prominent position with bishops than even the elders. Soon, however, because of the rapid expansion of the Church, and the consequent inability of bishops to be in every local Church, elders assumed this function of local pastor, with deacons assisting them as well as assisting the bishops.

    After the Council, the office of permanent deacon—married and unmarried—was restored to prominence. Thus, the Catholic Church once again restored married clergy. In many cases, deacons have been a needed blessing for the service and administration of the Church.

    The process of ordaining one to Holy Order is also called ordination. A bishop is needed for ordination.

Ordained Ministry: a Life of Service

Sunday of Deceased Priests
Mt 25:14-20

The *Qolo* of the *Hoosoyo* for the Monday liturgical commemoration (in the absence of a particular feast) has the following stanzas:

Behold, Christ is distributed by human hands.
He allowed himself to become a sacrifice
for the sake of sinners
that they may live by him.
In his mercy, he gave the priesthood
the power to break his body
and to give his living blood
for the Church, his Bride.

From the italicized words above three ideas emerge:

❖ It is through God's mercy towards us that we have the priesthood—as well as any good gift—from heaven. God takes the initiative in grace in bestowing the ministry on the Church in the first place.

❖ One of the two essential functions of the ordained ministry is the bringing about the Divine Eucharist in the midst of the Church. The other, of course, is the ministry of the Word.

❖ The ordained ministry exists in and for the sake of the Church, which is the Bride and Beloved of Christ. In other words, the Holy Orders of the Church—that of bishop, priest and deacon—exist for service to the rest of the priestly members of the Body of Christ.

The Council recognized these very Syriac and Maronite ideas:

Though they differ essentially and not only in degree, the common priesthood of the faithful and the ministerial or hierarchical priesthood are nonetheless interrelated; each in its own way shares in the one priesthood of Christ (*LG* 10).

The *Sedro* for the ordination liturgy for a presbyter expresses God's call of the candidate to service. It also forms a sort of blueprint for that call:

You called him to the holy call of your lordship:
may he be the steward of your divine mysteries,
a chosen priest and a trustworthy leader;
a teacher wise in all virtue for the sake
of your flock;
a ministering priest, alert and diligent,
to whom you entrusted the keys of
the heavenly Kingdom,
that he may open the doors of repentance
to those who are brought back to you;
a praiseworthy priest,
who increases the evangelical talent
thirty-, sixty- and one-hundred-fold;
a chosen priest, who is concerned with keeping
your divine precepts.

The Centrality of Eucharist for Ordained Ministry

The connection between ordination and the Eucharist is seen in the placing of the ordination ceremony within the Divine Liturgy after the reception of Holy Communion of the Celebrant and concelebrants and before Its distribution to the Congregation. (The regular time in the Liturgy for special ceremonies and blessings is after the homily; the only other exception is the Kneeling Rite on Pentecost Sunday, which also occurs after the Celebrant's Communion.) During the ordination ceremony the bishop will more than once place his left hand on the chalice and paten holding the Body and Blood of Jesus and place his right hand on the head of the candidate. It is as if the bishop is the channel through which the power of the Eucharist flows into the candidate. In a real sense, the Eucharist accomplishes ordination, just as ordination accomplishes the Eucharist. The Eucharist establishes the Church, just as the Church celebrates the Eucharist.

This intimate relationship between the Eucharist and the ordained priesthood points to a deeper and more fundamental theological and spiritual reality: Just as the ordained priest is "defined" by the Eucharist, the "Head" (Foundation) of the other sacramental Mysteries, so the priest, by his ordination, acts in the Name of Christ, Head of the Church.

In an interesting turn of phrase, the *Sedro* for the Sunday of Deceased Priests speaks of the residual power of the Eucharist, which priests have distributed during their lives, helping them even in death. The idea can well apply to all who in taking the Eucharist are faithful to the Body and Blood of Christ:

> *... May the marks of your Holy Mysteries*
> **shelter and protect them on their journey to you....**

This liturgical thought occurs in a text that is significant for the liturgical season during which it appears: near the end of the Epiphany Season, when we commemorate and renew our Initiation commitment. In Baptism we have entered the Church. In Chrismation we have been called to its service and to witness to Christ. And in the connection between Eucharist and ordained ministry, Initiation is highlighted in a special way by the priest's duty to accomplish and distribute the Eucharist. It is as if the very handling of the Eucharist has left "marks" on the priest's hands; or perhaps the nail marks from the crucifixion—from the Death of the Lord, which the Eucharist makes present. He looks to his own nourishment by means of taking the Bread of Life with all other faithful;

but he also feeds God's People with this Bread and Wine, Body and Blood.

Because of this strong emphasis on the connection between Eucharist and ordained ministry, the Maronite Church has not—at least in recent centuries—allowed any but a presbyter (priest) normally distribute Communion, with permission possible to deacons. This is supported in general in general Eastern Law (**Can. 709, §1**). (However, the Introduction to the *Qoorbono* states that in previous times other ways of taking the Eucharist were permitted. Thus, **Can. 709, §2** states that Eucharistic ministers other than a priest or deacon may be commissioned, as pastoral need demands).

An Effect of *Epiclesis*

Epiclesis is nothing less than the invocation—and recognition—of the power of the Holy Spirit working effectively in our lives. In ordination the Holy Spirit overshadows the candidate at the *epiclesis* of the bishop. When the bishop places his hands on the head of the deacon at priestly ordination, he affirms:

> ***The Divine Grace and Heavenly Gift***
> ***of our Lord Jesus Christ,***
> **which at all times satisfies our needs,**
> **cures our infirmities, heals our wounds,**
> **forgives our sins, and attends to the children**
> **of the holy Church,**
> ***is calling and electing this servant of God,***
> **N., here present,**
> **who stands before this holy altar.**
> **It presents him from the order of deacons**
> **and elevates him to the order of priests,**
> **as he betroths the holy altars**
> **of the Eparchy of (N).**

Three Processions, Three Priestly Functions

Ordained ministry is a life of vocation of service to the Church. Two themes are present in the prayers of the ritual: that ordained ministry exists for the peace and up building of the Church, and that one is ordained for the service of the altar.

These themes are ritually summed up by three processions in the ordination ceremonies for Holy Order. In each the newly ordained is led in procession around the church by an already ordained sponsor (or two sponsors), to whom he has just become brother and with whom a colleague and collaborator. Each procession illustrates the duties of the deacon or presbyter:

❖ **Procession with the censer.** Since incense carries the multiple symbolism of petition for forgiveness/purification as well as praise to God, this procession reminds us of the duty of the presbyter (priest) to forgive sins through the Mystery of Penance and the call to presbyter and deacon to lead the congregation in worship. A traditional Maronite incense hymn, very often used in the incensing of the Offerings after their transfer to the altar before the *Anaphora* begins, expresses these ideas quite aptly indeed:

> **Lover of the penitent,**
> **show your mercy in our day.**
> **This pure incense, Lord, accept,**
> **that these priestly hands now raise,**
> **as gifts by the faithful of your Church**
> *to atone and praise.*
> **And as you received the ram**
> **sacrificed by Abraham,**
> *Lord, receive this incense, which,*
> *we pray, may win*
> *mercy and release from sin.*

❖ **Procession with the Book of the Gospels**. This reminds us that the ministry of the Word is central to the work of the bishop—charged with guaranteeing the faithful transmission of the Word of God; the work of the presbyter—to preach the Word; and the deacon—the work of the deacon to serve the needs of the faithful in the spirit of the Word. Their duty is to study the Scriptures, learning better how to interpret them properly. Then they will preach that Word as effectively as possible in order to bring others into the knowledge and love of the Word of God. As the Council taught:

> The People of God is formed into one in the first place by the Word of the living God, which is quite rightly sought from the mouth of priests. For since nobody can be saved who has not first believed, it is the first task of priests as co-workers of the

bishops to preach the Gospel of God to all men. In this way they carry out the Lord's command, "Go into all the world and preach the Gospel to every creature" (*Mk* 16:15) and thus set up and increase the People of God (*PO* 4).

❖ **Procession with the chalice containing the Eucharist**. While the newly ordained holds the chalice on his head, the third procession takes place. The Body of Christ, placed in a covered, empty chalice, is placed above his head. Thus, as he stands under the Eucharist, he is called to understand the meaning of the Eucharist for the life of the Church and to serve it well.

Of all the responsibilities in the Church, bishops and presbyters are called to certain tasks: the ministry of the Word, the ministry of the Eucharist, and the ministry of healing. Only the bishop and priest may do a liturgical *Epiclesis* over the bread and wine, beseeching the Spirit to change them to Body and Blood of Jesus; only they can sacramentally forgive sins (in the Divine Liturgy, which they conduct) and outside of Liturgy, in confession; only they may anoint the sick and dying. In addition, in the East the priestly blessing is necessary for Crowning; thus, no other is delegated. And only the bishop or priest may normally baptize. (However, in an emergency laypersons may also baptize). Only the presbyter—not the deacon—baptizes because Chrismation follows baptism, and no other chrismates but the bishop or priest. In the East, the role of the priest is central to the sacramental Mysteries.

Kinds of Presbyters
Until the 18th century there were basically two kinds of priests in the Maronite Church: ordained monks and married priests. These were under the supervision of the bishop, but bishops were most often monks themselves, often living in community with the Patriarch. The eparchial model changed after 1736 to the model more recognized today: a stable bishop at the center of his eparchy (refer to **Chapter 8, "The Synod of Mt. Lebanon"**).

Ordained pastoral ministry changed at this time as well. Now, a third type of presbyter—married or celibate—began to emerge. Because he was responsible to the eparchial bishop (rather than to the abbot of the monastery), he became known as an "eparchial" (diocesan) priest. Because he was not bound by the vows of monastic life he was also referred to as a member of the "secular" clergy.

Imposed Celibacy

In 1929, Rome imposed celibacy on secular/diocesan priests outside of the Eastern Church homelands, particularly in the Americas and Australia. Consequently, three generations have mistakenly come to think that God has decreed that non-monastic priesthood had to be celibate. But the unbroken tradition of the Eastern Churches in their homelands proves otherwise, as does the permitting of Protestant ministers admitted into full communion into the Latin Church to remain married and functioning, albeit in the case of the latter in a limited fashion.

The laws imposing celibacy are human laws and may be easily reversed. Pastoral need, as well as the restoration of legitimate tradition, may change this situation, especially in view of unity with the Orthodox Churches, which have always universally sustained a married clergy along with priest-monks.

The Positive Witness of Celibacy

To this day, the Church values the positive witness of celibacy, seeing in it a more focused concentration on the pastoral life of the Church, coupled with the greater availability of the celibate presbyter, who does not have the immediate needs of family life to attend to. For those who can sustain this life witness, the rewards are great in the satisfaction they can derive for their single-mindedness. The benefits to the Church are great for the increased attention to pastoral life that a celibate is free to bring to it.

Married Clergy: Two Complementary Mysteries

It is simply incorrect to say that the Catholic Church does not allow married clergy. In growing numbers, in the Eastern and the Western Churches, married men in major Orders—deacons and presbyters—are serving the needs of the Church.

We should not, as a rule, speak of "priests being able to marry," for this has never been the constant tradition of the Church. Rather, we should clearly acknowledge that the Church *ordains married men*. In this way we will maintain the proper language about this tradition.

With the exception of the Syro-Malabar Church and Syro-Malankara Church in India, the Tradition of the Eastern Churches in general preserves the practice of ordaining married men to Holy Order, in both the Presbytery (priests) and the Diaconate (deacons). At this writing nearly half (47 per cent) of Maronite presbyters in Lebanon are married. By ordaining men already married, the Church has always been wisely concerned that the marriage relationship was stable first, before the candidate took on the added responsibilities of Holy Order.

There is a complementarity between these two Mysteries of Vocation: serving the Bride while loving a bride. Though not without difficulties, marriage and family as "domestic Church," even in the married ministry of the ordained, reflects the bigger picture of the Church, namely, parish and eparchy—family life is an integral part of all three of these aspects of the Church.

The Church Needs Ordained Priests

The Church as a whole benefits from all the forms of ordained priesthood. Thus, we are asked to pray for our priests, who serve at the invitation of the Gracious Lord, as well as for vocations to the ordained ministry. Parents have a duty, according to the Fourth Commandment, to respect a vocation in their children to the ordained ministry and the religious life, as well as other forms of ministry in Christ's Church.

This invitation to pray for the priest is built into the very structure of the *Qoorbono*. Twice during the Divine Service, at the entrance to the sanctuary at the very beginning of the Service, and at the approach to the altar at the opening of the Pre-*Anaphora*, the Celebrant beseeches the people: **"Pray to the Lord for me."** The people respond: **"May the Lord accept your offering and have mercy on us through your prayer."**

By extension the Liturgy asks people to pray for priests who have worked everywhere and at all times of the Church's history. Particularly poignant is the petition (elsewhere in the Tradition) to pray for priests who have no one to pray for them.

At the same time we cannot nor should we pass up the opportunity to pray for the Lord's living servants. The following text from the Sunday of Deceased Priests can as well be applied to the living:

> **O Lord God,**
> **allow us to approach the treasury of your mercy**
> **with confidence**
> **and to worship in your presence,**
> *as we petition you on behalf of the deceased servants*
> *of your altar.*
> *May those who shared in the power of the holy apostles*
> *to bless, forgive, and grant life to your people,*
> *now share in the rewards which you have prepared*
> *for your good and watchful servants.*

**We will glorify you, O God,
now and for ever. Amen.**

STUDY QUESTIONS:
1) How can it be said that all Christians share in the priesthood of Christ?
2) What are the three Orders of ordained ministry making up Holy Order, and how are they each related? What is the function of each Order?
3) In what way(s) is the Eucharist related to the ordained ministry?

Chapter 26:
The Mysteries of Vocation II: Holy Crowning

Marriage, a Courageous and Godly Decision

The second Mystery of Vocation to be considered touches the overwhelming majority of persons who, with clergy, make up the Church: married people. It

> **4ᵗʰ Sunday after Holy Cross**
> **Mt 18:23-35, or**
> **Lk 16:9-15**

is the Church's task to help people see that to marry in the Lord is indeed a godly decision and also to help them prepare well for it. After marriage takes place, it is also the Church's task to help couples remain committed by support and encouragement.

Marriage, a Joyful Human Reality

People have always become enthused about a wedding. There is happiness for the parents and families, joy for the couple (see *Song* 8:6-7), and the anticipation of the fun at the wedding reception. The *'Etro* of the Crowning ritual expresses this:

> **Praised are you, O Jesus Christ, our Lord,**
> **the God of Abraham, Isaac and Jacob;**
> *you gave joy to the groom and bride*
> *at the wedding banquet of Cana of Galilee.*
> **Now, O Lord,**
> **accept the perfume of this incense.**
> **Bless the groom, N., and the bride, N.,**
> **their witnesses and all their guests,**
> **as you blessed the just and their children.**
> **To you be glory, now and for ever. Amen.**

The Second Vatican Council talked about marriage in this way:

The Lord, wishing to bestow special gifts of grace and divine love on married love, has restored, perfected, and elevated it. A love like that, bringing together the human fand the divine, leads the partners to a free and mutual self-giving, experienced in tenderness and action, and permeating their entire lives; this love is actually developed and increased by its generous exercise. This is a far cry from mere erotic attraction, which is pursued in selfishness and soon fades away in wretchedness (*GS* 49).

Context: The Kingdom as a Wedding Banquet

Jesus spoke of the Kingdom of Heaven in terms of a wedding banquet to which all are invited (see **Chapter 14, "A New Earth and a New Heaven"**). Not only did he speak of it, he lived it, enjoying the company of others. He even made it a point to reveal his divinity and glory first at a wedding celebration—at Cana in Galilee.

Our Maronite Church commemorates this event as the opening of the Lenten Season. At first glance this seems to be very unlikely: beginning a penitential season with the joyous celebration of marriage. As always, and like a parable, the liturgical tradition has the capacity to surprise us and to make us reflect upon the mystery of the Kingdom.

The answer comes in the linking of the goal of Lent—Easter transformation through purification—with the happiness of the Kingdom, symbolized by the image of a wedding banquet. Why do we fast? So that we may better prepare ourselves to see the Kingdom in our daily life and one day to experience its fullness with God for ever. From the *Sedro*:

> **O Christ our God,**
> **you called your righteous guests**
> **to your spiritual banquet,**
> **and your beloved children to your kingdom.**
> *On earth you lived as one of the children of men:*
> *you associated with them, ate and drank with them,*
> *blessed their eating and drinking,*
> *their deeds and lives.*
> **You enriched them with the abundance**
> **of your heavenly gifts**
> **and your divine wisdom.**

We give thanks to you, O good One,
who are compassionate toward the work of your
hands.

St. Ephrem, in stanza 15 of his *Hymn on Paradise, VII*, says that even such a one as a virgin, who has in life foregone the pleasures of marriage, if faithful attains a place at the Heavenly Wedding Banquet:

> The virgin who rejected
> the marriage crown that fades
> now has the radiant marriage chamber
> that cherishes the children of light,
> shining out because she has rejected
> the works of darkness.
> To her who was alone
> in a lonely house
> the wedding feast now grants tranquility:
> here angels rejoice,
> prophets delight,
> and apostles add splendor.

God wills us to be happy forever with him in the Blessed Kingdom, and God also wants us to be happy here on earth. Weddings are one of those joyful times, and the Church knows how to celebrate them.

The Maronite Meaning of Crowning

In the Eastern Traditions, the marriage ceremony is called Holy "Crowning." In the rituals of many of the Eastern Churches, crowns of some form are placed on the heads of at least the bride and groom. There are several symbolic meanings of crowning.

First, the crowns symbolize fertility and creation. Look at the Blessing of the Crowns:

> *Like a crown, God has adorned the earth with flowers,*
> *the heavens with stars,*
> *and the land with the sea.*

The idea of fertility is expressed in Psalm 128, assigned to the Crowning ceremony:

Your wife will be like a fruitful vine within
your house; your children will be like olive
shoots around your table (*Ps* 128:3).

It is also expressed earlier in the *Sedro*:

O Lover of all people,
with your right hand now bless your servants,
**   N. and N.,**
who are betrothed to one another.
Confirm them in faith, hope, love and just deeds.
Make their marriage as honorable as the marriages
**   of the righteous and just of old.**
They served you in justice
and you multiplied their descendants
like the stars of the sky
*   and the grains of sand on the seashore.*
As they brought forth priests, kings, prophets,
apostles, preachers and teachers of your good news,
so likewise grant your servants, N. and N.,
to bear the fruits of justice.

The Council expressed this idea clearly when it spoke of the ends
of marriage:

By its very nature the institution of marriage and married
love are ordered to the procreation and education of the
offspring and it is in them that it finds its crowning glory.
Thus the man and the woman, who "are no longer two but
one" (*Mt* 19:6), help and serve each other by their marriage
partnership; they become conscious of their unity and
experience it more deeply from day to day. The intimate
union of marriage, as a mutual giving of two persons, and
the good of the children demand total fidelity from the
spouses and require an unbreakable unity between them
(*GS* 48).

The second meaning of the crowns lies in references to kings and
queens in the past as types of the two who stand before the priest and the
altar. Again from the Blessing of the Crowns:

> **With a crown he has shown the special calling**
> **given to the holy kings, priests, prophets and apostles.**
> **In his bountiful mercy may he bless + these crowns**
> **through the prayers of the Mother of God**
> **and all the saints.**

Here, two images come together to show the rich theology of the Crowning Service: the Kingdom as wedding banquet and the crowning of the couple. The linking of these two images shows that the couple is crowned precisely to further the work of the Kingdom in the midst of Church and society. They are indeed set aside for this task just as the ancient, righteous ones of old—the patriarchs and their wives—for God's service. This is their vocation as married—crowned—Christians.

Having matured, St. John Chrysostom expressed his view that the bride and groom are crowned as winners: winners over selfishness, in a lifetime of commitment to one another.

Fulfillment of the Chrismational Mission of the Couple

This calling then is a fulfillment of the mission that was given at the Chrismation of each. Just as Jesus went from his baptism out into the public world of his ministry, so the couple now go forth, strengthened by the effects of Chrismation, as well as by the graces of the Mystery of Crowning, to witness to the Heavenly Bridegroom in this vocation. Their witness extends first to each other, as they share their life of joy and mutual self-giving; to their children, who will constitute not only their family but also a "domestic Church"; and to the world outside the circle of the family.

Marriage Is a Covenant

One of the things that strike a visitor to a Maronite church for a Crowning Service is the abundance of references to the Hebrew Scriptures. In fact, this Old Testament emphasis is characteristic of the Service. It serves to expose the deep Old Covenant background of the reality of Christian marriage fulfilled in New Covenant.

The covenant of God with Israel is the supreme type, or model, used to convey the understanding of Christian marriage. There are several references in the Crowning ceremony, but the priestly blessing on the couple's hands (resting on the Book of the Scriptures, the foundation of marriage) expresses this idea clearly: that God's covenant was reflected in the covenant between the Patriarchs and their wives:

> **By the hand of God and his holy Word,**
> **our son, N., and our daughter, N., are joined**
>   **in marriage,**
> **in the name of the most Holy Trinity:**
> **Father, Son, and Holy Spirit,**
> **the One and only true God.**
> *May their marriage be as firm as the covenant*
>   *by which heaven and earth were created,*
> *and be blessed as was the covenant*
>   *by which Sarah was joined to Abraham,*
> *Rebecca to Isaac, and Rachel to Jacob,*
> *so that nothing shall separate them but death.*

Even the first canon on marriage (**Can. 776, §1**) in the *Code of Canons of the Eastern Churches* expresses this relationship in terms of "covenant." Thus, the relationship of man and woman constitutes the first form of communion between persons:

> The matrimonial covenant, established by the Creator and ordered by His laws, by which a man and a woman by an irrevocable, personal consent establish between themselves a partnership of the whole of life, is by its nature ordered toward the good of the spouses and the generation and education of the offspring.

Just as the Old Covenant carried with it rights and responsibilities between the covenanters (God, Israel), so too, in the New Covenant—of which Christian marriage is a symbol—are there rights and responsibilities to be observed.

Fidelity. As God was faithful to Israel, and as he expected Israel to return that fidelity, so too are the couple to be faithful to each other ("Let nothing separate them but death"), to Christ, to the Church and to their children.

Love. This is not to be the kind of exaggerated and superficial love of pop culture—cheap love, but rather "tough love," love that lasts for ever and sustains in the difficult times of the marriage relationship.

This is a mature love, which the couple knows to be godly and strong, while being gentle and giving. It is the ideal kind of love that Jesus held up as his standard:

I give you a new commandment, that you love one another. Just as I have loved you, you also should love one another. By this everyone will know that you are my disciples, if you have love for one another (*Jn* 13:34-35).

Duty. This is not talked about much in our day; but it was a big part of the foundation of the marriage relationship of earlier generations. It is related to fidelity and love. Duty is also the sign of a mature Christian, for one knows that in times of difficulty as well as in times of joy and ease, there are simply things which must be done, often without question, if the relationship is to survive. This becomes especially true when children come into the marriage. It also becomes important when serious illness enters the marriage. But it also applies in doing everything that enhances the relationship and avoiding everything that harms it.

Equality and respect are necessary for a marriage. God created human beings equal, in the divine image. Thus, any thought of domination of one over the other is out of the question. The opposite of domination is respect, the mutual respect of spouses.

Christian Marriage

In his *Letter to the Ephesians* (5:25-27) St. Paul speaks of the relationship of husband and wife as a human symbol of the relationship between Christ as the Bridegroom and the Church as Bride. This comparison shows us the intimacy Christ enjoys with us, his Bride, in a relationship of love. This idea is reflected in the *Proemion* of the Crowning ceremony:

> *May we be worthy to offer praise and thanksgiving*
> *to Jesus Christ, the heavenly Bridegroom.*
> *In his love, he betrothed the Church of all peoples*
> *and nations;*
> **by his Cross he sanctified her and made her**
> **a glorious bride.**
> **To him are due glory and honor,**
> **now and for ever. Amen.**

In the end this sacramental Mystery has as its ultimate goal the divinization of the spouses and their family and the final dwelling in the everlasting Covenant with the Glorious and Loving Trinity. This is accomplished precisely through the joyous and sacred union of the spouses in true love and the living out of the crowned life. As the final prayer of the Crowning ritual so fittingly expresses it:

> **May God bless you:**
> **groom, bride and witnesses,**
> **and protect this community by his glorious cross.**
> *May you begin and end your married life in justice.*
> *May you bring forth children pleasing to God in*
> *this world.*
> *And in the world to come,*
> *may you reach the harbor of eternal life. Amen.*

The Purposes of Christian Marriage

While some older Catholics may have grown up with the exclusive view that the purpose of marriage was the generation and education of children, the Council corrected this. Today, in the theology of marriage, we clearly add a second: the good of the spouses.

This is a healthy corrective. When we look at the deep meanings of Crowning as described above—chrismational mission, love, fidelity, duty and trust—we see that Christian marriage, properly entered into, serves to help the partners grow and mature. Each brings gifts to the relationship, and these gifts can improve the other, helping the partner to mature. This is not the cheap love of contemporary media. Rather, it is the love of which Paul speaks in *1 Cor* 13:1-13: love that is patient, kind, never rude, not holding grudges, but love that lasts for ever.

Canonical Considerations

The requirements and preparations for sacramental marriage should be entered into seriously for both the spiritual and Church Law requirements. Both eparchies of the United States Maronite Community have six-month preparation programs, designed to review the important aspects of Catholic, sacramental teaching, as well as to familiarize the couple with Maronite Tradition.

In addition, the Law of the Church requires that couples meet with the officiating priest, in order for him to ask them questions, under oath, from the Pre-nuptial Questionnaire. The answers, recorded in writing, become a part of the couple's permanent file at the church of the Crowning. (Refer to **Appendix I** for a brief description of these details.)

The Special Calling to Be a Hermit

Maronite Tradition recognizes the worth of the solitary life in its valuing of the life of the hermit. Far from being a life of anti-social withdrawal, people like St. Maron chose the solitary life in order to focus better on the will of the Lord and in turn re-focus on the spiritual and even physical needs of others, with the help of God. The *Proemion* for the feast of St. Maron, Solitary, expresses this:

> **May we be worthy to glorify, praise and confess**
> **the one, holy Father, who summoned faithful followers**
> *to lead a solitary life;*
> **the Only Son, who taught them** *the ways of perfection;*
> **the one, Holy Spirit, who** *crowned their struggles*
> *with miraculous deeds.*
> **To the Good One are due glory and honor,**
> **now and for ever. Amen.**

The Vocation to the Single Life

While the Church has designated a sacramental Mystery each to the two life callings of marriage and ministry, and has found a place in its theology and spirituality for consecrated men and women religious (women and men religious; hermits), it has not always paid enough attention to those who, for reasons of their own, have not chosen any of the above and yet have remained single.

In addition, in recent times there has been a trend toward being single, whether by choice or not. Such people are often quite good persons, and we should not make the presumption that they are merely living a selfish life. On the contrary, many choose, for example, to remain at home to care for an ailing parent, a life that often calls for heroism. We can also think about single parents, who make great sacrifices to feed and educate their children; nor should we ignore widows and widowers.

To be sure, not all single people are hermits. Nevertheless, being single for the higher reason of selfless dedication to a good cause, particularly if it is a spiritual one, can be a noble calling. We must recognize in such individuals a special following of Christ in a valuable way. They need our understanding, acceptance and support.

> Then he said to them all, "If any want to become my followers, let them deny themselves and take up their cross daily and follow me. For those who want to save their life

will lose it, and those who lose their life for my sake will save it. What does it profit them if they gain the whole world, but lose or forfeit themselves?" (*Lk* 9:23-25)

Homosexuality

Another example of unmarried persons is homosexuals. The psychological genesis of the exclusive or even predominant attraction to the same sex remains largely unexplained. Nevertheless, recent Vatican documents have made it abundantly clear that homosexuals are in the first place—as are all who are born into the world—*persons*. They deserve the respect due to the children of the Father. They also enjoy the same right not to be discriminated against in the work place as any one else.

Because it follows the Biblical ideal of heterosexual married relationship, the Church condemns active homosexual genital activity and lifestyle as contrary to natural law. Such acts close the sexual act to the gift of life and are therefore seen as "intrinsically disordered" (*CCC* 2357).

However, in their public lives (work, Church, other organizations) and their private lives, homosexuals have every right to form relationships that—as for all Catholics—are consistent with the message of the Gospel and the teachings of the Church. Homosexuals, who, with all other Christians, take Christ as a supreme model of chastity and honestly seek to live a good life, are not to be degraded in any way. Rather, they, like all people of good will, deserve our understanding, love and support.

STUDY QUESTIONS:

1) What is the significance of the descriptive name *Crowning* for the wedding ceremony?
2) Why can Christian marriage be described as a "covenant"? What are some fundamental elements (i.e., qualities) of the marriage covenant?
3) What are the purposes of Christian marriage?

Chapter 27:
Living a Moral Life I:
Biblical Morality

What is Morality?

When we are born, we are not only called to life but *to live and live well.* Having been gifted freely by the Creator with human existence, we seek the best

> **2nd Sunday of the Holy Cross**
> **Lk 17:20-37, or**
> **Mt 22:1-14**

way to live out that existence. Such a phrase like "quality of life" is important indeed.

There are, in fact, many ways to live life. Some people choose to live life badly, not advancing themselves, or caring for the wellbeing of others. On the other hand, the history of humanity is full of stories of individuals who have sacrificed their very lives for the good of others.

What motivates them?

The principles—or "norms"—by which one lives and their application in effective living are called "morality." If we live well by good and widely recognized principles, we are living a moral life.

Thinkers have for centuries recognized that one of the basic principles for living a moral life may be summed up in the saying, "Do good and avoid evil." On the surface, this sounds right: do what is good, avoid what is evil. Upon deeper reflection, however, we can see that there is a problem built into the *application* of this basically sound advice: How do we know what in fact is "good" and what is "evil"?

We have all heard the expression, "One person's junk is another's treasure." This judgment is made according to each individual's viewpoint. Similarly, what is good to one person may be wrong or bad to another. The task of those who reflect upon moral issues has always been to find what is objectively acceptable—"good"—by all. This is not easy.

Perhaps now we can see a bit better the complexity of the seemingly simple, truly sound, phrase, "Do good, avoid evil." This challenging reflection is at the heart of moral judgment.

Moral philosophers speak not only of "the good," as if there is only one single, true, good thing to do. They also speak of objective *norms*, principles that are always and everywhere valid for our acting and our living. Not everyone agrees what these norms might be; and there are even those who would deny the existence of such norms. This is part of the difficulty in speaking about human morality.

The Catholic Church has always been a leading force in the world in providing answers to these difficulties. For example, in addition to actions that are considered objectively good, the Church teaches that there are concrete acts that it is always wrong to choose, because their choice is a disorder of the will, i.e., a moral evil. One may not do evil so that good may result from it (*CCC* 1761).

Morality is very much a concern of the Church, which she finds in the inspired Word of the Scriptures (biblical morality) and in the lived-out experience of faithful believers (Tradition). Specifically, in our Maronite Tradition, this idea is reflected in the Prayer of the Veil of the *Anaphora of St. Sixtus:*

> **Through this prayer of offering, O Lord,**
> **may these holy mysteries *make us strangers***
> > ***to the passions of sin***
> **and familiar with deeds of justice.**
> **We will glorify you, O Father,**
> **now and for ever. Amen.**

We are to avoid evil and do good.

The Ten *Commandments*, Not the "10 Suggestions"

The Bible—both the Hebrew Scriptures and the New Testament—tells us about how God wants us to live. Many books have been written about biblical morality. But a few great and long-held examples of biblical principles will help here.

One of the things a young Catholic learns in religious education is the Ten Commandments, also known as the *Decalogue* (Greek: "Ten Writings"). These "terms" in the covenantal agreement (found in the *Book of Exodus*, chapter 20) between God and his People Israel, and given to them by the great Teacher Moses, are principles we Catholic Christians still honor today. Although these Commandments had their human expression in ancient, Middle Eastern customs and understandings, both Jews and Christians—followers of the so-called "Judeo-Christian" Tradition—realized that the Decalogue was God's revealed word and have sought to apply these Ten Commandments to the changing circumstances of life throughout the ages.

Such is the high place that the Church keeps for the Ten Commandments in our Christian life. Although one may be amused by the words of a well-known news commentator to the effect that many people treat the Commandments as the Ten "Suggestions"—as if they were nice, but not binding—they are in fact central to a biblical morality and still express for us today the will of God for knowing the good and avoiding evil.

The first three Commandments have to do with the love of God; the last seven, with our relationships to neighbors. Jesus was quoted as saying:

> ..."You shall love the Lord your God with all your heart, and with all your soul, and with all your strength, and with all your mind; and your neighbor as yourself" (*Lk* 10:27).

THE TEN COMMANDMENTS OF GOD
(*Ex* 20:2-17; *Dt* 5:6-21)

Please note: In keeping with the intent of this text to present basic instruction, the explanations given after each Commandment are basic summaries of the teaching of the Judeo-Christian tradition and of the moral teaching of the Church. They are not meant to be exhaustive. A fuller treatment of this same material may be found in the part of the **Catechism of the Catholic Church** *on the Commandments. Since Eastern Church theology has not traditionally treated moral questions in the same depth or in the same way that Western theology has, consulting the* **Catechism** *on this topic is recommended.*

1. **I am the LORD your God,** who brought you out of the land of Egypt, out of the house of slavery; **you shall have no other gods before me.** You shall not make for yourself an idol, whether in the form of anything that is in heaven above, or that is on the earth beneath, or that is in the water under the earth. You shall not bow down to them or worship them; for I the LORD your God am a jealous God, punishing children for the iniquity of parents, to the third and the fourth generation of those who reject me, but showing steadfast

love to the thousandth generation of those who love me and keep my commandments.

The temptation to worship idols is as old as recorded religion. When God revealed divinity to humanity, it was not in a tangible way, like the false gods of non-believers, idols made of wood, stone or clay. God is pure spirit, to whom only are all worship, adoration and prayer due. This includes the worthy veneration of images of God and the Saints.

Contemporary humans consider themselves too sophisticated to make idols in the ancient way; but it is good at making other things today, such as money, power, and wrongful use of sex, into the gods of this world. This is idolatry of a different—but no less insidious—form. Anything that we put ahead of God in our love is an idol. In the words of Paul, "Be sure of this, that no fornicator or impure person, or one who is greedy (that is, an idolater), has any inheritance in the kingdom of Christ and of God" (*Eph* 5:5).

Also forbidden are superstition, magic, sacrilege, simony and atheism.

Positively, the First Commandment challenges all to believe in God, to hope in God and to love God above all else. Also, under the virtue of religion is the fulfilling of promises and vows made to the Good One.

2. You shall not make wrongful use of the name of the LORD your God, for the LORD will not acquit anyone who misuses his name.

We live in days when using the names "God" and "Jesus"—as well as the names of Mary and the Saints—are used callously and offensively. This is otherwise known as *blasphemy*. Since we acknowledge Jesus as our Lord and King, we must always strive to use the Name with the utmost reverence. This is commanded by the Second Commandment. In the section about God-talk and naming the nameless One (**Chapter 2**), we saw how human beings struggle to find adequate words to speak about God. We then who should know better would not want to risk condemnation:

Everyone therefore who acknowledges me before others, I also will acknowledge before my Father in heaven; but whoever denies me before others, I will also deny before my Father in heaven (*Mt* 10:32-33).

Also included here is the avoidance of profanity, and all other language not befitting a person who is a Temple of the Holy. Perjury is also forbidden.

3. **Remember the Sabbath day, and keep it holy.** Six days you shall labor and do all your work. But the seventh day is a Sabbath to the LORD your God; you shall not do any work—you, your son or your daughter, your male or female slave, your livestock, or the alien resident in your towns. For in six days the LORD made heaven and earth, the sea, and all that is in them, but rested the seventh day; therefore the LORD blessed the Sabbath day and consecrated it.

The word *Sabbath* derives from the Middle Eastern languages for "seven." The Bible states that after the six days of creation God rested on the seventh. Hence, we imitate God by resting on the seventh day. However, the seventh day of the week is Saturday.

Because Jesus was raised on Sunday, the Church changed its day of rest to Sunday very early in Christian history. For Catholics—and the vast majority of Christians—Sunday is the Sabbath.

Going to worship on the appointed days (Sundays and holy days of obligation) should not be seen as a bother or even a duty. Rather, we who love God should welcome the opportunity to come together and praise God in a common fellowship, especially in countries where free worship is protected by law. Doing so should be our joy.

We are asked to look at these specified days of our lives even more deeply, namely as a chance to rest from the pressures of the work week, a time to relax and play (see **"Eastern Christian Duties,"** in **Appendix I**). In fact, in an earlier time (and even today in some countries) holy days were seen as festival days. We begin Sunday with the Word and the Eucharist, and we extend these graces and effects throughout the day.

Thus, we need to be nourished regularly on the Word and the Bread of Life. Only the gravest reason will excuse us.

4. **Honor your father and your mother, so that your days may be long in the land that the LORD your God is giving you.**

This Commandment is not only for children. In fact, it was not originally written merely for children but rather for a society (the Israelites) who highly prized family life and respected elders. Thus, anyone who exercises legitimate authority—not only parents—must be obeyed as well as govern in a godly manner. The Church highly encourages healthy family life as the foundation of society and even as the mirror of the Mystery of the Church (see **"The Domestic Church," in Chapter 28**).

In many societies, particularly in the West, senior citizens are shunted off to nursing homes and forgotten. This Commandment promises blessings to anyone who honors those who gave life.

5. You shall not murder. *(NRSV)*

The Church has traditionally restricted to the absolute minimum the instances when life may be taken: legitimate defense of self and of society. Recently, John Paul II has stated that the circumstances under which the State may take a life in capital punishment are "...very rare, if non-existent."

The other arena in which killing was more traditionally seen as permitted but that is seriously questioned today by the Church is war and the so-called *just war theory*. Nuclear holocaust, made possible by the unchecked arms race, as well as the technologizing of the means of war, render medieval images of hand-to-hand combat ludicrous and unconscionable. In the words of the *Catechism*:

> Because of the evils and injustices that all war brings with it, we must do everything reasonably possible to avoid it (*CCC* 2327)...The Church and human reason assert the permanent validity of the moral law during armed conflicts. Practices deliberately contrary to the law of nations and to its universal principles are crimes (*CCC* 2328)...The arms race is one of the greatest curses on the human race and the harm it inflicts on the poor is more than can be endured (*CCC* 2329)

No matter how it is rationalized, abortion remains in the Church's teaching an act of murder against defenseless life. This crime against life carries with it a penalty of excommunication. *In vitro* fertilization is not permitted by the Church because in the process of fertilizing the eggs in a petri dish, more than one egg successfully treated become zygotes and capable of growing into viable embryos. Hence, when they are discarded human life is too.

Biogenetics is a new and largely uncontrolled area. While scientists possess an increasing capability for good through better technology, the question still remains: how is this to be monitored and by what moral and ethical standards?

Euthanasia is often whitewashed as "mercy-killing"; it is prohibited here as is suicide "with the intention of setting an example" (*CCC* 2282). However, in very many cases, other circumstances—such as psychological or emotional—come into play.

This commandment also forbids the abuse of the body, mind and spirit and safety. Included are abuses of alcohol and drugs. The public sector has finally caught up to the moral wisdom of avoiding smoking, which has been proven to harm one's own health and the health of others (in secondary smoke). Any reckless, irresponsible behavior is forbidden as contrary to the service of life.

Since the opposite of death is life, we recognize here that the Catholic Church is a Church which respects life, from beginning to end, in the words of the late Cardinal Joseph Bernardin, a "seamless garment" (see **"A Consistent Ethic of Life,"** in **Chapter 28**).

Here we must also consider non-physical violence as well. Thus anything which degrades or diminishes the dignity of another is forbidden. This includes prejudice of any sort, notably, racism and sexism. Scandal, which leads another to do evil, is also forbidden. In short, any kind of violence is forbidden by the 5th Commandment.

As usual, Jesus pushes the point to its extreme, to an ideal that always challenges:

You have heard that it was said, "An eye for an eye and a tooth for a tooth." But I say to you, Do not resist an evildoer. But if anyone strikes you on the right cheek, turn the other also; and if anyone wants to sue you and take your coat, give your cloak as well; and if anyone forces you to go one mile, go also the second mile. Give to everyone who begs from you, and do not refuse anyone who wants to borrow from you. You have heard that it was said, "You shall love your neighbor and hate your enemy." But I say to you, Love your enemies and pray for those who persecute you, so that you may be children of your Father in heaven; for he makes his sun rise on the evil and on the good, and sends rain on the righteous and on the unrighteous (*Mt* 5:38-45).

He also said: "Blessed are the peacemakers, for they shall see God."

6. You shall not commit adultery.

Adultery violates the trust that stands at the heart of the marriage commitment. When this Commandment was given, it was to protect the sacredness of family life, which included the love and respect spouses were to have for one another. When one of the parties committing adultery is married, it is bad; if both are married (not to each other), it is double jeopardy.

Divorce is forbidden, because by it the bond between spouses and society's bonds of family life and broken.

Pre- and extra-marital sexual relations, however sincere, do not express the full commitment called for by truly Christian marriage.

Of particular concern is the growing acceptance of unmarried Christian people cohabitating. It is widely but wrongly assumed today that engaged persons may live together and carry on an active sexual life without sin. It is claimed that doing so enables people to get to know each other better and thus the couple will have a better marriage. The realities point to the opposite. Couples often break up bitterly when they really learn truths about themselves that they don't like; yet the emotional scars of undisciplined sex remain. In addition, cohabitating sends the wrong message to the very young that promiscuity is acceptable.

The Church teaches that the gift of sex is to be used within the context of a committed, Christian marriage; and anything outside of that context is forbidden. This includes: fornication, masturbation, polygamy, the use of pornography, prostitution, rape (actually a sin of violence), incest and any abuse by adults perpetrated on children.

While the Church condemns the use of artificial contraception, including sterilization and vasectomy, it does not prohibit the regulation of procreation by natural methods, such as natural family planning. The reliability of natural family planning methods has improved greatly.

Considered under this Commandment are the virtues of chastity and temperance, which help us to control our strong sexual drives toward improper use of them and towards impurity. By this Commandment

Christians are urged to use modesty, patience and discretion in dress and speech, for modesty protects the person's intimate center (*CCC* 2533).

7. You shall not steal.

The goods of creation are meant for all, even when we own private property. In every case, justice and charity must govern the distribution of goods. Envy and greed are forbidden.

Stealing is stealing, whether the furtive taking of tools and supplies from work or the rationalized piracy in stock brokering and embezzling. Not giving a full day's work for our wages is forbidden. The other common area is that of cheating in matters of taxes and insurance, as well as other kinds of fraud. Irresponsible gambling is also forbidden.

All that is stolen, big and small, must be returned; this is called "making restitution," and some form of it is to be demanded by the priest in the confessional. Since willful damage—or vandalism—is also forbidden, restitution must be made in this case as well.

Balanced against stealing is the real concern for the poor that committed Christians must have. If somehow I am living at the expense of helping the poor from my abundance, I have the duty to examine my self and my motives in not assisting them.

Since we live in a clearly more materialistic age, the urging to share is appropriate and just. (See *"Philanthropia,"* in **Chapter 28**.)

8. You shall not bear false witness against your neighbor.

The ancient philosophers reflected on the nature of Truth as the goal of their efforts. Jesus—the Way, the Truth and the Life—speaks about truth, too:

> As he was saying these things, many believed in him. Then Jesus said to the Jews who had believed in him, "If you continue in my word, you are truly my disciples; and you will know the truth, and the truth will make you free" (*Jn* 8:30-32).

Christians have a duty, by this Commandment, to be dedicated to knowing the truth and speaking it and also to be honest in everything, for society has the right to the truth. This commandment forbids all forms of lying, which may be defined as saying what is false with the intention of deceiving one's neighbor.

The words "false witness" refer to perjuring oneself in a court of law. Since the Ten Commandments are a legal code in the Covenant with God, we are dealing here with a commandment that sought to safeguard the moral health of the Israelite Community. But it also applies to other dealings with our in neighbors and friends—and with all. Defamation of character is forbidden.

We are also commanded to stand up for the truth when confronted by the all forms of dishonesty, and to make reparation if one violates the truth.

An issue closely related to the discussion of truth is that of the so-called "seal of confession." This is a very important matter of sacramental discipline by which a priest-confessor may never reveal something that is told in confession, even in a court of law. If he does so, Church law provides that his priestly faculties are suspended by the bishop. Knowing this ought to encourage people to seek God's and the Church's forgiveness for any sin, no matter how great, in the Mystery of Penance.

You shall not covet your neighbor's house; you shall not covet **9.) your neighbor's wife**, or male or female slave, or ox, or donkey, or **10.) anything that belongs to your neighbor.**

These two Commandments forbid the desire for things that don't belong to us and are related to the 7th Commandment's prohibition against stealing.

In the Israelite culture of the Middle East of the time of the giving of the Commandments, women were legally considered little more than possessions. (The reality was different within the home life; see, for example, *Proverbs* 26, esp. v. 16). Thus, the two Commandments seem to lump together wife and possessions. Nevertheless, the intent of the Commandments is still valid: do not even desire that which is not yours.

Envy and greed are forbidden by these Commandments.

On the positive side, the Commandments encourage a real regard for voluntary poverty. This means a real freedom from the *attachment* to material possessions that directs our gaze away from God and the spiritual life. Instead of being obsessed by a spirit of materialism, the Gospel-minded Christian recognizes that he or she strives to live within one's means, not *beyond* them.

We are also commanded here to the virtue of purity, especially regarding matters of sexuality.

Covenant: the Heart of Biblical Morality

As believers, we are not merely people bound by commands. This would amount to mere legalism. If we understand the nature and purpose of the Commandments given to us by God, we would know that they are meant to reflect *relationship*: to God (first three Commandments) and to others (last seven Commandments).

> When the Pharisees heard that he had silenced the Sadducees, they gathered together, and one of them [a scholar of the law] tested him by asking, "Teacher, which commandment in the law is the greatest?" He said to him, "You shall love the Lord, your God, with all your heart, with all your soul, and with all your mind. This is the greatest and the first commandment. The second is like it: You shall love your neighbor as yourself. The whole law and the prophets depend on these two commandments" (*Mt* 22:34-40).

Jesus' people, the Jews, knew well the covenant relationship with God. There had been the covenant with Noah, signified by the rainbow; and with Abraham and the promise of many descendants. Moses had received the Commandments, summing up the Old Covenant. But Jesus himself would ratify the New Covenant with God's People:

> This is my commandment: love one another as I love you (*Jn* 15:12).

Thus, because we are bound to the relationship of covenant, we are people who value living in community, especially the Community of the Church (see **Chapter 3, "Image and Likeness"** on communion as image of God).

The Beatitudes: New Law of Christ

When we turn to the New Testament, primarily the teaching of Jesus we find much that is powerful for knowing and doing the good.

The author of Matthew's Gospel (*Mt* 5:1-11) gives us a portrait of Jesus as the New Moses ascending the mountain and imparting the will of

God to the people. These new "laws" of living are not like the Old Covenant, which had its binding force in a legal contract. Rather, they respond to the human desire for happiness, fulfill the promises of previous covenants, and direct those faithful to Christ toward the Kingdom. They are, in fact, ways of acting that cause the one putting them into practice to be "blessed" (the Latin word for "blessed" is *beatus*, hence, "Beatitudes").

The Beatitudes are a sort of New Law of Christ:

1) Blessed are the poor in spirit, for theirs is the kingdom of heaven.
2) Blessed are those who mourn, for they will be comforted.
3) Blessed are the meek, for they will inherit the earth.
4) Blessed are those who hunger and thirst for righteousness, for they will be filled.
5) Blessed are the merciful, for they will receive mercy.
6) Blessed are the pure in heart, for they will see God.
7) Blessed are the peacemakers, for they will be called children of God.
8) Blessed are those who are persecuted for righteousness' sake, for theirs is the kingdom of heaven.
9) Blessed are you when people revile you and persecute you and utter all kinds of evil against you falsely on my account.
10) Rejoice and be glad, for your reward is great in heaven, for in the same way they persecuted the prophets who were before you.

Other Biblical Principles

The Beatitudes are certainly a key teaching of the Jesus; but the New Testament is rich and full of principles for a Christian morality.

Chief among these other biblical principles is the so-called "Golden Rule," stated in *Mt* 7:12:

In everything do to others as you would have them do to you; for this is the law and the prophets.

Perhaps few other biblical sayings are so widely accepted as a rule of living as this one. This is probably true because, far from being original with Jesus, it was in fact long accepted in other times and cultures in one form or another, including the Israelite religion. What Jesus did was to change the saying from its negative, Jewish phrasing ("What you don't

WHY CAN'T I DO IT IF IT'S LEGAL?

In the discussion about law so far two great examples have been presented: The Law given by God to Moses, which is what is usually meant by "The Law" in the Hebrew Scriptures and the Gospels, and the New Law of Christ, part of which is summarized in the Beatitudes, and part of which is Jesus' commandment to love (see *Jn* 13:34). These can be thought of as religious law systems determined by God's revealing them to us through Moses and Jesus.

When we think of law(s) today, most likely we think of the civil laws that govern countries and societies. These have usually been formulated by wise persons, who know that the positive function of law is to help structure and manage society for the greatest good of persons. Thus, even civil law generally serves a good purpose.

Yet, there is a possible danger here when it comes to acting in relationship to the law: the distinction between what is legal and what is moral. A growing number of persons today (particularly among the young but not limited to them) wrongly judge that just because something is permitted in the civil law of the land that it is also moral. Ideally, laws should be based on values commonly held by the society they seek to serve. Sometimes, as in the case of abortion, for example, they do not. Thinking that "legal is always moral" betrays an immature attitude toward acting rightly, i.e., according to God's Law. Equally irresponsible is the idea that it's OK to do something illegal as long as I don't get caught.

To act morally, Christians must realize that moral law always transcends mere civil considerations and rejoice when the civil law is in line with God's.

wish for yourself…") to the positive: "Do to others…" Clearly this meets the demands of a positive, Christian morality.

The Parables of Jesus

The parables of Jesus, which are widely accepted as among the most authentic of his sayings found in the New Testament, are good sources of principles for a Christian morality. One immediately thinks of the answer to the (Mosaic) lawyer in the Gospel who asks Jesus what he must do to gain eternal life:

> Just then a lawyer stood up to test Jesus. "Teacher," he said, "what must I do to inherit eternal life?" He said to him, "What is written in the law? What do you read there?" He answered, "You shall love the Lord your God with all your heart, and with all your soul, and with all your strength, and with all your mind; and your neighbor as yourself" (*Lk* 10:25-27).

Jesus then follows with the classic story of the "Good Samaritan" (*Lk* 10:31-35), a pointed story about going out of one's way to show kindness and caring for others, especially when it is least expected.

We cannot ignore, either, the famous parable about the judgment of the "king" in Matthew's parable of The Sheep and the Goats (*Mt* 25:31-46).

Forgiveness

Forgiveness as a way of life, and a condition for being forgiven, is stated clearly in the only prayer that the New Testament records Jesus teaching his followers, the "Our Father":

> …and forgive us our debts, as we also have forgiven our debtors… (*Mt* 6:12).

> …and forgive us our sins, for we ourselves forgive everyone indebted to us… (*Lk* 11:4).

The Three Theological Virtues

There are three virtues, which are given to us for a right relationship to the Trinity. They are the three "theological virtues" of *faith, hope and love.* Although they are found in places in the Scriptures, let us attend to the words of St. Paul:

> But strive for the greater gifts. And I will show you a still more excellent way... Love is patient; love is kind; love is not envious or boastful or arrogant or rude. It does not insist on its own way; it is not irritable or resentful; it does not rejoice in wrongdoing, but rejoices in the truth. It bears all things, believes all things, hopes all things, endures all things. Love never ends... but when the complete comes, the partial will come to an end. When I was a child, I spoke like a child, I thought like a child, I reasoned like a child; when I became an adult, I put an end to childish ways. For now we see in a mirror, dimly, but then we will see face to face. Now I know only in part; then I will know fully, even as I have been fully known. And now faith, hope, and love abide, these three; and the greatest of these is love (*1 Cor* 12:31; 13:4-8a, 10a-13 13:4-8a, 10a-13).

In the opening to this passage, Paul urges us to "strive for the greater gifts." He concludes with the observation that in this life "faith, hope and love abide." This passage from Paul is one of the classic passages speaking of the theological virtues.

In paragraph 1841 the *Catechism* describes these virtues as the three "theological virtues," and teaches that they "inform all the moral virtues" and gives them life.

The Primacy of Love

Returning to the passage from *First Corinthians* above, we see that for Paul—as for Jesus and the early Church—the most important virtue is love:

> And now faith, hope, and love abide, these three; and the greatest of these is love (*1 Cor* 13:13).

It is commonplace today to recognize that there are many different "definitions" of love, particularly in popular culture, ranging from the most base to the loftiest. We cannot pin love down to one meaning—the ancients Greeks at least had different words for "love." Yet here, with Paul, and with other New Testament writers, particularly the Fourth

Evangelist (John), love is primary. They echo the teaching of the Master, who even went so far as to encourage his followers to love their enemies and do good to those that persecuted them (see *Mt* 5:44).

Above anything, our world needs people who live with love as their guide. In daily living we must at all times seek to act with human kindness, for it is increasingly being forgotten. Deep, God-centered, people-caring love is at the heart of the Gospel. Above all, this love constitutes the Christian moral life.

> Little children, let us love, not in word or speech, but in truth and action…And this is his commandment, that we should believe in the name of his Son Jesus Christ and love one another, just as he has commanded us (*1 Jn* 3:18, 23).

The Bible has much to teach about upright living.

STUDY QUESTIONS:
1) What is the basic principle of morality?
2) Why are the 10 Commandments fundamental to Judeo-Christian morality?
3) Why is love so basic to Christian morality? What did Jesus mean by "love"?

Chapter 28:
Living a Moral Life II:
Morality in Church Tradition

Living Out Biblical Moral Principles
Since Tradition is the lived-out experience of God's Word in history, the Church has naturally reflected upon what constitutes living that Word in every age. Each generation that makes up the Church seeks to interpret God's will for Christian living according to the situation and circumstances of its age. Biblical morality—especially centered on the Gospel—is one of the pillars that support our Christian life.

Spirituality
Before any discussion about living out the Christian life, we do well to consider the important question of spirituality. Spirituality is nothing less than living in the spirit of the Gospel with the help of the Holy Spirit, who helps us remember the words and deeds of Jesus:

> I have said these things to you while I am still with you.
> But the Holy Spirit, whom the Father will send in my
> name, will teach you everything, and remind you of all that
> I have said to you (*Jn* 14:25-26).

Spirituality may take different forms. Also, there are common elements that make up a spirituality as well. Some basic elements of a Maronite and Eastern spirituality are:

❖ *The Word of God.* Fundamental to any Christian spirituality is a deep knowledge of and prayerful devotion to the Message of the Bible.
❖ *A lively liturgical life.* For a Maronite, as for all Eastern Church believers, the liturgical tradition is a basic way to define spirituality. This includes: the Divine Liturgy; the Lectionary and Liturgical Year;

the seven sacramental Mysteries; the Divine Office, and liturgical devotions.

❖ *The teachings of the Fathers.* Through the writings of these Teachers we experience the underpinnings of our individual and common Christian heritage. (See Brock, *Syriac Fathers...,* in Bibliography.)

❖ *Participation in the life of the Church,* especially in the living parish, is essential to a healthy spirituality. In the parish we can be affirmed in our common faith; learn about our spiritual heritage; hear the Word of God preached; deepen our religious education, and find opportunities to serve the wider community, especially the poor.

Sunday of Bartimaeus the Blind Man
Mt 10:46-52

Conscience

In any basic discussion of morality, an essential question is implied: *How do we know* the good to do and the evil to avoid? Or, put in another way: How do we know right from wrong?

From the earliest we can remember, we are taught that there are things we may do and things we may not. When we are young, our parents monitor our actions, reinforcing the good and discouraging the bad. We depend on them. Yet, it is inescapable that somehow this ability to sense the difference between right and wrong is within us from the moment of our birth.

There comes a time, however, in our young lives when we begin to exercise a judgment by ourselves about the rightness or wrongness of an action. Often this has been referred to in the past as reaching the "age of reason." By the time we have reached this age (about seven years old, but different with every individual's growth and maturity), many things have already been fed into our inner selves, and the ability to make our own judgments sharpens.

This inner, critical ability to tell right from wrong is called *conscience.*

Some people think of conscience as a burden, for when we know that something is wrong, and yet do it anyway, something inside accuses us; we feel guilty. Note here that two aspects of our inner selves come into play: our judgment of what is right or wrong, and our feeling of guilt or remorse at the bad choice. This interplay is critical about conscience.

On the other hand, conscience is a great source of joy and confidence for the mature person, for in making us aware of what is right, as well as what is wrong, we can respond positively, thus avoiding a bad decision and its consequent remorse and guilt.

When we are born into this world, conscience is put into us by the Wisdom of the Divine Guide, who wishes us to act uprightly. To quote the Council:

> Deep within their consciences men and women discover a law which they have not laid upon themselves and which they must obey. Its voice, ever calling them to love and to do what is good and to avoid evil, tells them inwardly at the right moment: do this, shun that. For they have in their hearts a law inscribed by God. Their dignity rests in observing this law and by it they will be judged. Their conscience is people's most secret core and their sanctuary. There they are alone with God whose voice echoes in their depths (*GS* 16).

So, every woman and man heeds the call deep within. We grow up and mature, and our life and choices become more difficult. This has always been true. However, in these days of rapid technological progress and the fast pace of life in general, we face problems that cannot easily be judged. How do we respond?

It would certainly be nice if we could rely simply and completely on the conscience built into us as we come into this world. But conscience is not like a computer in the sense that all we need to do is click a mouse and the answer is flashed on a screen.

> The days are surely coming, says the LORD, when I will make a new covenant with the house of Israel and the house of Judah. It will not be like the covenant that I made with their ancestors when I took them by the hand to bring them out of the land of Egypt—a covenant that they broke, though I was their husband, says the LORD. But this is the covenant that I will make with the house of Israel after those days, says the LORD: I will put my law within them, and I will write it on their hearts; and I will be their God, and they shall be my people (*Jer* 31:31-33).

Our Conscience Needs to Be Developed

Like the rest of our inner processes—intellect, emotions, and spirit—our conscience needs to be developed (*CCC* 1783-85). In fact we have a serious obligation to do this. We simply cannot rely upon inadequate data for conscience decisions—too much is at stake. The Council taught:

> Hence, the more that a correct conscience prevails, the more do persons and groups turn aside from blind choice and endeavor to conform to the objective standards of moral conduct (*GS* 16).

In developing our conscience, some of the important elements a Christian can rely upon are:

- ❖ Prayer, especially to the Holy Spirit
- ❖ Fruitful reception of the Mysteries, especially the Mystery of Penance
- ❖ The Word of God in the Holy Scriptures
- ❖ The teachings of the Church
- ❖ Responsible professional literature (e. g., medical information)
- ❖ The writings of respected theologians
- ❖ A trusted counselor or friend, including a clergyman or trusted family member

Maronite Liturgy refers to conscience in many places. An important reference is found in the prime Maronite *Anaphora of the Twelve Apostles*, at the closing of the Trinitarian Prayer section. Placed here, incidentally, the reference to conscience is seen in the context of the *Epiclesis*, thus relating conscience to the action of the Holy Spirit:

> **May these Holy Mysteries**
> **be for the pardon of our faults,**
> **the cure of our souls and bodies,**
> **and *the strengthening of our consciences,***
> **so that none of your faithful may perish.**
> **Rather, *may we live by your Spirit,***
> **lead a pure life,**
> **and give you glory,**
> **now and for ever. Amen.**

Once we have examined all the necessary elements that go into a mature conscience decision, *we have the duty to follow that decision* and, as the *Catechism* teaches in paragraph 1970, to act against this decision would be to condemn oneself. However, this is not the same as saying "I'm doing this because my conscience is telling me to," without having done the hard work of correct decision-making. This would only be fooling ourselves; but we cannot fool God.

A Greek philosopher once said that "the unexamined life is not worth living." Christians serious about living a moral life know that God is always calling us to be the best we can. This applies to conscience.

The Person Comes First

One of the insights gained in the thought of recent years is that in making moral judgments the dignity of the human person is to be considered first. This is important in an era in which systems—political, economic, national, institutional—threaten to dominate people. Examples are well documented. Perhaps the last in a long line of dangers to the human person is technology, some aspects of which seem out of control.

Over against the depersonalization that results from these negative influences, the Church stands on the side of the dignity of the person as a norm for moral judgment. Leaders of all religious traditions have spoken clearly in defense of human dignity and human rights. Related to this is the Church's condemnation of the enslaving nature of some commercial and all totalitarian actions (*CCC* 2455).

The basis for this recognition of the human person's dignity as fundamental is that we are created in the image and likeness of God (see **Chapter 3, "Image and Likeness"**). Every life—from the moment of conception to one's last breath—is precious in the Lord's eyes and should be in ours as well (see **"A Consistent Ethic of Life"** below).

This concept is at the heart of what is called *Christian anthropology*. By this study, the implications of just what it means to be a human touched by the grace of God become clearer.

Epikeia

"Teacher, which commandment in the law is the greatest?" He said to him, "'You shall love the Lord your God with all your heart, and with all your soul, and with all your mind.' This is the greatest and first commandment. And a second is like it: 'You shall love your neighbor as yourself.'" (*Mt* 22:37-39).

Because human beings are created in God's image, are endowed with conscience and free will, and are charged with living a moral life, sometimes decisions must be made—for the good of an individual or for the common good—that run counter to an established law *that is unjust.* Going against such legitimate authority for a just cause is called *epikeia,* a Greek word that means "reasonable," or "of just measure." This principle has been known in the moral theology of both the East and the West. This idea is reflected in *CCC* 2256.

It is to be stressed that *epikeia* is permitted in *rare circumstances of necessity or urgency;* is never against a just law; must be considered for only the gravest of reasons, and never to be the result of rationalization or mere convenience. One must also be prepared to undergo the consequences of such a decision as well. For such a decision it is altogether appropriate to seek careful guidance from a spiritual authority and should never be made without much reflection and prayer.

Epikeia is opposed to legalism. In its biblical meanings it is related to the gentleness characteristic of the Beatitudes (*2 Cor* 10:18) and to the great mercy of God (see *Bar* 2:27, *Dan* 3:42).

The Cardinal Virtues

One of the traditional teachings of the Church in this area of morality concerns the virtues. The *Catechism* (¶1834) defines human virtues as "firm attitudes, stable dispositions" that "govern our actions" and "make possible ease, self-mastery, and joy in leading a morally good life."

Four human virtues, called "cardinal virtues" because of their importance, are recognized as fundamental for Christian living. They are found not only in human life but are described in many places in the Christian Tradition. They are:

❖ *Temperance*—which moderates pleasurable attractions
❖ *Prudence*—which helps us discern the true good and the right means to achieve it
❖ *Justice*—which helps us give God and our neighbor their due
❖ *Fortitude*—by which we are strengthened in difficulties and constant in the pursuit of the good.

These, plus the "theological" virtues, can be helpful in making moral decisions and are essential to the formation of a correct conscience.

SEXUAL SANITY

The virtue of temperance is crucially needed in our day, particularly with regard to sexual morality. After the so-called "sexual revolution" of the 1960s, the whole world has been faced with the specter of sexual license, instead of true, Christian freedom regarding the God-given gift of our sexuality. Pope Paul VI was indeed prophetic when he saw the coming of a "contraceptive mentality" into our world. The relative abandoning in Western nations of the ideal of enjoying sex only in the context of marriage has brought about horrible moral and physical consequences: widespread fornication and adultery; sexually transmitted diseases (STDs), especially AIDS; babies born with AIDS; abortion, in itself and as a method of birth control; the use of sex as a weapon, particularly in an economic setting; the weakening of family life; a misguided notion of so-called "reproductive rights." While a daunting challenge, only a return to more Gospel-motivated (and healthy) view of sex and sexuality can turn the tide toward away from the abuse of this precious human gift.

> **May these holy Mysteries**
> **Be for the pardon of faults,**
> *The cure of our souls and bodies*
> *and the strengthening of our consciences,*
> **so that none of your faithful may perish.**
> *Rather, may we live by your spirit,*
> *lead a pure life,*
> **and give you glory,**
> **Now and for ever. Amen.**
> (Anaphora *of the Twelve Apostles)*

Virtues Inspired by Monasticism and the Life of the Hermit

What might the life of monks and hermits have to do with most of us who are NOT monks and nuns? The connection might be clearer when we as Maronites remember our spiritual roots. Not only the specific life of St. Maron but the whole era in which he lived saw the beginnings of what would become full-blown soon afterwards as the monastic movement; and within that movement the heroic and sacrificial life of the hermit. One need only think of saints other than Maron, for example, Pachomius, Simon the Stylite, or Anthony the Great. From the Opening Prayer of the Feast of St. Anthony:

> **O Lord God,**
> **make us worthy to honor the memory**
> **of blessed Anthony of the desert**
> **with faith and *humility*.**
> **Because of his love for you,**
> ***he renounced the world,***
> **embraced mortification and suffered for**
> **the truth.**
> **We glorify the One Who *perfected him in virtue,***
> **Father, Son and Holy Spirit,**
> **now and for ever. Amen.**

In our time we Maronites would see the canonization of the hermit, Joseph Makhlouf, now known as St. Sharbel, and of Sister Rebecca (Rafqa) Ar-Rayes.

Monasticism has played a great role in the formation and development of all the Eastern Churches. Even today, one of the clear differences between the Church Law of the East and the West is that there is definitely more legislation in the Eastern Law for monks and nuns.

Many of the spiritual and liturgical practices of the religious life have influenced how we have come to know ourselves as Church. In fact, one of the present-day challenges of our Church in its renewal has been to see how we can "be" Church in a non-monastic setting, especially in Maronite Communities established outside Lebanon.

Three virtues worth remembering and cultivating for our Christian living from this monastic context may be seen in *simplicity of life, humility,* and *fear of the Lord.*

Especially in our day, when consumerism and materialism have so permeated all aspects of life (and not only in the West but increasingly in the East as well), the *simple life* of the hermit continues to stand as a constant challenge to our obsession with possessions. Seeing the life of hermits such as Sts. Maron and Sharbel, or of Saint Rebecca (Rafqa), makes us realize that simplicity of life is still possible if we want it. Our only really necessary "possession" is God (Who in the end possesses us!). As Jesus once said:

> Therefore I tell you, do not worry about your life, what you will eat or what you will drink, or about your body, what you will wear. Is not life more than food, and the body more than clothing? Look at the birds of the air; they neither sow nor reap nor gather into barns, and yet your heavenly Father feeds them. Are you not of more value than they? And can any of you by worrying add a single hour to your span of life? And why do you worry about clothing? Consider the lilies of the field, how they grow; they neither toil nor spin, yet I tell you, even Solomon in all his glory was not clothed like one of these. But if God so clothes the grass of the field, which is alive today and tomorrow is thrown into the oven, will he not much more clothe you—you of little faith? Therefore do not worry, saying, 'What will we eat?' or 'What will we drink?' or 'What will we wear?' For it is the Gentiles who strive for all these things; and indeed your heavenly Father knows that you need all these things. But strive first for the kingdom of God and his righteousness, and all these things will be given to you as well. So do not worry about tomorrow, for tomorrow will bring worries of its own. Today's trouble is enough for today (*Mt* 6:25-34).

Humility is naturally related to the virtue of living simply. It is what Matthew meant when he spoke of being "poor in spirit" (*Mt* 5:3). Humility is a necessary condition for Christian living that comes right from the Gospel. It is a helpful virtue, for we live in an age today of an unhealthy individualism that is a distorted result of the overemphasis on freedom. We are free, yes. We are also called to be individuals in the sense of maturity and self-confidence. However, these good aspects of ourselves get out of hand when they are not focused on God and the divine will. We do well, in humility, to realize our own submission to the will of God in Christ for our lives and lifestyles.

Maronites need to cultivate the virtue of humility, for one of the characteristics of the Mediterranean culture is a rugged individualism, which can easily degenerate into selfishness and disregard for anything but our own will. The examples of holy religious women and men, especially of hermits, in our Tradition can serve as a corrective to an excessive individualism.

As an antidote to excessive independence, might we not consider instead the concept of *interdependence*? We are, when all is said and done, social beings. We have attained our best achievements as a species when we have worked together for the common good. By considering interdependence over individualism, we see that it is but one other face of the community of life, which the Church teaches and preaches. When we are moving through our life's journey in community and interdependence, we can as the Church be a sign "to the nations" of the saving will of God for the world.

Related to humility is *fear of the Lord.* As the Scripture says:

The fear of the LORD is the beginning of wisdom, and the knowledge of the Holy One is insight (*Prv* 9:10).

The fear of the LORD is the beginning of wisdom; all those who practice it have a good understanding. His praise endures for ever (*Ps* 111:10).

As any devout believer knows, the fear that is being spoken of in these verses is not the ordinary animal fear that causes one to cower in fright but rather the fear of offending the great majesty and great love of the Gracious One. We indeed should be aware of God's Presence in our lives and wish to live as if we knew that Presence. Fear of doing anything against this Great Lover has always been a powerful motivation for true, Christian living. As we say in each Divine Liturgy, in the introductory verses before the "Holy, Holy,":

Cel:	**Let us lift up our thoughts, our minds and our hearts.**
Cong:	**They are raised to you, O God.**
Cel:	*Let us thank the Lord with fear and worship him with humility.*
Cong:	**It is right and proper.**

"Maronite Virtues": Hospitality and Family Life

One of the beauties of the diverse Traditions of the Catholic Communion are the many aspects those individual Traditions bring to the whole. Each culture values things in a way others may not. When this is positive, it is enriching. It is in a real sense, then, that people throughout the ages have recognized a "Maronite Culture." Undoubtedly originating the Middle East, largely in Lebanon, specific cultural values have been carried beyond the original borders and still influence Maronite Communities all over the world today. As this fact relates to living a moral life, two "Maronite virtues" stand out.

The first virtue is *hospitality*. No doubt clearly a Middle Eastern—and certainly Lebanese—trait, it has strong support in the Bible. The author of the *Letter to the Hebrews* says:

> Do not neglect to show hospitality to strangers, for by doing that some have entertained angels without knowing it (*Heb* 13:2).

Jesus is quoted as being even more specific:

> Whoever is not against us is for us. For truly I tell you, whoever gives you a cup of water to drink because you bear the name of Christ will by no means lose the reward (*Mk* 9:40-41).

Whether it is visiting neighbors, visiting the sick, welcoming new members into the parish, or greeting people in the lobby of the church, hospitality should remain a cherished virtue.

Ask any Maronite family or any family of Middle Eastern background about family, and you're likely to find hospitality for hours! Possibly, a Maronite invented the bumper sticker: "Ask me about my grandchildren"! *Family life*, surely an Eastern trait, but even more widely Mediterranean, is a virtue to be cultivated more than ever today. The Church again has been in the forefront of championing respect for family life. So there is something innate about a healthy and holy concern about preserving family values.

The Council describes the Christian family in noble terms:

> In what might be regarded as the domestic church, the parents are to be the first preachers of the faith for their children by word and example (*LG* 11).

Put in simpler words, when a family lives according to God's plan, sharing a firm relationship of faith, love and respect, the Church—and all it stands for—becomes real. We seek support for our faith in the Assembly of the Church; the members of a Christian family have a right to find that same support in the bonds that should unite them. This "Church-at-home" is what is meant by the *Domestic Church*.

"Men and Women of Peace"

In the Middle East, not a day goes by without the word "peace" being spoken. Whether it is an introductory greeting or a farewell—"Peace be with (to) you"—peace is the often-talked-about, not-always-achieved wish of persons of this culture.

Jesus wished the same for his disciples during a very special time, the time of his Resurrection appearances:

> When it was evening on that day, the first day of the week, and the doors of the house where the disciples had met were locked for fear of the Jews, Jesus came and stood among them and said, "Peace be with you." (*Jn* 20:19)…A week later his disciples were again in the house, and Thomas was with them. Although the doors were shut, Jesus came and stood among them and said, "Peace be with you" (*Jn* 20:26).

Thus, it is with good reason that our Maronite Church links the virtue of peace with the Easter wish of the risen Lord. In fact, the ceremony composed by the Tradition is specifically called the "Rite of Peace" and is a necessary part of the Resurrection celebration. After the procession with the Cross draped in white or the Easter Icon (either may be carried in procession), from within the sanctuary the Celebrant blesses the four directions of the compass with the following Trinitarian blessing:

Facing east:

Cel: May the *peace* of God the + Father

Cong: Amen.

Facing west:

Cel: and the *tranquility* of the + Son

Cong: Amen.

Facing south:

Cel: and the *reconciliation* of the Holy + Spirit

Cong: Amen.

Facing north:

Cel: be with us and among us all the days of our + life.

Cong: Amen.

Clearly, this prayer expresses the biblical teaching that true peace—Christ's peace, not the negotiated cease-fires and temporary political settlements of the secular world—is the result of the reconciliation brought about by the loving sacrifice of Christ on the Cross.

Peace I leave with you; my peace I give to you. I do not give to you as the world gives. Do not let your hearts be troubled, and do not let them be afraid (*Jn* 14:27).

The Rite of Peace on Easter concludes:

O Lord Jesus,
you are the source of tranquility and peace
and the great treasure of blessing.
Bestow upon us and among us your peace and
tranquility.
Extend your merciful right hand **on this place**
and on this congregation here present,
as they bow their bodies and souls before you.
Bless them with your heavenly blessing.
Bind us all together
and make us worthy to glorify you...

Just as Christ wishes peace for the Disciples (including us, of course), we are bound to be people of peace. We need to absorb this message into the deepest places of our being and try with all our might to make it a reality in our lives—for ourselves, and for others. By being people of peace that we shall enter the Kingdom:

> Blessed are the peacemakers, for they will be called children of God (*Mt* 5:9).

As the *Anaphora of St. Sixtus* expresses it, at the time in the Divine Liturgy when the Peace of Christ is to be exchanged by the Congregation:

> **Send your blessing upon us, O Lord,**
> **that we may be worthy of the happy death**
> ***reserved to men and women of peace.***
> **We will glorify you, O God,**
> **now and for ever. Amen.**

Finally, the Celebrant wishes to unite himself as a man of peace to the ministry of the altar, the symbol of peace, in the concluding prayer of the Divine Service, a prayer reserved to him:

> ***Remain in peace, O holy altar of God,***
> ***and I hope to return to you in peace.***
> **May the offering I have received from you**
> **forgive my sins**
> **and prepare me to stand blameless**
> **before the throne of Christ.**
> **I know not whether I will be able**
> **to return to you again**
> **to offer sacrifice.**
> **Guard me, O Lord, and protect your holy Church,**
> **that she may be the way to salvation**
> **and the light of the world. Amen.**

Peace and Justice: the Church's Social Ministry

Before the dismissal of the Congregation in the *Anaphora of St. Mark*, the Celebrant extends his right hand over the people and prays:

> **O Lord our God, Jesus Christ,**
> **extend your blessing and pardon to the priests,**
> **the stewards of your people and your holy Church,**

> **to the ministers of your divine Mysteries,**
> **and to the faithful who have participated**
> **in this sacrifice.**
> *Provide for orphans, assist widows,*
> *sustain the poor and distressed,*
> *and satisfy the hungry.*
> *Protect those who call upon your name in every place*
> *from sin and guilt...*

What is the Church's teaching behind all these prayers cited? Clearly, they betray an awareness of the needs of the less fortunate within the Body of Believers, as well as the Gospel command to help them. While these prayers ask God to help, the implication is that we as committed Christians have to help God accomplish the task.

Lack of food, of decent housing, adequate property, of a safe national homeland—these cause people to use means that are not peaceful, and often violent, to obtain them.

Another way of saying this is that people have human rights. This is not due to any thought of selfishness. Rather, because of the dignity human beings possess in being made in God's image, certain basic rights must be valued—so that people may live life with basic comfort and dignity. All institutions are called to recognize these basic human rights, and criticism of their neglect is appropriate and just.

Pope Paul VI once said, "If you want peace, work for justice." He was challenging us to see that justice and peace go together.

The Church cannot idly sit by and wistfully hope that others—including God—will accomplish the necessary task of helping the poor and the unprotected. They will not simply go away. Jesus predicted that the poor would always be with us (*Mk* 14:7). The *Letter of James* says:

> Come now, you rich people, weep and wail for the miseries that are coming to you. Your riches have rotted, and your clothes are moth-eaten. Your gold and silver have rusted, and their rust will be evidence against you, and it will eat your flesh like fire. You have laid up treasure for the last days. Listen! The wages of the laborers who mowed your fields, which you kept back by fraud, cry out, and the cries of the harvesters have reached the ears of the Lord of hosts.

You have lived on the earth in luxury and in pleasure; you
have fattened your hearts in a day of slaughter. You have
condemned and murdered the righteous one, who does not
resist you (*Jas* 5:1-6).

The Deacon Ephrem the Syrian made a life of serving the poor,
particularly during the vicious wars that tore apart his city of Nisibis. The
famous bishop of Constantinople (originally from Antioch), John
Chrysostom, put this value of helping the poor into such practice that the
royalty of the city, who stood condemned for life of luxury at the expense
of the poor, exiled Bishop John. He paid the price for his whole-hearted
dedication to serving the poor and his challenge to those who neglected
them. For this he died in exile. In his typical fashion, he lashes out at those
who care more for their fine clothes than for clothing the needy. His words
sting:

> How ridiculous and absurd to thread your shoes with silk
> laces… What form of madness can be worse?… He who
> ought to bend his thoughts and eyes heavenward casts them
> down upon his shoes instead. His chief care, as he walks
> delicately through the Forum, is to avoid soiling his boots
> with mire or dust. Will you let your soul grovel in the mire
> while you are taking care of your boots? Boots were made
> to be soiled; if you cannot bear this, take them off and wear
> them on your head instead of on your feet. You laugh when
> I say these words, but I rather weep for your folly (quoted
> in Carroll, p. 123).

These two lights of the Eastern Tradition demonstrated the need to
help the needy.

On the second last Sunday before the end of the Epiphany Season,
the Maronite Church celebrates the Sunday of the Righteous and the Just,
which is the Syriac Tradition's designation for the feast of All Saints. The
Gospel for the day is the famous parable of the Last Judgment (*Mt* 25:31-
46):

> When the Son of Man comes in his glory, and all the angels
> with him, then he will sit on the throne of his glory. All the
> nations will be gathered before him, and he will separate

people one from another as a shepherd separates the sheep from the goats, and he will put the sheep at his right hand and the goats at the left. Then the king will say to those at his right hand, "Come, you that are blessed by my Father, inherit the kingdom prepared for you from the foundation of the world; for I was hungry and you gave me food, I was thirsty and you gave me something to drink, I was a stranger and you welcomed me, I was naked and you gave me clothing, I was sick and you took care of me, I was in prison and you visited me." Then the righteous will answer him, "Lord, when was it that we saw you hungry and gave you food, or thirsty and gave you something to drink? And when was it that we saw you a stranger and welcomed you, or naked and gave you clothing? And when was it that we saw you sick or in prison and visited you?" And the king will answer them, "Truly I tell you, just as you did it to one of the least of these who are members of my family, you did it to me" (*Mt* 25:31-40).

Philanthropia: **The Corporal and Spiritual Works of Mercy**

The Church teaches that to meet this need, one must live by the so-called Corporal and Spiritual Works of Mercy, which come from this parable (see **Appendix I** for a full listing of these). In the East, the virtue that motivates our going out to serve the needs of others is known by the Greek word *philanthropia*, or the "loving of all." This term is above all applied to our God, the Lover of All, a phrase often used in the liturgical tradition. If used of God, it is also properly used of us insofar as we are called to imitate the Gracious One. No living out of the moral life—doing good and avoiding evil—can be complete without acting upon these principles.

Let mutual love continue. Do not neglect to show hospitality to strangers, for by doing that some have entertained angels without knowing it (*Heb* 13:1-2).

Do not neglect to do good and to share what you have, for such sacrifices are pleasing to God (*Heb* 13:16).

In the second prayer of thanksgiving in the *Anaphora of St. John*, the Apostle of Love, before the Congregation is blessed and dismissed, the Celebrant prays:

We adore you, bless you and thank you,
O Jesus Christ, our Lord and God.
We implore your goodness and mercies
for the safekeeping of the living
and the rest of the dead;
for the feeding of the hungry
and the support of the needy;
for the visitation of the sick
and the consolation of the grieving.
Look kindly upon them
and give them abundant life.
Bless your people
and shield your flock with your cross....

Catholic Social Teaching

Catholic Social teaching is based solidly on the Gospel commands of Jesus and in the teaching within its Tradition. Recent centuries have seen much development in this area.

---

10 MAJOR LESSONS OF CATHOLIC SOCIAL TEACHING
(Source documents at the end of each paragraph)

1) Link of Religious and Social Dimensions of Life

The "social"—the human construction of the world—is not "secular" in the sense of being outside of God's plan, but is intimately involved with the dynamic of the Reign of God. Therefore faith and justice are necessarily linked closely together (*The Church in the Modern World*).

2) Dignity of the Human Person

Made in the image of God, women and men have a preeminent place in the social order, with inalienable rights, both political-legal and social-economic (*Peace on Earth*).

3) Option for the Poor

A preferential love should be shown to the poor, whose needs and rights are given special attention in God's eyes. "Poor" is understood to refer to the economically disadvantaged who, as a consequence of their status, suffer oppression and powerlessness (*Call to Action*).

---

4) Link of Love and Justice

Love of neighbor is an absolute demand for justice, because charity manifests itself in actions and structures that respect human dignity, protect human rights, and facilitate human development. To promote justice is to transform structures that block love (*Justice to the World*).

5) Promotion of the Common Good

The common good is the sum total of all those conditions of social living—economic, political, cultural—which make it possible for women and men to readily and fully achieve the perfection of their humanity. Individual rights are always experienced within the context of promotion of the common good (*Christianity and Social Progress*).

6) Political Participation

Democratic participation in decision-making is the best way to respect the dignity and liberty of people. The government is the instrument by which people cooperate together in order to achieve the common good (Pius XII, Christmas Message, 1944).

7) Economic Justice

The economy is for the people and the resources of the earth are to be equitably shared by all. Human work is the key to contemporary social questions. Labor takes precedence over both capital and technology in the production process. Just wages and the right of workers to organize are to be respected (*On Human Work*).

8) Stewardship

All property has a "social mortgage." All people are to be respected and share the resources of the earth. By our work we are co-creators in the continuing development of the earth (*On Human Work*).

9) Global Solidarity

We belong to one human family and as such have mutual obligations to promote the development of all people across the world. In particular, the rich nations have responsibilities toward the poor nations and the structures of the international order must reflect justice (*The Development of Peoples*).

10) The Promotion of Peace

Peace is the fruit of justice and is dependent upon right order among humans and among nations (*Peace on Earth*).

—Excerpted from ***Our Best Kept Secret: The Rich Hertitage of Catholic Social Teaching,*** by Michael J. Schultheis, Edward P. DeBerri and Peter J. Henriot (Washington, DC: Center of Concern, 1987), pp. 21-23.

A Consistent Ethic of Life

In this context of respect for human life that the late Cardinal Joseph Bernardin once coined the famous phrase that has become part of the vocabulary of morality: the "seamless garment" of a *consistent ethic of life.* He was referring to *Jn* 19:23-24, which describes how the soldiers who crucified Jesus decide not to tear Jesus' tunic apart, but keep it whole—it was seamless—and gamble for it. Just so, Bernardin suggested, our whole moral stance as Christians should be consistent, from decisions involving the very beginning of life to those of the end. As another theologian has put it: "The Catholic vision runs from womb to tomb."

Moral Issues, Ancient and Contemporary

People ask what the Bible has to say about dealing with moral issues that the people of the New Testament could not have foreseen, such as nuclear war or genetic engineering. The answer is that the principles Jesus taught are timeless, but the job of the Church—particularly the Magisterium—is to interpret these principles for our daily Christian living.

The Maronite Catholic Moral Response

As should be the case with all Catholics, Maronites should be able to say, when confronted by negative challenges to truly moral living, "I am a Maronite Catholic; that's not how I act."

How we act in life, how we behave, says a lot about who we are. Maronites, with all other Catholics, believe that guidance for Christian living comes from a gracious God, who reveals through Word and Tradition, and who loves us and wants only our good. In the words of the Prophet Micah:

> He has told you, O mortal, what is good;
> and what does the Lord require of you
> but to do justice, and to love kindness,
> and to walk humbly with your God? (*Mic* 6:8).

STUDY QUESTIONS:

1) What is conscience? By what specific means does our conscience grow and develop?
2) What is virtue? Name and describe some specific virtues.
3) Reflect upon the necessity of social justice in the Church's teachings on morality.

Concluding Word

The aim of this text has been to attempt to show how, through its rich and beautiful Tradition, especially in its liturgy, the Maronite Church is fully Catholic, expressing that Catholic identity clearly. While not denying any of the other Traditions and Churches of the Catholic Communion, and being aware of the necessary relationship to the other Catholic Churches with whom she or he is in communion, a Maronite lives Catholic life fully within a living Maronite experience.

Within the Catholic Communion, we share the teachings basic to all Catholics. As Eastern, we recognize the common elements of the East. As a Syriac Church with roots in the Antioch of both Peter and Paul, Maronites share the spiritual wealth of Antiochene and Syriac Teachers like Theodore of Mopsuestia and Ephrem, while expressing a simple life inspired by the hermit and monk, St. Maron, enriched by the culture of the Middle East, notably Lebanon.

This book has tried to present the basic teachings of the Catholic Church within the framework of the four basic parts of the Maronite Divine Liturgy. In summarizing the thought of Theodore of Mopsuestia on the Christian life, Rowan Greer makes the following observation that relates to the scope of this text:

> In conclusion, we may summarize the Christian life as Theodore envisaged it. The redemption wrought by Christ is mediated to Christians through the Church and the sacraments. By these means Christians everywhere participate in the good things of the future age. This participation is in a mode conforming to our present state, but it is nevertheless a real participation in the sense that some mystic foretaste of salvation and immortality is vouchsafed to the believer. This participation is evidenced also by the community of which the Christian life is a part; the *koinonia* of the Spirit is a reality, even though a

reflection of the future perfection. In speaking of the Christian life in terms of participation in the sacramental life and in the Christian fellowship, Theodore never for a moment loses sight of the importance of morality and the good life. Just as a considerable portion of his Christology is governed by this notion, so the Christian life is pictured as one of freedom and grace (p. 84).

As we wait in joyful hope for the Coming of our Savior Jesus Christ, we Maronites try to live our lives in such a way as to show that Christ's Kingdom is not only ahead of us in God's future but also present to us as revealed by the earthly life and ministry of Jesus of Nazareth, the Christ of Faith, King of our lives, and in the Church he founded.

Keeping in mind, then, this hope of the coming of the Kingdom, already-and-not-yet, we reflect on this fitting way to end this work by praying this Prayer from *Noohro*, the "Hymn of Light" from Morning Prayer:

> **Our King comes in majestic glory.**
> **Let us go forth to meet him with lighted lamps.**
> **Let us find our joy in him, for he has found**
> **joy in us.**

A SELECT BIBLIOGRAPHY

PART I

Books

Beggiani, Seely J. *Early Syriac Theology, with Reference to the Maronite Tradition*. Lanham, MD: University of America Press, 1983.

_____. *Introduction to Eastern Christian Spirituality: the Syriac Tradition*. Scranton: University of Scranton Press, 1991.

Brock, Sebastian. *The Luminous Eye: the Spiritual World Vision of St. Ephrem the Syrian*. Kalamazoo, MI: Cistercian Publications, 1985.

_____. *The Syriac Fathers on Prayer and the Spiritual Life*. Kalamazoo: Cistercian Publications, 1987.

Brown, Raymond E., and Meier, John P. *Antioch and Rome: Cradles of Catholic Christianity*. New York: Paulist Press, 1983.

Di Berardino, Angelo, ed. *Encyclopedia of the Early Church*. New York: Oxford University Press, 1992.

Dib, Pierre. *History of the Maronite Church*. Trans. Seely Beggiani. Detroit: Maronite Apostolic Exarchate, 1971.

Downey, Glanville. *A History of Antioch in Syria: from Seleucus to the Arab Conquest*. Princeton, NJ: Princeton University Press, 1961.

Faris, John D. *Eastern Catholic Churches: Constitution and Governance* (Introduction, pp. 1-12, 44-66). New York: St. Maron Publications, 1992.

Finn, Thomas M. *Early Christian Baptism and the Catechumenate: West and East Syria*. Collegeville, MN: The Liturgical Press, 1992.

Flannery, Austin, OP. *The Documents of Vatican Council II: The Basic Edition: Constitutions, Decrees and Declarations*. Collegeville, MN: The Liturgical Press, 1997.

Garosian, Nina, Mathews, Thomas F. and Thomson, Robert W., eds. *East of Byzantium: Syria and Armenia in the Formative Period.* Washington, DC: Dumbarton Oaks, 1982.

God with Us Publications. *Light for Life: Part One, the Mystery Revealed.* Pittsburgh, 1994.

John Paul II. *Orientale Lumen.* Vatican City: Libreria Editrice Vaticana, 1995.

_____. *Ut Unum Sint.* Vatican City: Libreria Editrice Vaticana, 1995.

Marthaler, Berard. *The Creed.* Mystic, CT: Twenty-/third Publications, 1993.

McBrien, Richard P., Gen. Ed. *The HarperCollins Encyclopedia of Catholicism.* San Francisco: HarperSanFrancisco, 1995.

McVey, Kathleen, Ed. *St. Ephrem the Syrian: Selected Prose Works.* Trans. Edward G. Matthews, Jr., and Joseph P. Amar. In *The Father of the Church*, vol. 91. Washington, DC: The Catholic University of America Press, 1994.

Meyendorff, John. *Byzantine Theology: Historical Trends and Doctrinal Themes.* New York: Fordham University Press, 1974.

_____. *Imperial Unity and Christian Divisions.* Crestwood, New Jersey: St. Vladimir's Press, 1989.

Murray, Robert. *Symbols of Church and Kingdom: a Study in Early Syriac Tradition.* London: Cambridge University Press, 1975.

National Conference of Catholic Bishops. *Eastern Catholics in the United States of America.* Washington, DC: United States Catholic Conference, 1999.

Nicols, Aidan, OP. *Rome and the Eastern Churches: A Study in Schism.* Collegeville, MN: Michael Glazier Books, 1992.

Nilson, Jon. *Nothing beyond the Necessary: Roman Catholicism and the Ecumenical Future.* New York: Paulist Press, 1995.

Pelikan, Jaroslav. *The Melody of Theology.* Cambridge, MA: Harvard University Press, 1988.

Perry, Ken, *et. al.*, eds. *The Blackwell Dictionary of Eastern Christianity.* Oxford: Blackwell Publishers, Ltd., 1999.

Pierini, Franco, SSP. *Catechism of Vatican II.* Staten Island: Alba House, 1967.

Pottmeyer, Hermann J. *Towards a Papacy in Communion.* New York: The Crossroad Publishing Co., 1998

Roberson, Ronald, CSP. *The Eastern Christian Churches: a Brief Survey.* (Revised 6th Edition) Rome: Pontifical Institute of Eastern Studies, 1996. Website: www.cnewa.org/ecc.htm.

Segal, J. B. *Edessa, 'The Blessed City.'* Oxford: Clarendon Press, 1970.

Zibawi, Mahmoud. *Eastern Christian Worlds.* Collegeville, MN: The Liturgical Press, 1995.

Articles (Series)

Beggiani, Seely. **"Aspects of Maronite History."** In *The Maronite Voice*, Newsletter of the Eparchy of St. Maron, Brooklyn, NY. Glen Allen, VA, 1996-99.

Videotape

Sawyer, Donald. **"Eastern Churches."** Austin, TX: Our Lady's Church, 1320 E. 51st St., Austin, TX, 78723, 1990.

PART II

Books

Bergant, Diane, and Karris, Robert, Eds. *The Collegeville Bible Commentary.* Collegeville, MN: The Liturgical Press, 1986.

Bratcher, Robert G. *Old Testament Quotations in the New Testament.* London: United Bible Societies, 1987.

Brown, Raymond E. *An Introduction to the New Testament.* New York, Doubleday, 1997

_____. *Biblical Exegesis and Church Doctrine.* New York: Paulist Press, 1985.

_____. *Responses to 101 Questions on the Bible.* New York: Paulist Press, 1990.

Carroll, Thomas C. *Preaching the Word.* In *Message of the Fathers of the Church, vol. 11.* Wilmington, DE: Michael Glazier, Inc., 1984.

Coggins, R. J., and Houlden, J. L., Eds. *A Dictionary of Biblical Interpretation.* Philadelphia: Trinity Press, International, 1990.

Greer, Rowan. *Theodore of Mopsuestia: Exegete and Theologian.* Westminster: The Faith Press, 1961.

Hall, Christopher A., Ed. *Reading Scripture with the Church Fathers.* Downers Grove, IL: InterVarsity Press, 1998.

Havener, Ivan. *Q: the Sayings of Jesus.* In *Good News Studies, 19.* Collegeville, MN: Michael Glazier/Liturgical Press, 1987.

LaVerdiere, Eugene. *The New Testament in the Life of the Church.* Notre Dame, IN: Ave Maria Press, 1980.

McCarthy, Carmel, RSM, Trans. *Saint Ephrem's Commentary on Tatian's Diatesseron.* Oxford: Oxford University Press, 1993.

McLeod, Frederick G. *The Image of God in the Antiochene Tradition.* Washington: The Catholic University of America, 1999.

Salim, Anthony J. *Homily Helps for the American Lectionary of the Syriac-Maronite Church of Antioch.* Flint, MI: Full-returning Word Publications, 1987.

Theodoret of Cyrus. *Commentary on the Psalms, 1-72.* Trans. Robert C. Hill. Washington, DC: Catholic University of America Press, 2000.

_____. *Commentary on the Psalms, 73-150.* Trans. Robert C. Hill. Washington, DC: Catholic University of America Press, 2000.

Trigg, Joseph W. *Biblical Interpretation.* In *Message of the Fathers of the Church, #9.* Wilmington, DE: Michael Glazier, 1988, especially pp. 31-38 and Chapter III (The Antiochene and Syriac Tradition).

Valee, Gerard. *The Shaping of Christianity: The History and Literature of Its Formative Centuries (100-800).* New York: Paulist Press, 1999.

Zaharopoulos, Dmitri Z. *Theodore of Mopsuestia on the Bible: a Study of His Old Testament Exegesis.* New York: Paulist Press, 1989.

Articles

McLeod, Frederick G., S. J. **"Theodore of Mopsuestia Revisited."** In *Theological Studies,* Marquette, WI, September 2000 (Vol. 61, No. 3).

Pontifical Biblical Commission. **"The Interpretation of the Bible in the Church."** In *Origins*, CNS Documentary Service. Washington, DC: Catholic News Service, 6 January 1994, vol. 23: No. 29.

Bible Commentaries

Bergant, Diane, and Karris, Robert, Eds. *The Collegeville Bible Commentary.* Collegeville, MN: The Liturgical Press, 1986.

Brown, Ramond E.; Fitzmyer, Joseph A., and Murphy, Roland E., Eds. *The New Jerome Biblical Commentary.* Englewood Cliffs, NJ: Prentice Hall, 1990.

Oden, Thomas C., Gen. Ed. *Ancient Christian Commentary on Scripture.* Downers Grove, IL: InterVarsity Press, 1998.

Bible Atlas

Pritchard, James B., Ed. *The Harper Atlas of the Bible.* New York: Harper and Row, 1987.

Bible Dictionary

Achtemeier, Paul J., Gen. Ed. *Harper's Bible Dictionary.* San Francisco: Harper and Row, 1985.

PART III

Books

Theodoret of Cyrrhus. *A History of the Monks of Syria.* Trans. R. M. Price. Kalamazoo, MI: Cistercian Publications, 1985.

'Zayek, Francis M. *Mary, Cedar of Our Catholic Faith.* Detroit: Diocese of St. Maron, 1975.

PART IV

Books

Beggiani, Seely. *The Divine Liturgy of the Maronite Church: History and Commentary.* 2nd Revised Edition. In *The Maronite Rite Series: Theology, Spirituality, Music, Culture, and History, Vol. VII.* New York: St. Maron's Publications, 1998.

Department of Liturgy, Trans. & Ed. *Qoorbono: the Book of Offering (5 Volumes).* Brooklyn, NY: St. Maron Publications, 1994.

Schultheis, Michael J., DeBerri, Edward P. and Henriot, Peter J. *Our Best Kept Secret: The Rich Heritage of Catholic Social Teaching.* Washington, DC: Center of Concern, 1987.

(Series)

Beggiani, Seely. **"A Commentary on the Holy Mysteries."** In *The Maronite Voice*, Newsletter of the Eparchy of St. Maron, Brooklyn, NY. Glen Allen, VA, 1995-96. (All seven sacramental Mysteries treated.)

APPENDIX I

Our Maronite Customs

Introduction

Note: This Appendix tells you about some of the more important customs and laws observed in our Maronite Church. Many of these are liturgical items regulated by the *Code of Canons of the Eastern Churches* and Maronite Particular Law. Some comments are pastoral in nature. Many are simply an explanation of things we see in and about the Maronite Church, which, because it is its own ritual Tradition, makes it distinct from other Traditions. Of course, many things will be shared in common with other Churches of the Eastern Tradition.

This section is important for a number of reasons. One is that when it comes to things prescribed in the law, we must be aware of a very significant event that occurred in 1991. In that year, for the first time in the history of the Church, a *complete* codification—or systematic organization—of laws governing the Eastern Churches went into effect. (There had been, throughout Church history, collections of laws, and even recently a partial codification for the Eastern Churches, but never complete.) This collection of laws—called "canons"—is known as the *Code of Canons of the Eastern Churches (CCEO)*, and has been referred to in the body of this text. The Code has canons that are common to both it and the separate Code for the Latin Church. In addition to common laws for all the Eastern Churches, each autonomous Eastern Church has (or will soon have) a "particular law," which governs the life of that Church.

Unfortunately, many people, including the clergy, are not fully familiar with all the ramifications of having two Codes for the Universal Church, though it is quite necessary to have two. It will take more time to adjust to this in the practical life of the Church. The Church has lawyers who have studied these sets of laws, and they can interpret and coordinate. When in doubt, your pastor can contact his Bishop's Chancery Office, whose trained staff will help explain the laws and resolve questions.

Some things, which you might expect to see in this Appendix, are found in other parts of the general text. Where this is the case, it is indicated by cross-referencing. Also, individual items may be found in the Index.

Canonical Considerations: the Sacramental Mysteries

BAPTISM

Admission of the Candidate into the Church

Since the earliest times, Baptism has been administered to children, for it is a grace and gift of God that does not presuppose any human merit; children are baptized in the faith of the Church. Some time before the baptism takes place, it is the custom for the parents (or just the mother) to bring the baby to the church for the rite of admission. (Compare this custom with the enrolling of an adult into the program of formation in the Catechumenate.) Traditionally, sometimes only the mother came for prayers after having a child. It is desirable to arrange for the blessing of the baby/candidate beforehand.

Determining Ritual Church Status

An important question with Baptism concerns the **ritual status of children**, i.e., to what Tradition/Rite and self-governing (*sui iuris*) Church do they belong? This is much misunderstood. In general, the presumption of the law is that if both parents are Catholic, but of different ritual Churches (for example, Maronite father, Melkite mother), the children assume the ritual Church of the father, **regardless of the Catholic "form" (ceremony/rite/ritual) used to baptize.** However, in the New Codes, there is a choice that is permitted: if both parents agree, and if they clearly state to the baptizing minister beforehand, the children may be members of the ritual Church of the mother. **If that choice has been made, it is necessary that it be entered into the baptismal record that the child is the ritual Church of the mother.** This is important for the future, especially when a Baptismal certificate is requested. Please remind the baptizing minister to record properly, and it may be helpful to state this on the baptismal certificate if one is given on the day of Initiation.

If only one parent is Catholic, the children are automatically the ritual Church of the Catholic parent.

Requirements for Baptism

The Law requires at least ONE sponsor for baptism, and provides criteria for being a good sponsor. He or she must be a practicing Catholic—this may be attested to by a certificate from the sponsor's proper parish pastor; he or she must have been fully initiated into the Church (have received all three Initiation Mysteries); must be living a good, Catholic life; be free of excommunication; not be mother, father or spouse, and be at least 18 years old. In general, the sponsor should be the kind of person who will support the parents in the duty of giving the child(ren) a Christian education and be a good example of Catholic life.

Insofar as it is possible, parents and godparents should attend pre-Jordan (pre-Baptism/Chrismation) classes, to review the teaching about these Mysteries, as well as to prepare them for their Christian duties in regard to the children's Christian upbringing.

As the child grows, pastoral care should be taken to ensure that he or she learn about not only his/her Baptism but also about Chrismation at an appropriate older age. Parents of children who have received both Mysteries should also make the staff of a Latin parish whose school the children may attend aware that both these Mysteries have been received, for neither Baptism nor Chrismation may be repeated.

Adult Initiation: the Catechumenate

Adults who wish to learn about Christianity should enter a **catechumenate** program (see **Chapter 15, "The Mysteries of Initiation"**). Care should be taken by the clergy and/or catechist to familiarize the catechumen as fully as possible with an Eastern and Maronite approach to Catholicism. In some East Syriac-speaking Churches the appropriate feast for reception of catechumens into the Church may have been 6 January (Baptism of the Lord). However, in Antioch the day for reception followed the custom of the Roman and Byzantine Churches, i.e., at the Easter vigil. Since Maronites derive from the West Syro-Antiochene Tradition, it can be concluded that Maronites would admit catechumens at the Easter Vigil as well.

Profession of Faith

Adults already validly baptized in another Christian Tradition and who seek to enter into full communion with the Catholic Church make what is known as a **"Profession of Faith."** Catechesis is done; however, this need not be of the same intensity or duration as for a catechumen, since there may already be a good foundation in faith. A sponsor is chosen, and a public ceremony of profession is made. All candidates except Orthodox and Polish Nationals are to be chrismated. The witnessing minister then records the event in the baptismal register.

In general, candidates enter the Catholic Church into their proper Tradition, Eastern Tradition (Orthodox, Oriental Orthodox, Church of the East) to Eastern, West (Protestant, Anglican, Episcopal) to the Latin.

Transfer of Ritual Church

Adults—and children 14 and older—may transfer to another ritual Church. This may be done in one of two ways:

1) *Petition.* A letter from the petitioning party, stating the legitimate reason(s) for the transfer, along with a cover letter from the pastor approving the reasons and recommending the transfer. The Chancery Offices of the two bishops involved will handle the rest.

2) *Election.* There are certain conditions in interritual marriage whereby a Catholic spouse-to-be may simply elect to change ritual Churches. Persons interested in doing so should consult with their pastor, who will inform them whether this simpler method applies.

Baptism in Danger of Death

Any person may perform an emergency baptism in danger of death. Hospital staff are trained to perform this also. This is how it is done:

Using clear water, the person baptizing pours the water over the head of the candidate, saying:

(*Name*) is baptized a lamb in the flock of Christ

(Water is poured the first time)

in the Name of the Father,

(Water is poured the second time)

and of the Son,

(Water is poured the last time)

and of the Holy Spirit for everlasting life. Amen.

CHRISMATION

Chrismation of Eastern Church children and adults occurs immediately after Baptism. According to the Eastern Code, the lawful minister of Chrismation is the presbyter (priest), who may chrismate anyone of any Rite at any time. If Chrismation occurs outside of Baptism, the candidate takes instruction about Chrismation, then chooses an appropriate sponsor (qualifications are similar to the Baptism sponsor) before the ceremony takes place.

+ + +

HOLY EUCHARIST

Note: Since the Mystery of the Holy Eucharist is necessarily bound up with the act of worship, all statements about It should have reference to some form of liturgy. Thus, as above, there will be both canonical as well as pastoral items below.

Reception of the Eucharist on Sundays and Holy Days—and indeed every time one attends the Divine Liturgy—is encouraged, provided one is properly disposed.

Regulations for the Communion Fast
The conditions for receiving Holy Communion are the state of grace (freedom from serious sin), the right intention (not out of routine or human respect, but for the purpose of pleasing God), and observance of the Communion fast.

This fast means that you must not eat anything (except medicine) or drink any liquid (other than water) one hour before the actual time of the reception of Communion. However, the sick and aged, even those not confined to bed or a home (and those caring for them who wish to receive Communion with them but cannot fast for an hour without inconvenience), can receive Holy Communion at any time.

How to Receive Holy Communion
Ideally, and as willed by Christ, Maronites receive both the Body and Blood of Christ in Holy Communion. This is done by "intinction," that is, by the priest, deacon or authorized subdeacon dipping the Sacred Host into the Precious Blood. As the communicant approaches, the hands are crossed over the chest. After the Distributor offers Communion, the communicant responds with a faith-filled "Amen." The communicant then receives Communion on the tongue.

HOLY CROWNING

A Brief Summary of Pastoral/Canonical Considerations

Note: Perhaps in no other sacramental Mystery are the laws about receiving this Mystery so complex. For a Crowning to be recognized by the Church, these regulations must be observed. The reason for this is bound up with the very complex development of Crowning in the history of the Church, East and West. This section doesn't pretend to present all the details. However, again, it is the responsibility of the witnessing minister to see to it that all conditions are fulfilled, particularly if the Crowning involves two parties of different ritual Catholic Churches; between a Catholic and a non-Catholic, or between a Catholic and a non-baptized person.

Pastorally, it is important to recognize that in a day of lessened sense of community in the Church, and lessened sense about commitment among people in general, effective pastoral preparation is essential. Most jurisdictions demand a six-month preparation program, in which the couple are introduced to the life of the local parish community and are also tested and directed concerning the quality of their commitment. This preparation must not be seen as a period of delay before the wedding can take place, but rather (positively) as an opportunity to prepare to marry well. All Catholic Crownings require certain procedures to be done—including necessary forms to be completed—before the wedding can take place. In addition to the requirements of the Church, the couple must also satisfy the demands of civil law as well; however, Crowning in the United States does not require a separate ceremony, as the State recognizes the authority of a Catholic minister in good standing to witness to the ceremony (in some states, the minister must register his ordination).

The requirements for Catholic Crowning are currently understood to be: at least one party must be a baptized Catholic; the couple must be free to be married in the Church (no existing marriages and no obstacles [known as "impediments"]; they must be the proper age; two witnesses (sponsors) are needed—these should be chosen in part for the support they can give to the couple; the Crowning is to take place in a sacred space—normally a Catholic church or chapel; before a priest in good standing with the Church, whose priestly blessing is needed. (Eastern-rite deacons may not solemnize a Crowning). The eparchial bishop may dispense with some of these requirements according to the laws of the Church.

In general, the Law still starts with the ritual Church of the groom, if he is Catholic, or reverts to the bride, if she is the only Catholic partner. If the groom is Eastern, jurisdiction is generally simpler. Unlike the Latin Rite custom of marriage in the bride's church (if both are Latin), in a mixed-Rite Crowning, the ceremony is expected to be in the parish of the groom. Dispensations for these and other details are possible, but must always go through the proper bishop's office.

Marriage between Catholics and Christians of other Traditions is, of course, possible; and such marriages have increased significantly in the days of ecumenism (see "**Ecumenism**" in **Chapter 6**) after the Council. In addition, it is possible to contract marriage with persons of other faiths, as well as non-baptized persons. Certain rules govern these weddings as well.

The ceremony is presumed to be completely in the Rite of the Catholic groom, and the prayers of the actual ceremony may not be changed, for example, to mix the prayers or gestures of another Tradition with the Maronite ritual, or to compose other words for the ceremony. The wedding ceremony in general should respect the proper Tradition, which includes the crowning—with flower crowns—of the bride and groom and witnesses; the placing of the rings on the fingers of the couple by the priest; the bride standing on the groom's right (the guests are also seated appropriately), and music proper to the Maronite service is to be used. Of course, only the Service of the Word and Crowning Ceremony are necessary for the church ceremony; the *Anaphora* and Communion are at times prayed when both partners are Catholic, but this is a recent innovation. Celebrating the Crowning without the *Anaphora* and Communion Rite is more traditional and may be desirable especially if one partner is non-Catholic, since neither the non-Catholic spouse nor his or her family may receive Communion. This will require careful, pastoral preparation and explanation.

Every couple accepted for Crowning in the Catholic Church must answer questions from the Pre-nuptial Questionnaire. These are to be asked individually of the groom and the bride, and under oath to ascertain the truth of the answers.

The Questionnaire has three sections: First are questions about the identity and sacramental background of the person. They include: proper age for marriage; Baptism and Chrismation, as well as a determination of the proper Rite (so as to determine proper jurisdiction). The second part seeks to determine whether there are any impediments to the marriage. These include previous marriages (this may necessitate an annulment process); the previous taking on of religious vows or ministerial ordination; emotional or psychological difficulties. The third part seeks to clarify the intentions of the bride and groom for the marriage, namely, whether they intend to be married to one another till death; whether they intend to have children, and if they intend to be faithful to one another exclusively.

The Pre-nuptial Questionnaire is a great help in determining whether or not the Crowning may take place.

The Betrothal/Engagement Ceremony

A traditional Eastern Church practice that has fallen into disuse in some parts of the Maronite Church is the Rite of Betrothal, or formal engagement. As with many Christian customs, this ceremony has its roots in the Jewish practice of Jesus' time (see *Mt* 1:18).

This ceremony is usually done in the home of the parents of the bride, but it may also be done in the parish church. It is a simple acknowledgment of the commitment of the couple, accompanied by the blessing of jewelry given to one or both of the couple.

Some pastors recently have seen in this ceremony an opportunity to initiate the six-month Crowning preparation program.

Annulment

Sometimes, what appeared to be a stable marriage breaks down, ending in a civil divorce. The Catholic Church does not recognize the ending of a marriage relationship by divorce, even though it is clear that the relationship can no longer be reconciled. In such cases one of the parties may petition the marriage tribunal of the Eparchy for a declaration of nullity of the bond. In other words, the tribunal will seek, through evidence submitted, whether there were grounds at the beginning of the marriage relationship that actually prevented a full Church marriage from occurring. If it can be proven that such grounds existed, the marriage may be declared "null and void," and BOTH parties—the one petitioning (the "Petitioner") and the other (the "Respondent") are free to be married in the Church. Usually the entire process takes about a year, and no date for a ceremony may be set until the declaration is actually in hand. The parish priest is usually the first person to turn to for assistance with an annulment case, though he may have other staff trained to handle cases.

Many misconceptions surround civil divorce and annulments. For example, the mere fact of a civil divorce does NOT prevent either party from receiving the Eucharist at Divine Liturgy—only when a divorced person *marries again without an annulment* is he or she prevented from Communion. Children of a Catholic couple who have divorced are NOT considered illegitimate. The fact of children born to a couple who have divorced does not necessarily mean that an annulment may not be granted. The grounds for granting a declaration of nullity have been expanded in recent years; thus, the chances for a positive judgment are greater than before. Tribunals try to treat the tragedy of divorce with a sense of compassion and no one should be afraid to try to seek an annulment.

PENANCE (Reconciliation)

Introduction

The precept to confess at least once a year is a reminder to receive the Mystery of Penance (Reconciliation) on a regular basis. If no serious sin has been committed in that time, confession is not obligatory. Other acts of penance may be done, such as fasting, extra time in prayer, almsgiving or acts of charity to satisfy the need to make up for our sins. However, frequent confession is of great value; it makes us more deeply conformed to Christ and more submissive to the voice of the Spirit.

The Mystery of Penance is a personal encounter with Jesus Christ represented by the priest in the confessional or reconciliation area. The penitent admits to God that he or she has sinned, makes an act of sorrow, accepts a penance (prayers, acts of self-denial, or works of service to others), and resolves not to sin in the future.

How to Go to Confession

Before going to confession, spend some time in prayer and reflection in humility before God for your sinfulness and on God's great mercy, which will be extended to you in this Mystery. Then you should make an examination of conscience to recall what sins you have committed since your last confession.

Such an examination should include all serious sins committed since the last confession; any faults (less serious sins) you have committed, especially those that are habitual and need particular attention and about which the priest can help you (especially if he is your regular confessor). You may consider the Ten Commandments as your guide; also, the Precepts of the Church. Some Scripture passages to consider are: *Mt* 25:31-46 (Corporal and Spiritual Works of Mercy); *Lk* 15:15-31 (The Prodigal Son/Forgiving Father); *Jn* 8:1-11 (The Adulteress Who was Forgiven); *Mt* 7:12 (The Golden Rule). Your pastor can help in providing a format for an examination of conscience suitable for your life circumstances.

Then you approach the place of confession:

❖ Father greets you kindly.
❖ You respond and then make and say the sign of the cross. You may ask the priest for a blessing or prayer for a good confession.
❖ You introduce yourself (not by name, just describe your situation) and tell how long it has been since your last confession. You then tell your sins. Each serious sin must be confessed as well as possible. It is useful to mention your most frequent and most troublesome faults. The priest will counsel you, then assign a penance. You next make an act of sorrow (see either p. 264 or p. 376 for an Act of Contrition.)
❖ Father then places his stole on your head (if face-to-face confession) or extends his right hand toward you and prays the Prayer of Forgiveness (i.e., the absolution).
❖ Father then dismisses you with the words, "Go in peace." Polite persons thank the priest.

It is important to note that the priest-confessor may not, under any circumstances, reveal what a specific person has confessed. Professional confidences are to be strictly kept as well. This is known as the "seal of confession." Breaking the seal carries severe penalties for the priest.

Fasting

Note: In Eastern Tradition in general, and in Maronite Tradition in particular, due to the rich heritage of monasticism, fasting has played a very important role in the life of the Church. Not only Friday, but Wednesday (and for some, Saturday) were seen as days of fasting. Beside the mandatory liturgical fast of Lent (called the "Great Fast"), other times, such as the fifteen days before the Assumption, or the nine days before Christmas, for example, have been considered "Little Fasts." It is in fact somewhat ironic that we Maronites have to have our fasting regulated, as it was very natural for our not-so-distant ancestors to do great acts of voluntary fasting. Strictly speaking the distinction between fasting and abstinence is foreign to Eastern practice. By doing these and other forms of penance, we can realize that interior change of heart that is so necessary for all Christians. In the United States the Latin regulation binding age is followed, but the actual fasting practice is Eastern. Thus, the current ritually mixed fasting discipline is given below:

Regulations for Lenten Fast and Abstinence

The law of abstinence (which binds Maronites generally) forbids the eating of meat or meat products. The law of fasting (which binds those from age 18 through 60) forbids everything except water and medicine from midnight till noon; meals in moderation afterward. The first Monday of Great Lent ("Ash Monday") and Great Friday are days of mandatory fast and abstinence; all other Fridays of Lent are days of abstinence only.

Pregnant women and people who are sick are not obliged to fast. Others who judge that they are unable to observe the laws of fast and abstinence should consult their parish priest or confessor.

How to Prepare for a Sick Call

When someone is confined to the home, and Communion and/or Confession is desired, you may prepare for the visit by having the following items at hand: a candle and matches; possibly a favorite icon; a copy of the Scriptures; a glass of water for drinking (if necessary) after the reception of Holy Communion. In addition, the general atmosphere should reveal that you know that the Lord is present—if the priest, deacon or subdeacon has the Eucharist with him—and all audio and video units should be turned off. If Anointing of the Sick is involved, it is desirable that several family members be present to join in prayer for the sick person.

+ + +

Funerals

The Service of the Incense (Wake Service)

The Service of the Incense is prayed on the eve of the funeral. It is brief, consisting of short prayers and centering on the chanting of the Incense Chant (*Shabahil Moryo*).

The *Jinnaaz* Service

The traditional funeral service on the day of burial is the *jinnaaz* (pl. *jinnaazaat*), which consists of prayers for the dead based upon a psalm-like structure, chanted from side to side.

Maronite Catholics express their sympathies by the phrase, *Allah yirhamoo* (for a man) and *Allah yirhama* (for a woman). This means, "May God have mercy on him/her." This phrase expresses a deep hope that our loving God will indeed show mercy to one who has lived faithful to the Gospel and has departed this world. Please note that by this custom Maronites do not presume that the deceased has already entered the Kingdom, but rather that God's mercy may, in God's good time, welcome the departed into eternal Light. This custom is in line with the custom of praying for the Faithful Departed.

Funerals are not prayed on Sundays.

Cremation of the body of the deceased is permitted in the Church, provided that the reasons for doing so do not in a public way go against the Church's teaching on respect for the deceased and the on the hope of resurrection of the body.

40-Day Memorial Service

The custom of celebrating the Eucharist 40 days after the death of the believer probably has its roots in the *refrigerium* service of ancient Christianity. The period of mourning came to last for forty days, after which the mourners shared the Eucharist; a common meal of physical and spiritual refreshment, and memories of the deceased. The number 40 is likely related to the biblical idea of 40 being a special number (Noah in the ark, Jesus' fasting in the desert).

Eastern Christian Duties

Please Note: The statements that follow are not exactly the same as what are known as "Precepts of the Church" in the Latin Tradition, although some may seem quite similar. The reason is that days of obligation vary with different sui iuris *Churches. You are encouraged to read these closely and to consult your pastor, deacon, religious education director or Chancery Office with questions.*

1) Worship on all Sundays and Holy Days of obligation.

Can. 881, §1. *Christian faithful are bound by the obligation to participate on Sundays and feast days in the Divine Liturgy, or according to the prescriptions or legitimate customs of their own Church* sui iuris, *in the celebration of the divine praises.*

§2. In order for the Christian faithful to fulfill this obligation more easily, available time runs from the evening of the vigil until the end of the Sunday or feast day.

Can. 880, §3. *Holy days of obligation **common to all the Eastern Churches**, in addition to Sundays, are:*

a) The Nativity of our Lord Jesus Christ (25 December)
b) The Epiphany (6 January)
c) Ascension Thursday (40 days after Easter)
d) The Dormition/Assumption of the Holy Mother of God
(15 August)
e) The Holy Apostles Peter and Paul (29 June).

However, the particular law of a Church sui iuris *can suppress the obligation of holy days or transfer them to a Sunday with approval by the Apostolic See.*

Maronite Particular Law adds other obligatory holy days. Chief among them is the *Feast of St. Maron*, observed on 9 February.

The others are:

a) New Year's Day
b) St. Joseph (19 March)
c) Great Friday of the Crucifixion
d) Monday of Bright Week (Easter Monday)
e) All Saints (1 November)
f) Immaculate Conception (8 December)
g) Parish Patronal Feast Day

Feasts in Particular Law added to the immovable common Eastern feasts may be moved by competent authority (the eparchial bishop) to the nearest Sunday.

In addition, please note the following observations about the list in the Particular Law:

A) The feasts of St. Joseph (19 March) and All Saints (1 November) are duplications from the Roman Calendar of the authentic Maronite celebrations of the Sunday of the Revelation to Joseph before Christmas and the Epiphany Season celebration of the Righteous and Just (the Syriac Church designation for All Saints). The recommendation of the Patriarchal Liturgical Commission that the texts of the authentic Maronite feasts be used for the Latin dates only highlights the fact of duplication.

B) A few of the feasts in the Particular Law also coincide with civil holidays in Lebanon, days on which Lebanese Maronites can easily get to their churches for worship. Thus, the eparchial bishop's competence to transfer feasts of the Particular Law—but not the five feasts common to all—by himself is pastorally sound.

Can. 881 §3: The Christian faithful are strongly recommended to receive the Divine Eucharist on these days and indeed more frequently, even daily.

Can. 883 §2: In families in which the parents are enrolled in different Churches sui iuris, it is permitted to observe the norms of one or other Church, in regard to feast days and days of penance. (Please note that when the Eastern Code was put into effect [1991], Catholic parents of two different ritual Churches may exercise an option of having the children baptized in the ritual Church of the mother, instead of the [presumed] ritual Church of the father. Refer to the section on canonical considerations in the discussion of Baptism above. If this option has been chosen, this canon [883, §2] applies.)

2) Enjoy the Lord's Day by refraining from business and work.

Can. 881 §4: The Christian faithful should abstain from those labors or business matters which impede the worship to be rendered to God, the joy which is proper to the Lord's day, or to the proper relaxation of mind and body.

3) Receive Holy Communion, particularly during Easter time (Sunday of the Resurrection to Trinity Sunday, i.e., Sunday after Pentecost).

Can. 708: The local hierarchs and the pastors are to see that with every diligence the Christian faithful are instructed concerning the obligation of receiving the Divine Eucharist in danger of death and also at those times which are established by a most praiseworthy custom or by particular law of their own Church sui iuris, especially at Easter time, during which Christ handed down the eucharistic mystery.

4) Receive the Mystery of Penance frequently, and as soon as possible if there is serious sin.

Can. 719: Anyone who is aware of serious sin is to receive the sacrament of penance as soon as possible; it is strongly recommended to all the Christian faithful that they receive this sacrament frequently, especially during the times of fasts and penance observed in their own Church sui iuris.

5) Observe the fasting and abstinence regulations on the appointed days.

Can. 882: On the days of penance the Christian faithful are obliged to observe fast or abstinence in the manner established by the particular law of their Church sui iuris.

6) Contribute to the support of the Church.

Can. 25, §1: The Christian faithful are obliged to assist with the needs of the Church so that the Church has what is necessary for its proper ends, especially for divine worship, for apostolic works of charity and for the decent sustenance of ministers.

> **Can. 1011:** *The competent authority has the right to require from the Christian faithful whatever is necessary to attain the ends proper to the Church.*

The Corporal Works of Mercy (For the Body)
1) Feed the hungry.
2) Give drink to the thirsty.
3) Clothe the naked.
4) Shelter the homeless.
5) Visit the sick.
6) Visit the imprisoned.
7) Bury the dead.

The Spiritual Works of Mercy (For the Heart, Mind, and Soul)
1) Help the sinner.
2) Teach the ignorant.
3) Counsel the doubtful.
4) Comfort the sorrowful.
5) Bear wrongs patiently.
6) Forgive all injuries.
7) Pray for the living and the dead.

Maronite Liturgical Customs and Objects

General Customs

As with all Eastern Christians, upon entering or leaving the church, Maronites bow reverently, rather than genuflecting, before the Tabernacle. In addition, there are times during the Divine Liturgy when the Congregation is exhorted to bow their heads—this instruction is to be observed literally.

The sign of the Cross is made tracing the hand from the left to the right.

The Gesture of Peace is given immediately before the Eucharistic Prayer (*Anaphora*) begins. This is faithful to the teaching found in *Mt* 5:23-24. The one who offers peace presents folded hands, and the person receiving it takes peace with open hands, then turns and offers peace to his neighbor with folded hands. Thus, peace is passed through the entire congregation. This custom is a sign of self-surrender and trust.

Only rarely does the liturgical Tradition call for kneeling: for example, on great Friday, at the Great Metany; on Pentecost, for the Kneeling Ritual. Maronites do not kneel for the Words of Institution. The general idea is that we stand in readiness for the Second Coming of the Lord; and since that is unknown, we need to be ready at all times. Thus, kneelers are not appropriate in Maronite churches.

When praying, Maronite Catholics extend their hands, palms upraised, in a gesture of supplication and readiness to receive God's blessing. This is done any time, but especially in the Divine Service at the Lord's Prayer and at the prayer "Make us worthy, O Lord..." before Holy Communion.

Like other Eastern Christians, Maronites cross their hands over their chest when receiving the Holy Eucharist.

Customs of the Liturgical Year

The beauty of any Tradition rests with the diverse customs that help to celebrate the events in the Liturgical Year. The following description of some of the customs of the Maronite Calendar will help show how we have a unique, Eastern Tradition. It should be noted that most of the special, seasonal, liturgical ceremonies take place after the homily of the Service of the Word. Exceptions are the Kneeling Rite on Pentecost (see below) and the ceremonies of ordination of Holy Order.

In general, Maronites greet one another at any feast of the Church with *'Eid Moobarak*, or "Happy Feast Day!"—but there are special greetings at some feasts.

Sunday(s) of the Church:

The Church, the Bride of Christ, is dressed in green and white for this time. Before the Divine Service has begun the sanctuary appointments have been removed. These would include such things as the altar cloths, candles, hand cross, liturgical books, and flowers. During the *'Etro* of the Service of the Renewal of the Church, these appointments from the altar and sanctuary that had been previously removed are then replaced, and the altar and sanctuary, as well as the walls of the church, are sprinkled with holy water and incensed.

Although it is not an established custom, it would certainly be appropriate to wish each other a "Happy New Year."

Season of the Glorious Birth of the Lord:

The Sunday celebrations center around the unfolding revelation of and preparation for the Birth of the Messiah, in the context of the human relatives of Jesus, as well as his legal status as Son of David through Joseph. In this season, there are no particular customs practiced until immediately before Christmas, except for voluntary fasting (especially in the nine days before the Feast).

The nine days before Christmas, commemorating the nine months that Jesus was in the womb of Mary, are celebrated by the "Rite of Preparation." Currently, the Eucharist is displayed for veneration, as simple prayers are recited, with the singing of traditional Christmas hymns. The earlier form of this devotion centered on the icon of the Nativity. On St. Barbara's Day (4 December), people plant winter wheat and other legumes, which will sprout just before Christmas. This sprouted wheat is placed before the Crib Scene. This is a reminder of the new life that is born for us this holy day. Midnight Divine Liturgy is the tradition.

The response to the *Trisagion* on Christmas is, "O Christ, born to the Daughter of David, have mercy on us!"

Maronites greet one another with the phrase (in Arabic) *Milaad Majeed*, which roughly translated means, "Glorious Nativity!" This greeting has more depth than the English, "Merry Christmas," although the intent is the same, of course. Undoubtedly, Lebanese Christians are just as likely to use the French, *Joyeux Noël*.

In the Syriac world of St. Ephrem Christians placed a garland over the door at Christmas to welcome the Holy Spirit (see *Hymns on the Nativity, 5:10*). This Syriac custom might be worth reviving, perhaps with the addition of a small icon of the Nativity placed within the garland.

Proper to the Eastern Churches, the day after Christmas is the "Congratulations to Mary" (*Theotokos*) for having borne the Savior.

1 January is traditionally the Feast of the Circumcision of Jesus. The secondary commemoration is of Saints Basil and Gregory.

Season of Epiphany (*Denho*):

The strong tradition of the East is to celebrate one's Initiation (Baptism/Chrismation/Eucharist) in the context of the Baptism of the Lord. During the Epiphany Service water is blessed. Burning charcoal, a symbol of the Holy Spirit—see the discussion on **"Fire and Spirit"** in **Chapter 19, "Initiation: Eucharist"**)—is placed into the water. With this water the pastor will go to the homes of the faithful to bless them; or at least the faithful may take containers of holy water to their homes from the church.

Certain Syriac-speaking Churches regard this as the time for the reception of catechumens into the Church. This season is the time for Maronites to reflect upon their Initiation commitment especially through Baptism and Chrismation.

The response to the *Trisagion* is, "O Christ, baptized by John, have mercy on us!"

Maronites traditionally make a pastry called *zlaabyeh*, dough fried in oil, probably popularly associated with Jesus' descent into the Jordan River.

The last three weeks of Epiphany focus on the destiny of those faithful to their Baptismal calling. These are the three Sundays of the Departed: Priests, Righteous and Just (the Saints), and the Faithful Departed in general. Although not a developed liturgical tradition, a good catechetical suggestion might be a celebration of the Saints on the eve or actual day of the Feast of the Righteous and Just, particularly as the patronal feast of St. Maron often occurs near this Sunday celebration.

Feast of St. Maron:

This feast occurs at the end of the Epiphany Season or at the start of Great Lent, depending upon how early Easter will occur (and how early, therefore, Lent will begin). This patronal feast of the Maronites is a holy day of obligation, and Maronites gather to honor God through the hermit and monk, Maron.

Great Lent:

This is above all the time of the Great Fast. Maronites, with all other Eastern Catholics, begin the Lenten fast on the first Monday (i. e., the day after Cana Sunday), on which ashes are used in the ritual (a latinization) to remind us of our mortality. Fasting, acts of penance and self-denial, as well as intense self-reflection, mark this season (see the **Regulations for Lenten Fast and Abstinence** in **Appendix I** above). Maronites refrain from eating meat and meat products on all Fridays of Lent; but many still observe abstinence from meat daily throughout the entire Lenten time; however, traditionally on both Saturday and Sunday in Lent one is not obliged to fast. Great Lent is the best and most fruitful time for confession of sins.

On Fridays of Lent, the traditional Veneration of the Holy Cross is prayed. Some parishes still pray the Latin "Stations of the Cross"; but increasingly, others are preceding the Veneration with Evening "Prayer of the Faithful" (*Ramsho*), which is, of course, more liturgical.

"Hosanna Sunday," the Sunday that closes the Third Weekday Cycle of Great Lent and that precedes Passion Week, is named for the joyous shouts of the people for Jesus the King. In Arabic, it is referred to as *Sha'neenee*. This joyous celebration focuses on the children of the parish, who are dressed in their best and carry highly decorated candles in the procession. People take the blessed palm branches home with them, and often weave them into intricate designs for display in homes and public places. The traditional greeting is *Sha'neenee Mbarakee*.

Passion Week:

Appropriately, the response to the *Trisagion* in Passion Week is "O Christ, crucified for us, have mercy on us!"

On the first three weekday evenings of Passion Week (Monday to Wednesday) the public, parish praying of Evening Prayer is encouraged.

On Thursday of Mysteries, the Ceremony of the Washing of the Feet is the prescribed Service. Adoration of the Blessed Sacrament follows. Some parishes involve the male candidates for reception of Holy Communion in this Service.

On Great Friday of the Crucifixion, the Liturgy of the Pre-Sanctified (the *Anaphora of the Signing of the Chalice*) is prayed. Also, at noon (or in the evening, if pastorally better) the Service of the Burial of the Lord is prayed. To this, the faithful bring cut flowers to be placed in the shroud used in the procession with the body of Christ, which has been removed from the crucifix and is placed in a replica of the tomb. During the Service, the faithful are invited to come forward in the church and kiss the feet of Christ before the procession.

On Great Saturday of the Light the *Qoorbono* may not be celebrated. Instead, there is the Service of Forgiveness, which includes confession.

Season of the Glorious Resurrection:

On Easter Sunday, the flowers that were brought to the church for the burial service are distributed to the faithful as they come forward to venerate the Cross or the Resurrection Icon by kissing or touching it. (For the meaning of this custom, please see the discussion in **Chapter 14, "A New Earth and a New Heaven."**)

Colored eggs are blessed, and there is a sort of game in which people try to crack each other's egg by tapping them on end—the one whose egg lasts longest unbroken is the winner.

During this most festive of times, and which is the focus of the liturgical year, the Cross is draped in white. The Congregation responds to the *Trisagion* with, "O Christ, risen from the dead, have mercy on us!"

Maronites, as all Eastern Christians, greet one another all through the six weeks of Easter with "Christ is risen!" and the reply, "He is truly risen!" (*Al Masseeh [q]aam! Ha[qq]an [q]aam!*).

The Resurrection Season includes, of course, the great Easter feast of Pentecost. During this Divine Liturgy, after the reception of Holy Communion by the Celebrant, the triple Rite of Kneeling takes place. The last of the three gestures is the kneeling on both knees by the entire congregation, including the Celebrant. We are to relate this gesture to the conclusion of the *Epiclesis* at every Divine Liturgy, when only the Celebrant kneels on both knees. Thus, this ritual on Pentecost, the feast of the overshadowing of the Holy Spirit, is partially repeated in each Liturgy at the invocation of the Holy Spirit.

In addition, water is again blessed and sprinkled on the people, and the faithful may take some home.

The Season of Glorious Pentecost:

This is the time in the Church Year when we are reminded of our walk with the Lord in the power of the Spirit, living his life. We also celebrate some of the more prominent, traditional feasts of the Saints: Peter and Paul (29 June); the Twelve Apostles (30 June); the Massabki Brothers (10 July); the Prophet Elias (Elijah) (20 July); Sharbel (23 July); the 350 Maronite Martyrs (31 July); the Assumption of Mary (15 August), which is commemorated by a small fast of 15 days leading up to this feast of our Lady; Simon the Stylite (1 September), and the Birth of Our Lady (8 September). The important feast of the Transfiguration of the Lord (6 August) also occurs during this Season. Some of these feasts are moved to the weekend, so that in areas where it is more difficult to get to the church for the weekday feast the faithful may more fully celebrate their significance.

There are customs connected to these feasts. For example, the Feast of the Assumption/Dormition is observed in a festive way in Lebanon, at the famous Shrine of Our Lady at Hareessa, above the Bay of Jounieh, in Lebanon. This famous shrine attracts Christian and non-

Christians alike all year. (Muslims highly revere Mary as the mother of the Prophet Jesus.) But on 15 August, and the days surrounding the Feast, pilgrims make their way to Hareessa to pray and be blessed.

In the United States, the Shrine of Our Lady of Lebanon, in North Jackson, Ohio, is a replica patterned on the great shrine at Hareessa. For the Feast, there is a three-day pilgrimage from 13 to 15 August, which attracts visitors from many long distances.

In Lebanon, on the vigil of the Feast of the Holy Cross (14 September), fires are burned on the tops of the mountains, celebrating the light of the Cross, which burns in the lives of faithful Christians.

The Season of the Glorious Cross:

This season begins on 14 September, the Exaltation of the Holy Cross. The feast has its basis in the legendary finding of the true cross by St. Helena, mother of the great emperor Constantine. On this feast, a procession is made with the Cross draped in white, and there is a blessing of water. During this season Maronites are urged to see the Cross as their standard of life and of salvation as they await the Second Coming of the Lord.

The ritual of the Feast calls for a procession with the Holy Cross around the Church (as at Easter), with its veneration by kissing or touching.

Commemorations for the *Qoorbono*

The liturgical books for the *Qoorbono* provide texts for the celebration of the Liturgy of the Word for both the Sunday and weekday commemorations as well as the texts for the feasts of the Liturgical Calendar. These fall into several categories:

❖ The Sunday commemorations are feasts of the Resurrection according to the seasons of the Liturgical Year (described in **Chapter 11, "The Liturgical Year"**). Some seasons simply repeat the Sunday text all week, except when a weekday feast replaces it. Such is the case, for example, in the Season of the Glorious Birth of the Lord and Epiphany Season.

❖ Great Lent presents a special situation. Here again the Sunday Services have their own texts, geared to fostering an awareness of their leading to the Resurrection Service on Easter. However, during the week are found three, separate penitential cycles: the First Weekday Cycle (three weeks); the Second Weekday Cycle (two "Weeks of Miracles"), and Hosanna Week leading up to Hosanna Sunday.

❖ Monday, Tuesday and Wednesday of Passion Week have one text for all three days. The remaining days—Thursday of Mysteries, Great Friday of the Crucifixion (*Anaphora of the Signing of the Chalice*), Great Saturday of the Light—are three of the most sacred days in the liturgical year. They have their proper texts. The celebration of the *Qoorbono* is not permitted on Saturday.

❖ The Weekday Cycle of commemorations—this applies to most of the Liturgical Year and not covered by any of the above—proceeds according to the following schedule: Monday, the Angels; Tuesday, two options—A) Memorial of Prophets, the Just (Saints), and Confessors and B) Memorial of Bishops, Priests, Doctors, and Monks; Wednesday, the Mother of God; Thursday, the Apostles and Four Evangelists; Friday, the Martyrs; Saturday, the Faithful Departed. This pattern is carried out except where replaced by a specific feast or memorial in the Liturgical Calendar.

*Anaphora*s and Their Seasonal Use

The Maronite liturgical manuscript tradition is rich in the number of Eucharistic *anaphora*s. Although not all of these are edited for use, the current text of the *Qoorbono* provides six *anaphora*s: *Twelve Apostles* (the representative *anaphora*); *James, Brother of the Lord* (the Maronite adaptation of the early Jerusalem model of the same name); *St. Sixtus*; *St. Mark, Evangelist*; *St. John, Apostle*; *St. Peter, Head of the Apostles.*

Special mention is made here about the *Anaphora of "Sharrar."* (*Sharrar* is the first word of this Eucharistic prayer and means "confirm." It is also known as the *Anaphora of Peter III.*) This is the oldest Maronite *anaphora* and has characteristics of the East Syriac Tradition. (The East Syriac *Anaphora of Addai and Mari* bears a strong resemblance to *Sharrar* but is later.) *Sharrar* is not currently in use but bears witness to the ancient period of the Maronite Tradition.

The *Qoorbono* suggests that *St. Sixtus* be used in the Season of Great Lent as well as for memorials for the Departed (such as the Sunday of the faithful Departed or a 40-day Memorial). In addition, the *Anaphora of the Signing of the Chalice* is assigned for Great Friday of the Crucifixion. Beyond this, any of the others may be used at the discretion of the Celebrant.

Maronite Liturgical Music

The music used in Maronite liturgical tradition is Syriac chant or based on it. This chant belongs to the earliest in the Church's music tradition. It shares the rhythms and spirit of its Jewish Temple ancestor. Through Romanus the Melodist Syriac chant influenced the development of the Byzantine and Latin chant systems.

Its proper modes are even indicated in liturgical manuscripts; note, for example, "tune: *ramremein*" or "tune: *bedoneh safro*" in the texts.

In addition, the metrical character of the chant is based on the systems developed by the liturgical work of the Syriac Teachers, such as Ephrem, Aphrahat and James of Sarug. Their compositions not only enriched the tradition in general but also left a legacy in the classification of certain melodies used at Liturgy. For example, one can hear a *yacoboyo* ("tune according to the meter of St. James") or an *efremoyo* ("according to St. Ephrem"; see *Ephremiaat* in the **Glossary**.)

For many centuries a purer form of this chant was the musical standard for the liturgy. However, as the Arabic influence of the culture came to predominate in the Middle East, the musical tradition adapted, taking on a more Arabic flavor.

After the Council a revival of interest in Syriac chant as the proper inspiration for Maronite liturgical music occurred. Authentic forms are better classified today. However, there is the growing recognition that new music composed for the Liturgy must take into account not only its proper Syriac roots but also the individual cultures into which the Worldwide Maronite Church now finds itself after the great immigrations of the beginning of the 19th century, particularly the Western countries.

Maronite Liturgical Art

The liturgical and church art tradition of the Maronite Church—icon, mosaic and manuscript illumination tradition—is based on Syriac and Antiochene roots. One must never forget, however, the general Byzantine and Persian contexts in which the icon tradition developed. (See Zibawi, *Eastern Christian Worlds*, for an excellent introduction to Syriac iconography.)

Although the Tradition became latinized, the true roots of the Maronite icon tradition seem go back to the Syriac icon tradition of the 6th/7th century. An important source is the Bible manuscript illuminations of the monk Rabboola of that time. This Bible manuscript was for many years in the possession of Maronite monks. Authentic Syriac-style church painting is found into the 13th century—a good example is the little church of St. Theodore in Bhaidat (Jbeil district), Lebanon.

The earliest example of a large authentic Maronite icon is that of Our Lady of Eeleej, named from the monastery in that place in Lebanon. This icon of the Mother of God dates from the 10th century and clearly stands in the tradition of the *hodegetria*, or "Guiding Lady" image of Mother and Child in which she points to her Son—she is the way to the "Way."

Like Maronite music, Maronite Church art is being adapted to the various Maronite cultures in the world today while attempting to remain true to its Syriac roots.

From the Antiochene heritage comes the tradition of exquisite stone carving for churches, an art still kept alive in cities like Aleppo, but too expensive to duplicate today.

Sacred Objects

1) The proper Eastern liturgical images are icons, paintings or mosaics—not statues, which are considered Western. (See **Maronite Liturgical Art**, above.)

2) Incense is used abundantly. There is a triple meaning: our prayers rising in honor and praise of God; and incense reminds us to seek forgiveness, as its fragrance "covers the foul smell of sin"; our purification (see **Glossary**). It is customary for those being incensed to bow and to make the sign of the Cross.

3) Incense is burned in a censer (see **Glossary**).

4) A small hand cross is used by the priest during the Divine Liturgy, for the sacramental Mysteries, for blessings and in sick calls to hospital and home. (See Glossary in **Appendix IV** for further explanation.)

5) Priestly vestments are Eastern, Syriac style. They include: a stole that hangs down the front, joined in several places; a belt of the same material; a cope clasped at the neck, and, traditionally, cuffs made of the same vestment material, worn over the ends of the sleeves of the undergarment (alb). Also worn is an "amice" (rectangular piece of lightweight, white material, to which is attached a piece of cloth the same

as the other outer vestments. The colors of vestments are not strictly regulated, as in other Traditions: namely, dark colors for penitential times (Great Lent; Great Friday) and white or gold for glorious times (Christmas, Epiphany, Thursday of Mysteries, Easter, Pentecost, Holy Cross).

Another robe is the *jibbee*. This is a long, black garment with wide sleeves that is an adaptation of the choir robes worn by monks when chanting the Divine Office. It is used by the clergy in the concelebrating of the *Qoorbono* and in the celebration of the seven sacramental Mysteries and liturgical services that do not include the Eucharist, such as Holy Crowning, Baptism (outside of *Qoorbono*), the *Jinnaaz*, or the chanting of the Divine Office.

Deacons and subdeacons wear stoles that are proper to their ministry.

6) A Cross with three bars at the top is frequently seen on books, in drawings, in churches, as pendants and necklaces, etc. Some have thought that this is a specifically Maronite form of the Cross, or even an "Antiochene Cross." Not so. It is basically a patriarchal Cross (signified by a double bar) used by the Pope (who added the third, smallest bar at the top) and adopted for use in the Middle Ages during the Crusades by the Maronite Patriarch, doubtless to show loyalty to Rome. In recent years in the U.S., this form of the cross was adopted as the so-called "Maronite Cross." However, most recently another cross, found in stone carvings in the lands of early Syriac culture adorns the official liturgical books from the Patriarchal Commission in Lebanon.

Blessings for Various Occasions

In addition, blessings and prayers for various objects, as well as persons, circumstances and occasions, may be found in the *Maronite Book of Blessings*. (Several of the traditional prayers in **Appendix II** were taken from this text.)

The custom of blessing objects such as homes, cars, religious jewelry does not imply a magical attitude toward these material objects. From ancient times religious persons have always respected certain places and objects as sacred dwellings for the divine. In our day blessed objects remind us of the protective power of God on those who possess them and of the faith needed to recognize this power and Presence.

In many parishes a special blessing of persons is given at Holy Communion. Those children who have not yet made their first Holy

Communion are blessed with the Holy Eucharist (paten and cup) when brought forward at Communion time in the Divine Liturgy. Of course, if a child has already received Holy Communion at Initiation, he or she continues to receive as usual.

The sick and homebound are regularly blessed with the hand cross.

Stipends (Stole Fees)

Before the contemporary policy—now recommended in the *Code of Canons*—of salaries and benefits for clergy, income for sacramental services was provided in part by free will offerings by the laity. Two instances stand out: offerings for praying of the Divine Service of the Holy Mysteries (*Qoorbono*)—intentions for the living or for the Faithful Departed; and for the administering of the sacramental Mysteries—in parish life this usually means the Mysteries of Initiation (Baptism, Chrismation, Eucharist [but not usually if First Eucharist is separated from infant Baptism]) and Holy Crowning. (These latter often involve a good deal of time on clergy's part involved in the preparation of the candidates for the Mysteries as well as the actual celebration of the sacramental ceremonies.)

In English-speaking countries a distinction is popularly made between *stipends* (offerings for the *Qoorbono*) and *stole fees* (offerings for the seven sacramental Mysteries; the Celebrant always wears a liturgical stole when celebrating these liturgies). These offerings may be made by the family of the sacramental recipients, or by the sponsors in Initiation or Crowning.

Particular Law or the Ordinary (eparch/bishop) of the eparchy can change the structure of income, and even eliminate the stipend system altogether. However, this has not been done in too many eparchies. While clergy income has improved in recent times, such traditional offerings still help. They also indicate a way of appreciating services rendered. Amounts of offerings are not fixed. In fact, the Law clearly indicates that offering be free will, and no one may be refused the opportunity to request an intention for the *Qoorbono* on the basis of inability to make an offering. Nevertheless, offerings should reflect the current standard of living in the country of offering.

Catholic Church law stipulates that the priest may accept only one stipend per offering of the *Qoorbono*. Also, many eparchies (and Latin dioceses) stipulate that the stipend of a second Divine Service prayed on the same day (called a *bination*) should go to the eparchial retirement fund for the clergy or some other charity (*CCEO*, Can. 715*)*. Unless otherwise provided for, a third *Qoorbono* on the same day (*trination*) is forbidden.

By Law, one *Qoorbono* per month must be offered without stipend for the intentions of the living and the repose of the deceased of the parish, especially on Christmas, Easter and the Sunday of the Faithful Departed before Great Lent begins. (This is often referred to by the Latin phrase, *Pro populo*, "For the [intentions of the] people."

The laity of some Eastern Churches make an offering to the priest for home blessings at Epiphany Season, as well as other occasions, but again, this is to be understood as a free-will offering to the priest.

APPENDIX II

Our Prayer Tradition

Prayer may be described as a conversation with God. As the introduction to the Lord's Prayer in the *Anaphora of St. John, the Apostle,* says:

> **God our Father,**
> *you accept prayers and answer petitions.*
> **Through your beloved Son,**
> *you taught us to stand before you*
> *and pray with purity and holiness.*
> *Grant that we may call upon you*
> *with pure souls and clear consciences,*
> *and to pray,* **saying:** …

We can see from the italicized words that God invites us to pray in sincerity, and the Divine One hears and answers our sincere prayers. It is clearly a matter of a two-way street, a conversation.

Maronite Tradition, with the rest of Catholic Tradition, values and encourages us to have this conversation with God. As with any dialog, there are times of speaking and times of listening.

When we speak to the Holy Trinity—or our prayer may even be addressed to one Person of the Trinity: the Father, Jesus, or Holy Spirit—we use basically two kinds of prayer: set formulas, or spontaneous prayer. The latter may or may not be a form of meditation. However, over the centuries, certain prayers have become fixed, and learned by heart. Some are expressed in a fixed way in the liturgical texts of a specific Tradition. Remember, too, the four kinds of prayer suggested in **Chapter 20**, in the section on prayer and praise as a response to faith, namely: adoration, petition, intercession and thanksgiving.

The Syriac Tradition of prayer is deep and spiritual, full of poetry and inspiring images, mystical. Besides Ephrem and Aphrahat, we can think of Philoxenus of Mabbug or Bishop Isaac of Nineveh. A good sampling of these may be found in Brock, *The Syriac Fathers on Prayer and the Spiritual Life*, and also Beggiani, *Introduction to Eastern Christian Spirituality*, in the Bibliography.)

This Appendix presents prayer formulas that are found in our Maronite prayer tradition and some which are common to all Catholics. These should be learned and used frequently as a way of sharing with other Maronites a beautiful way to have a conversation with God.

1) The Sign of the Cross
(Common to all Catholics)

Note: The Sign of the Cross is not traced on the body in the same way by all Eastern Christians. At the words, "... and of the Holy Spirit," the majority of Eastern Christians move the hand horizontally from the right shoulder to left. This was the universal custom of the Catholic Church, East and West, into the Middle Ages. For example, Pope Innocent III in the 13th century directed that the sign of the Cross be traced in this way by all Catholics, with two fingers and the thumb of the right hand joined (see the New Catholic Encyclopedia [1967], p. 479). Sometime later in the West the direction was reversed to movement of the hand from the left to the right. It appears that the Maronite Church followed suit.

The joining of two fingers and the thumb was a reaction to the Monophysite heresy (see "The Syriac Catholic Church" in Chapter 7), which denied the two natures of Christ, signified by the two fingers. With the addition of the use of the joining of the thumb and two fingers the Trinity is signified. This heresy began in the Syriac Antiochene area (the area of the origins of the Maronite Tradition). Since Maronites defended the true teachings regarding the natures of Jesus, it would seem logical that Maronites should restore the practice of making the Sign of the Cross with the two fingers and thumb joined.

**In the name of the Father, and of the Son, and of the Holy Spirit.
Amen.**
(Said at the beginning and at the end of prayers.).

2) The Lord's Prayer (Common)

Note: According to the New Testament Jesus taught the Lord's Prayer to the Twelve Apostles. Therefore, it has become the most universally known and cherished prayer among Christians in history, and rightly so. However, its form varies, even in English translation. This is due to the fact that translations themselves change, according to the tastes of the time, but more importantly according to the greater ability of each age to translate more accurately. For example, the most common way to pray this prayer is based on the seventeenth-century, British translation of the Bible. English was not spoken as we in the contemporary world speak English, as any student of Shakespeare knows: note, for example, the use of "thou" and "thee" for "you," as but a minor illustration. Further, the ending, "For the kingdom, the power and the glory are yours, now and for ever," is a time-honored, liturgical ending, based on the spirit of the prayer, which the early Church added to it.

*Especially the Eastern Traditions have preserved this ending; but in recent times the Latin Tradition has also incorporated it into the context of the Lord's Prayer, with a small "liturgical reflection" (*embolism*) dividing this ending from the main body of the prayer.*

Given below are the two versions of the New Testament, from Matthew and from Luke (note how they differ) from the New Revised Standard Version. The form of the Lord's Prayer from Matthew is more easily recognizable as the one known by most Christians.

> *Our Father in heaven,*
> *hallowed be your name.*
> > *Your kingdom come.*
> > *Your will be done,*
> > *on earth as it is in heaven.*
> *Give us this day our daily bread.*
> *And forgive us our debts,*
> > *as we also have forgiven our debtors.*
> *And do not bring us to the time of trial,*
> > *but rescue us from the evil one.*
> > *(Mt 6:9-13)*

> *Father, hallowed be your name.*
> > *Your kingdom come.*
> *Give us each day our daily bread.*
> *And forgive us our sins,*
> > *for we ourselves forgive*
> > *everyone indebted to us.*
> *And do not bring us to the time of trial.*
> > *(Lk 11:2-5)*

> **Our Father, (who are) in heaven,**
> > **hallowed be your name;**
> > **your kingdom come;**
> > **your will be done**
> > **on earth as it is in heaven.**
> **Give us this day our daily bread;**
> **And forgive us our trespasses**
> > **as we forgive those who trespass against us;**
> **And lead us not into temptation,**
> > **but deliver us from evil.**
> **For the kingdom, the power and the glory are yours,**
> > **now and for ever. Amen.**

3) Prayer of Praise (Doxology) (Maronite)

Glory be to the Father, and to the Son, and to the Holy Spirit,
now and for ever. Amen.

4) Prayer to the Mother of God

Note: While this form of the Prayer to Our Lady is widely known in the Catholic Church, it is not used by all Traditions. The first half of the prayer is based in the angel's greeting to Mary at the Announcement of the Incarnation (Lk 1:28). The second half uses the early title for Mary, "Mother of God," and emphasizes her intercessory role for us, especially at death.

Hail, Mary, full of grace!
The Lord is with you.
Blessed are you among women,
and blessed is the fruit of your womb,
　　　Jesus.
Holy Mary, Mother of God,
pray for us sinners,
now, and at the hour of our death. Amen.

5) Hymn of the *Trisagion*
(Common Eastern Tradition)

Note: This beautiful petition is a standard element of the Eastern Liturgies. It is said to have been introduced into the Byzantine Rite by the emperor-theologian Justinian. While historically there has been debate as to whether the Trisagion is addressed to the Holy Trinity, or solely to Christ, the clear witness of the Syriac Tradition is that it is addressed to Christ at some times, and to the Trinity at other times. Maronite Tradition makes this clear in the varied seasonal responses to the Trisagion (given below). The prayer is to the One who is "thrice- (Greek: tris, "three") holy ([h]agios)." This hymn is always sung three times.

In Maronite liturgy, Qolos are sometimes based on the Trisagion.

Holy are you, O God!
Holy are you, O Strong One!
Holy are you, O Immortal One!

Have mercy on us!

There are also seasonal ending for the Trisagion:

Christmas: O Christ, born to the Daughter of David, have mercy on us!
Epiphany: O Christ, baptized by John, have...
Passion Week: O Christ, crucified for us, have...
Easter: O Christ, risen from the dead, have...

+

6) The Apostles' Creed (Common)

Note: The early centuries of Catholicism developed several Creeds, which summarized the teachings of the Faith. In our day, the two most commonly used are the Nicene-Constantinopolitan Creed (used at the Divine Liturgy) and the Apostles' Creed. The latter is given below:

I believe in God, the Father almighty,
creator of heaven and earth.
I believe in Jesus Christ,
his only Son, our Lord.
He was conceived by the power
of the Holy Spirit
and born of the Virgin Mary.
He suffered under Pontius Pilate,
was crucified, died, and was buried.
He descended to the dead.
On the third day he rose again.
He ascended into heaven, and is seated
at the right hand of the Father.
He will come again to judge
the living and the dead.
I believe in the Holy Spirit,
the holy Catholic Church,
the communion of saints,
the forgiveness of sins,
the resurrection of the body,
and the life everlasting. Amen.

7) A Morning Prayer (Maronite)

Glory to you, Creator of the light
        that dispels darkness
        and gives joy to your creatures.
Create in us, Lord, works of light;
disperse the clouds of sin
        and fill us with the glorious radiance
        of your grace,
for in you we find refuge
and call upon you,
our Lord and our God,
to you be glory for ever. Amen.

— *Second Prayer,* Safro, *Tuesday of Season of Glorious Pentecost*

+

8) Prayer before a Meal (Maronite)

Leader: Glory be to the Father, and to the Son,
                       and to the Holy Spirit,
               now and for ever.

All: Amen.

Leader: O Lord God,
               may your plenty, blessing, + and
                       prosperity
               come down upon this meal
               prepared by your worshipers,
               and bestow upon those who partake of it
               the abundance of your favors.

All: Amen.

—*From the* Maronite Book of Blessings and Prayers

Or

Prayer Before a Meal (Roman Catholic)

All: **Bless us, O Lord, and these your gifts,**
             which we are about to receive from your bounty,
             through Christ our Lord. Amen.

9) Thanksgiving after a Meal (Maronite)

All: **May food abound and never fail;**
             may it remain plentiful,
             through the prayers of Our Lord's Mother,
             and the prayers of the righteous and just,
             who pleased the Lord with their deeds.

             O Lord,
             you are a good God,
             and we praise and thank you,
             Father, Son and Holy Spirit,
             now and for ever. Amen.

—*From the* Maronite Book of Blessings and Prayers

10) Act of Contrition

Note: To date, one of the two sacramental Mysteries that the Maronite Church has not yet revised is the procedure of auricular confession (confession heard privately by the priest). The other Mystery is Anointing of the Sick. These revisions are being studied by the Patriarchal Commission.

The formal Act of Contrition Prayer currently being used is that found in the Rite of Reconciliation of the Latin Church (given below), unless one chooses to pray a prayer spontaneously. What should be expressed is a sincere sorrow for offending God's love for us and a realization that God is not only just but merciful, and a firm intention not to sin again.

(Please refer to the discussion of the Eucharist as forgiving sin—see Chapter 19, "Holy Things for the Holy." There is a common absolution of the Congregation in the Rite of Forgiveness just before Holy Communion in the Qoorbono.) A valuable alternate to the prayer below is the Prayer of St. Ephrem, on p. 264, which may be used as a Prayer of Contrition in confession.

My God,
I am sorry for my sins with all my heart.
In choosing to do wrong,
and failing to do good,
I have sinned against you,
whom I should love above all things.
I firmly intend, with your help,
to do penance, to sin no more,
and to avoid whatever leads me to sin.
Our Savior, Jesus Christ,
suffered and died for us.
In his name, my God, have mercy. Amen.

—From the Roman Rite of Reconciliation

✝

11) The Jesus Prayer (Eastern)

Lord Jesus Christ, Son of David, have mercy on me, a sinner!

✝

12) Prayer for the Faithful Departed (Maronite)

O true Hope who never fails,
plant the true hope of your resurrection
among those who have died
and have fulfilled their lives hoping in you.
Grant the power of your resurrection to their bodies
and the forgiveness of sins to their souls.
Lead them into your kingdom,
that they may be with you.
And they will glorify and praise you, O Christ,
your Father, and your living and Holy Spirit,
now and for ever. Amen.

—Opening Prayer, Sunday of the Faithful Departed

✝

13) Night Prayer (Maronite)

O Lord,
the night and the day are yours;
you uphold the light and the sun.
Through your power you direct
        the sequence of the seasons.
O Lord,
you have brought the day to its close
        and called forth the night.
Be for us that great Day that never ends.
In the evening let your light shine in our hearts,
and in the darkness of the night,
enlighten us with the knowledge of your truth.
And so, through all the days of our lives,
we will praise you, now and for ever. Amen

—*From* Ramsho

14) Prayer for the Sick (Maronite)

In your kindness, O Lord, visit the sick,
and in your mercy, heal the afflicted.
Grant wholeness of body and soul
to all who suffer from illness and grief,
and seek compassion and mercy from you.
Praise be to you, Father, Son,
        and Holy Spirit,
now and for ever. Amen.

—*From the* Maronite Book of Blessings and Prayers

✝

15) Prayer before Holy Communion (Maronite)
(Always prayed in the Divine Service)

Make us worthy, O Lord God,
to sanctify our bodies with your holy body
and to purify our souls
          with your forgiving blood.
May our Communion be for
          the forgiveness of our sins
          and for eternal life.
O Lord, our God,
to you be glory, for ever. Amen.

+

16) Prayer for Vocations

O God,
you have called us at this moment in our lives
to be parents in the larger family of our Church.
Like Anne and Joachim,
the parents of Mary,
we want to be people of faith.
Help us, like them, to support your hand
at work in the lives of our families
and all the young members of the Church.
Use our prayers and sacrifices,
and the example of our lives,
to nourish your life within them.
Help them to know where you are
calling them to serve.
Give them your grace to answer
          "Yes."
                                        Amen.

—Anne-Joachim Vocation Prayer Ministry

17) The Rosary (Common)

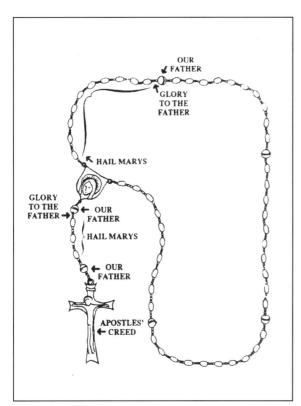

Note: The recitation of the Rosary is not originally part of Eastern Tradition in general. However, it has become a common prayer of all Traditions.

The full rosary is composed of fifteen decades, but it is divided into three, distinct parts, each containing five decades. The first part consists of five joyful events in the life of Jesus and Mary; the second part recalls five sorrowful, and the third part, five glorious events.

One begins by making the Sign of the Cross. Then one says "The Apostles' Creed," one "Our Father," three "Hail Marys" on the small chain. Then the following: Recall the event, say one "Our Father," ten "Hail Marys" and one "Glory Be to the Father." This completes one decade, and all the other decades are said in the same manner with different event meditated during each decade.

The events of the rosary are called the *"Mysteries of the Rosary"* (not to be confused with the proper Eastern term for the Sacraments, which are the sacramental "Mysteries"). They are events from the life of Jesus and Mary. By meditating on these sublime truths, we come to a better understanding of our religion: the Incarnation of the Lord, the Redemption, and the Christian life, present and future.

In the following outline the words in parentheses indicate practical applications to our daily lives.

The Joyful Mysteries of the Rosary

1) The messenger of God announces to Mary that she is to be the Mother of God. (Revelation)
2) Mary visits and helps her cousin Elizabeth. (Evangelization)
3) Mary bears Jesus in a stable in Bethlehem. (Incarnation)
4) Jesus is presented in the Temple. (Obedience to God's Will)
5) Jesus is found in the Temple. (Divine Fatherhood of Jesus)

The Sorrowful Mysteries of the Rosary

1) Jesus undergoes his agony in Gethsemane. (The Will of God)
2) Jesus is scourged at the pillar. (Jesus suffered for us)
3) Jesus is crowned with thorns. (Jesus, our true King)
4) Jesus carries the Cross to Calvary. (Discipleship)
5) Jesus dies on the Cross for our sins. (Salvation)

The Glorious Mysteries of the Rosary

1) Jesus rises from the dead. (Cornerstone of our faith)
2) Jesus ascends into heaven. (The glory of God)
3) The Holy Spirit comes to the Apostles and the Blessed Mother. (God is Love)
4) Mary is taken up into heaven. (Believers' Resurrection)
5) Mary is crowned Queen of heaven and earth. (Intercessory Prayer)

APPENDIX III

LITURGICAL OBSERVANCE/DOCTRINE COORDINATION

Please Note: This list of Sunday observances of the Liturgical Year includes those from the Sundays of the Season of the Holy Cross and those from the Renewal of the Church until Trinity Sunday (Sunday after Pentecost). This covers approximately nine months, the usual length of time of the average parish yearly religious education program. In any case, in the current Lectionary the Sunday Gospels between Trinity Sunday and the 1st after Holy Cross do not exhibit the same richness as the Seasons within these nine months (especially the Seasons of the Glorious Birth of the Lord and of Great Lent.). The linked themes presented in the list below present an overview of the basic teachings of the Catholic Faith in a nine-month period, for preaching or for catechesis.

Liturgical Observance	*Doctrinal Theme*

Season of the Glorious, Holy, Life-giving Cross
Seasonal Theme: The Cross as Our Standard as We Await Christ's Return

1) 1ST SUNDAY AFT. HOLY CROSS	Living between the Two Appearances of Christ, p. 171
2) 2ND SUNDAY AFT. HOLY CROSS	Living a Moral Life, Chs. 27, 28
3) 3RD SUNDAY AFT. HOLY CROSS	Living an Unrepentant Life: Hell, pp. 178-79
4) 4TH SUNDAY AFT. HOLY CROSS	The Mysteries of Vocation: Holy Crowning, Ch. 26
5) 5TH SUNDAY AFT. HOLY CROSS	Ecumenism and Interfaith Dialog, pp. 74, 76, 79
6) 6TH SUNDAY AFT. HOLY CROSS	Religious Life: Monasticism, p. 71
7) 7TH SUNDAY AFT. HOLY CROSS	Why Worship?, p. 231

Sundays of the Church
Seasonal Theme: The Renewal of the Church through Our Own Renewal

8) RENEWAL OF THE CHURCH	The Church, Icon of Christ, pp. 57-62

9) CONSECRATION OF THE CHURCH
(Some years not celebrated—see **PART II,**
"The Liturgical Year")   The Eastern Catholic Churches
                                              (treated in the previous Sunday
                                              when this Sunday is not
                                              celebrated), Chapter 7

Season of the Glorious Birth of the Lord
(*Soboorey*, "Happy Announcements")
Seasonal Theme: God's Intimate Revelation of the Birth of the Messiah.

10) ANNOUNCEMENT TO ZECHARIAH   Faith and Doubt, pp. 7-8

11) ANNOUNCEMENT TO MARY   The Incarnation, pp. 36-39

12) VISITATION TO ELIZABETH   Evangelization, pp. 216-218

13) BIRTH OF JOHN THE BAPTIZER   Revelation and Faith, pp. 5-6

14) REVELATION TO JOSEPH   Divine Providence, pp. 30-32

15) GENEALOGY SUNDAY   Scripture & Tradition, pp. 124-
                                              25

16) SUNDAY AFTER THE BIRTH OF THE LORD
(Some years not celebrated)   The Incarnation *(treated in*
                                              Announcement to Mary when
                                              this Sunday is not celebrated),
                                              pp. 36-39

17) FINDING IN THE TEMPLE   God the Father, pp. 25-27

Season of Epiphany (*Denho*)
Seasonal Theme: Our Life through the Mysteries of Initiation.

18) FIRST SUNDAY OF EPIPHANY   The Sacramental Life,
                                                  pp. 188-91

19) SECOND SUNDAY OF EPIPHANY   Initiation: Baptism and
                                              Chrismation, pp. 193-218

20) THIRD SUNDAY OF EPIPHANY

Image and Likeness
(treated in previous Sunday if Easter is early and Sunday is omitted), pp. 29-30

21) FOURTH SUNDAY OF EPIPHANY
(Other Sundays of Epiphany may be observed, depending upon the date of the beginning of Great Lent)

The Mysteries of Initiation: The Holy Eucharist, ch. 19

22) SUNDAY OF THE PRIESTS

The Mysteries of Vocation: Holy Order, pp. 271-82

23) THE RIGHTEOUS AND JUST

Mary and the Righteous and Just, pp. 157-170

24) THE FAITHFUL DEPARTED

Death and Judgment, pp. 173-74

Great Lent
Seasonal Theme: Our Conversion and Transformation to New Life by Fasting

25) CANA SUNDAY

A New Earth/Heaven, 181-82

26) THE MAN WITH LEPROSY

Communion of Saints, pp. 174-78 (Life after Death)

27) THE HEMORRHAGING WOMAN

Sin: The First Sin; Personal and Communal Sin, pp. 249-54

28) THE PRODIGAL SON

The Mysteries of Healing: Penance, Ch. 23

29) THE MAN WHO WAS PARALYZED

Mysteries of Healing: Anointing of the Sick and Dying, Ch. 24

30) THE MAN WHO WAS BLIND

Correct Conscience, pp. 310-12

31) HOSANNA SUNDAY

Christ our King, pp. 42-43

Season of Resurrection
Seasonal Theme: Our Sharing in the Easter Victory of Christ

32) RESURRECTION SUNDAY

The Resurrection, pp. 46-50

APPENDIX IV

A

ALTAR/TABLE OF PREPARATION: A small altar or table at the right side of the sanctuary at which the offerings of bread and wine used in the *Qoorbono* are prepared.

ANAMNESIS (an um NEE sis) (Greek: "remembrance"): The part of the *Qoorbono* after the *Words of Institution which recall the saving deeds of the Lord for His people. However, far from being mere recollection, this special kind of remembrance invites the worshiper to realize that the Eucharistic Banquet is the sacramental and mysterious participation in the Lord's Last Supper and Death on the Cross, made present again in the *Eucharistic Prayer, through the power of the Holy Spirit.

ANAPHORA (an APH or a) (Gr.: "offering"): The *Eucharistic Prayer of the *Qoorbono. The *Anaphora* is the central prayer of thanksgiving of the Liturgy in which the Trinity is invoked to accomplish the sanctification of the *Offerings. The *Anaphora* is the second basic part of the worship service (the *Service of the Word being the first). While trinary in structure, the emphasis differs in the East and West. In the Eastern *Liturgies, the trinary pattern of prayers is Father-Son-Spirit, culminating in the *Epiclesis*; while in the West, the pattern is Father-Spirit-Son, culminating in the *Consecration, a decidedly Christological emphasis.

ANTIOCH (AN tee ok): Prominent Roman Imperial city in northwestern *Syria which played an important role in the development of early *Church expansion. St. Paul writes about his travels to the Church at Antioch, and St. Peter evangelized there. Here, the followers of Jesus were first called "Christians" (*Acts* 11:26). Antioch also became an influential center of Christianity, where a very famous theological school was established. It eventually became the center of an important Eastern Church *Tradition, the *Antiochene Tradition, which includes the three West *Syriac Churches, of which the *Maronite Church is one. It also later became the seat of certain Patriarchates, Catholic—such as the *Maronite Patriarchate of Antioch—and others. Antioch produced such famous men as Bishop *Ignatius and *John Chrysostom.

ANTIOCHENE (an tee oh KEEN) (Also designated, "ANTIOCHIAN" [an tee oh KEE un]): of or relating to *Antioch.

ANTITYPE: See **TYPOLOGY.**

APHRAHAT (AF ra hat): Called the "Persian Sage," Aphrahat was a contemporary of St. *Ephrem. A convert to Christianity, he became a cleric. More important, he was a profound writer on Christian subjects, and his most famous work was entitled the *Demonstrations*. He is the earliest and one of the most renowned Fathers/Teachers of the *Syriac *Church.

ARAMAIC (air a MAY ic): The language of the ancient Aramaean people. This language survived down through our Lord's time and into the seventh century as a spoken language. It was then gradually replaced with Arabic with the Arab conquerors. Aramaic developed different dialects, divided into eastern and western Aramaic. While on earth, Jesus spoke a western (Palestinian) form of the language, although his exact (spoken) language is not known today. Closely related to Aramaic is *Syriac.

B

BEMA (BAY ma)(Syriac): Following Jewish Temple roots, some *Syriac church buildings—found from *Antioch to Mesopotamia—contain a special place or area at which the Scriptures were read. This U-shaped structure was located often in the midst of the congregation, in front of the curtain of the sanctuary area of the church. This area was called the *bema*, and many *Antiochene and Syriac texts attest that the *Service of the Word was conducted here. Scholars are divided over the existence of the bema in *Maronite churches.

BYZANTINE (BIZ an teen): Pertaining to that *Tradition of the *Church which had its beginnings in the city of Constantinople (present-day Istanbul), otherwise known in ancient times as "Byzantium" (biz AN tee um). This largest Eastern *Tradition of the Church embraces 13 *sui iuris* (self-governing) Churches, such as the Ukrainian Church, the Melkite Church, and the Ruthenian Church. Christians of the Byzantine Tradition are either Catholic or Orthodox.

C

CANTOR: The person who chants liturgical responses, often in the absence of a deacon.

CATECHUMEN (kat a KYOO men): An adult who is in the process of preparing for the reception of the Mysteries of Initiation. In the early *Church, the process for such preparation usually took two years, and culminated in key times of the Liturgical Year. For the largest part of the Church this was the Easter Vigil Liturgy, which followed Great Lent, a time of purification. In some Syriac Churches this time of reception was the Feast of the Baptism of the Lord (6 January). Today, the Latin Church has revived the process; it is known as the Rite of Christian Initiation of Adults (RCIA).

CELEBRANT: The leader of a religious service, especially of the Divine *Liturgy. It is usually a priest or *deacon, but not necessarily so.

CENSER: A decorated metal container which holds burning charcoal, onto which incense is placed for fragrant smoke in liturgical services. In Eastern Churches, there may be bells on the chains that support the bowl.

CHORBISHOP (kor BISH op): *Chor-* is from the Greek, *khora*, meaning "country," or "field." In the earliest times of the Syriac Church, this was a bishop who pastored Christians in country areas outside the large metropolitan centers (where the main bishop was referred to as a "metropolitan").

CHURCH: This term has two basic meanings: its most universal meaning is that of the Community of Believers in Jesus, which finds its fullness in the Catholic Communion. In a more narrow, yet no less important sense, "church" also means a group of Catholics who are 1) *sui iuris*, or otherwise known as a *"Particular Church," or self-governing (by their own hierarchy: patriarch, major archbishop, exarch or metropolitan), and 2), if also in communion with the See of Rome, is "Catholic."

    A "church" is to be distinguished from a "rite." A rite is a liturgical tradition, which members of a Particular Church follow. For example, members of the Melkite Church follow the *Byzantine Rite; members of the Syro-Malabar Church (India) follow the Chaldean Rite (Church of the East); members of the Maronite Church follow the West Syro-Antiochene Rite. (For a listing of the six, basic Rites of the Catholic Communion, see **TRADITION**.) See *SUI IURIS*.

CONCELEBRATION: A Divine *Liturgy in which other priests join the *Celebrant.

CONSECRATION: Traditional Latin *Rite term for the *Words of Institution—or Institution Narrative—of the Last Supper.

D

DEACON: In Holy Order, the major ministerial order that precedes that of *Presbyter (Priest). In the early *Church, deacons were called upon to take care of the needs of the poor, orphans, widows. They soon gained a position of service second only to the bishops. Many often remained deacons, even after the Order of Presbyter gained prominence over deacons. Deacons had a special role in the Divine *Liturgy, especially so in the *Byzantine Church. Today, the order of permanent deacon—many are married—has been re-established. St. *Ephrem was a deacon.

DIAKONAL (dee AK o nal) **PROCLAMATION**: Any liturgical proclamation made by a *deacon. It may be a statement of church order ("stand," "sit," etc.), a response (see *KOROOZOOTO*), or the proclaiming of the *Diptychs. Important diakonal proclamations are the reading of the Holy Gospel and preaching.

DIPTYCHS (DIP tiks)(Greek: Petitions or Intercessions): The intercessory prayer of the faithful, usually proclaimed by the *deacon or, in the absence of a deacon, the *presbyter, who in any case always prays the first and last intercessions.

DOXOLOGY: From the Greek, "a speech of glory" or "of praise." It usually begins with such words as, "Glory be to the Father...."

E

EDESSA (e DESS a): An ancient city in northeastern *Syria, between the Tigris and Euphrates Rivers (ancient province of Osrhöene), which was the center of a very famous school of theology. Many saints and theologians came from this city, and it was to Edessa that St. *Ephrem eventually went to live and write. The School of Edessa had a considerable influence on the formation of *Maronite *Tradition, especially through the writings of Ephrem.

'EED L'KABEER (eed l'ka BEER)(Arabic: "the Greatest Feast"): In at least the *Maronite *Church, the traditional Arabic designation for the Feast of the Resurrection.

EPHREM (EF rem): Famous 4th-century spiritual Father/Teacher and *deacon of the *Syriac *Church. Born in *Nisibis, he moved to *Edessa. He wrote many prose theological treatises and commentaries on the Scriptures. He is equally famous for his composition of metrical verses (*memre*, pronounced, "memray"), which found their way into the *Syriac liturgical *Tradition. The quality of this metrical work is widely judged to be so fine as to credit Ephrem as one of the greatest liturgical poets of the Universal Church. In addition, Ephrem is considered a (theological) Doctor of the Universal Church.

EPHREMIAAT (ef rem ee AT)(Arabic): Arabic name for verses attributed to *Ephrem, and used in the *Syriac *Liturgies, including the *Maronite *Tradition.

EPICLESIS (ep i KLEE sis, or e PIK le sis) (Gr.: "invocation"): The calling upon the Holy Spirit in a sacramental prayer context for the purpose of sanctification or enlightenment. In the Eucharistic *Liturgies of the East, the *Epiclesis* occurs very soon after the *Words of Institution and is distinctly noticeable; while in the Latin *Mass an abbreviated *invocation is found, though not as distinguishable or pronounced. The reason for this is that the theologies of the East have always laid greater liturgical emphasis on the action of the Spirit in the Holy *Mysteries.

'ETRO (ET ro)(Syr.: "perfume [of incense]"): The usual final part of the *Hoosoyo*. The *'Etro* acts as kind of summary of the ideas of the *Hoosoyo*, petitioning God to accept the incense offered and answer the prayer of the faithful, in the spirit of the theme of the day.

EUCHARIST: From the Greek word, *eucharistain* (yoo khar is TANE), "to give thanks": to the Heavenly Father for giving us the Divine Son, Jesus, for salvation and for the Eucharist Itself, in which we meet Jesus again.

EUCHARISTIC PRAYER: The central prayer of the Divine *Liturgy, which follows the *Service of the Word. It centers on the notion of thanksgiving for the mystery of Christ-made-present. See ***ANAMNESIS; ANAPHORA*; TRINITARIAN PRAYER.**

F

FENQITHO (fen KEE to)(Syr.: "a treasury of feasts"): A collection of liturgical texts for feast days of Our Lord, Our Lady and the Saints. It is also called the ***"SANCTORAL CYCLE."*** The texts of the *Fenqitho* are coordinated with the Liturgical Calendar.

FETGOMO (fet GO mo)(Syr.): The Alleluia verse after the First Reading(s) of the *Service of the Word. It is variable with the text of the feast or commemoration.

H

HAND CROSS: A small cross used by some Eastern *Traditions for blessing in the Divine *Liturgy, in the sacramental Mysteries and other occasions. In the *Maronite Tradition, ribbons or a scarf—often white or gold, but other colors may be used—are attached the hand cross. These materials on the hand cross are a symbol and reminder of the strong Eastern emphasis on the Resurrection, as well as St. John's theological idea that the Cross IS Resurrection.

HOMILY: A preaching on the *Lectionary Readings and on the theme of the day's Service, in a clear, conversational style.

HOOSOYO (hoo SOY o)(Syr.: "prayer of forgiveness"): This is the most important prayer of the *Introductory Rites of the *Syriac *Liturgies. The *Hoosoyo* has liturgical and exegetical functions: A) it highlights the character of forgiveness God offers to the penitent; B) it commemorates the special feast or saint of the day, and expresses its liturgical theme; and C) full of Scriptural allusions, often in Syro-*Antiochene *typology, the *Hoosoyo* actually provides a liturgical commentary on at least the Gospel of the Feast or commemoration. Thus, one can look to the *Hoosoyo* as the foundation of *Maronite liturgical scriptural interpretation.

The *Hoosoyo* is traditionally divided into four parts: the *Proemion*, the *Sedro,* the *Qolo* and the *'Etro*.

I

ICON (EYE kon)(from the Gr.): A stylized painting or *mosaic depicting Christian religious persons or events. The style differs with the different Eastern *Traditions. The most prominent use of icons is found in the *Byzantine Church, but it is by no means limited to that Tradition. After long disuse, due to latinization, some Churches, such as the Maronite Church, are in the process of restoring their icon tradition. For example, see Zibawi, *Eastern Christian Worlds*, in the Bibliography, for a source on the non-Byzantine icon tradition.

ICONOSTASIS (eye kon o STAH sis, or, eye kon AH sta sis)(Gr.): In some Eastern *Churches, the screen or wall that divides the altar area from the main body of the church and into which *icons are placed. In the Syriac Church, a curtain separates the sanctuary from the body of the church; however, its use in *Maronite churches is still debated by scholars.

IGNATIUS OF ANTIOCH: Second-century bishop (d. *ca.* 110) of that city whose theology of the Church and ministry—especially the triple orders of bishop, *presbyter, *deacon as fundamental—has been revived in current theology. An early martyr for the Faith, he was the first to apply the term "Catholic" ("Universal") to the Christian *Church.

INCENSE: Fragrant-smelling smoke produced by grains of various resins placed on burning charcoal in a *censer. An indispensable element of Eastern *Liturgies, incense in the East has various meanings. The Introduction to the *Qoorbono* mentions three: A) praise of the Lord: this meaning came from the custom in the Roman Empire of burning incense before the image of a god, or of a deified emperor; B) purification, covering up the "foul stench of sin", and C) forgiveness. Especially these last two meanings are seen clearly in the *Hoosoyo*: as we acknowledge our sinfulness, we seek to be pardoned and purified to heed the lessons of the Word of God. Of all the *Traditions, the East uses incense more frequently.

INTRODUCTORY RITES: In the *Maronite *Qoorbono*, those prayers and actions that lead to the *Service of the Word. They include: the *Preparation of the *Offerings; the *Lighting of the Church; the Opening Chant (often a Psalm or *Qolo*); ministers' Entrance into the Sanctuary; Opening Prayers; *Hoosoyo*; *Trisagion*. These rites have as their purpose to bring the worshiper to a change of heart and to purification (*metanoia*), so as to move the worshiper to be able more fruitfully to hear God's Word.

INVOCATION (of the Holy Spirit): See *EPICLESIS*.

J

JAMES OF SARUG (sa ROOG): 5th/6th-century theological writer (d. 521) whose writings about the *Mother of God are considered by some to rival those of St. *Ephrem. His influence on *Maronite *Tradition is considerable, and he is considered one of the spiritual Fathers/Teachers of the *Syriac *Tradition. A Maronite *Anaphora* is named after him.

JOHN CHRYSOSTOM (KRIZ os tum): 4th/5th-century contemporary of St. *Maron. St. John was born in *Antioch and there wrote many commentaries on the Gospels. He was subsequently chosen bishop of Constantinople. He was dedicated to eradicating the considerable decadence of the City, especially in the Emperor's court, and imperial neglect of the poor. John paid the price for this by being exiled by the Emperor to Komana, where he died in 407. The most frequently used *Anaphora* of the *Byzantine *Rite is named after him. *Chrysostom* means "Golden Mouth" in Greek. John was so named because of his prodigious preaching ability.

JOHN MARON: Elected Bishop of the Maronites in 685 A.D., John filled the previously vacant Chalcedonian See of *Antioch, establishing the *Maronite Patriarchate of Antioch in the 8th century.

K

KOROOZOOTO (kor oo ZOO to)(Syr.): Diaconal proclamation in liturgy.

L

LECTIONARY: A systematic pattern of Scripture Readings, for Sundays, weekdays, feasts and special occasions, according to a proper liturgical *Tradition. The distinctive way in which a lectionary organizes its Readings reveals a Tradition's uniqueness.

LIGHTING OF THE CHURCH: The first action of the *Introductory Rites of the *Maronite *Qoorbono. During the lighting, a hymn such as the "Hymn of Light" is sung.

LITURGY: From the Greek word *leitourgia* meaning "a work of the people." In ancient times, liturgy was very often a public action in civil events, such as the dedication of a public building, although it could have religious meaning as well. In specifically Christian, religious terms, it refers to the liturgical action of the *Church: Eucharistic (Divine) Liturgy, Divine *Office, the seven sacramental *Mysteries, and devotional prayers.

LITURGY, DIVINE: The proper general term for the Eucharistic Service in Eastern *Traditions. In the *Maronite Tradition, the Divine Liturgy is also known properly as the *"Service of the Holy Mysteries," or *Qoorbono, as it is called in Syriac.

M

MARON: The 4th/5th-century hermit-monk from Northwest *Syria (d. *ca.* 410), who journeyed from the area of the city of Antioch to the banks of the Orontes River near Apamea. He is said to have lived a life of extreme austerity and self-denial, and to have had powers of miracles—spiritual and physical. Literary evidence exists from Bishop Theodoret of Cyrrhus, who acknowledges the existence and sanctity of St. *Maron in his *History of the Monks of Syria*; also a fragment of a letter from John *Chrysostom to his "friend and fellow priest Maron."

MARONITE: Referring to that *Church of the *Antiochene *Syriac *Tradition that claims the discipleship of St. *Maron; to the tradition of the great monastery which was established in Maron's name after his death, and to the Catholic Community that became autonomously established in the 8th century under the leadership of Bishop John Maron of Kfarhai (present-day Lebanon).

MASS: Latin *Rite term for the Eucharistic worship service, from the Latin, *missa*. See **LITURGY, DIVINE.**

MAZMOORO (maz MOOR o)(Syr.: "psalm of praise," or "psalm of the Readings"): In the **Qoorbono* variable verses before the First Scripture Reading that alternate between Congregation and *Celebrant.

METANOIA (met a NOY a)(Gr.: "change of heart in total conversion"): An important biblical concept (see, for example, *Mk* 1:15, or *Mt* 4:17), *metanoia* is a central idea to Eastern *Liturgy, especially in the *Syriac **Hoosoyo*.

MONASTIC: Referring to monks and monasteries. Because the *Maronite *Tradition had its origins with the monk St. *Maron, a knowledge of monasticism is essential for not only a theological understanding of the Tradition but also its liturgical life and spirituality. Monastic themes permeate Maronite liturgical tradition. It is also seen in the way the Psalms and **Qolos* are chanted from side to side, antiphonally.

MOTHER OF GOD: Mary, the Virgin Mother of Jesus. A focus of great devotion in the Eastern Churches, she is venerated as Mother of God; Model of the Church; Model of faith and discipleship; Protectress of the Church and the People of God; among the Saints the greatest Intercessor to her Son. She goes by a myriad of titles, many of which express theological reflection about her See THEOTOKOS, *OOM ALLAH*; see also **Chapter 13.**

MOSAIC (mo ZAY ik): A form of artistic image using small stones of different colors, worked into a design pattern. Mosaics were a prominent art form of the ancient world, and consequently became a prominent expression of religious art of the Christian *Church, found in all *Traditions. Very fine examples of mosaics existed at *Antioch.

MYSTERY: An important concept of Eastern theologies, "mystery" denotes the otherness, the hiddenness of God, who chose to reveal Divinity Itself, most especially in Jesus, the *Icon of God, through the enlightenment, in our lives of the Holy Spirit. Mystery also signals the proper attitude of the Eastern Christian when reflecting upon the encounter of the Lord in the sacramental *Mysteries. See *ROZO*.

MYSTERIES, HOLY, or SACRAMENTAL: An Eastern *Church way of naming the *Sacraments. Opposed to a static view, Eastern Christians refer to these special times of the Christian life as sacramental *Mysteries*, realizing that the Lord visits his people in a totally free and gratuitous manner, often indefinable by human standards. It might be said that the Eastern Christian "participates in the Mysteries" rather than the more properly Latin "receives the *Sacraments."

N

NISIBIS (NIZ i bis): With *Edessa, this city formed one of the two focal points of East *Syriac Christianity. Located in the frontier province of Adiabene, this province and city of the Roman Empire frequently came under Persian attack and rule. Nisibis was the first home of St. *Ephrem and academic home of *Aphrahat and was the site of a famous Catechetical School dominated by the influence of "*The* Interpreter (of the Bible)," Theodore of Mopsuestia.

O

OBLATIONS: Another word for the *Offerings of bread and wine at the *Qoorbono*.

OFFERINGS: In liturgical terms, the bread and wine used in the Divine *Liturgy. At one time, in all of the liturgical *Traditions, the bread the wine were brought to the church by the people, and the *Celebrant selected them personally for the Service. Some of the Traditions still maintain this practice.

OFFICE, DIVINE: The prayer traditionally chanted by men and women religious and the laity in all *Traditions, coinciding with certain hours of the day and based on the Psalms. For this reason, the Divine *Office has also been known as the *"Liturgy of the Hours," or in the *Maronite Church as the "Prayer of the Faithful." The purpose of this pattern of prayers is the sanctification of the entire day through prayer. Outside of the monastery only Evening and Morning Prayer are usually prayed.

OOM ALLAH (oom UL lah): Arabic for *"Mother of God." See ***THEOTOKOS***.

P

PARTICULAR CHURCH: See ***SUI IURIS***.

PRE-*ANAPHORA*: The section that precedes the *Service of the Eucharist (*Anaphora). It consists of the transfer of the *Offerings, (i.e., procession, with accompanying hymn), Prayers of Offering and Commemoration, Prayer of the Veil, Incensing and *Service of Peace. In this third part of the Divine *Liturgy we commemorate both the living and departed, as well as reflecting on our eternal destiny.

PREPARATION OF THE OFFERINGS: At the very beginning of the Divine *Liturgy, even before it begins, the bread and wine used for the Service are prepared at the *Altar of Preparation. As each is prepared, a prayer is recited; then, the *Offerings are covered with veils.

PRESBYTER (PRES bi ter)(Gr.: "elder"): In the early *Church bishops were the principal *celebrants of the Divine *Liturgy, aided by the *deacons. It was not until later, as the Church expanded, that the position of presbyter (already attested in the New Testament) became more prominent, for then the presbyter became the local head of a congregation in the place of the bishop. Thus, in terms of church administration, the original ordering of the three Holy Orders was bishop, *deacon presbyter; then, as the churches demanded different administration, this order to changed to what we today understand as the ordering: bishop, presbyter, deacon.

PROEMION (pro AY mee on)(Syr.: "introduction"): The *Proemion* is the first part of the *Hoosoyo. Its function is to introduce the *Hoosoyo* of the feast or day. Usually beginning with a note of praise, the *Proemion* continues with a statement of one or another aspect of the person or event commemorated. This section is very often an expanded *doxology to the Holy Trinity.

Q

QOLO (KO lo)(Syr.: "hymn"): The *Qolo* is a metrical hymn, used at various parts of liturgical services. One prominent use of the *Qolo* in Maronite Liturgy is as the third section of the **Hoosoyo*, where it amplifies the theme of the feast or day.

QOORBONO (koor BO no)(Syr.: "offering"): This is the *Syriac word for the Maronite *Service of the Holy Mysteries. This term captures the meaning of the nature of the *Eucharistic Prayer: an offering in thanks.

R

RA'BONO (ra BO no)(Syr.: "pledge"): Among the many elements of the *Maronite *Service of the Holy Mysteries, the notion of *ra'bono* is important. As Christians await the Second Coming of their Lord in glory, they find themselves in, but not totally of, the world. The reception of the Lord in sacramental *Mystery stands as a present pledge of future triumph with the Lord. This lends to the notion of Christians as a pilgrims on the way to heaven, a journey on which they travel, not unaided, but full of hope with the Pledge of Life Eternal. (See the *Letter to the Hebrews* for the notion of Christian as pilgrim.) This latter notion was taken up by the Second Vatican Council in its description of the Christian life. The idea of *ra'bono* is clearly seen in Maronite *Tradition in the *Trinitarian Prayer in the "Holy, holy … ," the *Words of Institution, and the thematic thrust of the liturgical Season of the Holy Cross.

RAMSHO (RAM sho)(Syr.): Evening Prayer of the West *Syriac *Churches. The *Maronite Church has its own proper form.

RITE: General word for ritual, or set order of prayers for worship. One may speak, for example, of the Rite of Initiation (Baptism, Chrismation and Eucharist); the Rite of Holy Crowning; the Rite of Ordination; the Rite of Kneeling on Pentecost. Formerly, *rite* was incorrectly used to describe a particular *Tradition of the *Church, for example, the "Ukrainian Rite." Doing so, however, too narrowly limited a particular expression of Catholicism to its liturgical expression, when in fact the reality of a particular Catholic Tradition is much broader. See **TRADITION**.

ROZO (RO zo)(Syr.: "mystery"): *Syriac term for sacrament. See **MYSTERY**.

S

SACRAMENT: Traditional Western (Latin) term for one of the seven sacramental *Mysteries.

SAFRO (SAF ro)(Syr.) Morning Prayer of the West *Syriac *Churches. The *Maronite Church has its own proper form.

SANCTORAL CYCLE. See *FENQITHO*.

SEDRO (SED ro)(Syr.: "rank," "order of petitions"): The *Sedro* is the second major section of the *Hoosoyo*. It celebrates the theme of the feast or day. In addition, according to its name, it presents a series of petitions—a kind of litany—based on the theme: As the Lord once did a gracious deed for his people, may the Lord again favor us. The *Sedro* is the heart of the *Hoosoyo*. Many Scriptural allusions are found in it, often in the form of *typology. It usually closes with standard *doxology.

SERVICE OF THE EUCHARIST: Another term for *Anaphora*.

SERVICE OF THE HOLY MYSTERIES: The *Maronite worship service. See *QOORBONO*.

SERVICE OF THE WORD: In *liturgy in general, the first of the two parts of the of the worship service (the second part is the *Anaphora*). It centers on the reading of and expounding upon the Holy Scriptures. (See **HOOSOYO, HOMILY, LECTIONARY**). In the *Maronite *Tradition, the Service of the Word of the *Qoorbono* begins after the *Introductory Rites and concludes with the *Trisagion*. The Service of the Word is consistently patterned on the canonical prayer hour of the Divine *Office.

SERVICE OF PEACE: In the *Syriac *Tradition, part of the *Pre-Anaphora*. It is the liturgical action that immediately precedes the *Anaphora*. The Service of Peace is done before the central action of the Eucharist, following (very logically) from St. Matthew's recording of Jesus' words: We should make peace with our neighbor before making our *offering at the altar (*Mt* 5:23-24).

SOOTORO (soo TOR o)(Syr.): Night Prayer of the West *Syriac *Churches. The *Maronite Church has its own proper form.

SUBDEACON: In the *Maronite *Church, the ministerial order before that of *deacon. Subdeacons are charged with "ministering at the altar," lighting the church and caring for the church building. In the *Qoorbono*, besides proclaiming some of the responses, subdeacons are charged with reading certain passages from the Scriptures. In the past, subdeacons have served in a liaison capacity between civil authorities and their religious communities in secular dealings affecting the villages in which they lived and served, particularly in the Middle East. Today, along with the temporary subdiaconate in seminary, a revived permanent subdiaconate exists.

SUI IURIS: From the Latin, meaning "of its own right"; also "self-governing," or "particular," as in *Particular Church*. Applied to a Catholic Church structural context, it means a group of Catholics of one of the six liturgical *Traditions of the *Catholic Communion of Churches that has its own hierarchy (for example, patriarch, or other high administrating bishop, and clergy), in communion with the Vatican. For example, the *Maronite Church is a *sui iuris* Church of the West Antiochene Tradition; the Ukrainian Church is a *sui iuris* Church of the *Byzantine

Tradition. In the Latin Church, "Particular Church" means the diocese.

SYRIA: For purposes of this book, the name *Syria* refers to the provinces of the Roman Empire located at the Eastern end of the Mediterranean Sea, extending eastward to Parthia (Persia, Mesopotamia). Syria was divided into smaller districts: the Northern, with its administrative capital at *Antioch, and the Southern, with its capital at Jerusalem. The eastern frontier, which included Adiabene and Osrhöene, included the famous cities of *Edessa and *Nisibis. These two frontier towns often found themselves as the pawns on the ongoing wars between Rome and the Persian Empire.

SYRIAC (SEER ee ak): A language closely related to *Aramaic. Syriac is divided into two basic dialects: eastern (centered in ancient *Nisibis and *Edessa, in modern-day southern Turkey), and western (centered in *Antioch and Palestine). Syriac survived as an academic language for several centuries, as many of the classics of Greek learning were translated into Syriac; and a whole body of original Syriac literature exists. It also served as a liturgical language in the Syriac *Churches (of which the *Maronite Church is one) even to this day. The metrical homilies of St. *Ephrem are a good example of the use of Syriac. See **ARAMAIC**.

T

TARGUM: A translation of the books of the Hebrew Bible (Old Testament) into Aramaic, made when Aramaic was the common spoken language in Palestine. They were produced between about 250 B.C. and 300 A.D. and were usually read in the synagogues.

THEOTOKOS (thay oh TOH kos): Greek word for *"Mother of God" (literally, "God-bearer"). See ***OOM ALLAH***.

TRADITION: A) The fundamental meaning of Tradition, in Catholic understanding, is the handing on of the Faith.

B) The collective, historic experience and life of the Christian Community. This includes many things: history, theology, spirituality, worship (*rite), customs, literature, law and discipline, and understanding of the Bible. Tradition, as a way of Christian life, involves a process of growth and development in continuity with the past. One speaks, for example, of the "Catholic Tradition."

Within Catholic Tradition are to be found particular Traditions, which have their origins in the historic and cultural circumstances to which they adapted in the early missionary expansion of Christianity, as well as their particular expressions of the elements named above. On recognizes here the six major Traditions of Eastern and Western Catholicism (tied to cities and regions in the Roman Empire): The five Eastern Traditions, with their areas and languages of origin, are: 1) *Antiochene, (West) Syriac Tradition (ancient *Syria/West Syriac; the *Maronite Church belongs here)—represented by three *sui iuris Churches; 2) Chaldean/East Syriac ("Church of the East"/Mesopotamia)—two Churches; 3) Alexandrine (Egypt, Coptic and Ge'ez)—two Churches; 4) *Byzantine (Constantinople/Greek, Old Slavonic)—13 Churches; 5) Armenian (Cappadocia/Armenia)—one Church. The Western Tradition is basically the Latin (Rome), and a few other, local Western Churches. From these 6 Traditions developed 22 self-governing (*sui iuris*) *Particular Churches of the present-day Catholic Communion of Churches, 21 of them Eastern. See diagram, p. 98.

One should not confuse this definition of Tradition with the older, less accurate and limiting understanding of the term *rite*. Compare **RITE**.

C) This is not to be confused with the more common understanding of traditions (with a lowercase *t*), by which is meant the particular customs that reflect the uniqueness and particularities of each Tradition and enhance one's appreciation of one's particular Tradition.

TRINITARIAN PRAYER: Strictly speaking, those prayers within the *Anaphora* that are addressed respectively to each Person of the Holy Trinity, from the beginning of the *Anaphora* until before the Rite of Communion. For the Eastern *Traditions, the Trinitarian part of the *Eucharistic Prayer preserves the Scriptural order of revelation of the Trinity: Father, Son, Holy Spirit. For example, in the *Maronite Divine *Liturgy these are the Praise of the Father, *Words of Institution Narrative of the Last Supper, and *Epiclesis*. The Latin *Tradition centers the Eucharistic action around the *Consecration: Preface (Father), Invocation (Spirit), Last Supper Narrative (Son). See *ANAPHORA*.

TRISAGION (tree SAH gee on): Greek word for "thrice (*tris*) holy ([*h*]*agios*)." This prayer, which begins, "Holy are You, O God, ..." (or in Syriac, *Qadeeshat Aloho*...), is a standard element of the Eastern *Liturgies. It has, at various times during the history of the *Church, been understood as addressed to the Trinity or only to the Christ. Both are correct. In *Maronite Tradition the response to the *Trisagion* varies with the liturgical season.

TYPE: See **TYPOLOGY**.

TYPOLOGY: The biblical literary device that links persons, places or events from the Hebrew Scriptures (Old Testament)—called a "type"—to New Testament persons (preeminently Christ), places or events—called an "antitype"—in such a way that the former things foreshadow the later ones. For example, the Israelites' crossing of the Red (Reed) Sea is a type of Christian Baptism, which is a journey from the slavery of sin to the freedom of forgiveness of sin (antitype). Typology was the preferred tool for biblical interpretation in the Syriac Church in general. However, the East *Syriac *Tradition (of Ephrem and Aphrahat) made more extensive use of typology than did the West Syriac Tradition of Antioch.

V

VERNACULAR: The language naturally spoken by the natives of an area.

VIATICUM (veye AT i kum) Latin word for "(that which is) with you on the way (to the Kingdom)." This word refers to the Holy Eucharist as received and remaining with the faithful, especially in the moments of death. *Viaticum* is one primary reason that the Eucharist is reserved in churches, especially for use in bringing to the sick. See **ZWODO**.

W

WORDS OF INSTITUTION (of the Eucharist at the Last Supper): In the *Eucharistic Prayer, the Narrative of the Last Supper wherein Jesus offered his sacramental Body and Blood, under the appearance of bread and wine, to be consumed by the believer for eternal life. The form of this Narrative is extremely varied among the *Rites of the *Church. See **CONSECRATION**.

Z

ZWODO (ZWO do)(Syr.: "pledge"): *Syriac word for *viaticum*.

APPENDIX V

ABBREVIATIONS OF THE NAMES OF THE SIXTEEN DOCUMENTS OF VATICAN II, AND A BRIEF SUMMARY OF THEIR CONTENTS

AA   *(Apostolicam Actuositatem)* "Decree on the Apostolate of the Laity," 18 November 1965: Everyone is called to holiness; involvement of the laity in the Church; bringing the Gospel into the world.

AG   *(Ad Gentes)* "Decree on the Church's Missionary Activity," 7 December 1965: All share in the missionary work of the Church; evangelization is more effective by example than by direct tactics.

CD   *(Christus Dominus)* "Decree on the Bishops' Pastoral Office in the Church," 28 October 1965: Collegiality of bishops as sharing authority with the Pope; calls for synods of bishops.

DH   *(Dignitatis Humanae)* "Declaration on Religious Liberty," 7 December 1965: A well-formed conscience as the basic norm for morality; dignity and rights of the human person; condemnation of all types of discrimination.

DV   *(Dei Verbum)* "Dogmatic Constitution on Divine Revelation," 18 November 1965: Scripture and Tradition as the main sources of revelation flowing from a common fount; primacy of the Word of God in both the Hebrew Scriptures (Old Testament) and the New Testaments; the *Magisterium* serves the Word of God.

GE   *(Gravissimum Educationis)* "Declaration on Christian Education," 28 October 1965: value of education to values; parents have the prime responsibility for the moral training of their children.

GS   *(Gaudium et Spes)* "Pastoral Constitution on the Church in the Modern World," 7 December 1965: Church and world as mutually related; dignity of all persons; marriage and family, culture, society, economics, politics, and peace issues.

IM   *(Inter Mirifica)* "Decree on the Instruments of Social Communication," 4 December 1963: Responsibility and challenges of the media; use of the media to promote faith and values.

LG *(Lumen Gentium)* "Dogmatic Constitution on the Church," 21 November 1964: The Church as the People of God; permanent diaconate restored.

NA *(Nostra Aetate)* "Declaration on the Relationship of the Church to Non-Christian Religions," 28 October 1965: Sees sacredness in non-Christian religions as valid approaches to the Divine; especially respects Judaism as the root of Christianity; anti-Semitism condemned.

OE *(Orientalium Ecclesiarum)* "Decree on Eastern Catholic Churches," 21 November 1964: Addressed to the Catholic Churches of the Eastern Traditions; recognizes diversity in rites and encourages retaining traditions.

OT *(Optatam Totius)* "Decree on Priestly Formation," 18 October 1965: Priestly training and continuing formation; calls for evaluation of seminary curricula.

PC *(Perfectae Caritatis)* "Decree on the Appropriate Renewal of the Religious Life," 28 October 1965: Calls to renewal of relevance and challenge to religious to live in conformity to Gospel values.

PO *(Presbyterorum Ordinis)* "Decree on the Ministry and Life of Priests," 7 December 1965: Priests are called to integrate their lives with work and spirituality; pastoral dimension of the priestly life.

SC *(Sacrosanctum Concilium)* "Constitution on the Sacred Liturgy," 4 December 1963: Liturgy as the focus of community worship and piety; liturgical renewal and more active participation of the laity.

UR *(Unitatis Redintegratio)* "Decree on Ecumenism," 21 November 1964: Encourages Christian unity; respects others' beliefs; sets forth guidelines for endeavors with other Christian denominations.

APPENDIX VI

DIRECTORY OF
EASTERN CATHOLIC EPARCHIES/EXARCHATES
IN THE UNITED STATES

N.B.: Population figures (following names of eparchies) are taken from the *Official Catholic Directory, Jubilee Edition*. P. J. Kenedy and Sons, Publishers. New Providence, NJ, 2000.

Armenian Catholic Exarchate of U.S.A. and Canada (pop. 26,000)
Chancery & Vicar General Office
110 E. 12th Street
New York, NY 10003-5395
(212) 477-2030 (Office)
(212) 477-2185 (Fax)
E-mail: dioceseofnewton@aol.com

❖ *Embraces Armenian Catholics residing in all States of the United States and all Provinces of Canada.*

Eparchy of Newton (Melkite-Greek Catholic)(pop. 27,629)
The Chancery
158 Pleasant St.
Brookline, MA 02446
(617) 566-4511 (Off)
(617) 566-4115 (Fax)
www.dsha.k12.wi.us/melkite/eparchy.htm

A) *Embraces Melkite Catholics living in all States of the U.S.*

Byzantine Eparchy of Parma (Ruthenian)(pop. 12,634)
Chancery Office
1900 Carlton Road
Parma, OH 44134
(216) 741-8773 (Off)
(216) 741-9356 (Fax)
www.parma.org

❖ *Embraces Ruthenian Catholics living in Illinois, Indiana, Iowa, Kansas, Michigan, Missouri, Nebraska, North Dakota, South Dakota and Wisconsin. Also the entire State of Ohio, including the Counties of Ashtabula, Trumbull, Mahoning, Columbiana, Carroll, Harrison, Guernsey, Noble, Morgan, Athens, Meigs, Gallia and Lawrence.*

Byzantine Catholic Eparchy of Passaic (Ruthenian)(pop. 38,668)
Chancery Offices
445 Lackawanna Avenue
West Paterson, NJ 07424
(973) 890-7777 (Off)
(973) 890-7175 (Fax)
www.members.aol.com/byzruth/index.htm/ E-mail: ECLnews@aol.com

❖ *Embraces Ruthenian Catholics residing in the States of New Jersey, Connecticut, Delaware, District of Columbia, Florida, Georgia, Maine, Maryland, Massachusetts, New Hampshire, New York, North Carolina, Rhode Island, South Carolina, Vermont, Virginia, and all Eastern Pennsylvania within the western boundaries of the Counties of Franklin, Juniata, Lycoming, Mifflin, Union and Tioga.*

Metropolitan Archeparchy of Philadelphia (Ukrainian)(pop. 68,000)
Chancery Office
827 N. Franklin Street
Philadelphia, PA 19123
(215) 627-0143 (Off)
(215) 627-0377 (Fax)
E-mail: srtom@catholic.org

❖ *Embraces Ukrainian Catholics residing in the District of Columbia, the States of Virginia, Maryland, Delaware, New Jersey, and eastern Pennsylvania to the eastern boundaries of the Counties of Potter, Clinton, Center, Mifflin, Huntington, and Fulton.*

Eparchy of Saint Josaphat in Parma (Ukrainian)(pop. 11,412)
Chancery Office
5720 State Road
P.O. Box 347180
Parma, OH 44134-7180
(440) 888-1522 (Off)
(440) 888-3477 (Fax)
E-mail: 110330.137@compuserve.com

❖ *Embraces all Ukrainian Catholics residing in the States of Ohio, Mississippi, West Virginia, Kentucky, Tennessee, Alabama, Georgia, North Carolina, South Carolina, Florida, and western Pennsylvania.*

Eparchy of Saint Maron of Brooklyn (Maronite)(pop. 30,000)
The Chancery Office
109 Remsen Street, Brooklyn, NY 11201
(718) 237-9913 (Off)
(718) 624-8034 (Fax)
www.stmaron.org

❖ *Embraces all Maronite Catholics residing in the States of New York, New Jersey, Pennsylvania, Florida, Georgia, No. Carolina, So. Carolina, Delaware, Virginia, Washington DC, Maine, New Hampshire, Vermont, Massachusetts, Rhode Island, Connecticut, Maryland.*

Eparchy of Our Lady of Lebanon of Los Angeles (Maronite) (pop. 24,054)
1021 10th St.
St. Louis, MO 63104
(310) 247-8322 (Off)
(310) 247-9297 (Fax)
www.eparchyla.org
E-mail: eparchy@aol.com

❖ *Embraces the faithful presently living in the states of Alabama, Alaska, Arizona, Arkansas, California, Colorado, Hawaii, Idaho, Illinois, Indiana, Iowa, Kansas, Kentucky, Louisiana, Michigan, Minnesota, Mississippi, Missouri, Montana, Nebraska, Nevada, New Mexico, North Dakota, Ohio, Oklahoma, Oregon, South Dakota, Tennessee, Texas, Utah, Washington, West Virginia, Wisconsin, Wyoming.*

Eparchy of Saint George in Canton (Romanian)(pop. 5,000)
Chancery Office
1121 44th Street N.E.
Canton, OH 44714-1297
(330) 492-4086) (Off)
(330) 493-1416 (Fax)
www.RomanianCatholic.org
E-mail: Romanian_Catholic@compuserve.com

❖ *Embraces all Romanian Catholics residing in the United States.*

Metropolitan Archeparchy of Pittsburgh (Ruthenian)(pop. 70,599)
Chancery Office
925 Liberty Avenue
Pittsburgh, PA 15222
(412) 281-1000 (Off)
(412) 281-0388 (Fax)
E-mail: archpitt.aol.com

❖ *Embraces Ruthenian Catholics residing in that part of the State of Pennsylvania west of the western boundaries of the Counties of Tioga, Lycoming, Union, Mifflin, Juniata and Franklin. In the State of Ohio, the Counties of Ashtabula, Athens, Belmont, Carroll, Columbiana, Gallia, Guernsey, Harrison, Jefferson, Lawrence, Mahoning, Meigs, Morrow, Morgan, Noble, Trumbull, and Washington. Also those Ruthenian Catholics residing in the States of Alabama, Arkansas, Kentucky, Louisiana, Mississippi, Oklahoma, Tennessee, Texas, and West Virginia.*

Eparchy of Saint Nicholas in Chicago (Ukrainian)(pop. 10,000)
Chancery Office
2245 W. Rice Street
Chicago, IL 60622
(312) 276-5080 or 276-4537 (Off)
(312) 276-6799 (Fax)

❖ *Embraces all Ukrainian Catholics residing west of the western borders of Ohio, Kentucky, Tennessee and Mississippi.*

Eparchy of Saint Thomas the Apostle (Chaldean)(pop. 75,550)
Chancery Office
25603 Berg Road
Southfield, MI 48034
(248) 351-0440 (Off)
(248) 351-0443 (Fax)
E-mail: cryst96@aol.com

❖ *Embraces all Chaldean Catholics residing in all states of the United States.*

Eparchy of Stamford (Ukrainian)(pop. 17,754)
Chancery Office
14 Peveril Road
Stamford, CT 06902-3019
(203) 324-7698 (Off)
(203) 967-9948 (Fax)
E-mail: BASILEOS@aol.com

❖ *Embraces all Ukrainian Catholics residing in the New England States and the State of New York.*

Eparchy of Van Nuys (Ruthenian)(pop. 3,050)
Chancery Office
8131 N. 16th Street
Phoenix, AZ 85020
(602) 861-9778 (Off)
(602) 861-9796 (Fax)
www.eparchy-of-van-nuys.org
E-mail: EVNizer@aol.com

❖ *Embraces Ruthenian Catholics residing in the States of California, Oregon, Washington, Idaho, Nevada, Arizona, Utah, Wyoming, Montana, Colorado, New Mexico, Alaska and Hawaii.*

Eparchy of Our Lady of Deliverance (Syriac Catholic)(pop. 12,100)
Chancery Office
P. O. Box 8366
Union City, New Jersey 07087-8262
(201) 583-1067 (Off)
(201) 583-0212 (Fax)
www.syriac-catholic.org
E-mail: frsyriac@aol.com

❖ *Embraces all Syriac Catholics in all States of the United States and all Provinces of Canada*

St. Thomas Syro-Malabar Catholic Diocese of Chicago
5000 St. Charles Rd.
Bellwood, IL 60104
(708) 544-7099 (Off)
(708) 544-0339 (Fax)
www.members.aol.com/DioceseofChicago
E-mail: georgemparampil@yahoo.com

❖   *Embraces all Syro-Malabar Catholics in the United States.*

APPENDIX VII

SUMMARIES OF THE BOOKS OF THE CATHOLIC BIBLE

The following are capsule summaries for each book of the Bible. These summaries are not exhaustive. They should, however, serve as a handy guide to the content of each book. The common abbreviation for a book's name is also given. **Deuterocanonicals designated by (†).**

THE OLD TESTAMENT (HEBREW SCRIPTURES)

GENESIS (Gn): In this book of beginnings the stories are about creation, early relationships between God and people, and God's promise to bless Abraham and his descendants.

EXODUS (Ex): The name *Exodus* means "departure." This book tells how God led the Israelites out of a life of slavery in Egypt. God made a covenant with them and gave them the Law to order their lives.

LEVITICUS (Lv): This book is named for the priestly tribe of Levi and is made up of laws concerning rituals and ceremonies.

NUMBERS (Nm): The Israelites wandered in the wilderness for 40 years before entering Canaan, the Promised Land. The name of the book comes from two censuses taken during the journey.

DEUTERONOMY (Dt): Moses gave three farewell speeches shortly before he died. In them he reviewed the laws of God for the Israelites. This book gets its name–"second law"–from this review.

JOSHUA (Jos): Joshua led the Israelite armies into victory over the Canaanites. The book ends with the division of the land among the tribes of Israel.

JUDGES (Jgs): The Israelites often fell away from God and into the hands of oppressors. God sent "judges" to lead and deliver them.

RUTH (Ru): Love and dedication between Ruth and her mother-in-law, Naomi, are the themes of this story.

1 SAMUEL (1 Sm): Samuel was the leader of Israel between the time of Judges and the time of Saul, the first king of Israel. When Saul's leadership failed, David was anointed by Samuel to be king.

2 SAMUEL (2 Sm): Under David's rule, the new nation was strong and unified. But after David committed adultery and murder, his family and nation suffered.

1 KINGS (1 Kgs): This book starts with stories about Solomon's reign over Israel. After the death of Solomon, the kingdom went to war with itself, north against south. The result was two nations, Israel in the north and Judah in the south.

2 KINGS (2 Kgs): Israel was conquered by Assyria in 721 B.C. Judah was defeated by Babylon in 586 B.C. These events were seen as judgment upon the people because they did not follow the laws of God.

1 CHRONICLES (1 Chr): This book begins with genealogies from Adam to David and then recounts the incidents of David's reign.

2 CHRONICLES (2 Chr): This book covers the same period as *2 Kings* but the emphasis is on Judah, the southern kingdom, and its rulers.

†PRAYER OF MANASSEH: This brief prayer is an excellent example of a Psalm of repentance.

EZRA (Ezr): God's people returned to Jerusalem after being held captive in Babylon for several decades. One of the leaders was Ezra. This book contains his charge to the people to be true to the law of God.

†1 ESDRAS: Esdras is the Greek form of the name Ezra and this book closely parallels the canonical Old Testament books of Ezra. It is a history of the Jews from the time of Josiah to that of Ezra. The author's purpose is to encourage the reform and renewal of Israel's worship life.

†2 ESDRAS: This book is not related to 1 Esdras. It is a series of visions and revelations which aims to reveal the future in ways that will help believers bear up under the suffering and persecution they must endure.

NEHEMIAH (Neh): After the Temple was rebuilt, the protective wall around Jerusalem was restored. Nehemiah brought this effort to completion. He also worked with Ezra to restore religious fervor among the people.

†TOBIT (Tb): The book of Tobit provides a clear picture of Jewish culture and religious life in the centuries before the time of Jesus. It weaves together two stories about Jewish life in Persia after the exile—that of the pious Tobit in Nineveh and the long-suffering Sarah in Ecbatana.

†JUDITH (Jdt): This book tells the story of Judith, a woman of great courage and faith in God who was able to carry out a bold plan to rescue her people by driving out the enemy troops who were attacking her city.

ESTHER (Est): This book tells the story of the Jewish queen of Persia who exposed a plot to destroy her people and thus saved all the Jews in that country from destruction.

†ESTHER (Greek version): The Book of Esther in Greek is a translation, adaptation, and expansion of the Book of Esther in Hebrew. The new material helps the reader better to see the religious dimensions of Esther's story.

†1 MACCABEES (1 Mc): This is a history of the Jewish revolt (168 B.C.) against the Seleucid rulers of Syria. It tells of the priestly family of Judas Maccabeus and the establishment of an independent Judea under Maccabean kings (134 B.C.). This book seeks to show that God, who had led and rescued Israel in former times of crisis, is just as active in their present day, and in the same ways.

†2 MACCABEES (2 Mc): This book is not a continuation of the history given in 1 Maccabees. Instead, it is a parallel account of the period covered in 1 Maccabees 1-7. The author is deeply interested in the meaning of martyrdom and resurrection.

†3 MACCABEES (3 Mc): This book appears in the ancient Greek Septuagint and in an appendix to the Latin Vulgate Bible and is recognized as Deuterocanonical Scripture by a number of Eastern Orthodox Churches. Its contents deal with the suffering of the Jews in Alexandria about a half-century before the Maccabean period in

Palestine (168–134 B.C.). Its aim is to console and guide the faithful of the first century B.C. in the midst of their difficulties.

†4 MACCABEES (4 Mc): In important manuscripts of the Greek Bible this book has been included as an appendix. It was early translated into Syriac and has had a deep influence on Eastern Christian religious thought. While using some historical events from the Maccabean era as examples, this book is really an extended lecture or essay on the power of reason to control human emotions.

JOB (Jb): The question, "Why do innocent people suffer?" is addressed in the story of Job.

PSALMS (Ps[s]): These 150 prayers and hymns were used by the Hebrew people to express their relationship with God. They cover the whole range of human emotions from joy to anger, from hope to despair.

†PSALM 151 (Ps 151): This psalm celebrates the abilities of the young David in his victory over Goliath. In most manuscripts of the ancient Greek Bible it follows the usual 150 psalms. In 1956 a Hebrew Psalms scroll containing Psalm 151 was found among the Dead Sea Scrolls. Until then this additional psalm had never appeared in any Hebrew manuscript.

PROVERBS (Prv): This is a book of wise sayings and ethical and common sense teachings on how to live a godly life.

ECCLESIASTES (Eccl): In a quest for happiness and the meaning of life, this writer, known as "the Philosopher," asks many questions that are still raised in today's society.

SONG OF SONGS (SONG OF SOLOMON) (Sg): This poem describes the joy and ecstasy of love. It has been understood both as a picture of God's love for Israel and of Christ's love for the Church.

†WISDOM OF SOLOMON (Wis): This book uses both traditional Jewish material and ideas from Greek philosophy to teach that God will reward the faithful and punish the wicked.

†SIRACH (ECCLESIASTICUS) (Sir): This book is a lengthy collection of wise advice on a wide variety of practical problems. It is very similar in style to the Old Testament book of Proverbs.

ISAIAH (Is): The prophet Isaiah brought the message of God's judgment on the nations, pointed to a future king like David, and promised a time of comfort and peace.

JEREMIAH (Jer): Before Babylon destroyed Judah, Jeremiah foretold God's judgment. While his message was largely of destruction, he also pointed toward a new covenant with God.

LAMENTATIONS (Lam): As Jeremiah had warned, Jerusalem fell to the Babylonians. This book records five "laments" for the fallen city.

†BARUCH (Bar): This book is set in the time of the Babylonian exile. It is comprised of a national prayer of confession, a wisdom hymn and a consolation poem in the style of Isaiah.

†THE LETTER OF JEREMIAH: While written in the form of a letter, this book is really more of a sermon about the foolishness of idolatry.

EZEKIEL (Ez): Ezekiel's message was given to the Jews held captive in Babylon. He used stories and parables to speak about judgment, hope and restoration.

DANIEL (Dn): Daniel remained faithful to God while facing many pressures as a captive in Babylon. This book includes Daniel's prophetic visions.

†PRAYER OF AZARIAH AND SONG OF THE THREE JEWS: This is an addition to the book of Daniel. It includes the prayer of Azariah, followed by a hymn of praise that the three friends of Daniel sang in the midst of the fiery furnace.

†SUSANNAH: This book is also an addition to the book of Daniel. It is the story of a narrow escape by an innocent victim of lust and lying, and is the basis of Daniel's enduring reputation as a brilliant judge.

†BEL AND THE DRAGON: This is the third of the additions to Daniel. It consists of two stories attacking idolatry. In each one Daniel shows that there is only one true and living God.

HOSEA (Hos): Hosea used his commitment to his wife in the face of her unfaithfulness to illustrate the "adultery" Israel had committed against God, whose faithful love never ceased.

JOEL (Jl): After a locust plague in Judah, Joel urged the people to repent.

AMOS (Am): During an era of prosperity, this Judean prophet preached judgment on the rich leaders of Israel. Amos urged them to consider the poor and oppressed rather than their own self-satisfaction.

OBADIAH (Ob): Obadiah prophesied judgment on Edom, a neighboring country.

JONAH (Jon): Jonah did not want to preach to the Ninevites, an enemy people. When he finally brought God's message to them, they repented.

MICAH (Mi): Micah's message to Judah was a prophecy of judgment as well as forgiveness and hope for restoration. Especially notable is his single verse summary of what God requires of us (6:8).

NAHUM (Na): Nahum announced that God would destroy the people of Nineveh because of their cruelty in war.

HABAKKUK (Hb): Habakkuk's book features a dialogue between Habakkuk and God about suffering and justice.

ZEPHANIAH (Zep): Zephaniah announced the day of the Lord, which would bring judgment on Judah and other surrounding nations. This coming day would be one of doom for many, but a humble and faithful remnant will survive to bless the whole world.

HAGGAI (Hg): After the people returned from exile, Haggai reminded them to give God their highest priority and to rebuild the Temple before working on their own homes.

ZECHARIAH (Zec): Like Haggai, Zechariah urged the people to rebuild the Temple, assuring them of God's help and blessings. His visions point to a glorious future.

MALACHI (Mal): After the exiles returned, they became complacent about their religious life. Malachi tried to stir them up by preaching about the day of the Lord.

✿✿✿

THE NEW TESTAMENT

MATTHEW (Mt): This Gospel includes many Old Testament quotations, thus appealing to a Jewish audience and presenting Jesus as the Messiah promised in the Hebrew Scriptures. Matthew told the story of Jesus from birth to resurrection and placed emphasis on his teaching.

MARK (Mk): Mark wrote a short, action-packed Gospel. He emphasized Jesus' miracles and his life of suffering. His aim was to deepen the faith and commitment of the community to which he wrote.

LUKE (Lk): In this Gospel the availability of salvation for all people is emphasized. Luke proclaimed this message by showing Jesus' involvement with people who are poor, needy, and on the fringes of society.

JOHN (Jn): The Gospel of John stands apart from the others. John organized his message around seven "signs" that point to Jesus as the Son of God. His writing style is reflective and filled with striking images.

ACTS OF THE APOSTLES (Acts): When Jesus left his disciples, the Holy Spirit came to abide with them. Written by Luke as the sequel to his Gospel, *Acts* records key events in the history of the work of the early Christian Church to spread the Gospel throughout the Mediterranean world.

ROMANS (Rom): In this important letter, Paul wrote to the Romans about life in the Spirit, which is given to believers in Christ through faith. The apostle tells them about God's great kindness and declares that because of Jesus Christ, God accepts us and sets us free from our sins.

1 CORINTHIANS (1 Cor): This letter deals with the problems the church in Corinth was experiencing: dissension, immorality, public worship, and confusion about spiritual gifts.

2 CORINTHIANS (2 Cor): In this letter, Paul wrote about his relationship with the church of Corinth and the effects of false apostles on his ministry.

GALATIANS (Gal): This letter addresses freedom from the law through Christ. Paul declares that it is by faith that all who believe are put right with God.

EPHESIANS (Eph): A central theme to this letter is that God's eternal purpose is to bring together from many nations and peoples the universal Church of Jesus Christ.

PHILIPPIANS (Phil): This letter emphasizes the joy found in any situation when a person believes in Christ. Paul wrote it while in prison.

COLOSSIANS (Col): In this letter Paul tells the people of Colossae to make Christ the center of their faith and to put aside their superstitions.

1 THESSALONIANS (1 Thes): In this letter Paul gives advice to the people of Thessalonica concerning Christ's return.

2 THESSALONIANS (2 Thes): This letter discusses the same topics as the first. Paul teaches the people a way to be ready for the Lord.

1 TIMOTHY (1 Tm): This letter served as a guide for Timothy, a young leader in the Church. It contains advice about worship, ministry, and relationships within the Church.

2 TIMOTHY (2 Tm): This is Paul's last letter. In it he offers a final challenge to his co-worker.

TITUS (Ti): Titus was ministering in Crete. In this letter Paul gave him advice on how to help Christians follow Christ.

PHILEMON (Phlm): In this letter Philemon is urged to forgive his runaway slave, Onesimus, and accept him as a friend in Christ.

HEBREWS (Heb): The letter to the Hebrews challenges new Christians to move beyond their traditional rituals and ceremonies and believe that Christ has fulfilled them all.

JAMES (Jas): James advises putting beliefs into practice and offers practical ways for Christians to live out their faith.

1 PETER (1 Pt): This letter was written to comfort early Christians who were being persecuted for their faith.

2 PETER (2 Pt): In this letter Peter warned against false teachers and urged Christians to stay loyal to God.

1 JOHN (1 Jn): This letter explains basic truths about the Christian life, with emphasis on the command to love one another.

2 JOHN (2 Jn): This letter, addressed to "the elect lady and her children," warns against false teachers.

3 JOHN (3 Jn): In contrast to 2 John, this letter states the need to welcome people who preach Christ.

JUDE (Jude): Jude warns against the influence of evil ones outside the fellowship of believers.

REVELATION (Rv): This book was written to encourage persecuted believers and affirm their faith that God will care for them. Using visions and symbols, the writer illustrates the triumph of good over evil and the creation of a new heaven and new earth.

INDEXES

INDEX OF SCRIPTURE CITATIONS
(In alphabetical order, and not as listed in the Bible)

HEBREW SCRIPTURES (OLD TESTAMENT)

NEW TESTAMENT

Acts of the Apostles

2:1-4	165
2:1-13	59
2:42	82
3:1-10	139
6:2	140
11:26	99, 389

Colossians

1:15	4

1 Corinthians

2:9-10	179
10:17	59
11:23-25	220
11:29-32	204
12:6-11	215
12:20	194
12:31	307
13:1-13	290
13:4-8a	307
13:10a-13	307
13:12	180
13:13	307
15:12-17	49
15:23-28	171
15:44	183

2 Corinthians

5:7	224
5:18-19	77
5:21	36, 39
10:18	314
11:14	203
13:13	245

Ephesians

2:4-7	208
5:5	296
5:8	205
5:25-26	58
5:25-27	289
5:32	58

Galatians

5:22-23	215
6:14	173

Hebrews

1:1-2	5, 188
1:1-4	35
1:3	21, 35
4:15-16	162
4:16	162
9:24-25	220
13:1-2	325
13:2	319
13:16	325

James

2:20-26	261
5:16	237
5:1-6	324

John

1:1-3	27
1:14	25
2:1-11	xviii
2:11	182
2:19	135
2:19-22	42
3:5	210
3:15	35
3:16	188
3:17	40
6:48-51	223
6:56	223
6:57	223
8:1-11	347
8:30-32	301
10:30	18
13:34-35	289
14:2	181
14:6	42, 78
14:9	35, 188
14:10	18
14:23	51
14:25-26	309
14:27	321
15:5-6	68
15:12	303
15:14-15	4
16:7	52
16:12-15	144

INDEX OF LITURGICAL PRAYERS CITED

GENERAL INDEX

Constitution on the Sacred Liturgy. *See* Second Vatican Council: Constitution on the Sacred Liturgy.

Contraception, 300, 315

Conversion, 254-56

Coptic Catholic Church: membership, 90

Coptic Orthodox Church, 96, 98

Corporal and Spiritual Works of Mercy, 325

Council of Chalcedon, 34, 48, 103, 159

Council of Ephesus, 159

Council of Florence, 85

Council, Second Vatican. *See* Second Vatican Council.

Covenant, 302

Creation, 27-30; as an expression of the Word of God, 5; new, 28

Creed, 22; definition, 11. *See* Apostles' Creed; Nicene Creed.

Cremation, 350

Cross, 220; Christ's sacrifice on, 38, 177; double meaning in Passion Week, 44; reconciliation of humanity through, 321; salvation through, 139; as symbol of transfiguration, 183; triumph of the, 172. *See also* Hand cross; Glorious Cross, Season of the.

Crowning, Holy, 191, 283-90; 344-46

Crowns: symbolism of, 285-87

Crucified Christ in Holy Week, A. See Brown, Raymond.

Customs, Maronite liturgical, 354-66

Cyrrhus: map, 92

De Revelatione. See Second Vatican Council: Dogmatic Constitution on Divine Revelation.

Deacon(s), 67, 274, 392

Deceased Priests, Sunday of, 136-37, 274, 357

Dead Seas Scrolls, 113, 122, 144

Death, Christian, 173-74

Decalogue. *See* Ten Commandmants.

Declaration on the Relationship of the Church to Non-Christian Religions. *See* Second Vatican Council: Declaration on the Relationship of the

Decree on the Apostolate of the Laity. *See* Second Vatican Council: Decree on the Apostolate of the Laity.

Decree on the Eastern Catholic Churches. *See* Second Vatican Council: Decree on the Eastern Catholic Churches.

Decree on Ecumenism. *See* Second Vatican Council: Decree on Ecumenism.

Decree on the Instruments of Social Communication. *See* Second Vatican Council: Decree on the Instruments of Social Communication.

Deemaan, 103

Deutero-canonical books, 114-15. *See also Apocrypha.*

Devil. *See* Evil One.

Devotion to the Mother of God, 170

Dew of mercy, 174. *See also* God's mercy.

Diakonal Proclamation, 392

Diatesseron, 119

Diocese. *See* Eparchy.

Diodore of Tarsus, 129-30

Diptychs, 392-93

Discipleship, 215-16

Divine Office: always begins with doxology, 17; Antiochene roots expressed in, 33; definition, 239, 400; part of public prayer of the Church, 236; Psalms form the backbone of, 238-239; texts not used in this work, 13. *See Ramsho, Safro.*

Divine Service of the Holy Mysteries. *See Qoorbono.*

Divinization, 34, 209-10

Divino Afflante Spiritu. See Pius XII.

Divorce, 300; and Communion, 346-47

Doctor of the Church: definition, 146

Doctrine, Catholic, 11-12

Dogmatic Constitution on the Church. *See* Second Vatican Council: Dogmatic Constitution on the Church.

Dogmatic Constitution on Divine Revelation. *See* Second Vatican

Liturgy, 195, 233-40, 398; Maronite, 241-48

Liturgy of the Pre-Sanctified. *See* Pre-Sanctified, Liturgy of the.

Logos. See Word.

Lord's Prayer, The, 239-40, 370-71

Love: one of the Theological Virtues, 307

Lumen Gentium. See Second Vatican Council: Dogmatic Constitution on the Church.

Lying, 301

Macomber, William: *East of Byzantium*, 234

Magi, 36, 38

Magisterium. *See* Teaching office of the Church.

Maifooq, 103

Makhlouf, Joseph. *See* Sharbel, Saint.

Malankara Orthodox Syrian Church, 96

Man with Leprosy, Sunday of the, 138, 174-76

Man Who Was Blind, Sunday of the, 138

Man Who Was Paralyzed, Sunday of the, 138

Manuscript illumination, 362-63. *See also* Rabboola.

Mariamists, 71

Marks of the Eucharist, 177, 276

Maron, Saint, 99, 257, 398; beginning of monastic movement, 316; Feast of, 137, 167, 357; founder of Maronite Church, 71; life of, 101-2, 130-31; monastery of, 103; simplicity of life, 317, 329

Maronite Church of Antioch, 329-30, 398; Antiochene roots, 33; hierarchy, 65; history of, 34, 39, 48, 91, 94, 99-108, 241; membership, 90; monastic influence on, 71; organization of, 70, 103, 106-7; parish boundaries, 67; relationship to Rome, 85-86, 104-6; "Rite" incorrect, 88; use of Scripture, 110

Maronite culture, 69, 104, 319

Maronite Nation, 104

Maronite Tradition, 22, 23, 89, 101, 130-31; in Bible interpretation, 147; marriage in, 290; on spirituality, 309

Marriage, 283-90; between Catholics and others, 345; as covenant, 287-89; in Maronite Tradition, 290; as mission, 287. *See also* Single life; Crowning, Holy.

Married clergy. *See* Clergy.

Martyrdom, 48

Martyrs, 48, 168; weekday commemoration of, 361. *See also* Massabki Brothers.

Mary (mother of Jesus), 13, 36, 103, 155; all-holy, 160-63; Assumption (Dormition) of, 13, 163-64; Cedar of Lebanon, 166; ever-virgin, 160; Feast of Assumption of, 359-60; first sharer in Resurrection, 163-64; as intercessor, 165-66, 169-70; Jesus' first disciple, 163; Mother of the Church, 164-65; as Mother of God, 157-66; on Pentecost, 59; as first among the Righteous and Just, 154, 157; as sinless, 199; titles of, 158

Mass, 398

Massabki Brothers, Feast of, 359; martyrs, 48, 168

Masturbation, 300

Materialism, 302

Matrimony. *See* Crowning, Holy.

Mazooro, 399

Melkite Catholic Church, 34; membership, 90

"Melkite": signifying Chalcedonian, 34; as term of derision, 34

Memorial of Bishops, Priests, Doctors, and Monks: weekday commemoration of, 361

Memorial of Prophets, the Just, and Confessors: weekday commemoration of, 361

Memra, Memre, 101, 130, 239, 393

Men religious (monks). *See* Religious.

Mercy of God, 173-76, 262-63

Messiah. *See* Christ.

Metanoia, 399; *See also* Conversion.

Metropolitan, 66
Midrashe, 239
Miracles of Jesus. *See* Jesus.
Mission: of the Church, 43; of the Laity, 68-71, 216. *See* Apostolate.
Missionaries of Kraim. See Kraimist Fathers.
Modesty, 301
Monasticism, 101, 399; influence on Eastern Tradition, 316; influence on Maronite Tradition, ix
Monks. *See* Religious.
Monophysitism: definition, 95
Monothelitism: definition, 39
Monsignor, 66
Mopsuestia: map, 92
Moral principles. *See* Morality.
Morality, 293-327; and law, 305; biblical, 293-308; principles of, 309; sexual, 315
Morning Prayer. *See Safro.*
Mosaic, 362-63, 399
Moses, 26
Most Holy Trinity. *See* Trinity.
Most Holy Trinity, Mystery of the, 12
Mother of God, 399; weekday commemoration of, 361
Mt. Lebanon, 103
Murder, 298-299
Music, Maronite liturgical, 362
Myron (*Myroon*), Holy. *See* Holy Myron.
Mysteries, Seven Sacramental. *See* Sacramental Mysteries.
Mysteries, Sacramental. *See* Sacramental Mysteries.
Mysteries of Healing, 249, 259, 265
Mysteries of Initiation, 193-96; and the Catechumenate, 341
Mysteries of Vocation, 271, 283; Crowning and ordained presbyters complementary vocations, 280
Mystery: in Eastern Tradition, 3, 399
N.A.M. *See* National Apostolate of Maronites.
National Apostolate of Maronites (N.A.M.), 71. *See also* Apostolate.

NCCB. *See* National Conference of Catholic Bishops (USA).
National Conference of Catholic Bishops NCCB.), 66
Nativity. *See* Jesus: birth of.
Nestorius, 94; on Mary, 159
New Adam, 200
New Sunday, 9, 46, 139
New Testament, 115; continuity with Old Testament, 128
Nicene Creed, 11
Nineveh Days, 136
Nisibis, 82, 94, 99, 400; center of East Syriac Christianity (with Edessa), 126; connection to St. Maron, 130-31; map, 92
Non-Chalcedonians, 34. *See also* Oriental Orthodox Churches.
Nostra Aetate. See Second Vatican Council: Declaration on the Relationship of the Church to Non-Christian Religions.
Nuns. *See* Religious.
Oblations, 400
Offerings, 68, 155, 177-78, 241, 245, 400
Oils. *See* Holy Oils.
Old Testament, 114
O.L.M. *See* Lebanese Maronite Order.
Ordained ministry, 271-82; functions of, 275, 277-78; levels of Order, 273. *See* Order, Holy.
Order, Holy, 191
Ordinary: of eparchy, 65
Ordination ceremony, 275-78
Oriental Congregation: *Instruction for Applying the Liturgical Prescriptions of the* Code of Canons of the Eastern Churches, 248
Oom Allah, 401
Orientale Lumen. See John Paul II: *Orientale Lumen.*
Orientalium Ecclesiarum. See Second Vatican Council: Decree on the Eastern Catholic Churches.
Oriental Orthodox Churches, 96
Origen, 149

Orthodox: designation for majority
Byzantine Tradition after the Schism
of 1054 A.D., 97; Churches, listing in
diagram, 98
Orthodox Assyrian Ch. of the East, 95
Orthodox Church, 84-85
Orthodox Church of "Czechoslovakia,"
98
Orthodox Tradition, 76
Our Father, The. *See* Lord's Prayer.
Our Lady of Eeleej, 363
Outline of the *Qoorbono*, 244-45
Overshadowing, 52-53, 190, 241, 359
Pachomius, Saint, 101, 316
Palestine, 93
Palm branches, 358
Palm Sunday. *See* Hosanna Sunday.
Papias, 125
Parables of Jesus. *See* Jesus.
Paraclete, 18
Paradox: biblical interpretational tool,
128, 131; as theological method, 189
Parents: first religious educators of
children, 207, 319; role in determining
ritual status of children, 340; role in
early conscience formation of
children, 310; to be cared for, 297; to
be obeyed, 297-98; single parents, 291
Parish, 67; boundaries, 67; participation
in the life of, 71, 310; patronal feast
day, 351; presbyters traditionally staff
as pastors, 66-67
Parishioner: definition of an active, 67
Parousia, 171
Particular Church. *See Sui iuris* Church.
Pascha. *See* Easter.
Paschal Mystery, 41-42, 221. *See also*
Eucharist.
Passion Week, 42-47, 138, 358
Passover, 183
Pastors, 66
Patriarch(s): definition, 64; Eastern, 65;
Five, in early Christianity, 64; Pope as
Patriarch of the West, 64
Patriarch, Maronite: in Lebanon, 66;
John Maron, first Patriarch, 103;
residence in Bkirkee, 103; takes

"Peter" in name, 103-04. *See also*
Patriarchal residences, Maronite.
Patriarchal Liturgical Commission,
Maronite, 248
Patriarchal residences, Maronite. *See*
Bkirkee; Deemaan; Maifooq;
Qannoobeen; Yanoo<u>h</u>
Patriarchate of Constantinople, 98
Patriarchate of Moscow, 98
Patriarchs of the Eastern Catholic
Churches. *See* Patriarch(s).
Paul, Saint, 58, 59, 99, 179-80, 194-95,
254; on evil, 202-03; Feast of, 359; on
fruit of the Holy Spirit, 215; on
Resurrection, 49
Paul VI, 75, 323
Peace and justice, 322-25
Peace, Rite of, 320-22
Peace, virtue of, 320-22
Penance, 183-84, 191, 347-48, 357
Penance, Mystery of, 259-63, 353
Penitential cycles, Great Lent, 357
Penitential Rite: in *Qoorbono*, 260
Pentarchy, 64-65
Pentateuch, 114.
Pentecost, 55, 59, 139, 359; Divine
Service of, 28; Sunday, 51, 139;
Sundays after, 139
Perjury, 297
Persia, 91
"Person": in Trinity. *See* Trinity.
Peshitta Version, 119. *See* Bible.
Peter, Saint, 99; Church established on
faith of, 58; Feast of Peter and Paul,
359
Petition, Prayer of. *See* Prayer, Types of.
Philanthropia, 325-26
Philo, 149
Pius XII: *Divino Afflante Spiritu*, 147
Plato, 149
Pneumatization, 182-85
Poetry: as language of God-talk, 16; of
St. Ephrem, 99
Polycarp, 125
Pope of Rome, 64-65
Pope of Alexandria, 64
Pornography, 300

Rite of Eastern Christian Initiation of
Adults (RECIA). *See* Christian
Initiation of Adults, Eastern, Rite of.
Ritual Church, 352; status, 340; transfer,
342
Robe of glory, 198-200, 204, 210, 211
Roman Curia, 65
Romanian Catholic Church:
membership, 90
Romanian Orthodox Church, 98
Romanus the Melodist, 362
Rome, 82, 84; map, 83
Roncalli, Archbishop Angelo. *See* John
XXIII.
Rosary, 379-80
Rozo (raza), 403. *See also* Mystery.
Russian Catholic Church: membership,
90
Russian Orthodox Church, 98
Ruthenian Catholic Church:
membership, 90
Sabbath, 297
Sacramental Mysteries, 189-91, 240,
340-49, 400; definition of Theodore of
Mopsuestia, 189; listing, 191; as
liturgical actions, 191; passive voice,
190; role of the Holy Spirit in, 190;
role of priests in, 278; sanctification of
life, 190. *See also* Mysteries of
Initiation; Mysteries of Healing;
Mysteries of Vocation.
Sacramentality, 189
Sacrament, 403; Latin term for
Mysteries, 62. *See* Sacramental
Mysteries.
Sacred objects, 363
Safro, 239, 403
Saints. *See* Righteous and Just.
Salvation, 40, 61; hope for, 176
Sanctoral Cycle, 133
Satan. *See* Evil One.
Sayings Gospels, 134
Schism, 61, 73, 75, 85-86, 97
Scripture. *See* Bible.
Scripture and Tradition, 124-25
Seamless garment. *See* Consistent ethic
of life.

Season of Epiphany. *See* Epiphany,
Season of.
Season of the Glorious Birth of the Lord.
See Glorious Birth of the Lord, Season
of the.
Season of Glorious Pentecost. *See*
Glorious Pentecost, Season of.
Season of the Glorious Resurrection. *See*
Glorious Resurrection, Season of the.
Season of the Holy Cross. *See* Holy
Cross, Season of the.
Seasonal Cycle, 133
Second Coming. *See* Christ: Second
Coming.
Second Vatican Council, 72-73; on
collegiality, 66; Constitution on the
Sacred Liturgy, 247; on Church, 59-
60; Decree on the Apostolate of the
Laity, 69; Decree on the Eastern
Catholic Churches, 65, 81, 86-88, 247,
248; Decree on Ecumenism, 12, 77;
Decree on the Instruments of Social
Communication, 217; Declaration on
the Relationship of the Church to Non-
Christian Religions, 77; Dogmatic
Constitution on the Church, 59, 165,
271; Dogmatic Constitution on Divine
Revelation, 4, 110, 124, 147-48; on
laity, 68; on marriage, 284, 286; on
Second Coming, 182
Sedro, 403. *See also* Hoosoyo.
See of Rome, 64
Seleucia-Ctesiphon, 94; map, 92
Senses of Scripture, 146-47
Septuagint, 118, 149
Service of the Holy Mysteries, Divine.
See Qoorbono.
Service of Peace, 404
Service of the Incense, 349
Service of the Word, 110, 404
Seven Sacramental Mysteries. *See*
Sacramental Mysteries.
Sex: extra-marital, 300; pre-marital, 300
Sexism, 299
Sha'neenee. See Hosanna Sunday.
Sharbel, Saint, 257; Feast of, 168, 359;
hermit, 316; simplicity of life, 317